中国法治论坛

CHINA FORUM ON THE RULE OF LAW

中国法治论坛
CHINA FORUM ON THE RULE OF LAW

人权保障与法治建设:
中国与芬兰的比较

Safeguarding Human Rights and Constructing the Rule of Law:
A Comparison between China and Finland

主　编/〔中国〕李林
　　　　〔芬兰〕基莫·诺迪欧
副主编/〔中国〕谢增毅

社会科学文献出版社
SOCIAL SCIENCES ACADEMIC PRESS (CHINA)

总　序

　　故宫北侧，景山东麓，一座静谧的院落。蕴藉当年新文化运动的历史辉煌与典雅的土地上，流淌着中国法律理论的潺潺清泉，燃烧着法治思想的不息火焰。多年来，尤其是1978年中国改革开放以来，一代代法律学者在这里辛勤劳作，各领风骚，用他们的心血和智慧，谱写了许多可以载入史册的不朽篇章。

　　为了记载和激扬法治学问，推动法治，继往开来，中国社会科学院法学研究所设立"中国法治论坛"系列丛书。一方面，重新出版最近20余年来有重要文献价值的论文集，如始于20世纪70年代末的关于人治与法治、法律面前人人平等、起草新宪法以及法律阶级性等问题的专项讨论，90年代初以来关于人权、市场经济法律体系、依法治国、司法改革、WTO与中国法、环境保护、反酷刑、死刑存废等问题的专项讨论；另一方面，陆续编辑出版今后有足够学术含量和价值、比较成熟的国际国内相关研究项目和会议的论文集。

　　法律乃人类秩序规则。法治乃当世共通理念。"中国法治论坛"不限于讨论中国的法律问题，也并非由中国社会科学院的学者独自担当。我们期望，这个论坛能够成为海内外学者、专家和广大读者、听众共同拥有的一个阐解法意、砥砺学问的场所，一片芳草茵茵、百花盛开的园地。

夏　勇

2003 年 6 月 6 日

Preface to China Forum
on the Rule of Law

To the north of the Forbidden City and east of Jingshan Hill lays a peaceful courtyard. It is the seat of the Institute of Law of Chinese Academy of Social Sciences, the most prestigious national institute in China devoted to legal research and legal education. On this small piece of land, rich in historical splendor and elegance of the New Culture Movement of 1919, flows an inexhaustible spring of Chinese legal theory and rages an inextinguishable flame of the ideal of the rule of law. Since several decades ago, especially since the "reform and opening up" in 1978, generations of Chinese legal scholars have been working diligently on this small piece of land and, with their wisdom and painstaking efforts, composed many immortal masterpieces of law that will go down in history.

China Forum on the Rule of Law is a series of books published by the Institute of Law with a view to carrying on the past and opening a new way for the future in the research of the rule of law and promoting the development of the rule of law in China. In this series, we will, on the one hand, republish papers published in China in the past 20 years which are of great historical significance, such as those relating to the discussions since late 1970s on the rule of man and the rule of law, the equality of everyone before the law, the drafting of the new Constitution, and the class nature of thelaw and those relating to debates since early 1990s on human rights, the legal system under the market economy, ruling the country in accordance with the law, judicial reform, WTO and China, environmental protection, eradication of torture, and abolition of the death penalty. On the other hand, we will edit and publish papers from future research projects and academic seminars, both in China and abroad, which are relatively mature and of sufficiently high academic value.

The law is the norms of order for all mankind and the rule of law a universal ideal of all peoples in the contemporary world. China Forum on the Rule of Law is not limited to the discussion of the legal issues in China, nor will it be monopolized by scholars of the Institute of Law. We sincerely hope that it will be able to provide an opportunity for scholars, experts, as well as readers to freely express their ideas and exchange their views on legal issues, a forum for a hundred schools of thoughts to contend, and a garden for a hundred flowers to bloom.

Xia Yong

6 June 2003

目 录

第三部分　法治政府建设与司法体制改革

CONTENTS

Part One: Economic and Environmental Rule of Law from the Perspective of Comparative Law

Part Two: Safeguarding Human Rights
through the Rule of Law

Part Three: Constructing a Law-Based Government and
Reforming the Judicial System

第一部分
比较法视野下的经济与环境法治

经济法治与经济风险的预防和治理

徐孟洲[*]

【摘要】2010 年以来，复杂多变的内外部多重因素使得中国经济持续下行，经济发展面临产生经济风险的巨大压力与严峻挑战。本文认为，加强防范经济风险并进行有效风险控制或治理是一种理性的应对；防控经济风险必须真正落实依法治国的基本方略，遵循经济法治思维，提高防范经济风险和风险管理意识，逐步建立预防与治理经济风险的具体制度及其相应的法律机制。

【关键词】经济风险　经济法治　防治

在市场经济体制下，经济社会的发展与法治之间存在密切关系。良好的法治环境可以引导、促进和保障整个市场经济健康、有序、持续发展。30多年的改革开放实践表明，中国在经济发展方面之所以能够取得今天这样举世瞩目的成就，很大程度上得益于不断改善的经济法治环境。我们知道，市场经济的自由发展会产生周期性的经济危机。在中国社会主义市场经济快速发展中，是否也会发生经济危机？如何防范或杜绝经济危机？可以采取什么样的风险控制和危机应对措施？今天，我想围绕这些问题，从法治角度谈几点浅见，供大家参考。

一　中国经济发展面临经济风险的严峻挑战

国家统计局的资料显示，改革开放 30 多年来，中国的经济发展创造了年均增速 9% 以上的奇迹。但是从 2010 年第一季度开始，中国经济增长的速度连续 13 个季度下滑，到 2013 年第二季度时，经济增速仅达 7.5%，这

---

* 徐孟洲，中国人民大学法学院教授。

是改革开放以后持续时间最长的增长放缓。目前中国经济发展面临发生严重经济风险的巨大压力，但中国经济不会崩溃①，在中国社会主义市场经济体制下不会发生经济危机。

我们知道，经济危机（economic crisis）是政治经济学上的一个概念，它指经济系统没有产生足够的消费价值，也就是在资本主义经济发展过程中周期性爆发的生产相对过剩的危机。大多由于一国宏观经济管理当局在没有准备的情况下出现经济的严重衰退或大幅度的货币贬值，从而引发金融危机，又进而演化为经济危机。例如，2008年美国金融危机引发经济危机，华尔街对金融衍生产品的"滥用"和对次贷危机的估计不足终酿苦果。此次金融危机迅速引发多米诺骨牌效应，使美欧各国特别是发展中国家的经济遭到重创。

而经济风险是指因经济前景的不确定性，使经济运行和经济主体经营活动时，蒙受重大经济损失的可能性。经济风险是复杂的，可以表现为多种形式，有多种分类方法。一般将经济风险划分为金融风险②、财政风险③、产业风险④和计划与规划风险⑤；按经济过程的不同阶段，经济风险可被分为投资风险、生产风险、销售风险等；经济风险按其产生的原因，还可被分为由于自然因素，如洪灾、火灾、地震引发的自然风险，因社会上的行为，如战争、政治动乱等引起的社会风险，因经营管理不善或市场供求剧

---

① 美国《福布斯》杂志网站2012年7月2日发表文章《思考中国》，该文做出中国经济即将遭遇"硬"着陆（经济增长从8%降至5%）的推测，对中国"经济崩溃"表示不安。美国"末日博士"鲁比尼也预言中国经济会崩溃。

② 金融风险：在加快经济金融全球化和信息网络化进程的同时，也给经济金融系统带来了巨大的风险。由于各国的金融业务和客户相互渗入和交叉，国与国之间的风险相关性加强，金融风险交叉"传染"的可能性上升；网上交易量出现瞬间剧增，加大了因交易环节中断而导致的支付、清算风险，并使补救成本增大，纠错余地缩小；由于电子货币流通速度快，其对基础货币的衡量和货币乘数都造成很大影响；电子货币的跨国界流动，使一国货币政策的独立性和金融监管受到严峻挑战。

③ 财政风险：财政风险的加剧源于财政收支不平衡、财政赤字过度、财政预算支出大、政府债务负担重、税收流失等。例如，地方政府债务危机、欧债危机等表现出来的就是一种财政风险。

④ 产业风险：由于政府产业政策不当，指导不力，以及网络经济强烈的不确定性和正反馈效应，使得产业在发展过程中形成的风险。近年来产生的"网络泡沫"，使很多企业充分体会到，在网络经济中，生与死、快乐与痛苦，只不过咫尺之遥。网络经济既充满了机会，又暗含着杀机。

⑤ 计划与规划风险：因国家计划与规划具有预测性、诱导性和规划性和一定指令约束性，对国民经济的影响很大，国家计划与规划不科学而出现问题，也会造成全局性的经济风险。

烈波动等因素引起的经营风险，等等。

2010 年以来，不少地方出现了大的经济泡沫，大量的资金都被卷到投机炒作房地产漩涡中，房地产价格连续高涨；部分农产品价格剧烈波动；艺术品和其他一些大宗商品都有金融化、资本化趋向，金融功能异化，造成以金融为代表的虚拟经济越来越脱离实体经济；网络经济秩序混乱。在 2012 年底举行的中央经济工作会议上，首次把"过剩产能"这一概念放在核心位置，并明确指出经济政策"要高度重视财政金融领域存在的风险隐患，坚决守住不发生系统性和区域性金融风险的底线"。

特别值得关注的是地方政府债务负担沉重。2013 年 6 月 10 日，国家审计署通过网站公布的审计结果显示，36 个地区 2012 年底债务余额共计 3.85 万亿元，比 2010 年增加 4409.81 亿元，增长了 12.94%。2012 年，有 9 个省会城市本级政府负有偿还责任的债务率超过 100%，最高的达 188.95%，如加上政府负有担保责任的债务，债务率最高的达 219.57%。这表明我国地方政府债务已经存在风险。

曾有学者预言"2013 年中国将爆发经济危机"。① 我认为，中国经济发展面临产能过剩、增长下滑、房地产价格连续高涨、地方政府债务巨大等重大经济风险是无法回避的事实，然而我们目前经济发展还有 7.6% 的增长，产业升级空间较大，有政府宏观调控，地方债务可控，因此，不会爆发经济危机。

二　实行经济法治是预防和治理经济风险的基本方式

经济发展与经济法治之间是相互影响相互作用的。经济法治是促使经济发展的一个重要的外在因素。良好的法治环境可以保障经济又好又快地发展，当经济处于一个全面快速的发展阶段时，经济发展对于法治有明显的需求，新型产业的发展需要新法规加以规制，新型法律纠纷需要与时俱进的司法解释加以解决。但是这并不意味着法治只为经济增速服务。当经济发展处于不景气或存在经济风险甚至发生经济危机时，经济法治也能发挥独特作用。

在西方国家有所谓危机应对经济法，就是说经济法的出现就是为"应

---

① 国务院发展研究中心资源与环境政策研究所副所长李佐军，于 2011 年 9 月 27 日，在齐鲁证券长沙营业部举行的一次内部报告会上做了题为 "2013 年中国将爆发经济危机" 的报告，预测中国 "可能是 2013 年，最可能是 2013 年 7、8 月份（下半年）爆发经济危机"。

付经济不景气或其他意想不到的危机而被动制定的"。① 现实中出现了什么社会经济问题需要解决，就制定什么样的经济法。由于出现的各种社会经济问题有特殊性，决定了所制定的经济法也各具特色。② 例如，20 世纪 30 年代的危机时期，美国罗斯福政府颁布了《国家产业复兴法》；美国奥巴马政府针对 2008 年金融危机的现实，于 2009 年 6 月正式公布了"全面金融监管改革方案"，2010 年 7 月，美国参议院通过了最终版本的《金融监管改革法案》（即"多德－弗兰克法案"），该法案被认为是"大萧条"以来最全面、最严厉的金融改革法案；1978 年日本政府在经济不景气的态势下，制定了《特定不景气地区中小企业对策临时措施法》和《特定不景气产业稳定临时措施法》等。可见西方国家大多采取制定经济法律、法规的措施来摆脱经济危机。

如何预防和应对经济风险？我认为实行经济法治是预防和应对重大经济风险的有效路径。政府必须真正落实依法治国基本方略，加强经济法治建设，提高运用法治决策思维和方法去解决经济风险的意识，逐步建立起积极预防和有效治理经济风险的经济法律机制。例如，适时制定和实施一些经济法规：不排除一些企业为了单纯的经济利益而做出铤而走险的逐利行动，这时国家就要制定禁止这类行为的经济法规；经济减速伴随经济结构调整，而且大减速往往能触发大调整、大改革，这就有可能产生大裁员和失业风险，这时国家就要运用产业政策法、劳动法和税法加以应对；刺激经济、扩大内需就要依靠财政预算法、鼓励民间投资法、中小企业促进法；等等。

实行经济法治是政府管控经济风险的基本方式。政府管理经济，防控经济风险有许多方式，既有经济手段、行政手段，也有政策工具和方法；既有对宏观经济的调控，也有对企业经营活动的规制等。但是政府管理经济，都必须依法行政，运用法治思维和方法，只有这样才能创造公平竞争的外部环境。

实行经济法治必须提高经济风险控制意识和经济法治理念。加入 WTO 以后，中国经济发展受国际市场影响增大，这就不可能完全摆脱国际金融危机的影响。在经济风险控制方面，我们一定要考虑到经济发展是会有风

① 刘文华主编《经济法》（第 4 版），中国人民大学出版社，2012，第 24 页。
② 参见邱本《关于经济法发展的几个问题》，载中国人民大学经济法学研究中心编《经济社会发展与经济法》，法律出版社，2011，第 59－63 页。

险的,要提高经济风险控制意识,增强对于国际金融危机及其产生经济波动所需要的应变能力、风险控制能力、宏观经济分析能力等。经济法治是预防与治理经济风险的基本方式,也是预防与控制经济风险的基本保障。因此,政府、生产经营者、消费者和一切利益相关者都应提高市场经济是法治经济的法治意识和理念。防控风险,"留住财富,别无他法,唯有法治"。①

总之,经济增长时期需要完善经济法治,减速时期同样需要防范经济风险的经济法治。法律的确定性、稳定性、规范性,使法律有预测、引导和制约作用。要使法律的这些功能和作用在经济管理和经营中充分发挥出来,防止重大经济风险发生,就必须实行经济法治。市场经济是法治经济。法治,特别是在经济领域实行的经济法治,是预防重大经济风险发生的有效路径。

三 识别和确认经济风险需要经济法律机制

为了防范和治理经济风险,首先要科学界定人们所要识别和确认的经济风险是什么。建立起识别经济风险的法律机制。对可能发生的不同类别的经济风险要进行标准化技术界定与识别,建立一套制度化的识别各类经济风险法律机制,使人们易于识别经济风险。

在法律上明确界定需要防范和治理的各种经济风险的概念、范围、主要特征及其表现,采用一定幅度的数据量化指标等,确立一套能够快捷识别经济领域内产生的各种具体类别的风险和综合经济风险的识别操作程序机制。

为了准确发现经济风险,还需增加一道认定经济风险的法律机制。在技术层面识别经济风险种种迹象的基础上,再运用法律具有确定性、规范性的独特功能,将经济风险的技术规范上升为法律规范,从而构建确认经济风险的经济法律机制。

当然,经济风险的不确定性、复杂性和偶发性,使其主要特征及其表现是动态的、互相转化的,用规范和指标完全固定经济风险特点、范围是十分困难的。有学者也认为:"风险所带来的不确定性、不可计测性却很难通过法律和政府举措来缩减,更不必说消除殆尽。换句话说,无论采取何

---

① 王琳:《法治:财富论坛的渊源与未来》,中国网,http://news.china.com.cn/live/2013 - 06/08/content_20459460.htm,最后访问日期:2013 年 6 月 8 日。

种方法来防止风险，总会存有'剩余风险'，所以规范预期不得不相对化，不得不以'风险 vs 风险'的状态为前提来考虑风险对策以及相关的制度设计。"① 所以，识别和锁定经济风险，还需要通过自我反省的机制调整法律形式与客观事实之间的关系。只有通过这种反省机制，适时修改、解释法律条文，并在执行中依照实质优先形式的原则进行操作，才有可能使规范预期经济风险与事实上的经济风险之间的裂痕渐次达到弥合。

四　经济法治与经济风险的监控与预防

1. 经济风险监控制度化是经济法治的要求

识别并确认经济风险以后，最为重要的就是持续监控暴露出的风险信息和事项。对经济风险监控不力，也无法治理经济风险。什么是风险监控？所谓风险监控，是指在决策主体的运行过程中，对风险的形成、发展与变化情况进行全程监督，并根据需要进行应对策略的调整。因为风险是随着内部外部环境的变化而变化的，它们在经济决策主体活动的推进过程中可能会增大或者衰退乃至消失，也可能由于环境的变化又生成新的风险。经济风险监控就是通过对经济风险的识别、确认、评估等，应对全过程的监视和控制，从而保证经济风险治理达到预期的目标，它是经济风险防控实施过程中最重要的一环。监控风险实际是监视经济运行的进展和经济环境变化，其目的是：核对经济风险防控策略和措施的实际效果是否与预见的相同；寻找机会改善和细化规避风险措施；获取反馈信息，以便使应对决策更符合实际。在风险监控过程中，及时发现那些新出现的以及随着时间推延而发生变化的风险，然后及时反馈，并根据对项目的影响程度，重新进行风险识别、评估和应对。

依经济法治的要求，解决经济风险，必须建立起积极预防和有效治理经济风险的一整套经济法律制度。经济风险监控制度就是治理经济风险的经济法律制度中的重要组成部分。经济风险监控制度一般包括确认监控主体与被监控主体的法律地位，明确二者相互关系，确定监控事项范围、监控手段或方式、风险评估内容与结果和监控程序、责任等。

2. 市场重要信息与经济风险监控事项的确定

市场重要信息能够反映和发现经济风险的迹象。依法收集、传递、反

---

① 季卫东：《依法的风险管理》，载李林主编《全面落实依法治国基本方略》，中国社会科学出版社，2009，第120－132页。

馈、公开和处理市场重要信息，对确定形成经济风险前后的发展与变化情况，对加强风险监控很有价值。在这里经济风险监控制度应当确定一定范围的市场重要信息为法定的经济风险监控事项。

3. 电子网络技术与经济风险监控与预防

采用经济法治解决经济风险，需要现代化技术手段的支持，所以普遍使用电子网络技术识别和处理经济风险监控事项，对于预防与监控经济风险具有重要应用价值。应当尽快建立有利于发挥互联网预防与监控经济风险的制度。

4. 建立经济风险监控报告制度

一切报告都是下级向上级机关或业务主管部门汇报情况和陈述事实，让上级机关掌握基本情况和工作进展的。通过报告让上级机关获得信息，掌握下情，为进行宏观决策和指导提供依据。经济风险监控报告是一种对经济风险监控的事项、情况和进展进行分析的例行报告。因此，建立经济风险监控报告制度，是预防与治理经济风险的有效措施。

五　治理经济风险的经济法治思维和方法

1. 治理经济风险必须树立经济法治思维

在市场经济条件下，市场主体从事经济活动需要经济法治思维，政府管理经济也需要经济法治思维，应对和治理经济风险同样需要经济法治思维。经济法治思维是指导各项经济法治活动的行动指南，是依法治国、依法行政、依法管理经济的必然要求，是克服拍脑袋决策等非理性行为的有效方法，是治理经济风险的法治。在首都各界纪念现行宪法公布施行30周年大会上，习近平总书记强调指出，要落实依法治国基本方略，加快建设社会主义法治国家，以宪法为最高法律规范，维护社会主义法制的统一和尊严，全面推进科学立法、严格执法、公正司法、全民守法进程，维护社会公平正义。2013年3月17日，李克强总理在会见采访"两会"的中外记者时强调，建设法治政府，要把法律放在神圣的位置，任何人、办任何事，都不能超越法律的权限，我们要用法治精神来建设现代经济、现代社会、现代政府。2013年5月13日，李克强总理在国务院机构职能转变动员电视电话会议上又强调指出，转变政府职能，就是要解决好政府与市场、政府与社会的关系问题，通过简政放权，进一步发挥市场在资源配置中的基础性作用，激发市场主体的创造活力，增强经济发展的内生动力；就是要把政府工作重点转到创造良好发展环境、提供优质公共服务、维护社会公平正义上来，用法治思维和法治方式履行政府职能。面对经济风险需要经济法治思维，要用经济法治思维应对与治理经济风险。

2. 在治理经济风险中经济法治的优势

在治理经济风险中，经济法治的方法与其他应对方法相比较而言，具有一定优势。因为作为经济法治主要法律部门的"经济法应对现实问题具有系统的理论解释力和有效的规则调整力。这是经济法的一贯特点。如对科学发展观、和谐社会、金融危机等等，经济法都可以做出自己独特的、不同于其他法律部门的理论解释和规则调整。经济法经过百来年的发展，已经初步形成了自己的理论体系和规则体系，具有科学的理论解释力和有效的规则调整力。如对金融危机，经济法可以从国家干预理论、宏观调控理论、金融监管理论等予以解释，并从财政法、金融法、投资法等予以调整"。①

在应对 2008 年国际金融危机时，中国为应对金融危机而增加的 4 万亿投资，其愿望是好的，但决策内容和程序之所以遭到国人的批评，就是因为没有严格遵循我国《预算法》等经济法律的有关规定，重大的经济决策缺乏经济法治思维和未采用法治方式，忽视国家宏观经济调控法律化作用，使社会经济发展遭受损失。

3. 政府治理经济风险应受经济法治约束

治理经济风险无疑必须充分发挥好政府的作用。从经济法治角度来看，政府使用的任何治理经济风险的工具，包括政府规制行为和政府调控行为，都应遵循以民主与法治为核心的经济法治的要求。政府依法治理，就是要求政府在决策行为与执行行为时不能忘记法治思维，不能脱离法治方式，即行政权力必须被限制。正如习近平总书记所言："要加强对权力运行的制约和监督，把权力关进制度的笼子里。"

政府治理经济风险应受经济法治约束。怎样约束？我认为可以通过两大方面实现：（1）强化人民代表大会制度对政府宏观调控权力的制约和监督。切实杜绝类似"4 万亿"投资预算不经全国人民代表大会批准的脱法行为。大力推动规划、产业调整、振兴、促进等方面的立法，尽量减少政府指令冻结、限购、补贴等直接干预的行政措施。（2）完善法定市场规则

---

① 邱本：《关于经济法发展的几个问题》，载中国人民大学经济法学研究中心编《经济社会发展与经济法》，法律出版社，2011，第 59 - 63 页。

体系，大力减少行政审批和企业税费负担，建立负面清单制度，增强经营者的自主权，激发社会投资活力和创造力，这是治理经济风险的根本之策。

4. 建立健全保护劳动者、消费者和中小投资者权益的制度

治理经济风险的首要目标就是要维护劳动者、消费者和中小投资者权益，保障民生。

劳动者是创造社会财富的生力军，遇到再大的风险和困难也要保护好劳动者，保存抗击风险的有生力量。在经济减速下滑，在面临经济结构大调整时期，伴随而来的就是大裁员和广失业，如何应对这些风险？从经济法治角度看，要完善劳动法和劳动合同法，建立社会保障法，健全破产法，适应转岗需要建立义务培训制度，培养与积蓄劳动力大军。

治理经济风险需要扩大内需，扩大内需就要扩大消费，扩大消费就要让广大消费者大胆放心消费、有钱消费，而要做到放心消费、有钱消费，就要公平分配，提高普通劳动者的工资使之有钱消费。建立可靠的社会保障制度，进一步健全消费者权益保护法律制度，使广大消费者放心消费。

治理经济风险需要扩大投资，当下特别需要鼓励民间投资，而要扩大投资，就要切实保障中小投资者权益。如何保障中小投资者权益？我认为：一是健全证券法，完善投资者保护制度；二是改革银行法律制度，允许民间资本进入银行业，创办民资银行，与此同时建立存款保险制度、金融机构破产制度等一套保护中小投资者权益的经济法律制度。

结　论

当前中国经济发展面临产生经济风险的巨大压力与严峻挑战，但是中国不会发生经济危机，国民经济也不会崩溃。加强防范经济风险并进行有效风险控制或治理，需要政府、企业经营者、劳动者、消费者、投资者共同努力，遵循经济法治思维，提高防范经济风险和风险管理意识，建立预防与治理经济风险的经济法律机制，真正采用法治方式防范和应对经济风险，在经济领域落实依法治国的基本方略，将市场经济活动、政府规制和调控行为纳入经济法治的轨道。

Economic Rule of Law and the Prevention and Management of Economic Risks

Xu Mengzhou *

【Abstract】 As a result of the combined effect of many complicated and changeable factors, China has been suffering from continuous economic downturn and faced with various economic risks since 2010. The author of this article holds that a rational response to these challenges is to strengthen the system of the prevention and effective management of economic risks and, in order to do that, China must truly implement the basic strategy of ruling the country by law, abide by the principle of economic rule of law, enhance the consciousness of economic risks and of management of economic risks, and gradually establish the concrete system of prevention and management of economic risks and the corresponding legal mechanisms.

【Keywords】 Economic Risks; Economic Rule of Law; Prevention and Management

---

* Professor, Law School of Renmin University of China.

Fit for the Governance of Global Value Chains?

—The Framework for Commercial Dispute Resolution in Finland from a Multiparty, Multi-Contract Perspective

Jaakko Salminen [*]

[Abstract] Global value chains, made up of multiple actors from diverse backgrounds and connected through several contracts, pose major problems for coordinated governance. One practical prerequisite is a dispute resolution forum that can take into account all the actors and contracts that are relevant from the perspective of a specific dispute. In this paper, I will discuss the legal framework for organizing commercial dispute resolution in Finland through arbitration and mediation. In particular, I will evaluate the framework from the perspective of multiparty and multi-contract situations typically in complex contractually organized value chains such as the ongoing Olkiluoto 3 nuclear power plant construction project. In this context, the relationship between the rule of law and the fragmented regulatory field of commercial dispute resolution seems ambiguous.

1. Introduction

Global value chains are made up of multiple actors from diverse backgrounds and connected through several contracts. They pose major problems for coordinated governance especially if disputes arise between actors that are not parties to the same

---

[*] Jaakko Salminen, University of Turku.

contract. One practical prerequisite for value chain governance is a dispute resolution forum that can take into account all the actors and contracts that are relevant from the perspective of a specific dispute. In this article, I will discuss the legal framework for organizing commercial multiparty and multi-contract dispute resolution in Finland with special reference to problems possibly faced by contractually organized value chains.

In Section 2, I will first use the Olkiluoto 3 nuclear power plant project as an example scenario where multiple parties and contracts have a vested interest in a dispute. Instead of its planned completion in 2009, the Olkiluoto 3 project has been delayed seven years and has given cause to multibillion-euroarbitration claims. I will follow this by laying out the general framework for multiparty and multi-contract international commercial dispute resolution.

In Section 3, I will examine Finnish regulatory approaches to multiparty and multi-contract dispute resolution from the perspective of global value chain governance. I will discuss Finnish cases on the scope of arbitration agreements, some multiparty and multi-contract aspects of the 2013 Arbitration Rules of the Finland Chamber of Commerce, and Finnish regulation on the enforceability of mediated agreements.

Finally in Section 4, I will discuss conclusions that can be drawn on the basis of the presented framework. States have shown little interest in regulating dispute resolution in global value chains even when these have a major impact on diverse actors nationally and internationally. Instead, parties' contractual arrangements and dispute resolution institutes, such as the ICC in Paris, the FCC in Finland, and CIETAC in China, have a major regulatory function that may leave open questions of transparency, legitimacy, and efficiency.

2. Governing Disputes in Value Chains

Value chains are typically organized in groups of contracts working towards a shared economic objective. ① It is unclear what the precise legal effects of a value chain are on the individual constituent contracts as this depends on many factors, such as the contents of the contracts and any practices that the value chain members

---

① Eg Gary Gereffi, John Humphrey, and Timothy Sturgeon, 'The governance of global value chains' (2005) 12 Review of International Political Economy 78 – 104.

may have established between themselves. ① Intuitively, however, the fate of the contracts making up a value chain reston the other contracts of the same value chain. The parties to one contract have a vested interest in the other contracts. A key problem in value chain governance is, thus, that the chain may cease to operate as a whole and instead fragment into actors who concentrate on individual contracts without oversight of the whole. ② One approach to remedy fragmentation-related problems is to establish methods of information sharing that transcend contract boundaries, thereby creating contract boundary spanning governance mechanisms. ③

In Section 2.1, I will use the Olkiluoto 3 nuclear power plant project as an illustrative example of the problems of a contractually organized value chain from the perspective of implementing a value chain spanning governance mechanism. Then, in Section 2.2 I will chart the framework for organizing a centralized dispute resolution forum as one important aspect of value chain governance.

2.1 Olkiluoto 3

Construction on Finland's fifth nuclear power plant, Olkiluoto 3, was supposed to be completed in 2009. At the time of writing, Olkiluoto 3 is expected to be ready at earliest in 2016. Simultaneously, the main parties are engaged in a multibillion-euro arbitration. ④ While there is little public knowledge about the dispute and the issues at stake, a study of the Olkiluoto 3 value chain published by the Finnish Nuclear and Radiation Safety Authority (FNRSA) in 2011 highlights some of the problems encountered during the project. ⑤ Unless otherwise stated, all information in this article on the Olkiluoto 3 project is based on that report.

Olkiluoto 3 is set apart from most value chains by the involvement in the project

---

① For one example, see Gunther Teubner, *Netzwerk als Vertragsverbund: Virtuelle Unternehmen, Franchising, Just-in-time in sozialwissenschaftlicher und juristischer Sicht* (Nomos 2004).

② For the problems of fragmentation, see Omri Ben-Shahar and James J. White, 'Boilerplate and Economic Power in Auto Manufacturing Contracts' (2006) 104 Michigan Law Review 953 – 982.

③ Peter Kajüter and Harri I. Kulmala, 'Open-book accounting in networks' (2005) 16 Management Accounting Research 179 – 204.

④ www. world-nuclear-news. org/C-Suppliers-raise-Olkiluoto-3-damages-claim-3110134. html.

⑤ 'Olkiluoto 3-varavoimadieselgeneraattoreiden (EDG) ja niiden apujärjestelmien ja laitteiden hankintaan kohdistuva tutkinta' (Säteilyturvakeskus 2011).

of a regulatory authority, the FNRSA. FNRSA's involvement has a fundamental impact on the constitution and operation of the nuclear value chain. The FNRSA oversees the construction of nuclear power plants in Finland, first, by regulating the procedures and quality criteria to be implemented throughout the value chain of nuclear power plant construction, and, second, by inspecting plans, materials, and construction to ensure that everything complies with safety requirements.

The regulations that FNRSA produced are open-ended so that they can reflect developing best practices and do not overly constrict the possibilities of commercial operators to choose from a number of available options. Due to this open-endedness, the regulations do not always provide direct guidance but instead need to be interpreted in the contexts of the specific plans and operations of each supplier and contractor involved in the project.

The FNRSA has a public law relationship to the company that has been granted a license to build and operate a nuclear power plant (licensee). In Olkiluoto 3, the licensee ordered a nuclear power plant on turnkey basis from the main contractor, a two-party consortium. Both consortium members organised their respective parts of the value chain, each comprising hundreds of suppliers and subcontractors from numerous countries.

Olkiluoto 3 has been an abject failure. One major cause of the failure, it seems, was in the design of the governance structure for mobilizing the FNRSA regulations to control contractor performance in the value chains. On the basis of the FNRSA report it seems that the licensee, in practice, outsourced the implementation of the FNRSA regulations to the main contractors who in turn did the same with their respective value chains.

Failure followed when various actors in the value chain misinterpreted the FNRSA requirements. The FNRSA maintained that it had a relationship only with the licensee and could not directly address issues raised by the other value chain members. It appears that the project had no centralized arrangements set up to ensure proper compliance with FNRSA regulations. Thus, the misinterpretations travelled from one value chain member to nodes further up in the value chain all the way to the FNRSA before they could be addressed and then sent back down through the contractual chain of command hierarchy. The non-functional communication arrangement contributed to the serious delays experienced in the project.

At first glance, decentralizing the responsibility to interpret the FNRSA regulations is a natural contract governance move. However, according to the FNRSA, ensuring compliance with FNRSA regulations was the duty of the licensee. The FNRSA had expected the licensee to establish a system of compliance beyond the level of individual contractor value chains. The licensee organized the project governance structure to make the main contractor responsible for compliance. The main contractor pushed responsibility further down and expected its suppliers and subcontractors to ensure compliance. The structure of delegating responsibility was replicated through the value chains.

Who, then, is to blame for delays caused by non-compliance with the FNRSA's requirements? Should the licensee have taken a more active role, or was the risk of non-compliance validly passed on to one or more of the other members of the value chain? There is no easy answer to the question, nor will I attempt to provide one. My focus turns procedural. Suppose, further, that some of the individual contracts in the value chain were breached in a way that could have been avoided had the value chain been organized as expected by the FNRSA. The ensuing dispute involves many if not all members of the value chain. As they all had a stake in the success of the contract boundary spanning governance mechanism requested by the FNRSA, they all also have a legitimate interest in participating in the dispute even though it may not be directly related to their own contracts. On an even more indirect level, such disputes also concern environmental, safety, and labour interests. Poor value chain governance may lead to oversight of necessary environmental and safety features, while the ensuing long delays cause labour management problems possibly leading to temporary or permanent layoffs.

Similar situations are not limited to the very specific scenario of a nuclear construction project in Finland. The question of organizing the governance of a value chain and the effects that different forms of value chain governance have on the individual contracts of the value chain is relevant in numerous other contexts such as automotive or aircraft manufacturing. [1] In all these contexts, a centralized

---

[1] Eg Kajüter and Kulmala, 'Open-book accounting in networks', Ben-Shahar and White, 'Boilerplate and Economic Power in Auto Manufacturing Contracts', and Matthew C. Jennejohn, 'Contract Adjudication in a Collaborative Economy' (2010) 5 Virginia Law & Business Review 173 – 237.

dispute resolution forum that could overcome the same contract boundaries as the contract boundary spanning governance mechanism would help mitigate the negative effects of governance failures.

2. 2 The current framework for centralized dispute resolution

A single centralized forum for dispute resolution is arguably a better solution than multiple proceedings if multiple parties under multiple contracts are involved in a dispute revolving around the same issues. The need for a single venue is particular pressing in value chains. Value chains are functional wholes. The chain actors must maintain amicable relationships to enable the chain to function.

The avoidance of contradictory judgments, increased overall efficiency, and increased willingness in finding an amicable settlement are advantages typically attributed to a centralized forum in multiparty and multi-contract arbitration. [1] Loss of efficiency for some parties and a possible lack of transparency and foreseeability in forum selection, on the other hand, are some often mentioned disadvantages. [2] Beyond these, a further factor to be taken into account is limitation periods. In long-term and severely delayed projects such as Olkiluoto 3 that comprise numerous actors in complex value chains, parties are often required to initiate proceedings that remain pending while waiting for the outcome of other proceedings in order to not lose their rights.

If a value chain implements contract boundary spanning governance methods, the situation is even more multifaceted. Olkiluoto 3 is an illustrative example. The fate of individual contract disputes may be dependent on a contested overall value chain governance mechanism. Yet the governance mechanism may have no link to the individual contractal beit the governance mechanism that is the root cause of the dispute. The problem is striking. If no centralized dispute resolution forum that can overcome contractual boundary lines exists, the overall efficiency of the value chain will suffer, but also transparency and legitimacy within the value chain will be torn apart.

---

[1]　Bernd von Hoffmann, 'Schiedsgerichtsbarkeit in mehrstufigen Vertragsbeziehungen, insbesondere in Subunternehmerverträgen' in Karl-Heinz Böckstiegel and others (eds), Die Beteiligung Dritter an Schiedsverfahren (Carl Heymanns Verlag 2005).

[2]　Ibid.

Despite the need, centralized dispute resolution forums are rarely found in contractually organized value chains. The reasons for their non-existence are often legal. In the following two subsections I will discuss the general framework of international commercial arbitration (Section 2.2.1) and mediation (Section 2.2.2) from the perspective of a centralized dispute resolution forum in multiparty and multi-contract proceedings.

2.2.1 Arbitration

Arbitration is almost without exception the dispute resolution method of choice in large-scale project contracts. To implement a centralized project dispute resolution forum using arbitration, two issues are crucial. First, all value chain actors must be bound by an arbitration agreement that subjects disputes to a single forum. Second, the procedural framework must be flexible enough to accommodate multiparty and multi-contract arbitration. The former question depends on contract law rules, while the latter is governed by applicable procedural rules such as a national arbitration law or the rules of an arbitration institute the parties agreed to use.

The simplest option to accommodate both issues is to draft an arbitration clause or agreement that specifically enables multiparty and multi-contract proceedings and have relevant parties sign it. ① Another option is to construct a conflict management system. Both options pose formidable challenges. All the relevant parties would have to be identified and induced to sign. Such agreement may be difficult to achieve in complex value chains. First, value chains are often dynamic and fluid, and consequently contract management is difficult. Second, different actors may have

---

① An example that highlights the complexity of such clauses is provided by the American Arbitration Association's 2007 Guide to Drafting Alternative Dispute Resolution Clauses for Construction Contracts:

The owner, the contractor, and all subcontractors, specialty contractors, material suppliers, engineers, designers, architects, construction lenders, bonding companies and other parties concerned with the construction of the structure are bound, each to each other, by this arbitration clause, provided that they have signed this contract or a contract that incorporates this contract by reference or signed any other agreement to be bound by this arbitration clause. Each such party agrees that it may be joined as an additional party to an arbitration involving other parties under any such agreement. If more than one arbitration is begun under any such agreement and any party contends that two or more arbitrations are substantially related and that the issues should be heard in one proceeding, the arbitrator (s) selected in the first filed of such proceedings shall determine whether, in the interests of justice and efficiency, the proceedings should be consolidated before that (those) arbitrator (s).

widely divergent objectives that may hamper the reaching of a consensus.

Without a single arbitration clause or a unitary conflict management system that extends to all relevant parties and contracts, finding a common dispute resolution forum to aid in value chain governance will be nearly impossible. A number of legal doctrines may, however, facilitate at least limited governance even if explicit value chain dispute resolution arrangements are missing.

If the different contracts of a value chain contain *compatible* dispute resolution agreements, a venue may be parsed together. In compatible dispute resolution agreements, technically separate agreements refer to the same institutional arbitration rules, which allow the interpretation that the parties had, in fact, intended that the various separate contracts constituted one multilateral transaction. ① Close connections between contracts and close links between reciprocal rights and obligations may be indicative of such. For example, according to Hanotiau, "the economic unity of the group [of contracts] is becoming one of the most important criteria in determining the scope of the arbitration agreement within the group, at least when it appears to be in line with the will of the parties" . ②

The compatibility solution is limited in its scope. If contracts in a value chain, for example, refer to different institutional arbitration rules and, consequently, contain *incompatible* dispute resolution agreements, no common intent of the parties to have a dispute resolved in a specific forum can be easily identified. ③ No saving grace exists. An innovative solution to lacking intention was developed by Teubner. He proposed that if a governance structure forms above the level of individual contracts, then this governance structure should be treated apart from the individual contracts. ④ Conceivably such a governance structure, perhaps similar to what the FNRSA requested to be implemented above and beyond individual contracts in the Olkiluoto 3 scenario, could provide a possibility for overriding

---

① Bernard Hanotiau, 'Multiple Parties and Multiple Contracts in International Arbitration' in Permanent Court of Arbitration (ed), *Multiple Party Actions in International Arbitration* (Oxford University Press 2009) p. 66 – 67.

② Ibid. p. 67 fn. 68, referring to François-Xavier Train, *Les contrats liés devant l'arbitre du commerce international* (L. G. D. J 2003).

③ Hanotiau, 'Multiple Parties and Multiple Contracts in International Arbitration' p. 66 – 67.

④ Teubner, *Netzwerk als Vertragsverbund: Virtuelle Unternehmen, Franchising, Just-in-time in sozialwissenschaftlicher und juristischer Sicht.*

incompatibilities between individual contracts.

The procedure followed in multiparty and multi-contract arbitrations depends on the institutional or ad hoc arbitration rules chosen by the parties and the applicable law. The problem is that applicable arbitration rules and laws may contain divergent regulations on, for example the role of parties in multiparty arbitrations, the possibility of and the prerequisites for multi-contract arbitration, joinder and consolidation. ① While some national arbitration laws do regulate multiparty and multi-contract issues, others remain silent and leave the issues up to the parties' choice of institutional or ad hoc rules. For example in Finland the local arbitration law does not cover multiparty or multi-contract issues, while the Arbitration Rules of the Finland Chamber of Commerce do regulate such issues in detail. I will compare these rules with other institutional approaches in Section 3. 1. 2 below.

2. 2. 2 Mediation

The regulation of mediation (or conciliation②) follows a pattern similar to arbitration. The scope of a mediation clause is dependent on interpretation of the parties' agreement while mediation procedure is based on applicable procedural law or any institutional or ad hoc mediation rules chosen by the parties.

Institutional mediation rules do not explicitly address multiparty or multi-contract issues even if mediation thought to have value in such disputes. ③ The key reason for this must be that mediators are by and large free to structure mediation proceedings as they see fit. ④ For example, according to Article 7 of the ICC

---

① By way of example, see Cristián Conejero Roos, 'Multi-party Arbitration and Rule-making: Same Issues, Contrasting Approaches' in Albert Jan van den Berg (ed), 50 *Years of the New York Convention*: *ICCA Internatonal Arbitration Conference* (Kluwer Law International 2009) for the differences in the extent of agreement required for joinder in various institutional arbitration rules.

② The terms mediation and conciliation are to an extent interchangeable. For example, UNCITRAL has a model law on international commercial conciliation, while the EU has adopted a directive on mediation, but both refer to non-binding, third party assisted procedures. Differences in usage exist locally. For example, under Swiss law conciliation refers to a court-directed procedure, while mediation refers to an out-of-court procedure.

③ Guide to Enactment and Use of the UNCITRAL Model Law on International Commercial Conciliation 2002, 2004, p. 25.

④ For comparison of one key procedural limit in institutional mediation rules, the right to terminate mediation proceedings, see Jaakko Salminen, 'The Different Meanings of International Commercial Conciliation' (2011) Nordic Journal of Commercial Law.

Mediation Rules, the mediator and the parties are free to structure the proceedings as they agree. ①

In general, mediation emphasizes the underlying business interests of the parties in a way that would not be possible in binding legal proceedings. ② Thus mediation proceedings as a non-binding, interest-based form of dispute resolution may be easier to establish in the multiple party and contract spanning disputes of a value chain even where no contractual obligation to do so exists. Should such proceedings lead to a mediated agreement, a specific enforcement advantage may be attainable over normal agreements depending on the national framework for enforcing mediated agreements. Finnish mediation law provides one example of this and it will be discussed in detail in Section 3. 2.

3. Value Chains and Finnish Regulatory Approaches to Dispute Resolution

In this section I look at how the general framework presented above in Section 2. 2 is reflected in current Finnish regulation on dispute resolution.

First, there is no explicit legislation on the scope of dispute resolution agreements in contractually organized value chains. A few cases where Finnish courts have dealt with parties' contractual dispute resolution arrangements in multi-contract settings provide the only guidance available. These cases are discussed in Section 3. 1.

The Finnish Arbitration Act regulates the general procedural aspects of arbitration in Finland. ③ It contains no explicit rules on multiparty or multi-contract disputes. The Arbitration Rules of the Finland Chamber of Commerce (FCC

---

① ICC Mediation Rules, effective 1 January 2014, available at www. iccwbo. org/products-and-services/arbitration-and-adr/mediation/rules/.

② Richard Hill, 'The Theoretical Basis of Mediation and Other Forms of ADR: Why They Work' (1998) 14 Arbitration International 173 – 184.

③ Laki välimiesmenettelystä (967/1992), available in English at www. finlex. fi/fi/laki/kaannokset/1992/en19920967. pdf. For English discussion see Jukka Peltonen, 'Intervention of State Courts in Finnish Arbitration-An Overview' (2011) Juridiska föreningens tidskrift 561 – 581, and Marko Hentunen, Anders Forss, and Jerker Pitkänen, 'IBA Arbitration Committee's Arbitration Guide on Finland', 2012.

Rules), on the other hand, do regulate multiparty and multi-contract proceedings. ① I will discuss the FCC Rules in Section 3. 2.

Finally, out-of-court mediation in Finland is based on the Mediation Directive (Directive 2008/52/EC of the European Parliament and of the Council of 21 May 2008 on certain aspects of mediation in civil and commercial matters). The directive was implemented in Finland through the 2011 Mediation Act (Act on mediation in civil matters and confirmation of settlements in general courts 394/2011). ② As of now the Finland Chamber of Commerce has not adopted rules on mediation. The Mediation Act contains almost no rules on the conduct of out-of-court mediation proceedings. Instead, the Act concentrates on the prerequisites that a mediated agreement must fulfil for to be recognized equal to a court judgment in enforcement. I will discuss these requirements in Section 3. 3.

3. 1 Finnish cases relating to the scope of dispute resolution agreements

Although privity of contract is the leading principle, non-signatories may also be bound by arbitration agreements under Finnish law. For example, the Finnish Supreme Court has found that a guarantor is entitled to refer an arbitration agreement in the construction contract to the performance of which was guaranteed. ③ Other examples include assignees, third party beneficiaries, and maritime insurance. ④

However, cases on multi-contract situations are meagre. The few available cases deal with multi-contract situations between the same parties, such as when two parties have entered into a number of different contracts all relating to the same general transaction. A framework agreement and purchase orders made under the framework agreement are typical examples.

In the Supreme Court case KKO 1990: 106 two parties had entered into a dealership agreement. The same parties then entered into an agreement on the sale

---

① The Arbitration Rules of the Finland Chamber of Commerce, in effect from 1 June 2013, in English at http://arbitration. fi/en/rules/.

② Laki riita-asioiden sovittelusta ja sovinnon vahvistamisesta yleisissä tuomioistuimissa (394/2011), in English at www. finlex. fi/fi/laki/kaannokset/2011/en20110394. pdf

③ Finnish Supreme Court decisions KKO 1930-II-555 and KKO 1939 – II – 424.

④ Finnish Supreme Court decisions KKO 1939 – II – 424, KKO 2007: 39, and KKO 2013: 84.

of equipment to be used under the dealership. The dealership agreement contained an arbitration clause, while the sales agreement contained a prorogation clause in favour of a local court. The Supreme Court found the two agreements independent from one another. Thus the dispute, which revolved around the sales agreement, was governed by the prorogation clause in the sales agreement.

In a more recent Supreme Court case, KKO 1997: 200, two parties had entered into a foreign currency credit agreement. Later on, the same parties entered into a credit restructuring agreement that covered all their previous agreements. The former agreement had no dispute resolution clause, while the latter had an arbitration clause. The Supreme Court found that the parties had intended to cover all disputes arising from their earlier credit agreements with the credit restructuring agreement, and, therefore, the arbitration clause extended to all disputes arising from under the earlier credit agreements.

Finally, in a case from 2011 the Helsinki Court of Appeal, the court found that where two or more agreements between the same parties form a single contractual entity (*sopimuskokonaisuus*), the presumption is that the parties have not intended to initiate separate dispute resolution proceedings for the different agreements. [1] An arbitration clause in one of the agreements was, thus, extended to another agreement that did not have an explicit dispute resolution clause.

Thus, only few conclusions can be made with regard to dispute resolution in value chains based these cases. Where agreements form a single contractual entity and do not contain incompatible dispute resolution agreements, the scope of an arbitration agreement may extend to all contracts in the entity. Other than that, little can be said with certainty. There are no cases involving multiple contracts with incompatible dispute resolution agreements where the different contracts would have been held to constitute a single contractual entity. Nor are there any cases suggesting the opposite. Neither are there cases involving multi-contract situations between multiple parties.

Some of the arguments used hint above by the Finnish Supreme Court in the cases that the Court could be likely to adopt a pragmatic approach to the scope of dispute resolution agreements. The dispute resolution clause most closely related to

---

[1]   Helsinki Appeals Court case HHO 17. 8. 2011 S 10/2248 nr 2426.

the dispute may be the preferred choice if dispute resolution agreements contradict each other. ① Again, it is unclear what this would mean for the scope of dispute resolution agreements in a contractual value chain with a contract boundary spanning governance mechanism. Could the mechanism be construed as a contract above the layer of the individual contracts of the value chain or, for example, as a special trust-based relationship, is unclear. Thus also whether issues related to such a governance mechanism might be settled in the forum most closely associated with the arrangement despite incompatible dispute resolution agreements otherwise is an open question.

In the meanwhile, the only certain way of organizing a centralized dispute resolution forum fora value chain is through an umbrella dispute resolution clause in all connected contracts. Alternatively, using compatible dispute resolution agreements in the separate contracts of the value chain might also work as long as the value chain constitutes a single contractual entity indicating the value chain members' intent to settle their disputes in the same proceedings.

3. 2 Arbitration Rules of the Finland Chamber of Commerce

The FCC Arbitration Rules seem to have borrowed their approach to multiparty and multi-contract proceedings from the 2012 ICC Arbitration Rules (ICC Rules). ② Consequently, I will compare the FCC Rules primarily to the ICC Rules while also commenting on a numberof alternative models.

Under the FCC Rules' multiparty arbitration regime, any party to a proceeding may raise a claim against any other party despite any nominal status as claimant or respondent. ③ Further, the claims need not be based on the same contract or

---

① In KKO 1990: 106 the Finnish Supreme Court emphasised among other things the lack of relationship between the claim and the contract containing the arbitration clause. In KKO 2013: 84 (on whether a third party beneficiary was bound by an arbitration agreement) the Supreme Court on the other hand emphasised the existence of a relationship between the dispute and a specific contract: That the calculation of damages required the application and interpretation of a contract supported the view that the dispute resolution clause in that contract extended to a non-signatory.

② Based on information received from the Arbitration Institute of the Finland Chamber of Commerce and the general likeness of the FCC and ICC Rules.

③ FCC Rules Art. 11.

arbitration agreement, as long as all claims arise under the FCC Rules. ① The right is not unconditional. For arbitrations based on one arbitration agreement, the rules require that the board of directors of the Arbitration Institute be prima facie satisfied that the agreement allows for all the claims to be heard in the same proceedings. ② If multiple arbitration agreements exist, the rules require that the board be prima facie satisfied that the arbitration agreements are not incompatible with one another and that the parties may have agreed that their claims can be determined in a single arbitration. ③ These requirements are in general similar to those in the ICC Rules. ④

Joinder of additional parties is possible without the agreement of all parties up until the moment when the case file is transmitted from the Arbitration Institute to the arbitral tribunal, while later requests for joinder require agreement from all parties. ⑤ This is also in line with the ICC Rules. ⑥ In any case, joinder is subject to the same requirements as multiparty arbitration. Before the board allows a joinder request to proceed it must be prima facie satisfied that claims against or from the party to be joined fall under an arbitration agreement governed by the FCC Rules. If multiple arbitration agreements are involved the board must be similarly convinced that no incompatible arbitration agreements are involved and that all the parties may have agreed to hear the disputes in the same proceeding.

Consolidation is possible either where, first, all parties agree to it, second, all the claims are made under the same arbitration agreement, or, third, where the claims are not made under the same arbitration agreement, when the disputes arise in connection with the same legal relationship and the arbitration agreements are compatible with one another. ⑦ The third option differs from the comparable rules in the ICC Rules. ICC requires in addition that the arbitrations be between the same parties. ⑧ With regard to consolidation the FCC Rules, thus, appear more

---

① FCC Rules Art. 12.
② FCC Rules Art. 14 (1).
③ FCC Rules Art. 14 (2).
④ ICC Rules 6 (4).
⑤ FCC Rules Art. 10.
⑥ ICC Rules Art. 7.
⑦ FCC Rules Art. 13.
⑧ ICC Rules Art. 10.

flexible than the ICC Rules.

Albeit that arbitral tribunals have the final say on whether or not they will assume jurisdiction in particular cases, the FCC board may decide whether it will allow a case to proceed to an arbitral tribunal in the first place if joinder, consolidation, multi-contract proceedings have been requested or any claim questioning the existence of a binding arbitration agreement or any objection to determination of multiple claims in a single proceeding has been raised. ① Also this is in line with the ICC Rules save for two exceptions. First, the ICC Rules allow for joinders and multi-party arbitration proceeding requests to automatically proceed to tribunal scrutiny if such requests go unchallenged. The International Court of Arbitration (the functional equivalent of the board of the FCC Arbitration Institute under the ICC Rules) has to make a prima facie decision on acceptability of the requests only if a party objects. Second, the ICC Rules explicitly state thatany party may appeal all decisions by the ICC Court except decisions on consolidation. ② In the FCC Rules there is no provision on whether decisions of the board can be appealed or not.

In sum, the FCC Rules generally follow the framework presented in Section 2.2 above. Multiparty arbitrations are possible as long as the arbitration agreement allows for claims from multiple parties. Multi-contract arbitrations are possible as long as there are no incompatible arbitration agreements and as long as the parties have intended for the claims to be determined in the same proceeding. When compared to other institutional rules, multiparty and multi-contract disputes are clearly and extensively regulated. For example, the CIETAC Rules allow consolidation only when all parties agree to it, while multi-contract settings or joinder are not addressed. ③ Similarly, the Stockholm Rules allow consolidation without agreement as long as the parties in both proceedings are the same while remaining otherwise silent on joinder and multi-contract proceedings. ④

---

① FCC Rules Art. 10. 18 and 14.

② ICC Rules 6 (5).

③ China International Economic and Trade Arbitration Commission (CIETAC) Arbitration Rules (CIETAC Rules), effective 1 May 2012, available at www. cietac. org/index/rules. cms.

④ Arbitration Rules of the Arbitration Institute of the Stockholm Chamber of Commerce (Stockholm Rules), effective 1 January 2010.

One general point of critique can, however, be raised. The relevant provisions in the FCC rules seem to borrow much of their content from the ICC Rules. No doubt the reasoning behind this has to do with the status of the ICC Rules as an internationally well-known standard. The ICC Rules also provide a flexible and up-to-date model for regulating multiparty and multi-contract arbitrations. For example, joinder under the ICC and FCC Rules does not require that all or some parties give their consent unlike under some other institutional rules. ① It is, nevertheless, questionable whether ICC rules are the optimal regime for dealing with joinders and multiparty and multi-contract arbitrations. For example, under the Swiss Rules requests for joinder are decided by the arbitral tribunal instead of the arbitral institute. Requests for joinder fall under identical rules independent of whether the requests were submitted prior to the constitution of the tribunal or later. ② Compared to the Swiss Rules, the ICC approach seems to have a number of drawbacks. It gives the arbitration institute significantly more power to direct arbitration proceedings by making crucial decisions on multiparty jurisdiction. As seen above, the FCC Rules take this approach even further.

Transferring some of the power to decide over multiparty and multi-contract issues from arbitral tribunals to arbitration institutes may be grounded in an effort to guarantee foreseeability in international commercial arbitration and the use of institutional rules. Foreseeability comes at a cost. The power transfer adds an additional layer of governance. This may affect the transparency and legitimacy of institutional arbitration by decreasing the level of control that parties have over the proceedings. Suppose that the board of the FCC Arbitration Institute refuses to

---

① See Conejero Roos, 'Multi party Arbitration and Rule-making: Same Issues, Contrasting Approaches', who notes that institutional rules that regulate multiparty disputes may be classified into those that require agreement from all parties to allow joinder, those that require agreement only between the requesting party and the party to be joined, and those that allow joinder even when all other parties oppose it.

② Swiss Rules of International Arbitration ("Swiss Rules"), effective June 2012, available at www. swissarbitration. org/sa/download/SRIA_ english _ 2012. pdf. According to Article 4 (2): *Where one or more third persons request to participate in arbitral proceedings already pending under these Rules or where a party to pending arbitral proceedings under these Rules requests that one or more third persons participate in the arbitration, the arbitral tribunal shall decide on such request, after consulting with all of the parties, including the person or persons to be joined, taking into account all relevant circumstances.*

forward a request for joinder to an arbitral tribunal because it is not convinced that the applicable contract law would allow the scope of an arbitration agreement to be extended to the party to be joined. The party requesting joinder is nonetheless certain that the contractual arrangement in question allows joinder. Who has jurisdiction over this pre-jurisdictional dispute? Could the party requesting joinder for example ask for a court injunction against the arbitration institute's decision?

From a value chain perspective, the FCC Rules are a major step forward compared to those arbitration rules that do not address questions arising in multiparty or multi-contract situations. The FCC Rules are similarly a step forward from institutional rules based on less flexible approaches requiring explicit agreement on procedural issues such as joinder or consolidation. However, the FCC Rules can also be criticized for the additional layer of governance they institute to multiparty and multi-contract arbitration by transferring some of the power to decide over the acceptability of claims from arbitral tribunals to an opaque organ of an arbitration institute.

3.3 The enforcement of mediated agreements

As noted in Section 2.2, mediation is a flexible alternative to arbitration. There are few binding rules on how mediation should be conducted. Mediators and parties are relatively free to structure their proceedings as they see fit. Nonetheless, in Finland a mediated agreement can be granted a distinct enforcement advantage that equates it with a court judgment. This requires a district court decision declaring the agreement enforceable, which in turn requires certain criteria to be met. I will discuss these criteria here as they de facto regulate the conduct of mediation proceedings in Finland.

First, there is no international framework for the enforcement of mediated agreements. While arbitration awards have a broad enforceability under the 1958 United Nations Convention on the Recognition and Enforcement of Foreign Arbitral Awards (New York Convention), the scope of the Finnish Mediation Act is jurisdictionally limited to two scenarios. The mediation must take place either in Finland or, if an EU cross-border mediation is involved, in another EU member state excluding Denmark. A EU cross-border mediation is one where the parties are domiciled in different EU member states. If for example a Chinese and Finnish party wish to resolve their dispute through mediation and have an agreement that is directly enforceable in Finland, the mediation must take place in Finland.

Second, the mediation process must be "a structured proceeding", structured proceedings are, according to the Mediation Act section 18, proceedings that are based on agreement, institutional mediation rules or "other similar arrangements", such as a decision to mediate. Somewhat counterintuitively, the mediation proceeding itself does not need to be structured. The Mediation Act contains few rules on how the mediation procedure is to be structured, save for excluding evaluative mediation, i. e. mediation where the mediator explicitly evaluates the strengths and weaknesses of the parties' legal positions, out of its scope. ① According to the Mediation Act, section 18, the Act "does not apply to procedures where the mediator as an expert makes decisions or recommendations for settlement of the dispute regardless of whether the decisions or recommendations are binding".

Third, the mediated agreement itself must fulfil a number of requirements. The agreement must be in writing and signed by all the parties and the mediator. Further, all parties must not only agree on the contents of agreement but also agree that it is directly enforceable. Only if such dual consent is received from all parties, can the district court confirm the enforceability of the mediated agreement. ②

Finally, the Act establishes a degree of content control. The mediated agreement may not be confirmed as enforceable if it is against the law, manifestly unreasonable, violates the rights of a third party, or cannot be enforced under the provisions of the Finnish Enforcement Code. ③

Meeting all these requirements provides a marked advantage. The agreement may then at any time be taken to the enforcement authorities and the authorities will directly initiate enforcement proceedings. The party seeking enforcement escapes the inconvenience of having to initiate court proceedings to procure an enforceable

① Jaakko Salminen, 'Intressiperusteinen riidanratkaisu verkostossa – sovintosopimus riidan hallinnan välineenä' in Ari Saarnilehto and others (eds), *Monimuotoinen verkosto-Johtamista ja juridiikkaa* (Lakimiesliiton kustannus 2013).

② For the possible forms such consent may take, see ibid.

③ Mediation Act § 23 and Ulosottokaari (705/2007, Finnish Enforcement Code).

judgment. But because there is no international framework for enforcing mediated agreements, this may be of little value from the perspective of global value chains unless the mediated agreement can be enforced in Finland, or in case the Mediation Directive's criteria for a cross-border mediation are fulfilled, in other EU member states.

Thus, in case the value chain is truly global, the avenue opened by the Mediation Act might not be the best alternative for enforcing mediated agreements. Alternatively, a mediated agreement may also be enforced in the same way as a normal contract. This would mean raising a claim of breach of contract at the relevant local court and enduring the possible lengthy court proceedings. A better alternative might be that where an arbitration tribunal can be constituted, the tribunal may adopt the mediated agreement as its award. This would have the advantage that a mediated agreement dressed up as an arbitral award has wide enforceability globally under the New York Convention.

4. Conclusion: The Rule of Law and Private Dispute Resolution?

The FCC would like to see Finland as the "problem-solver of the world" by 2030. ① Whether the highly ambitious goal can be attained depends crucially on whether Finland has a world-class dispute resolution infrastructure. I have in this article looked at the framework for international commercial dispute resolution in general and in Finland in particular from the perspective of multiparty and multi-contract issues that may arise in global value chains.

No simple solutions exist for constituting a centralized forum for dispute resolution in global value chains. Contractual arrangements, institutional rules, and the skills of mediators in organizing and managing proceedings, all embedded in national and international law on contracts, arbitration, and mediation, work together to create a complex framework. As seen above, all these aspects also have their individual challenges. It is uncertain how contract law will treat dispute

---

① Edilex Uutiset 25. 10. 2012, 'Keskuskauppakamari: Suomalaisessa välimiesmenettelyssä itää satojen miljoonien arvoinen kansainvälinen bisnes' (2012).

resolution agreements in global value chains that simultaneously constitute a whole while being built up from individual contracts. Institutional arbitration rules are being updated to better account for multiparty and multi-contract situations. Amidst the porous, uncertain and changing rules, arbitration institutes seize some of the jurisdictional power that has traditionally belonged to arbitral tribunals, creating added layers of governance. Mediation faces different kinds of challenges. The lack of a fixed procedural framework places emphasis on the training of mediators to recognize and structure multiparty and multi-contract procedures, while the enforceability of mediated agreements is put in question by the lack of an international enforcement regime.

The international commercial dispute resolution framework transfers a considerable amount of decision-making power from national legislators and courts to arbitration institutes, mediators, and the parties themselves. The relationship between the multiple parties' different intentions in making (or having to accept) particular contractual arrangements and choosing certain sets of institutional rules has a profound impact on the way their disputes will be settled. These choices affect the efficiency, transparency, and legitimacy of dispute resolution proceedings. In cases like the Olkiluoto 3 scenario that is not only limited to the parties directly involved in a value chain, but may also have repercussions on for example environmental, safety and labour issues. Due to their broad societal impact, particular attention should be paid on the many governance aspects of international commercial dispute resolution in global value chains as a whole, all the way from legislative, contractual, and arbitration institute perspectives to the training of mediators.

适合全球价值链的治理？

——从多方多合同的视角看芬兰商业纠纷解决框架

亚科·萨尔米宁[*]

【摘要】 由来自各种不同背景的多个行为者组成，并通过数个合同相连接的全球价值链给协同治理带来了很大的问题。协同治理的一个实际先决条件就是存在一个能够考虑到与具体争议相关的所有行为者和合同的争议解决机制。本文讨论了芬兰通过仲裁和调解的方式解决商业纠纷的法律框架，特别是从对于复杂的、通过合同组织起来的价值链来说，很典型的多方多合同的情况——如目前正在进行中的奥尔基洛托核电站建设项目的角度评估了这一框架。在这一语境中，法治与商业纠纷解决这一分散的规制领域之间的关系似乎变得模糊了。

---

* 亚科·萨尔米宁，图尔库大学。

中国 《著作权法》 的近期修订与建议

李明德*

【摘要】 本文结合中国社会科学院知识产权中心的专家建议稿和国家版权局向国务院提交的《著作权法》修改草案送审稿，讨论了《著作权法》修改中的一些问题，包括废除《计算机软件保护条例》，重新梳理著作权的权利体系，突出规定相关权，以及强化对于著作权和相关权的保护。本文认为，我国《著作权法》的第三次修订，应当面向实务，解决问题，促进文化产业的发展。

【关键词】 计算机程序 著作权 相关权 著作权和相关权的保护

2011 年 7 月 13 日，国家版权局宣布《著作权法》第三次修订全面启动，同时委托中国社会科学院知识产权中心、中南财经政法大学知识产权研究中心、中国人民大学知识产权学院分别起草《著作权法》第三次修订的专家建议稿，提供给国家版权局参考。在上述三个专家建议稿的基础上，国家版权局于 2012 年 3 月 31 日公布了《著作权法》修改草案，向社会公众征求意见。在征求公众意见的基础上，国家版权局形成第二个征求意见稿，于 2012 年 7 月 6 日公布征求意见。[①] 2012 年 12 月 18 日，国家版权局向国务院提交了《著作权法》修订送审稿。[②] 根据全国人大常委会的立法规划，《著作权法》的修订将在本届人大完成。

---

* 李明德，中国社会科学院法学研究所研究员。

① 国家版权局：关于《中华人民共和国著作权法》（修改草案）公开征求意见的通知及其附件。国家版权局：关于《中华人民共和国著作权法》（修改草案第二稿）修改和完善的简要说明。（http://www.ncac.gov.cn/）以上两个文件，收录于李明德、管育鹰、唐广良《〈著作权法〉专家建议稿说明》，法律出版社，2012。

② 国家版权局：关于报请国务院审议《中华人民共和国著作权法（修订草案送审稿）》的请示，2012 年 12 月 18 日。

　　本文将结合中国社会科学院知识产权中心的专家建议稿（以下简称"专家建议稿"）和国家版权局向国务院提交的《著作权法》修订草案送审稿（以下简称"送审稿"），探讨《著作权法》与《计算机软件保护条例》、著作权和相关权的权利体系，以及对于著作权和相关权的保护等问题，以期对于《著作权法》的进一步修订有所助益。①

一　废除《计算机软件保护条例》

　　中国现行的著作权法体系由以下法律文件构成：《著作权法》；《著作权法实施条例》，《计算机软件保护条例》，《著作权集体管理条例》，《信息网络传播权保护条例》；国务院和国家版权局等行政部门发布的相关规定和办法；② 最高人民法院发布的相关司法解释；③ 省、自治区、直辖市一级的高级人民法院发布的审判指导意见；④ 各级人民法院判决的典型案件；等等。在这样一个法律体系中，《著作权法》的任务是规定著作权和相关权保护的基本原则和重大问题。至于具体的细节问题则应当由其他法律文件予以规定。

　　《著作权法》修订伊始，曾经有个别专家主张，将现行的《著作权法》、《著作权法实施条例》、《计算机软件保护条例》、《著作权集体管理条例》和《信息网络传播权保护条例》加以整合，形成一部著作权法，就像德国、法国或者日本著作权法那样。然而，中国的知识产权法，包括著作权法，在体系上都是由"法、条例、规定、办法、司法解释"等一系列文件构成。如果将《著作权法实施条例》、《著作权集体管理条例》和《信息网络传播权保护条例》的内容纳入《著作权法》中，就会改变目前的著作权法律体系，而且与同属知识产权的专利法体系、商标法体系迥然不同。同时，将这几个条例纳入《著作权法》中，也会造成《著作权法》有关集体管理和信息网络传播方面的内容过于庞大，造成《著作权法》在相关内容的规定上不平衡的问题。所以，"专家建议稿"认为，没有必要改变目前的著作权法体系，进而制定一部"全面"的著作权法。

　　尽管如此，"专家建议稿"认为，在现行的著作权法体系中，《计算机

---

① 中国社会科学院知识产权中心的专家建议稿已经出版，见李明德、管育鹰、唐广良《〈著作权法〉专家建议稿说明》，法律出版社，2012。

② 例如，国务院于 2009 年 11 月发布的《广播电台电视台播放录音制品支付报酬暂行办法》。

③ 例如，最高人民法院于 2002 年发布的《关于审理著作权民事纠纷案件适用法律若干问题的解释》。

④ 例如，北京市高级人民法院于 2005 年发布的《关于确定著作权侵权损害赔偿责任的指导意见》。

软件保护条例》似乎有些多余。按照世界贸易组织《与贸易有关的知识产权协议》（简称 TRIPS 协议）第 10 条，计算机程序应当作为文字作品予以保护。世界知识产权组织《版权条约》第 4 条也做出了类似的规定。[1] 当然，计算机程序作为文字作品受到保护，也有一些不同于传统意义上的文字作品的特点。例如，计算机程序可以由人类阅读的源代码构成，也可以由机器阅读的目标代码构成。又如，计算机程序复制件的合法持有者，为了避免机器失灵或者操作失误而造成的损失，可以制作备份。再如，为了计算机程序兼容的问题，程序的使用者可以对相关的程序做出必要的修改。

正是基于这样的原因，美国于 1980 年修订《版权法》，只规定了两个内容，就提供了对于计算机软件的保护。一是在《版权法》第 101 条中规定了计算机软件的定义："计算机软件是一系列陈述或指令，可以直接或间接地适用于计算机，以达到某种特定的结果。"二是在《版权法》第 117 条中规定了有关权利的限制，计算机软件复制件的合法所有人，可以为了备份和兼容的目的而复制有关的软件。[2] 其余的问题则完全适用《版权法》的有关规定。

中国在制定《著作权法》的同时制定了《计算机软件保护条例》，于 1991 年 10 月 1 日起实施。随后，《计算机软件保护条例》又于 2002 年做了修订。然而，仔细比较《著作权法》和《计算机软件保护条例》的规定，就会发现《计算计软件保护条例》除了有关软件的定义和权利的限制之外，其他的规定都与《著作权法》的相关规定雷同。基于此种情形，学术界很多人都建议，在《著作权法》中增加计算机程序的定义和必要的权利限制，然后废除《计算机软件保护条例》。[3]

根据以上考虑，"专家建议稿"在相关的条文中增加了两个内容。第一，在有关作品的第 3 条中，规定了更为准确的"计算机程序"而非"计算机软件"，同时在"计算机程序"之后增加了"包括源程序和目标程序"几个字。这相当于计算机程序的定义。第二，将《计算机软件保护条例》中有关权利限制的第 16 条直接纳入《著作权法》中。具体说来，就是计算机程序复制件的合法持有人，可以将计算机程序装载入计算机，可以制作备份，可以为了兼容而做出必要的修改。[4] 在此基础之上，计算机程序作为

---

① 参见世界贸易组织 TRIPS 协议第 10 条、世界知识产权组织《版权条约》第 4 条。

② 参见《美国版权法》第 101 条和 117 条。

③ 参见李明德《著作权法概论》，辽海出版社，2005，第 285 - 287 页。

④ 参见《计算机软件保护条例》第 16 条。

文字作品，与其他文字作品一样，获得相应的保护。

"专家建议稿"认为，针对计算机程序做出这样的修订，符合中国加入的《伯尔尼公约》、TRIPS 协议和世界知识产权组织的《版权条约》，同时也与大多数国家将计算机程序作为文字作品予以保护的做法相似。事实上，"专家建议稿"主张废除《计算机软件保护条例》，绝不意味着弱化对于计算机程序的保护。在这方面，"专家建议稿"还特别规定，侵犯计算机程序的著作权，可以追究侵权者的民事责任、行政责任和刑事责任。

就国家版权局的"送审稿"来看，显然已经接受了"专家建议稿"的上述思路。首先，"送审稿"第 3 条第 15 项规定："计算机程序，是指以源程序或者目标程序表现的、用于电子计算机或者其他信息处理装置运行的指令，计算机程序的源程序和目标程序为同一作品。"这相当于是计算机程序的定义。其次，"送审稿"第 44 条规定计算机程序的合法授权使用者，可以将计算机程序装载入计算机，可以制作备份，可以进行必要的修改。第 45 条规定，为了学习和研究，可以通过安装、显示、传输或者存储等方式使用计算机程序。第 46 条规定，为了兼容的必要，可以复制和翻译该程序中与兼容性信息有关的内容。①

显然，在做出了上述规定以后，继续保留《计算机软件保护条例》的必要性就不存在了。当然，"送审稿"关于计算机程序的规定是否恰当，还可以在《著作权法》进一步的修订中加以讨论。同时，"送审稿"第 45 条的规定，为了个人学习和研究而使用计算机程序，显然多余。因为，按照现行《著作权法》第 22 条第 1 项，为了个人学习、研究或者欣赏，使用他人已经发表的作品，不属于侵权。此外，"送审稿"第 46 条的规定，为了兼容的必要而复制和翻译程序中相关的信息，完全可以与第 44 条中为了使用的修改合并在一起。

二　重新梳理著作权的权利体系

现行《著作权法》对于著作权内容的规定，存在着一些问题。例如，将著作权规定为人身权和财产权，而没有规定为作者的精神权利和经济权利。又如，将作者享有的经济权利分解为 12 项，过于分散，不利于权利人主张自己的权利。在这方面，"专家建议稿"对著作权的权利体系做了较大的改动。一是将著作权分为作者的精神权利和经济权利，明确规定作者的

---

① 参见国家版权局"修改草案"第 41 条、42 条和 43 条。

精神权利归属于创作作品的作者，不得转让，保护期没有限制。二是将作者的经济权利归纳为复制权、发行权、演绎权、传播权、展览权和出租权，规定这些权利归属于创作作品的作者，但可以通过法律规定、合同约定、赠与和继承等方式归属于他人所有。

（一）　明确规定作者的精神权利和经济权利

现行《著作权法》第 10 条将著作权规定为人身权和财产权，深受民法学者的影响，而与相关的作品保护国际公约相悖。

《伯尔尼公约》第 6 条之二规定了署名权和保护作品完整权，而这一条的小标题就是"精神权利"。关于复制等权利，公约虽然没有使用"经济权利"的小标题，却在规定精神权利的时候说"不依赖于作者的经济权利，乃至在经济权利转让之后"，作者仍然享有署名权和保护作品完整权。[①] 这表明，《伯尔尼公约》将作者的权利界定为精神权利和经济权利。除此之外，《法国著作权法》也从精神权利和经济权利的角度规定了作者的权利。例如《法国著作权法》第二编的标题是"作者权利"，其中第一章的小标题是"精神权利"，第二章的小标题是"经济权利"。[②] 至于《德国著作权法》，则从著作人身权和各项使用权的角度，规定了作者的精神权利和经济权利。[③]

按照著作权法体系的精神，作者的精神权利不可转让，专属于作者所有。这是因为，作品中所体现的精神或者人格，属于特定的作者。即使有人加以转让，例如更换署名，体现在该作品中的精神或者人格，仍然是创作作品的作者的精神和人格，不可能变成更换了署名的那个人。同时，按照著作权法体系的精神，就作品的创作而产生的经济权利，从源头上归属于作者所有。但是，这类经济权利，可以因为法律的规定或者合同的约定而归属于其他自然人、法人所有。

现行《著作权法》第 10 条将著作权划分为著作人身权和著作财产权，存在着两个问题。第一，著作人身权不属于财产权，著作人身权不具有财产权的性质。显然，这样的规定方式，违反了著作权法体系将精神权利和经济权利视为财产权，认为精神权利具有财产权性质的精神。第二，使用"著作人身权"，很容易导致过于宽泛的理解。很多望文生义的研究者，从

---

① 参见《伯尔尼公约》第 6 条之二。
② 参见《法国知识产权法典》第一部分第二编第一章、第二章。
③ 参见《德国著作权法》第二章。

作者人身权的角度出发，甚至将民法意义上的人格权、名誉权、姓名权等都纳入"著作人身权"的范围。

（二）删除发表权和修改权

现行《著作权法》第 10 条规定了四项精神权利，即发表权、署名权、修改权和保护作品完整权。然而《伯尔尼公约》则在第 6 条之二中仅仅规定了署名权和保护作品完整权。[①]

《伯尔尼公约》为什么没有规定作者的发表权？这是因为，作者的发表权与经济权利密切相关。当作者第一次行使自己经济权利的时候，例如复制、发行、表演、展览自己作品的时候，就在同时行使了发表权利。大体说来，法律在规定作者的各种经济权利的同时，又规定或承认作者的发表权，只是为了强调作者精神权利的这一个方面，强调只有作者本人可以决定自己的作品是否发表和以何种方式发表。正是由此出发，《伯尔尼公约》没有规定作者的发表权，很多国家的著作权法也没有规定作者的发表权。这样，删除发表权，不会对作者行使自己的权利造成影响。

至于作者的修改权，本身就是保护作品完整权的一个内容。根据郑成思教授的说法，规定"修改权"的本意是，一旦作品出版发行，作者不能行使收回作品权。但是，当作品再次印刷之时，出版者应当通知作者，让作者对自己的作品加以修改。[②] 现在已经很少有人知道《著作权法》制定之时的讨论，进而对修改权做出了很多望文生义的解释。既然修改权就在保护作品完整权的范围之内，删除修改权也不会产生什么问题。

基于以上考虑，"专家建议稿"删除了作者的发表权和修改权，仅仅保留了署名权和保护作品完整权。

（三）将经济权利归纳为复制权、发行权、演绎权、传播权、展览权和出租权

现行《著作权法》第 10 条规定了 12 项经济权利，如复制、发行、出租、展览、表演、放映、广播、信息网络传播、摄制电影、改编、翻译、汇编。这种规定方式存在着两个问题。一是权利的规定过于琐细，例如放映、信息网络传播、翻译等。二是有关的权利有交叉。例如放映和广播，可以纳入表演的范围。又如，摄制电影可以纳入改编的范围。除此之外，由于规定了 12 项权利，一旦发生了侵权，著作权人很难确切知道自己的哪

---

① 参见《伯尔尼公约》第 6 条之二。
② 参见郑成思《知识产权法》（第 2 版），法律出版社，2003，第 319 – 321 页。

一项权利或者哪几项权利受到了侵犯。

　　大体说来，现行《著作权法》第 10 条关于经济权利的规定，过于跟随《伯尔尼公约》的规定。例如，《伯尔尼公约》第 8 条规定了翻译权，第 9 条规定了复制权，第 11 条规定了公开表演权、广播权和公开朗诵权，第 12 条规定了改编权，第 14 条规定了电影摄制权。[①] 这些规定，除了公开朗诵权，都纳入了现行《著作权法》第 10 条之中。然而，《伯尔尼公约》对于作者权利的规定，有一个历史的演变。有的因为新技术的发展而规定，例如广播权、电影摄制权；有的因为认识发生变化而做出规定，例如翻译权、公开朗诵权。在这方面，中国《著作权法》只要将有关的规定或者作品的使用方式容纳到相关的权利之中就可以了，而不必亦步亦趋地跟随《伯尔尼公约》的字词。

　　在对于经济权利的规定方面，《法国著作权法》只规定了复制和表演 2 项权利。[②]《美国版权法》第 105 条规定了复制、发行、演绎、表演和展览 5 项权利。[③] 至于《德国著作权法》，则根据有形使用和无形使用的方式规定了经济权利，前者包括复制、发行、展览，后者包括表演、公开提供、播放等。[④] 显然，我们不能说法国、美国、德国所规定的经济权利少于中国《著作权法》的规定，就认为这些国家的著作权或者版权保护不如中国。

　　在对于作者经济权利的规定方面，"专家建议稿"对现有的 12 项经济权利做出归纳，规定为复制权、发行权、演绎权、传播权、展览权和出租权。其中，复制权、发行权、演绎权和传播权，适用于所有的作品，展览权仅仅适用于美术作品和摄影作品，出租权仅仅适用于电影作品和计算机程序。当然，出租权也适用于表演和录音制品，这在"相关权"部分做了具体规定。"专家建议稿"认为，使用复制权、发行权、演绎权、传播权、展览权和出租权六个概念，基本可以容纳现行《著作权法》中的经济权利。同时，这样的规定也便于著作权人在诉讼中主张自己的权利，便于法官判定被控侵权人是否侵犯了原告的经济权利，包括侵犯了哪一项经济权利。

　　国家版权局的"送审稿"，就著作权分为作者精神权利和经济权利的建议来说，仍然沿袭了原有的规定，没有采纳"专家建议稿"的意见。例如，"送审稿"第 13 条规定，"著作权包括人身权利和财产权利"。又如，著作

---

① 参见《伯尔尼公约》第 8 条至 14 条。
② 参见《法国知识产权法典》第 122 条。
③ 参见《美国版权法》第 105 条。
④ 参见《德国著作权法》第 15 条。

权中的人身权利包括发表权、署名权和保护作品完整权。当然在这方面，"送审稿"还是删除了原来的修改权，将其含义纳入了"保护作品完整权"①。然而在进一步归纳经济权利方面，则在很大程度上接受了"专家建议稿"的思路。例如，"送审稿"第13条将作者的经济权利归纳为复制权、发行权、出租权、展览权、表演权、播放权、信息网络传播权、改编权、翻译权等9项权利。不过在本人看来，其中的播放权和信息网络传播权可以纳入"表演权"的范围，翻译权可以纳入"改编权"的范围。

三　突出规定相关权

现行《著作权法》第四章是关于相关权的规定，涉及了版式设计、表演、录音、录像和广播。然而，纵观现行《著作权法》第四章的整体内容，至少存在着三个问题。

第一，现行《著作权法》第四章在规定版式设计、表演、录音和广播的同时，还就出版合同、表演合同、录音合同、广播合同做出了一系列规定。"专家建议稿"认为，应当将有关合同的内容剔除出来，放在"著作权和相关权合同"一章中，做出统一规定。这样，这一章就成了专门规定相关权的章节。同时，就《著作权法》的整体结构而言，按照突出权利的思路，可以先规定著作权，再规定相关权，然后规定著作权和相关权的合同。正是基于这样的思路，"专家建议稿"将"相关权"一章放在了"著作权"一章之后。其具体顺序是第一章总则，第二章著作权，第三章相关权，第四章著作权和相关权合同，第五章著作权和相关权的保护。

第二，现行《著作权法》第四章第三节在规定录音的同时，还加上了录像。然而，国际上保护邻接权或者相关权的《罗马公约》，仅仅提供了对于表演者、录音制作者和广播组织的保护，并没有涉及录像。在这方面，只有德国等一些大陆法系国家，在保护电影作品的同时，提供了对于录像的保护。② 根据这些国家的保护标准，如果相关的录像或者视听具有独创性，可以作为电影作品获得著作权的保护。如果不具有独创性，则可以作为录像获得相关权的保护。值得注意的是，德国等大陆法系国家保护录像，已经超出了《罗马公约》的要求，反映了这些国家提供较高水平的著作权

---

① 其具体规定是："保护作品完整权，即允许他人修改作品以及禁止歪曲、篡改作品的权利。"

② 参见《德国著作权法》第95条。

保护和相关权保护的现实。

　　基于以上考虑，"专家建议稿"认为应当删除有关录像的保护。按照"专家建议稿"的思路，如果有关的录像或者视听达到了独创性的要求，构成了电影作品，可以获得著作权的保护。如果有关的录像或者视听没有达到独创性的要求，则不予保护。在这方面，我们没有必要自我拔高相关权的保护水平。

　　第三，版式设计作为出版者的权利，是中国《著作权法》的一个特色。因为就相关权来说，无论是有关相关权保护的《罗马公约》，还是世界贸易组织的 TRIPS 协议和世界知识产权组织的《表演与录音制品条约》，都没有提及版式设计。尽管如此，中国自 1991 年以来就有了对于出版者版式设计的规定。例如，1991 年《著作权法实施条例》第 38 条规定："出版者对其出版的图书、报纸、杂志的版式、装帧设计，享有专有使用权。"到了 2001年修订《著作权法》时，又在第 35 条规定："出版者有权许可或者禁止他人使用其出版的图书、期刊的版式设计。""前款规定的权利的保护期为十年，截止于使用该版式设计的图书、期刊首次出版后第十年的 12 月31 日。"①

　　是否对版式设计提供相关权的保护，是一个值得讨论的问题。在"专家建议稿"起草的过程中，很多专家提议删除版式设计的规定。然而，"专家建议稿"基于尊重现实的考虑保留了有关版式设计的规定。

　　大体说来，在对于相关权的规定方面，国家版权局的"送审稿"基本接受了"专家建议稿"的思路。例如，"送审稿"第三章规定了出版者、表演者、录音制作者和广播电台电视台的权利，同时剔除了有关出版合同、表演合同、录音合同和广播合同的内容。这些内容则被放入了"送审稿"的第四章中。又如，"送审稿"在规定相关权的时候，没有涉及"录像制品"，这表明删除了对于录像的保护。再如，"送审稿"第三章的题目叫作"相关权"，紧跟"著作权"一章之后，突出了对于权利的保护。

　　当然，"专家建议稿"在相关权的规定上，其顺序是表演、录音、广播和版式设计。而"送审稿"的顺序是出版者、表演者、录音制作者和广播电台电视台。应该说，这种顺序上的差异不会成为问题。但是，"专家建议稿"所说的广播组织，不仅包括了广播电台、电视台，而且包括了卫星广

---

① 2001 年《著作权法》第 35 条没有提到图书、期刊的"装帧设计"，这是因为"装帧设计"本身就属于美术作品，不应当纳入相关权的范围。

播组织、有线转播组织和网络广播组织。显然，从广播组织权保护的现状来看，不应当仅仅局限于广播电台和电视台，而且应当包括卫星广播组织、有线转播组织和新兴的网络广播组织。

四　强化著作权和相关权的保护

现行《著作权法》第五章的标题是"法律责任和执法措施"，主要规定侵权的法律责任和执法措施。其中的侵权责任，包括侵犯作者精神权利的责任、侵犯经济权利的责任，以及可以给予行政处罚和追究刑事责任的侵权行为。其中的执法措施，包括责令停止侵权、损害赔偿、诉前的临时措施，以及著作权纠纷的调解、仲裁等。

"专家建议稿"认为，应当将第五章的标题改为"著作权和相关权的保护"，突出对于权利的保护。同时，针对现行《著作权法》第47条将侵犯作者精神权利、经济权利和相关权放在一起规定，在第48条中将侵犯著作权和相关权的民事责任、行政处罚和刑事责任放在一起规定的做法，"专家建议稿"使用专门的条文分别规定了侵犯精神权利和经济权利的行为。同时，在侵犯经济权利的范围内，进一步规定了承担民事责任的行为、可以受到行政处罚的行为、可以追究刑事责任的行为。在此基础之上，又以专门的条款规定了某些违法行为，例如规避技术措施、删除或篡改权利管理信息。具体如下。

"专家建议稿"规定，侵犯他人署名权和保护作品完整权的，应当承担停止侵害、消除影响、赔礼道歉、赔偿损失等民事责任。其中，关于保护作品完整权的规定是，歪曲、篡改他人作品或表演，对作者或者表演者的声誉造成损害的，才追究责任。① 这就意味着，侵犯作者的精神权利，仅追究民事责任，与行政处罚和刑事责任无关。

"专家建议稿"规定，侵犯作者经济权利、表演者权、录音制作者权、广播组织权和出版者权的，应当承担停止侵害、赔偿损失等民事责任。侵犯作者经济权利和相关权，同时损害社会公共利益的，可以由著作权行政管理部门给予行政处罚，包括责令停止侵权，没收违法所得，没收、销毁侵权复制品和处以罚款等。

在刑事责任方面，"专家建议稿"将追究的范围限定在了计算机程序、电影作品、录音制品和擅自出版他人享有专有出版权的图书上。根据规定，

① 参见《伯尔尼公约》第6条之二。

未经著作权人许可复制、发行、传播其计算机程序和电影，未经许可复制、发行和通过信息网络传播其录音制品的，除了追究民事责任和给予行政处罚，还可以追究刑事责任。在这方面，"专家建议稿"还沿袭了现行《著作权法》和《刑法》中的规定，对于擅自出版他人享有专有出版权图书的，可以追究刑事责任。① 这样，就把刑事责任的承担，限定在了计算机程序、电影作品、录音制品和擅自出版他人享有专有出版权的图书上，这有利于集中有限的刑事司法资源，有效地打击社会影响面较大的盗版行为。

"专家建议稿"认为，技术措施和权利管理信息是因为数字技术和网络技术，才纳入了著作权法的体系。但是，技术措施和权利管理信息不是因为作品的创作，或者表演、录音、广播信号的产生而产生。在这方面，世界知识产权组织的《版权条约》和《表演与录音制品条约》都规定，成员有义务保护技术措施和权利管理信息。② 这也表明，保护技术措施和权利管理信息，不属于著作权和相关权的范畴。此外，现行《著作权法》中加以禁止的制作出售假冒他人署名的作品的，也与著作权和相关权无关。有鉴于此，"专家建议稿"草拟了一个专门的条文，规定规避技术措施、删除或者改变权利管理信息，以及制作和出售假冒他人署名的作品，属于违法行为，可以追究民事责任，可以给予行政处罚。如果构成犯罪，则可以追究刑事责任。

针对权利人强烈呼吁的维权难，以及维权成本高而侵权成本低的情形，"专家建议稿"在损害赔偿的规定上做了两点改变。一是规定法定赔偿金为一万元以上、一百万元以下。现行《著作权法》的法定赔偿金是五十万元以下。这样，"专家建议稿"不仅将法定赔偿的上限提高到了一百万元，而且规定了一万元的最低限额。③ 规定一万元的最低限额，一方面可以让提起侵权诉讼的权利人至少获得一万元的赔偿，另一方面又不至于起到鼓励诉讼的作用。二是规定了损害赔偿的"倍数"。根据规定，为了有效地制止侵权，对于一年以内实施两次以上侵犯著作权行为的，可以判处两倍或者三倍的赔偿。在损害赔偿的计算方面，"专家建议稿"首先规定了权利人的损失和侵权者的利润所得，其次规定了法定损害赔偿，然后规定了损害赔偿金的倍数，这就意味着前三者都可以适用损害赔偿金的倍数。显然，这样

---

① 参见现行《著作权法》第 48 条、《刑法》第 217 条。

② 参见《版权条约》第 11 条、《表演与录音制品条约》第 18 条。

③ 参照《美国版权法》第 504 条，法定损害赔偿的最低数额为 750 美元，最高数额为 3 万美元。

的规定可以在某种程度上遏制反复侵权和恶意侵权的行为。

在著作权和相关权的保护方面，对于其他的措施，例如诉前的责令停止侵权、财产保全等，"专家建议稿"未做修改。

就国家版权局的"送审稿"来看，已经部分接受了"专家建议稿"的思路。例如，"送审稿"第 72 条规定了侵犯著作权、相关权的民事责任，第 77 条规定了侵犯著作权和相关权的行政处罚和刑事责任。又如，"送审稿"第 78 条针对技术措施和权利管理信息的保护，做了专门的规定，不再与侵犯著作权和相关权的责任混同在一起。再如，"送审稿"第 76 条将法定赔偿的上限提高到了一百万元以下，规定了对于两次以上故意侵犯著作权和相关权的，可以根据赔偿数额确定两至三倍的赔偿数额。

然而，"送审稿"在法定赔偿的问题上虽然确立了一百万元的上限，但没有确定最低限额。这是因为，有人担心一旦确定了一万元的下限，可能会起到鼓励诉讼的作用。不过，面对维权成本高、侵权成本低的现状，确立法定赔偿的最低数额本身就有鼓励维权的意味。当然，如果认为一万元太高，也可以是 5000 元或者 3000 元。至少，确定一个最低的法定赔偿数额，对于潜在的侵权者具有一定的威慑。

此外，是否分别规定侵犯精神权利、经济权利的民事责任，是否可以将刑事责任限定在电影作品、计算机软件、录音制品和专有出版权方面，也值得在《著作权法》的进一步修订中加以讨论。

五　结语

中国现行的《著作权法》制定于 1990 年，于 1991 年生效。中国加入世界贸易组织以前，于 2001 年 10 月进行了第一次修订。2010 年 2 月，针对世界贸易组织争端解决小组的裁定，又进行了第二次修订，删除第 4 条第 1 款，同时规定以著作权出质的应当登记。① 目前正在进行第三次修订。

如果说《著作权法》的前两次修订是基于外来的压力，那么目前进行的第三次修订则是基于我国经济社会现实的需要而进行的主动修订。在这样一个修订过程中，我们应当面向实务，着力解决司法和行政执法中发生的问题，切实保护著作权和相关权，进而鼓励作品的创作和传播，实现文化产业的繁荣发展。

---

① 全国人民代表大会常务委员会《关于修改〈中华人民共和国著作权法〉的决定》，2010 年 2 月 26 日。

Proposals on the Upcoming Revision of the Chinese Copyright Law

*Li Mingde**

【Abstract】 This paper, based on the "Expert Suggestions for the Third Amendments of the Copyright Law of China" by Intellectual Property Center, China Academy of Social Sciences, and the Drafting Amendments of the Copyright Law of China by National Copyright Administration of China, discusses some issues in the revision of the Law, including to repel "Regulations for the Protection of Computer Software", to rearrange author's moral rights and economic rights, to clarify the related rights concerning performance, sound recording, broadcasting, and typographical design, and to strengthen the protection of author's rights and related rights.

【Keywords】 Computer Program; Author's Rights; Related Rights; Protection of Author's Rights and Related Rights

* Professor, Institute of Law, Chinese Academy of Social Sciences.

Finnish Private Law: Statutory System without a Civil Code[*]

Teemu Juutilainen[**]

【Abstract】 Finland counts as a civil law jurisdiction, but Finnish private law is not based on a comprehensive civil code. As in the other Nordic countries, codification of private law has taken place in the form of statutes, that is, various individual acts. General principles and other contents of the "general part" of private law are largely uncodified and will most likely remain so. The absence of a civil code and a comprehensive statutory general part leaves the system of private law open-ended, which accounts for several aspects of the Finnish overall approach to private law. These concern interpretation and application of law, the relative weight of different sources of law, the role of legal science, and the openness of law to external influence. Despite the absence of a civil code, Finnish lawyers perceive domestic private law as a systematic whole, a doctrinal structure. Systematisation is entrusted to legal science, rather than predetermined by legislation.

---

[*] A slightly updated version of the author's chapter "Finnish Private Law: Statutory System Without a Civil Code", in *The Scope and Structure of Civil Codes*, Ius Gentium: Comparative Perspectives on Law and Justice, vol. 32, ed. Julio César Rivera (Dordrecht: Springer, 2013), 155 – 180. © Springer Science + Business Media Dordrecht 2013. Reproduced with kind permission from Springer Science + Business Media B. V. The text has greatly benefited from comments by Katri Havu and Janne Kaisto (Faculty of Law, University of Helsinki) and language editing by Christopher Goddard (Riga Graduate School of Law).

[**] Doctoral Candidate, Faculty of Law, University of Helsinki.

I. Overview of Private Law

A. *Implications of the Absence of a Civil Code*

Finnish law is a statutory system. [1] Legislation is strongly emphasised as the primary source of law, and application of written law is regarded as the paradigmatic model for legal decision-making. In these respects, Finnish law follows the Continental European tradition. However, legal-culturally Finland is first and foremost a part of the Nordic (less precisely: Scandinavian) legal community, together with Sweden, Norway, Denmark, and Iceland. Thus, many general characteristics of Finnish law are shared by the other Nordic legal systems. [2]

As opposed to the Continental European tradition, Finnish private law is not based on a comprehensive civil code. That is, with respect to the organisation of law, Finland has no equivalent, say, to the French *Code Civil*, the German *Bürgerliches Gesetzbuch*, or the Dutch *Burgerlijk Wetboek*. As discussed below, certain

---

[1] In this article, references to statutes are given with their respective numbers in the Statutes of Finland, for example, the Contracts Act (228/1929). The latter part of the number indicates the year when the statute was published, which is usually also the year of enactment. Most of the statutes referred to have been amended several times, but the numbers do not reveal amendments. The statutes can be found in their original form as well as in their amended and consolidated form, indicating the dates of amendment, in the Finlex data bank (http://www.finlex.fi/en/). While Finnish statutes are official only in the Finnish and Swedish languages, the databank provides unofficial translations in other languages, mostly in English. These translations, when available, have been used in the present article.

[2] Thomas Wilhelmsson, *Critical Studies in Private Law: A Treatise on Need-Rational Principles in Modern Law* (Dordrecht: Kluwer Academic Publishers, 1992), 15 – 17. See Ulf Bernitz, "What is Scandinavian Law? Concept, Characteristics, Future", in *Scandinavian Studies in Law*, vol. 50, ed. Peter Wahlgren (Stockholm: Stockholm Institute for Scandinavian Law, 2007), 17 – 20. For reasons of geography and history, Finnish law is more similar to Swedish law than the laws of the other Nordic countries. Finland was a part of the Kingdom of Sweden from the 13th century to 1809. Nevertheless, significant differences exist even between Finland and Sweden. For example, see Johanna Niemi-Kiesiläinen, "Comparing Finland and Sweden: The Structure of Legal Argument", in *Nordic Law-Between Tradition and Dynamism*, eds. Jaakko Husa, Kimmo Nuotio, and Heikki Pihlajamäki (Antwerp: Intersentia, 2007). Niemi-Kiesiläinen compares these legal systems with respect to the theory of legal sources and legal argumentation.

parts of Finnish private law are codified in various individual acts. Other parts, notably when it comes to general principles of law, are uncodified and expected to remain so. To be sure, a comprehensive codification of the "general part" of private law would be at odds with the Nordic tradition. ①

This open-ended structure has shaped certain aspects of the Finnish overall approach to private law. First, legal norms of a general nature are thought to exist even without a statutory "general part". These norms can be developed by doctrine, and then applied by courts. Moreover, particular existing rules can be applied by way of analogy. ② Indeed, due to the central role of legislation and the absence of a comprehensive civil code, the "inductive" method of constructing general principles on the basis of analogies from pieces of legislation has become natural. Hence, it is relatively common to ask whether given provisionsexpress a general principle, despite their limited scope. ③

Second, in the absence of a comprehensive civil code, other accepted sources have gained more significance. This holds true for the application of individual acts and the construction of general principles alike. Considerable weight is placed on *travaux préparatoires* as well as legal practice, especially precedents of the Supreme Court. Also noteworthy is the weight of so-called "real arguments", that is, substantive arguments concerning the expected consequences of a decision. These arguments are often associated with Scandinavian Legal Realism and its emphasis on legal science as a form of social engineering. The breakthrough of social engineering and the strengthening of the position of "real arguments" in private-law research took place in Finland in the 1940s, which is later than in other Nordic countries. ④ Notwithstanding the fact that private-law research eventually came to adopt many

---

① Wilhelmsson, *Critical Studies*, 17 - 18. See Bernitz, "Scandinavian Law", 20 - 22; Aulis Aarnio, "Introduction", in *An Introduction to Finnish Law*, 2nd ed. , ed. Juha Pöyhönen (Helsinki: Talentum Media, 2002), 12 - 13.

② Jan M. Smits, "Nordic Law in a European Context: Some Comparative Observations", in Husa, Nuotio, and Pihlajamäki, *Nordic Law*, 62 - 63. Smits suggests that reasoning by analogy may be more common in Nordic countries than in jurisdictions with comprehensive civil codes.

③ Wilhelmsson, *Critical Studies*, 18. Generally on interpretation and gap-filling in Finnish law, see Aulis Aarnio, "Statutory Interpretation in Finland", in *Interpreting Statutes: A Comparative Study*, eds. D. Neil MacCormick and Robert S. Summers (Aldershot: Dartmouth, 1991), 131 - 144.

④ Wilhelmsson, *Critical Studies*, 18 - 19.

methodological tenets of Scandinavian Legal Realism,① the realist impact on Finnish law in general remained rather modest. ②

Third, legal science has relatively great latitude, and authority, in building theoretical structures of law. Arguably, this would be less so if these structures were predefined in a comprehensive civil code or other statutory " general part " . ③ If theoretical structures of law are understood as concepts and principles, this role of legal science can be illustrated by paradigm shifts that occurred in Finnish private-law research in the course of the 20th century. Without going into too much detail, reference can be made to two schools of thought, namely, analytical and post-analytical.

A grand project of the analytical school was to break up "lump" concepts, which *Begriffsjurisprudenz* ("conceptual jurisprudence") had used for deductive purposes, into more refined "relational" or "functional" concepts. The aim of this exercise was to clear space for new kinds of research questions, to be then answered by argumentation based on positive law. Post-analytical scholars approve the heuristic role that the analytical school assigned to concepts, but fill the opened argumentative space differently; that is, these scholars emphasise application of principles. The focus of their doctrinal work is on principles rather than concepts, and the work is often explicitly tied in with its societal context (the welfare state) . ④

Fourth, an open-ended structure is likely to be more open to external influence than a comprehensive civil code. Avenues for that influence are legislative co-

---

① Markku Helin, *Lainoppi ja metafysiikka: Tutkimus skandinaavisen oikeusrealismin tieteenkuvasta ja sen vaikutuksesta Suomen siviilioikeuden tutkimuksessa vuosina* 1920 – 1960 (Vammala: Suomalainen Lakimiesyhdistys, 1988), 423 – 425.

② Toni Malminen, "So You Thought Transplanting Law is Easy? Fear of Scandinavian Legal Realism in Finland, 1918 – 1965", in Husa, Nuotio, and Pihlajamäki, *Nordic Law*, 82 – 87. Malminen's main explanation for this is the legacy of the Finnish Civil War of 1918, and in particular the ideology of the winning "Whites", which was the side of the propertied class. Scandinavian Legal Realism was often suspected of being socialist ideology in a legal disguise.

③ Wilhelmsson, *Critical Studies*, 19 – 20.

④ Kaarlo Tuori, *Oikeuden ratio ja voluntas* (Helsinki: WSOYpro, 2007), 216 – 218. See Niemi-Kiesiläinen, " Comparing Finland and Sweden ", 95 – 97. Some post-analytical studies are representative of "alternative" or "critical" legal dogmatics. On these approaches, see Jaakko Husa, Kimmo Nuotio, and Heikki Pihlajamäki, "Nordic Law-Between Tradition and Dynamism", in Husa, Nuotio, and Pihlajamäki, *Nordic Law*, 35; Wilhelmsson, *Critical Studies*, 4 – 11.

operation, conventions, doctrine, and court practice. Legislative co-operation between the Nordic countries was lively in the 20th century. In several instances, the different countries enacted, as normal national legislation, acts that share not only almost the same content, but also the same section-by-section structure. ① The potential of conventions can be exemplified by the United Nations Convention on Contracts for the International Sale of Goods (CISG), which has strongly influenced Nordic acts on the sale of goods, including the Finnish Sale of Goods Act (355/1987). ② As for doctrine, references to foreign legal materials are well accepted. Thus, import of dogmatic constructions and arguments takes place. Courts do not generally cite foreign legal material when deciding a case on Finnish law, but such material may have *de facto* weight. In most cases, courts are influenced by foreign legal material indirectly through legal doctrine. ③

In relation to the matter of external influence, an additional point can be made concerning the Europeanisation of private law. As a Member State of the European Union, Finland is subject to its legislation. A common topic among private-law scholars in Member States is the fragmentary effect of European Union legislation on national systems of private law. This effect is mainly perceived as a problem

---

① Thomas Wilhelmsson, "Harmonization of Private Law Rules-a Finnish Perspective", in *The Finnish National Reports to the XIIIth Congress of the International Academy of Comparative Law*, Montréal 19 – 24 August 1990, eds. Kaarina Buure-Hägglund, Heikki E. S. Mattila, and Karla Kilpeläinen (Helsinki: Institutum Iurisprudentiae Comparativae Universitatis Helsingiensis, 1990), 1 – 7, 11. Examples of Finnish acts with close counterparts in the other Nordic countries include the Contracts Act (228/1929), the Promissory Notes Act (622/1947), the Act on Gift Promises (625/1947), and the Sale of Goods Act (355/1987). See Stig Strömholm, "General Features of Swedish Law", in *Swedish Legal System*, ed. Michael Bogdan (Stockholm: Norstedts Juridik, 2010), 12 – 13; Severin Blomstrand, "Nordic Co-operation on Legislation in the Field of Private Law", in *Scandinavian Studies in Law*, vol. 39, ed. Peter Wahlgren (Stockholm: Stockholm Institute for Scandinavian Law, 2000); Jan Hellner, "Unification of Law in Scandinavia", *The American Journal of Comparative Law* 16, no. 1 – 2 (1968).

② For example, the "control liability" defined in Article 79 of the CISG, which had previously been unknown in Finnish law, was adopted in the act, and has later spread to other parts of Finnish contract law as well. On this, see Wilhelmsson, "Harmonization of Private Law", 9 – 10.

③ Ibid. , 11 – 17. Particularly in doctrine, legal material from other Nordic countries has a special position. In some cases, its weight is almost comparable to domestic sources. The influence of German law was strong until the Second World War. Since then, a shift has occurred towards Anglo-American law. See Husa, Nuotio, and Pihlajamäki, "Nordic Law", 20 – 21.

caused by directives,① the type of legislative act that requires Member States to achieve a particular result, but leaves the choice of form and methods to the national authorities. ② In Finland, and in other Member States without a general civil code, the problem of fragmentation is almost entirely about the substantive content of private law. By contrast, in Member States with a general civil code, the problem comes with an additional layer, namely, the question whether directives should be implemented within or outside the civil code.

Professor Jan Smits sums up the Dutch discussion on this point as follows: "there is no easy way out of the dilemma posed by the Europeanization of private law: a coherent implementation inside the Civil Code is never fully possible, whereas implementation outside the Code would damage the idea of the Code as a complete and consistent whole. "③ Of course, it would go too far to argue that an open-ended structure of private law is better equipped than a comprehensive civil code to function in the context of a transnational multi-level system like the European Union. Still, to a Finnish private lawyer, who has no "code idea" to be concerned about, ④ the question of within or outside of the civil code may give a feeling of a pseudo-problem.

B. Main Sources of Private Law

In Finnish legal science, the sources of law have been sorted into groups on the basis of their stating grounds and binding force. The stating grounds refer to the distinction between authoritative and substantive sources of law. Authoritative sources derive their importance from the social position of the institution from which they originate, whereas substantive sources derive theirs from the perceived significance of their content. Binding force determines how difficult it is for the interpreter to set aside the source of law in question. The distinction between strongly binding, weakly binding, and permitted sources is used for this

---

① See Jan Smits, "Dutch Report: Coherence and Fragmentation of Private Law", *European Review of Private Law* 20, no. 1 (2012): 157 – 160.

② Article 288 of the Treaty on the Functioning of the European Union.

③ Smits, "Dutch Report", 163.

④ As elaborated in section I. C below, Finnish private law is perceived as a systematic whole despite the absence of a general civil code.

purpose. The interpreter may deviate from a strongly binding source only exceptionally. Deviating from a weakly binding source is allowed, but such a decision is considered as properly made only if the interpreter gives solid reasons for the deviation. Permitted sources may be used in interpretation, and it is not necessary to give special reasons for doing or not doing so. ①

Authoritative strongly binding sources are written law. Authoritative weakly binding sources are *travaux préparatoires* and court decisions (precedents). Authoritative permitted sources are works of legal science. Substantive strongly binding sources are established custom. Substantive permitted sources form an open-ended category, including general principles of law, morality, and factual arguments ("real arguments"). ②

The status of written law and established custom as strongly binding sources is stated in Chapter 1 Section 11 of the Code of Judicial Procedure (4/1734):

A judge shall carefully examine the true purpose and grounds for the law and render judgment accordingly, and not following his own opinions against the law. In the absence of statutory law, the custom of the land, if not unreasonable, shall also be his guide.

Established custom is of very limited importance in practice. National statutes form the following hierarchy: Constitution > act ("ordinary law") > decree > decision of the Council of Ministers > decision of a Ministry > other authoritative instructions. A lower-level statute may only be given if it can be based on an entitling or justifying provision in a higher-level statute. According to Chapter 6 of the Constitution of Finland (731/1999), the power to enact acts belongs to the Parliament and to the President (the former passes the contents of acts and the latter confirms them), and issuing decrees may be a function of the President, the Council of Ministers, or a Ministry. ③

Section 107 of the Constitution concerns the hierarchy of national statutes with respect to their application:

---

① Pekka Timonen, "Sources of Law and Material on the Sources of Law", in Pöyhönen, *Introduction to Finnish Law*, 24 – 25; Aulis Aarnio, *Laintulkinnan teoria: Yleisen oikeustieteen oppikirja* (Porvoo: WSOY, 1989), 218 –222.

② Timonen, "Sources of Law", 25; Aarnio, *Laintulkinnan teoria*, 218 –247.

③ Timonen, "Sources of Law", 26.

If a provision in a decree or another statute of a lower level than an act is in conflict with the Constitution or another act, it shall not be applied by a court of law or by any other public authority.

A significant part of private law legislation is non-mandatory, which means that contracting parties are free to agree on deviations from the obligations or procedures set by law. This is the case, for example, with the Sale of Goods Act (355/1987). In addition, some areas of private law remain wholly or largely unregulated. Building contracts provide an example of this. While building contracts are subject to the general Contracts Act (228/1929), which is fragmentary and partly outdated, no special legislation exists on this type of contract. [1] Consequently, disputes concerning these contracts may have to be considered in the light of the contract itself, possible private sources of norms (for example standard terms), earlier court decisions, and the general doctrine of contract law. [2]

Travaux préparatoires are said to express the legislator's meaning, and to derive their authority as a source of law from the Parliament. Although many of these documents are produced outside the Parliament (for example in the relevant Ministry), their importance is based on the idea that the Parliament has processed them. They contain information on the purposes of the new enactment and its relationship to existing legislation. Essential material in legal interpretation might be, for example, government proposals that include detailed grounds for each section and subsection of the proposed enactment. The most important group of *travaux préparatoires* are printed parliamentary documents, that is, government proposals, reports of the Parliamentary Committees, and statements given and suggestions accepted during the plenary session of the Parliament. Significant or politically sensitive enactments are often prepared in committees and task groups. Their reports may also become significant in interpretation. [3] In practice, the more recent the enactment is, the more significant the *travaux préparatoires* are in its interpretation. However, they should not be seen as an exhaustive source or a basis

---

① However, the Consumer Protection Act (38/1978) includes a chapter on the sale of building elements (installation-ready construction parts) and construction contracts.

② Timonen, "Sources of Law", 26.

③ Ibid., 28.

for conclusions *e contrario*. That is, the fact that a certain interpretive option is not mentioned does not usually justify the conclusion that the option is meant to be excluded. [1]

Of court decisions, the most important as sources of law are those of the Supreme Court and the Supreme Administrative Court. The decisions of these courts are called precedents. Although precedents are not legally binding sources, they are very important in practice. It is a task of these two courts to unify and guide court practice, and they admit cases partly on the basis of the importance that the legal question is assumed to have when it comes to deciding other similar cases. In view of the limited number of cases processed by the Supreme Courts, decisions of lower courts may become significant sources of law as well. In addition, special courts (such as the Market Court) and boards (such as the Consumer Disputes Board) produce important legal source material. [2]

The position of legal science as a source of law derives from its function to research (that is, to systematise and interpret) the content of the legal system. With respect to its own object of research, legal science is an authoritative institution. [3] Yet, in an interpretive situation, the weight of proposals by legal science should only depend on how convincing they are as to their substance. [4]

Substantive permitted sources are in practice clearly more important than their classification as "less than weakly binding sources" might suggest. The more room for interpretation and the more alternative outcomes the case at hand involves, the more a good judge considers these sources, even without being formally obliged to do so. The sources are solely substantive, and often derive their importance from ideas of justice and morality, as perceived in the interpretive situation under consideration. General principles as a source of law may concern, for example, legal certainty, equality before the law, and fairness. Morality in this context refers primarily to general arguments of justice and public consciousness of what is just. Factual arguments, then, involve assessment of expected consequences when

---

[1]   Jarno Tepora, *Johdatus esineoikeuden perusteisiin* (Helsinki: Helsingin yliopiston oikeustieteellinen tiedekunta, 2008), 7.

[2]   Timonen, "Sources of Law", 29.

[3]   Ibid. , 30.

[4]   Tepora, *Johdatus esineoikeuden perusteisiin*, 8 – 9.

choosing between interpretive options. [1]

The above description focuses on domestic sources of law. However, a complete picture would require inclusion of European Union law, which has been binding on Finland since it became a Member State in 1995. The European Union has no direct and general competence to legislate in the field of private law, but measures adopted in the context of specific European Union policies, relating above all to creation of the internal market, have included private law elements. In some cases, the principal treaties, particularly the Treaty on the Functioning of the European Union, have a direct impact on private law. This is most notable in competition law. In most cases, though, the impact comes through secondary legislation, that is, directives or regulations. Directives have to be implemented in national law, whereas regulations are binding as such. An example of a field that has been heavily influenced by the European Union is consumer law. The Court of Justice of the European Union plays an important interpretive role. [2]

C. System of Private Law

From a structural viewpoint, Finnish lawyers perceive domestic law in the Continental European manner as a systematic whole. That is, despite the absence of a general civil code, the law is thought to form a doctrinal structure. [3] Finnish accounts of the systematisation of law often begin with the distinction between the legal order and the legal system. The legal order is the entirety of valid legal norms at a given moment, whereas the legal system is the result of systematisation efforts by legal science. Systematisation efforts involve, above all, organising legal norm material into fields of law. It is commonly thought that the general doctrines of a field of law are decisive for its existence and identity, that is, its concepts, principles, and theories. In other words, in addition to a specific regulatory object, a field of law needs concepts that structure its normative material, principles that

---

[1]　Timonen, "Sources of Law", 30.

[2]　Christian Twigg-Flesner, "Introduction: Key Features of European Union Private Law", in *The Cambridge Companion to European Union Private Law*, ed. Christian Twigg-Flesner (Cambridge: Cambridge University Press, 2010), 1 – 3.

[3]　Wilhelmsson, *Critical Studies*, 19.

condense its normative contents, and theories that combine concepts and principles. ①

Legislation does not predetermine the systematisation of Finnish private law. The task of system building is largely entrusted to legal science. To be sure, systematisations created by legal science change over time. Furthermore, different scholars may have differing views as to how the system should be built, at least when it comes to details. However, the following outline of the fields of private law is well established and generally accepted.

Finnish private law is first divided into two parts, namely, general private law (or "civil law") and special private law (or "economic law"). General private law consists of the law of persons, patrimonial law (here, "patrimonial" refers to a person's property in general), family law, and inheritance law. Special private law, which is not the main concern of this chapter, includes commercial law, labour law, and environmental law. Patrimonial law, then, consists of the law of obligations, property law, and the law of intellectual property. ②

Two different ways of thinking affect the present division between the law of obligations and property law. According to the older and perhaps somewhat old-fashioned view, the law of obligations concerns rights to receive something from another person, whereas property law concerns rights in physical things (literally, the Finnish word for property law, *esineoikeus*, means "the law of things"). The newer view maintains that both fields of law concern relations between persons, yet different kinds of relations. While the law of obligations deals with relations between contracting parties, or other relations *inter parties*, property law deals with relations *ultra parties*, that is, relations between a contracting party and a third party. According to the newer way of thinking, property law is about questions of third-party protection in the exchange

---

① Tuori, *Oikeuden ratio ja voluntas*, 105 – 110; Lars Björne, *Oikeusjärjestelmän kehityksestä* (Vammala: Suomalainen Lakimiesyhdistys, 1979), 1 – 3. Differing views have been presented on the prospects of creating coherence within a field of law by developing general doctrines. See Thomas Wilhelmsson, " Yleiset opit ja pienet kertomukset ennakoitavuuden ja yhdenvertaisuuden näkökulmasta", *Lakimies* 102, no. 2 (2004): 203 – 207.

② Janne Kaisto and Tapani Lohi, *Johdatus varallisuusoikeuteen* (Helsinki: Talentum, 2008), 16 – 18; Tepora, *Johdatus esineoikeuden perusteisiin*, 12 – 13.

of rights, and its objects are not confined to rights in physical things.[1] For example, with respect to assignment of claims, the relation between assignor and assignee would belong to the law of obligations, whereas potential relations between the assignee and the assignor's creditors and between the assignee and a competing assignee (double assignment) would belong to property law.

Generally, the greater the detail of systematisation, the greater the differences between divisions suggested by different scholars. The law of obligations is further systematised in two somewhat overlapping ways. On the one hand, its field is divided into a general part and a special part. The general part includes legal norms and doctrines common for all obligations, whereas the special part deals with specific types of obligations. When it comes to details, different scholars have drawn the line differently. Nonetheless, the general part is usually thought to include the content (correct fulfilment), sanctions, alteration and cessation of obligations. The special part, then, is usually related to the different types of contracts and other dispositions, debts, and means of payment. The refund of benefit by unjust enrichment is in most cases dealt with in the special part, but it has been considered to fit into the general part, too.[2] On the other hand, the law of obligations is divided into the fields of contract law, the law of compensation for (non-contractual) damages, and the refund of benefit by unjust enrichment.[3] Section IV. C below gives a picture of the subfields of property law. The law of intellectual property, which is the third field of patrimonial law, is divided into two main fields, namely, copyright and industrial rights (for example patents and trademarks).[4]

II. Historical Context

A. *Explanations for the Absence of a Civil Code*

Legal history offers some plausible explanations for the absence of comprehensive civil codes in the Nordic countries. The explanations have been developed by

---

[1] Kaisto and Lohi, *Johdatus varallisuusoikeuteen*, 22 – 24; Tepora, *Johdatus esineoikeuden perusteisiin*, 13 – 16.

[2] Erkki Aurejärvi and Mika Hemmo, *Velvoiteoikeuden oppikirja*, 3rd ed. (Helsinki: Edita, 2007), 7 – 9.

[3] Heikki Halila and Mika Hemmo, *Sopimustyypit*, 2nd ed. (Helsinki: Talentum, 2008), 2.

[4] Pirkko-Liisa Haarmann, *Immateriaalioikeus*, 4th ed. (Helsinki: Talentum, 2006), 3 – 4.

contrasting the situation in the Nordic countries with the legal, social and political reasons for the emergence of codifications elsewhere in Europe during the same period.

At least three factors account for the codification movement. First, codifications were aimed at remedying the abundance of competing legal sources. Continental European legal systems had become extremely complex in the early modern period. Roman law had absorbed canon law, customary law, and the *lex mercatoria*. Local princes and cities had been issuing their own statutes. Complicated legal doctrines were needed to determine the relation between the different sources. On top of all this had grown an immense mesh of privileges. Second, codifications were seen as tools for modernising societies and changing social structures. In this sense, codifications provided national lawgivers with an easier and more effective way to steer the course of their nations. In contrast to *ius commune*, which had been above all a product of academe, codifications could easily be changed according to political will. Courts and citizens could follow codifications more easily than the old law. Importantly, judiciaries also had to follow the codified law. Third, codifications could serve nationalist purposes. Indeed, national codifications could be seen as important as national languages or literature. ①

The Nordic countries were never burdened by such an abundance of legal sources. The legal landscape and the social structure were relatively simple. Separate city laws, manorial law, and local princely legislation were unknown. The content of customary law was not clearly established, partly because it remained unwritten. Canon law had ceased to exist as a separate body of law after the Lutheran Reformation. Most importantly, *ius commune* was never received as the subsidiary body of law; the number of trained lawyers was simply too small for full reception. ②

All this left ample space for the so-called proto-codifications, namely, *Danske Lov* of 1683 (Denmark), *Norske Lov* of 1687 (Norway), and the Swedish Law of the Realm of 1734. These collections of laws are called proto-codifications because they were, unlike the Prussian *Allgemeines Landsrecht* and the French *Code Civil*,

---

① Husa, Nuotio, and Pihlajamäki, "Nordic Law", 18 – 19.
② Ibid. , 19.

and others, not products of the scientific environment of natural law and conceptual jurisprudence. Although they were not codifications in the modern sense, they served similar needs. Furthermore, as Denmark-Norway and Sweden-Finland came to resemble typical nation states in the 19th century, the proto-codifications were already national in character. ①

In sum, because of the fewness of competing legal sources, the existence of proto-codifications, and the absence of Roman law to be cleared out the way, 19th century Nordic societies felt no need for modern codifications. As the century advanced and the Nordic countries began to compile their laws and practices in statutory form, statutory law as such, even without the form of codification, could cater for the modernisation needs of these societies. ②

B. Closest Counterpart to a Civil Code: The Law of 1734

Finland has never had a general civil code in the modern sense of the term. The closest historical counterpart is the Swedish Law of the Realm of 1734 ("the Law of 1734"). ③ Until 1809, Finland was the eastern half of the Kingdom of Sweden, thereafter an autonomous part of the Russian Empire, and declared independence in 1917. ④ The first five of the nine codes (or "beams", as they were named; in Swedish: *balk*) of the Law of 1734 concern private law, namely, marriage, inheritance, real property, building, and trade. This law did not deal with abstract legal institutions and their effects. Instead, it was built by the casuistic method, and thus provided rules for concretely described situations. ⑤ Some of its original provisions (in the codes of building, trade, and judicial procedure) are still in

---

① Husa, Nuotio, and Pihlajamäki, "Nordic Law", See Ditlev Tamm, "The Nordic Legal Tradition in European Context-Roman Law and the Nordic Countries", in *Nordisk identitet: Nordisk rätt i europeisk gemenskap*, ed. Pia Letto-Vanamo (Helsingfors: Institutet för internationell ekonomisk rätt vid Helsingfors universitet, 1998), 22 – 24.

② Husa, Nuotio, and Pihlajamäki, "Nordic Law", 19 – 20.

③ See the remarks on this and the other so-called proto-codifications in section II. A above.

④ On codification attempts during the Russian Era, see section XII below.

⑤ Jukka Kekkonen, "Suomen oikeuskulttuurin suuri linja 1898 – 1998", in *Suomen oikeuskulttuurin suuri linja: Suomalainen Lakimiesyhdistys 100 vuotta* (Helsinki: Suomalainen Lakimiesyhdistys, 1998), 19.

force in Finland, but most of them are of very little practical importance. ① Legal historians tend to emphasise the significance of this law as a carrier of legal tradition. ②

III. Comparative Classifications

René David and John E. C. Brierley include Finnish and the other Nordic legal systems in the Romano-Germanic legal family. They admit, though, that the diversity within this legal family may necessitate secondary groupings. In their view, Nordic (Scandinavian) laws could be recognised as a secondary grouping, alongside Latin, Germanic, and Latin American laws, and so on. However, they do not seem to seriously pursue this idea. While they discuss certain particular features of Nordic laws, such as the absence of modern codifications, these legal systems generally merge into their account of the Romano-Germanic legal family. ③

A more detailed, and today arguably more influential, classification is presented by Konrad Zweigert and Hein Kötz. They remark that the Nordic legal systems expose difficulties with the usual implicit assumption that the Western legal systems belong either to the common law or to the civil law. According to them, Nordic laws cannot be allocated to the common law because their development has been quite independent of English law and because they display few, if any, indications of the common law, such as the typical methods of finding law and the strong emphasis on judicial decisions in important areas of private law. They have doubts about allocating Nordic laws to the civil law either, due to the fact that Roman law has played a relatively modest role in the legal development of the Nordic countries, and because of the absence of comprehensive civil codes. Nevertheless, they conclude that Nordic laws belong to the civil law, but "by reason of their close interrelationship and their common 'stylistic' hallmarks, they must undoubtedly be admitted to form a special legal family, alongside the Romanistic

---

① An exception to "very little practical importance" is mentioned in section IV. C below.

② Kekkonen, "Suomen oikeuskulttuurin suuri linja", 18 – 19.

③ David and Brierley, *Major Legal Systems in the World Today: An Introduction to the Comparative Study of Law*, 3rd ed. (London: Stevens & Sons, 1985), 34, 112 – 113.

and German legal families". ①

Zweigert and Kötz's view comes close to the prevailing opinion, which is also shared by Nordic jurists. The prevailing opinion is that the Nordic legal systems form a separate legal family distinct not only from the common law but also from the civil law, in spite of the considerable Continental European influence. A typical justification for this opinion is the long and continuing Nordic legal tradition which, to name some of its reputed characteristics, attaches relatively little importance to legal formalities and construction of large theoretical systems, and avoids undue conceptualism. It is often suggested that the absence of comprehensive civil codes contributes to an atmosphere of concrete and pragmatic thinking, as opposed to the more abstract and systematic thinking of Continental Europe. ②

IV. Patrimonial Law Legislation

A. Contract Law

The great bulk of Finnish contract law legislation is contract-type specific. The most important exception is the Contracts Act (228/1929), ③ which is a general act on concluding contracts, authorisation to conclude contracts, and invalidity and adjustment of contracts. ④ No general legislation exists on other central matters such as the content of contractual obligations, breach of contract, and contractual

---

① Zweigert and Kötz, *An Introduction to Comparative Law*, 3rd ed. , trans. Tony Weir (Oxford: Oxford University Press, 1998), 277.

② Tamm, "Nordic Legal Tradition", 17. For discussion of Nordic laws against the backdrop of methodological questions of comparative classifications, see Husa, Nuotio, and Pihlajamäki, "Nordic Law", 2 – 10. For a critical "outsider's view" of the alleged pragmatism of Nordic laws, see Smits, "Nordic Law", 61 – 63.

③ A more accurate translation would be "Act on Juridical Acts in the Field of Patrimonial Law". Some provisions of the act seem to represent the view that the concept of contract is an instance of the concept of juridical act.

④ See Christina Ramberg, "The Hidden Secrets of Scandinavian Contract Law", in Wahlgren, *Scandinavian Studies in Law*, vol. 50, 250. According to Ramberg, the Nordic contracts acts, one of which is the Finnish Contracts Act, are fragmentary and unable to address modern contractual problems. In Finland, a committee report on the need to reform the Contracts Act was published in 1990. However, the project was then halted, partly because wishes were expressed that the reform should be undertaken as Nordic co-operation. On this, see Mika Hemmo, *Sopimusoikeus* I, 2nd ed. (Helsinki: Talentum, 2003), 39 – 40.

remedies. Contracts unregulated by legislation are subject to relatively uniform general principles. However, the content of general principles varies according to the following distinctions: standard-term contracts and individually negotiated contracts, consumer contracts and contracts between businesses, and transactions and long-term contracts. General principles also complement regulation of those contract types that are subject to special legislation, unless the relevant legislation provides otherwise. [1]

Since the end of the 1980s, contract law legislation has remarkably expanded. As a consequence, the position of written law as a source of contract law has strengthened. Examples of this legislation include the Sale of Goods Act (355/ 1987), the Act on Commercial Representatives and Salesmen (417/1992), the Act on the Regulation of Contract Terms between Entrepreneurs (1062/1993), the Act on Residential Leases (481/1995), the Act on the Lease of Business Premises (482/1995), the Housing Transactions Act (843/1994), the Insurance Contracts Act (543/1994), the Package Travel Act (1079/1994), the Code of Real Estate (540/1995), the Payment Services Act (290/2010), the Act on Guaranties and Third-Party Pledges (361/1999), the Act on Real Estate and Housing Agency Services (1074/2000), and the Employment Contracts Act (55/ 2001). [2]

B. The Law of Compensation for (Non-contractual) Damages

The general act regulating compensation for non-contractual damages is the Tort Liability Act (412/1974). In matters unregulated by this act, such as causality and unforeseeable damages, the case law of the Supreme Court is of particular importance. [3]

Special legislation is common in this field. Examples include the Employment Accidents Insurance Act (608/1948), the Traffic Insurance Act (279/1959), the Nuclear Liability Act (484/1972), the Act on Compensation for Crime Damage (1204/2005), the Act on Compensation from State Funds for the Arrest or

---

[1] Hemmo, *Sopimusoikeus I*, 28 – 37.

[2] Ibid. , 38 – 39. Some of these acts replaced previous regulation on the same subject matter.

[3] Mika Hemmo, *Vahingonkorvausoikeus*, 2nd ed. (Helsinki: WSOYpro, 2006), 15.

Detention of an Innocent Person (422/1974), the Patient Damages Act (585/1986), the Occupational Disease Act (1343/1988), the Product Liability Act (694/1990), the Act on Compensation for Damage Caused by Ordnance to a Civilian (1213/1990), the Act on Compensation for Environmental Damage (737/1994), the Environmental Damage Insurance Act (81/1998), the Rail Traffic Liability Act (113/1999). ①

C. Property Law

The law of real property is largely covered by the Code of Real Estate (540/1995). The code includes provisions on sale and transfer of real property, the registration system, ② registration of title and special rights, and real estate liens and mortgages. It has been discussed whether the principles and rules of this code could be generalised within the field of property law, that is, whether they could be applied beyond the law of real property. Other central statutes in the law of real property are the Real Estate Register Act (392/1985), the Real Estate Formation Act (554/1995), and the Land Use and Building Act (132/1999). ③

No general legislation or provisions exists, on ownership, except the Act on Certain Co-ownership Relations (180/1958). Besides real property, registration legislation exists on book-entry securities: the Act on the Book-Entry System (826/1991) and the Act on Book-Entry Accounts (827/1991). In addition, legislation on industrial rights, such as patents and trademarks, includes provisions on registration of these rights. Registration also plays a role with respect to certain non-possessory security rights over movable property (mortgages). Legislation exists on mortgages over aircraft, vessels, and certain kinds of cars, albeit that the respective acts have long needed reform. The Enterprise Mortgage Act (634/1984) enables businesses to use their tangible movables and intangibles as "floating" security for credit. No general legislation exists on rights to use and rights of severance, but special legislation has been enacted on leases: the Act on Residential

---

① Mika Hemmo, *Vahingonkorvausoikeus*, 15 - 16. Some of these acts are insurance-based or other special non-fault compensation systems.

② A country-wide real estate register is maintained in accordance with the Real Estate Register Act (392/1985).

③ Tepora, *Johdatus esineoikeuden perusteisiin*, 3 - 4.

Leases (481/1995), the Act on the Lease of Business Premises (482/1995), and the Act on the Lease of Land (258/1966). Some provisions of the archaic and casuistic "Trade Code" of the Law of 1734 still apply to matters of movable property. For example, good faith acquisition is based on these provisions. The Promissory Notes Act (622/1947) regulates the transfer and pledge of negotiable and ordinary promissory notes, and applies to receivables by way of analogy. Furthermore, many provisions relevant to substantive property law are found in insolvency legislation. [1]

V. Commercial Law Legislation

Finland does not have a commercial code in the sense of a comprehensive codification. Still, a field of law called commercial law exists. Its systematic place is in special private law (see section I. C above), and its subfields are rather heterogeneous. The central subfields are the law of business organisations, market law, and consumer law. Sometimes, especially in university curricula, the law of intellectual property is also included in commercial law.

Many matters of a commercial nature, such as specific types of commercial contracts, negotiable instruments, means of payment, and security rights (security for credit) are traditionally dealt with in the relevant fields of general private law (patrimonial law). As a matter of fact, one of the common characteristics between the Nordic legal systems is that no sharp distinction exists between civil law and commercial law. [2]

Central statutes in the law of business organisations are the Partnerships Act (389/1988), the Act on European Economic Interest Grouping (1299/1994), the Limited Liability Companies Act (624/2006), the Act on European Company (742/2004), the Co-operatives Act (1488/2001), and the Act on European Cooperative Society (906/2006). In market law, central statutes of general application are the Competition Act (948/2011), the Unfair Business Practices Act (1061/1978), and the Act on the Right to Practice a Trade (122/1919). Additionally, market law includes sector-specific legislation on, for example,

---

[1]   Tepora, *Johdatus esineoikeuden perusteisiin*, 4 – 6.

[2]   Tamm, "Nordic Legal Tradition", 17.

energy markets, communications, postal services, transport, financial services and insurance. ① Consumer law is discussed in more detail in the following section.

VI. Consumer Law Legislation

A. Overview

Finnish consumer law legislation consists of several statutes. In recent years, this field has been heavily influenced by European law. It has been estimated that at least three fourths of the provisions are based on European Union legislation. ②

The core statute of the field is the Consumer Protection Act (38/1978). In its present form, the act includes provisions on its scope of application, which largely define the scope of consumer law in general, as well as chapters on regulation of marketing, regulation of contract terms, adjustment and interpretation of a contract, sale of consumer goods, door-to-door selling and distance selling, distance selling of financial services and instruments, consumer credit, certain consumer service contracts, sale of building elements (installation-ready construction parts) and construction contracts, and time-share and long-term holiday products. Other consumer legislation includes the Act on Real Estate and Housing Agency Services (1074/2000), the Housing Transactions Act (843/ 1994), the Package Travel Act (1079/1994), the Consumer Safety Act (920/ 2011), and the Product Liability Act (694/1990). Additionally, decrees have been issued that specify some acts.

The following statutes concern the consumer authorities: the Act on the Consumer Agency (1056/1998), the Act on the Consumer Disputes Board (8/ 2007), the Act on Financial and Debt Counselling (713/2000), the Market Court Act (1527/2001), the Act on Certain Procedures before the Market Court (1528/2001), and the Act on Class Actions (444/2007).

In addition, certain statutes of a general nature contain special provisions concerning consumer relations. Examples include the Electricity Market Act (386/1995), the Insurance Contracts Act (543/1994), and the Interests Act (633/1982).

---

① Pentti Mäkinen et al. , *Markkinaoikeuden perusteet*, 2nd ed. (Helsinki: Talentum, 2006).
② Tuula Ämmälä, *Suomen kuluttajaoikeus* (Helsinki: Talentum, 2006), 1.

B. Consumer Contracts

Consumer contracts are concluded between a business (entrepreneur) and a consumer. These contracts concern consumer goods or services, that is, "goods, services and other merchandise and benefits that are offered to natural persons or which such persons acquire, to an essential extent, for their private households" (Consumer Protection Act, Chapter 1 Section 3).

Consumer contracts do not belong to the traditional systematisation of contract law, which is based on recognition of different contract types. In that respect, the concept of the consumer contract can be said to have a fragmenting effect on the traditional system. On the one hand, the concept of the consumer contract splits traditional contract types into two parts. For example, instead of speaking of sales contracts as a unitary type, consumer sales have to be distinguished from "ordinary" sales. On the other hand, the concept of the consumer contract includes several traditional contract types: consumer sales, consumer services, and so on. It should be also noted that the significance of the concept of the consumer contract is not limited to the scope of application of the Consumer Protection Act. That is, the concept plays a role in general doctrines of contract law and the law of obligations (see section VI. C below). [1]

The Consumer Protection Act includes some general provisions that concern all consumer contracts. These are found in Chapter 3 on regulation of contract terms, according to which a business may be enjoined from using a contract term which is to be deemed unreasonable from the point of view of consumers, and in Chapter 4 on adjustment and interpretation of a contract. Additionally, the provision of Chapter 10 Section 5 of the Code of Judicial Procedure (4/1734), which concerns jurisdiction as to claims based on consumer protection legislation, concerns all consumer contracts. However, the main part of the more specific regulation concerns specific types of consumer contracts. A common feature of the special provisions on consumer contracts is that they are usually mandatory. For example, Chapter 5 (Sale of Consumer Goods) Section 2 of the Consumer Protection Act prescribes: "A contract term differing from the provisions of this

---

[1]   Thomas Wilhelmsson, "Kuluttajasopimukset", in *Encyclopædia Iuridica Fennica I: Varallisuus-ja yritysoikeus*, eds. Heikki E. S. Mattila et al. (Helsinki: Suomalainen Lakimiesyhdistys, 1994), 377 –378.

chapter to the detriment of the buyer shall be void unless otherwise provided below. " That is, deviations from the provisions are allowed if they improve the consumer's position. Similar examples are Section 3 (2) of the Insurance Contracts Act and Section 25a (1) of the Electricity Market Act. ①

The general aim of regulation of consumer contracts, which holds true for consumer law as a whole, is to improve the consumer's position in relation to the entrepreneur, who is generally assumed to be the stronger party both in terms of bargaining power and information. Because this regulation is based on the formal statuses of consumer and business, the protection it offers is sometimes criticised for over-and under-inclusiveness, that is, of having too little regard for the contracting parties' actual need for protection. ②

C. Relationship Between General Contract Law and Consumer Contract Law

In the wake of consumer legislation, consumer law, with its strong public law elements, has emerged as a field separate from general private law. The same can be said about the relationship between consumer contract law and general contract law. This can also be seen in matters unregulated by legislation. It is considered clear that general principles of contract law and the law of obligations may be applied differently depending on whether the issue at hand concerns a relation between a consumer and a business or a relation between businesses. ③

---

① Thomas Wilhelmsson, "Kuluttajasopimukset", in *Encyclopædia Iuridica Fennica I: Varallisuus-ja yritysoikeus*, eds. Heikki E. S. Mattila et al. (Helsinki: Suomalainen Lakimiesyhdistys, 1994), 379 – 380; Halila and Hemmo, *Sopimustyypit*, 5.

② See Halila and Hemmo, *Sopimustyypit*, 5 – 8. They remark that consumer protection is not the only instance of weaker-party protection in Finnish contract law. For example, according to Section 3 (2) of Insurance Contracts Act, the mandatory provisions protect not only the consumer but also "another natural person or legal person that in terms of the nature and scope of its business or other activities or other circumstances can be compared to a consumer". In addition, the Act on Residential Leases (481/1995) protects the lessee as the weaker party irrespective of whether the lessor is an entrepreneur, and the substantive provisions of the Hire-Purchase Act (91/1966) seem to be based on the view of the buyer as the weaker party. Perhaps the most obvious example, however, concerns employment contracts.

③ Thomas Wilhelmsson, "Kuluttajaoikeus", in *Encyclopædia Iuridica Fennica I: Varallisuus-jayritysoikeus*, eds. Heikki E. S. Mattila et al. (Helsinki: Suomalainen Lakimiesyhdistys, 1994), 359; Wilhelmsson, "Kuluttajasopimukset", 377 – 378.

However, this separateness is only relative. That is, many provisions of general contract law legislation, such as the Contracts Act, apply to consumer contracts and other contracts alike, as *lex generalis*. As regards consumer sales, the provisions of Chapter 5 of the Consumer Protection Act have been squared with those of the general Sale of Goods Act. The provisions of Chapter 5 of the Consumer Protection Act are the primary source as *lex specialis*. Additionally, Section 29 of the same chapter explicitly states that the provisions of the Sale of Goods Act apply to a sale referred to in the chapter, unless otherwise provided in the Consumer Protection Act. The section includes a list of provisions of the Sale of Goods Act which do not apply at all to consumer sales. [1]

It has also been argued that isolation of consumer contract law from general contract law would be undesirable. According to this view, consumer contract law provides important impulses to the development of general contract law. Regulation of marketing liability in the Sale of Goods Act has been referred to as an example of these impulses because the provisions of the Consumer Protection Act served as one of its models. [2] Furthermore, it has been argued that some provisions of Chapter 8 of the Consumer Protection Act on certain consumer services (repair and manufacture) may also become applicable in relations between businesses by way of analogy or as general principles of the law of obligations. [3] In conclusion, the influence between consumer contract law and general contract law seems to go both ways.

VII. Labour Law Legislation

Most labour law can be divided into three subfields, namely, employment contract law, the law of collective agreements (collective bargaining) and employee participation, and the law of occupational safety and health. [4] The core

---

[1] See Wilhelmsson, "Kuluttajaoikeus", 359; Ämmälä, *Suomen kuluttajaoikeus*, 37 – 67.

[2] Wilhelmsson, "Kuluttajaoikeus", 359.

[3] Halila and Hemmo, *Sopimustyypit*, 94.

[4] Kari-Pekka Tiitinen, *Työoikeuden pääasiat* (Helsinki: Helsingin yliopiston oikeustieteellinen tiedekunta, 2005), 1. See Niklas Bruun, "Labour Law and Non-discrimination Law", in Pöyhönen, *Introduction to Finnish Law*, 175 – 176. An example of a statute that may be difficult to fit into these categories is the Act on the Right in Employee Inventions (656/1967).

statute of employment contract law is the Employment Contracts Act (55/2001). This regulates, among other things, employer and employee obligations, family leave, lay-offs, termination and cancellation of employment contracts, invalidity of employment contracts and unreasonable terms, international aspects of employment contracts, and liability for damages. Employment contracts are also regulated in the Seafarers' Employment Contracts Act (756/2011) and the Act on the Employment of Household Workers (951/1977). Additionally, the provisions on apprenticeship in the Act on Occupational Training (630/1998) can be included in employment contract law. ①

Central statutes in the law of collective agreements and employee participation are the Collective Agreements Act (436/1946),② the Act on Collective Agreements for State Civil Servants (664/1970), the Act on Collective Agreements for Local Government Officials (669/1970), the Act on Confirmation of the General Applicability of Collective Agreements (56/2001), the Mediation in Labour Disputes Act (420/1962), the Act on the Labour Court (646/1974), the Act on Co-operation within Undertakings (334/2007), the Act on Personnel Funds (934/2010), and the Act on Personnel Representation in the Administration of Undertakings (725/1990). ③ In the law of occupational safety and health, central statutes include the Occupational Safety and Health Act (738/2002), the Radiation Act (592/1991), the Occupational Health Care Act (1383/2001), the Young Workers' Act (998/1993), the Working Hours Act (605/1996), and the Annual Holidays Act (162/2005). ④

Furthermore, labour law has important intersections with non-discrimination law and social security law. The issue of discrimination is addressed in Section 6 of the

---

① Tiitinen, *Työoikeudenpääasiat*, 10 – 11.

② An important contact point between the law of collective agreements and (individual) employment contract law is the principle of the general applicability of collective agreements. That is, as provided by Section 7 of the Employment Contracts Act, even employers who are not members of an employer organisation and not a party to any collective agreement are still obliged in certain cases to follow the relevant collective agreement. See Bruun, "Labour Law", 183 – 184.

③ Tiitinen, *Työoikeuden pääasiat*, 132 – 158.

④ Ibid. , 158 – 182.

Constitution of Finland (731/1999), [1] and further concretised in the Employment Contracts Act and the Act on Equality between Women and Men (609/1986). [2] Social security law is often considered to include both employment related and general social security law. Employment related social security law includes legislation on accident insurance, employment pension, wage guarantee in the case of employer insolvency, and unemployment benefits. [3]

VIII. Family and Inheritance Law Legislation

Family law, which encompasses several statutes, is divided into the subfields of child law, name law, guardianship law, and relationship law. Inheritance law consists of statutory succession law and testament law (the law of wills). [4]

In child law, central statutes are the Paternity Act (700/1975), the Act on Assisted Fertility Treatments (1237/2006), the Act on Legal-Genetic Paternity Test (378/2005), the Adoption Act (153/1985), the Child Custody and Right of Access Act (361/1983), the Act on the Execution of a Decision on Child Custody and Right of Access (619/1996), the Act on Child Maintenance (704/1975), the Maintenance Support Act (580/2008), and the Child Welfare Act (417/2007). The core statute of name law is the Names Act (694/1985). In guardianship law, central statutes are the Guardianship Services Act (442/1999), the Act on the Arrangement of Guardianship Services (575/2008), and the Continuing Power of Attorney Act (648/2007). Central statutes in relationship law are the Marriage Act (234/1929), which applies to couples of the opposite sex, the Act on Registered Partnerships (950/2001), which applies to same-sex couples, and the Act on the Dissolution of the Household of Cohabiting Partners (26/2011). As for inheritance law, the core statute is the Code of Inheritance (40/1965), which covers statutory succession law and testament law alike.

---

[1] When it comes to protection of union activities, Section 13 of the Constitution, on freedom of assembly and freedom of association, is relevant.

[2] Bruun, "Labour Law", 204 – 210.

[3] Tiitinen, *Työoikeuden pääasiat*, 1.

[4] Urpo Kangas, *Perhe-ja perintöoikeuden alkeet* (Helsinki: Helsingin yliopiston oikeustieteellinen tiedekunta, 2006), 3 – 7.

IX. Regional Private Law Legislation：Åland

Finland is a unitary state and, generally speaking, a unitary jurisdiction with respect to private law legislation. That is, as a starting point, the same private law applies in all parts of the country. The only exceptions stem from the autonomous status of the Region of Åland. The region is located in the Åland Islands, an archipelago in the Baltic Sea, at the entrance to the Gulf of Bothnia. The Åland Islands are demilitarised, and the region is monolingually Swedish-speaking. The population is approximately 28, 000 people.

The region's autonomous status includes competence to enact regional legislation in matters specified in Section 18 of the Act on the Autonomy of Åland (1144/ 1991). Of these matters, at least the following may directly concern or touch upon private law：

7) building and planning, adjoining properties, housing; 8) the appropriation of real property and of special rights required for public use in exchange for full compensation… 9) tenancy and rent regulation, lease of land; 10) the protection of nature and the environment, the recreational use of nature, water law; 11) prehistoric relics and the protection of buildings and artifacts with cultural or historical value; 12) health care and medical treatment … 14) education, apprenticeship, culture, sport and youth work; the archive, library and museum service… 15) farming and forestry, the regulation of agricultural production… 16) hunting and fishing, the registration of fishing vessels and the regulation of fishing industry… 18) the maintenance of the productive capacity of the farmlands, forests and fishing waters; the duty to transfer, in exchange for full compensation, unutilised or partially utilised farmland or fishing water into the possession of another person to be used for these purposes, for a fixed period; 19) the right to prospect for, lay claim to and utilise mineral finds; 20) the postal service and the right to broadcast by radio or cable in Åland… 21) roads and canals, road traffic, railway traffic, boat traffic, the local shipping lanes; 22) trade… 27) other matters deemed to be within the legislative power of Åland in accordance with the principles underlying this Act. ①

---

① Exceptions to the listed matters are omitted.

To give but one example, which directly concerns contract law, the region has enacted an act on the lease of apartments and other premises, *hyreslag för landskapet Åland* (1999: 19). By contrast, Section 27 of the Act on the Autonomy of Åland includes a list of matters in which legislative competence belongs to the State of Finland. The list includes, among other things, the following matters:

6) surname and forename, guardianship, the declaration of the legal death of a person; 7) marriage and family relations, the juridical status of children, adoption and inheritance ⋯ 8) associations and foundations, companies and other private corporations, the keeping of accounts; 9) the nation-wide general preconditions on the right of foreigners and foreign corporations to own and possess real property and shares of stock and to practice trade; 10) copyright, patent, copyright of design and trademark, unfair business practices, promotion of competition, consumer protection; 11) insurance contracts; 12) foreign trade; 13) merchant shipping and shipping lanes; 14) aviation ⋯ 16) the formation and registration of pieces of real property and connected duties; 17) mineral finds and mining ⋯ 21) labour law ⋯ 40) telecommunications ⋯ 41) the other matters under private law not specifically mentioned in this section, unless the matters relate directly to an area of legislation within the competence of Åland according to this Act; 42) other matters that are deemed to be within the legislative power of the State according to the principles underlying this Act. ①

Another aspect of the region's autonomous status, which clearly has implications for private law, is the so-called right of domicile, regulated in Chapter 2 of the Act on the Autonomy of Åland. The right of domicile is a form of regional citizenship, introduced with a view to protecting the local culture and Swedish language as well as keeping the land in Ålandic ownership. The right of domicile can be acquired by birth or application. Acquisition by application normally requires that the applicant, who must be a Finnish citizen, has lived in Åland for at least five years, and has a satisfactory command of the Swedish language. Persons without the right of domicile are subject to restrictions on the right to acquire real property and the right to practice a trade. The former restrictions are laid down in the Act on the Acquisition of Real Property in Åland (3/1975), and the latter restrictions in

---

① Again, exceptions are omitted.

regional legislation. ①

In conclusion, the instances where the autonomous status of the Region of Åland may concern private law are limited and rather disjointed. They do not form a coherent whole, let alone being able to create a complete system of private law. The general framework and great bulk of private law applied in Åland is the same as in mainland Finland.

X. Private International Law Legislation

At present, Finnish private international law is largely based on European Union legislation. The core of this field consists of the Regulation (EC) 593/2008 on the law applicable to contractual obligations (Rome I) and the Regulation (EC) 864/2007 on the law applicable to non-contractual obligations (Rome II), which provide uniform conflict rules. ② Both regulations are applied universally in the sense that the law specified by the regulation will be applied whether or not it is the law of a European Union Member State.

Conflict rules and other private international law regulation on specific types of contracts are also found in individual domestic acts. Examples include the Act on the Law Applicable to Certain Insurance Contracts of International Character (91/ 1993), the Maritime Act (674/1994), the Act on Negotiable Promissory Notes (242/1932), the Act on Cheques (244/1932), the Act on the Law Applicable to Sale of Goods of International Character (387/1964), the Consumer Protection Act (38/1978), and the Posted Workers Act (1146/1999). ③

---

① *Åland in the European Union* (Helsinki: Europe Information, Ministry for Foreign Affairs of Finland, 2005), 14 – 15.

② Depending on the definition of private international law followed, Regulation (EC) 44/2001 on jurisdiction and the recognition and enforcement of judgments in civil and commercial matters ("Brussels I") may also be mentioned, as well as Regulation (EC) 2201/2003 concerning jurisdiction and the recognition and enforcement of judgments in matrimonial matters and the matters of parental responsibility ("Brussels IIA"). Regulation (EC) 44/2001 will be replaced in 2015 by the recast Regulation (EU) 1215/2012.

③ See Ulla Liukkunen, "Recent Private International Law Codifications", in *Studies on the Finnish Legal System: Finnish Reports to the 18th Congress of the International Academy of Comparative Law (IACL) Washington D. C. 25th July-August 1st 2010*, ed. Erkki J. Hollo (Edilex database, Edita, 2011), 131 – 132, http://www. edilex. fi/lakikirjasto/8059. pdf.

Before the Rome II Regulation entered into force, Finnish conflict rules on non-contractual obligations were unwritten and ambiguous. ① This is still largely the case for conflict rules on property law matters. ② The unwritten general rule for rights in immovable and tangible movable property is the *lex rei sitae* rule. An open question is the law applicable to third-party effectiveness of an assignment of claims.

Finnish international family law was quite thoroughly reformed in 2002. The new provisions are found in Part V of the Marriage Act (234/1929) and Chapter 26 of the Code of Inheritance (40/1965). ③

XI. Private Law Legislation, the National Constitution, and Public International Law

A. Relationship Between Private Law and the Constitution

The relationship between private law legislation and the Constitution of Finland (731/1999) is too complicated a topic to be thoroughly discussed in this article. Therefore, suffice to mention just some of their contact points. These can be found in legislative work, application of law by courts, and systematisation efforts by legal science.

First and foremost, private law legislation, like legislation in general, must be enacted in accordance with the Constitution. The rules on enactment of legislation are included in Chapter 6 of the Constitution. If the legislation to be enacted restricts a fundamental right (Chapter 2 of the Constitution), the following list of preconditions compiled by the Constitutional Law Committee of the Parliament has to be fulfilled: the restriction has to be enacted by an act (not a lower-level statute), the scope of the restriction and its limits have to be exact, the grounds for the restriction have to be acceptable (pressing societal need), the core of the fundamental right in question has to remain untouched, the

---

① See Ulla Liukkunen, "Recent Private International Law Codifications", in *Studies on the Finnish Legal System: Finnish Reports to the 18th Congress of the International Academy of Comparative Law (IACL) Washington D. C. 25th July-August 1st 2010*, ed. Erkki J. Hollo (Edilex database, Edita, 2011), 131 – 132, http://www. edilex. fi/lakikirjasto/8059. pdf.

② For one exception, see Section 5a (4) of the Act on Book-Entry Accounts (827/1991).

③ See Tuulikki Mikkola, *Kansainvälinen avioliitto-ja jäämistöoikeus* (Helsinki: WSOYpro, 2009), 53 – 61.

restriction has to be proportionate, "protection under the law" in accordance with Section 21 of the Constitution has to be available, and Finland's international human rights obligations have to be adhered to. According to Section 22 of the Constitution, the public authorities shall guarantee the observance of fundamental rights and human rights. This provision seems to set some requirements as to the content of private law legislation. For example, it has been argued that when it comes to fundamental rights of a personal and economic nature, one of the most central means of protection is compensation for damage. ①

In the application of law by courts, Section 106 of the Constitution may also become relevant with respect to private law legislation. According to this section, if applying a provision of an act would be in evident conflict with the Constitution, the court has to give primacy to the Constitution. The requirement of an "evident conflict" underlines the exceptionality of these situations. ②

Furthermore, private law legislation may be touched by the requirement of fundamental-right conforming interpretation. This relates to the horizontal effect of fundamental rights, that is, the effect between private parties. In this respect, the starting point of the Finnish system of fundamental rights is the so-called indirect horizontal effect, which means that the effect of fundamental rights between private parties takes place primarily through ordinary legislation. When applying legislation, courts have to choose the outcome alternative which best promotes realisation of fundamental rights. Thus, fundamental rights provide arguments and supplementary aspects for adjudication that applies ordinary legislation. ③ However, it is common that in a dispute both parties are able to invoke their "own" fundamental rights. For example, in a damages case, the claimant may rely on the right to personal integrity (Section 7), the right to privacy (Section 10), or protection of property (Section 15), whereas the defendant may rely on the right to work and the freedom to engage in commercial activity (Section 18), or freedom of expression (Section 12). Since the Constitution includes no order of priority as to fundamental rights, the court has to weigh the parties' arguments. Generally,

① See Päivi Tiilikka, *Sananvapaus ja yksilön suoja: Lehtiartikkelin aiheuttaman kärsimyksen korvaaminen* (Helsinki: WSOYpro, 2007), 146 – 159.
② Ibid. , 160 – 162.
③ Ibid. , 162 – 165.

arguments that concern the core of a fundamental right weigh more. [1]

In legal science, Professor Juha Pöyhönen (Karhu) has outlined a theoretical resystematisation of Finnish private law (patrimonial law) in accordance with fundamental rights. Instead of the mere concept of freedom, which has been the core of the traditional system, the new system would be founded on the entire system of fundamental rights. [2]

B. Relationship Between Private Law and Treaties

Finland adheres to the so-called dualist theory, which perceives national law and international law as separate systems. Therefore, the provisions of treaties or other international obligations are not formally considered as a part of the Finnish internal legal system until they have been implemented into it, that is, until they have been brought into force. [3] Before implementation, an international obligation would not, as a rule, be applied by Finnish courts or other authorities, nor would it affect the rights or obligations of a person within Finland's jurisdiction. Section 95 (1) of the Constitution prescribes as follows: "The provisions of treaties and other international obligations, in so far as they are of a legislative nature, are brought into force by an act. Otherwise, international obligations are brought into force by a decree." Implemented international obligations occupy the same hierarchical position as Finnish domestic legislation, and they will be applied similarly. [4]

In practice, implementation is usually achieved by so-called blanket acts or decrees, which merely state that the treaty in question is brought into force, and the text of the treaty is annexed to the act or decree. [5] As regards norm conflicts between implemented treaties or between an implemented treaty and ordinary national legislation, the prevailing view (already formed before the present Constitution was

---

[1] Hemmo, *Vahingonkorvausoikeus*, 16 – 17. See Tiilikka, *Sananvapaus ja yksilön suoja*, 165 – 169.

[2] Pöyhönen, *Uusi varallisuusoikeus*, 2nd ed. (Helsinki: Talentum, 2003).

[3] European Union membership entails exceptions to this. See section I. B above.

[4] *Valtiosopimusopas: Kansainvälisten ja EU-sopimusten valmistelua ja voimaansaattamista koskevat ohjeet* (Ulkoasiainministeriö, 2012-ennakkoversio, päivitetty maaliskuussa 2012), 6, 70 – 71. As for treaties concluded by or in the context of the European Union, see ibid., 7 – 15, 80 – 81.

[5] Kari Hakapää, *Uusi kansainvälinen oikeus*, 3rd ed. (Helsinki: Talentum, 2010), 22. Hakapää notes that the use of blanket acts and decrees does not represent dualism in its pure form, but is rather somewhere between dualism and monism.

enacted) has been that the norm-hierarchical level of an implemented treaty follows the norm-hierarchical level of its implementing enactment. Then, the usual principles of *lex superior*, *lex posterior*, and *lex specialis* can be applied. However, these principles should not be taken too rigidly. It has been suggested as a strong presumption that the legislator cannot have meant a binding international obligation to be derogated (for which Finland could become liable). Conflicts can, and should, usually be avoided by way of harmonising interpretation. ①

XII. Codification Attempts and Prospects

Comprehensive codification of law, including private law, was attempted in Finland in a project that began seriously in 1835. At that time (between separation from the Kingdom of Sweden in 1809 and the declaration of independence in 1917), Finland was an autonomous Grand Principality ("Grand Duchy") of the Russian Empire. The project was an offshoot of Russian efforts, directed by Mikhail Speransky, that had resulted in the *Svod Zakonov Rossiskoj Imperii* codification of 1832. ②

Finnish law was to be codified according to the Russian model. From the Russian authorities' viewpoint, this project was about rationalisation, essentially for Finland's own good. Unlike later Russian policies towards the Grand Principality of Finland, it was not motivated by Russian nationalism and Pan-Slavism. Nevertheless, Finns perceived the Russian measures as a policy of oppression. ③

The project faced firm opposition in Finland, and was eventually rejected. However, the Finnish response was not unanimous. ④ Proponents of

---

① Allan Rosas, "Kansainvälinen normisto ja Suomen oikeusjärjestelmä", in *Kansainvälinen normisto Suomen oikeusjärjestelmässä*, eds. Allan Rosas and Catarina Krause (Helsinki: Lakimiesliiton Kustannus, 1993), 20.

② Kekkonen, "Suomen oikeuskulttuurin suuri linja", 24.

③ Osmo Jussila, *Suomen perustuslait venäläisten ja suomalaisten tulkintojen mukaan 1808 – 1863* (Helsinki: Suomen Historiallinen Seura, 1969), 196 – 197.

④ It should be noted that even though the aims and general framework of the project were imposed by the Russians, the detailed plans were drafted in Helsinki. The work commenced with a plan by Carl Evert Ekelund, Professor of Roman and Russian law at the Imperial Alexander University of Finland (renamed in 1917 as the University of Helsinki). In this plan, the second of the two main parts concerned civil law. See Jussila, *Suomen perustuslait*, 195 – 196.

codification saw a chance to reform out-dated legislation, and to organise the large body of existing norms in a more manageable way. Opponents claimed that codification would discontinue the Swedish-Finnish legal tradition, stir confusion in legal practice, and open the door for Russification of Finnish law. Finally, the opposing arguments convinced the Russians to set the project aside "for the time being" . [1] The stability of the Grand Principality was regarded as more important than codification and unification. [2] Codification plans were resumed on some later occasions, but they never led to concrete results. [3]

Apparently, enactment of a comprehensive civil code has not been planned or seriously discussed in Finland during its independence. In 1948, Frederik Vinding Kruse, a Danish professor, presented his own proposal for a Nordic Civil Code. [4] However, as Professor Ulf Bernitz states, " this project was hardly taken seriously" . [5] Recently, Finnish scholars have participated in discussions on the need for and feasibility of a European Civil Code. [6]

---

[1] Kekkonen, "Suomen oikeuskulttuurin suuri linja" , 24 – 25. Kekkonen remarks that the debate has some parallels with the German Thibaut-Savigny controversy.

[2] Jussila, *Suomen perustuslait*, 204 – 208.

[3] Matti Klinge, *Keisarin Suomi*, trans. Marketta Klinge (Espoo: Schildts, 1997) , 295 – 296.

[4] Fr. Vinding Kruse, *En nordisk lovbog: Udkast til en fælles borgerlig lovbog for Danmark, Finland, Island, Norge og Sverrig* (København: Centraltrykkeriet, 1948).

[5] Bernitz, "Scandinavian Law" , 20.

[6] For a culmination of the discussions, see Christian von Bar and Eric Clive, eds. , *Principles, Definitions and Model Rules of European Private Law: Draft Common Frame of Reference (DCFR)*, vols. I-VI (Oxford: Oxford University Press, 2010). Despite being essentially an academic undertaking, the DCFR resembles a civil code. In addition to a book entitled "General provisions" , it includes six books on the law of obligations and three books on property law.

芬兰私法：一个没有《民法典》的成文法体系

泰穆·尤蒂莱宁[*]

【摘要】虽然芬兰算是一个民法法系国家，但是芬兰的私法却并不是建立在一个全面的民法典之上的。就像在其他北欧国家一样，私法的法典化是通过制定法，即不同的单行法律的形式实现的。私法的一般性原则以及其他"通则"多数都没有被法典化，并且这种情况很可能不会改变。由于没有一部民法典和综合性的通则，芬兰民法是一个开放性的系统。这也解释了芬兰对于私法所采取的整体方法的一些方面，包括法律的解释与适用、法学的作用以及法律对外部影响的开放性。尽管芬兰没有一部民法典，但是芬兰法学家们将国内私法看作一个系统的、由法律原则所组成的整体结构。私法的系统化不是由立法所预先决定的，而是由法律科学所完成的。

---

* 赫尔辛基大学法学院博士研究生。

State Ownership and Corporate Social Responsibility Agenda in International Instruments

—Coping with Conflicting Regulatory Rationales?

Mikko Rajavuori *

【 Abstract 】 The article discusses state ownership from a corporate social responsibility (CSR) perspective. It suggests that states, acting in corporate owner capacity, are starting to utilize the accomplishments and imbalances of global economic liberalization at an unprecedented scale. This development has, in turn, prompted enhanced regulatory interventions to reduce undue state influence over corporations with the aim of securing a level playing field in global markets. As a corollary, the intersections between state ownership and issues of CSR have also increased. These intersections raise several difficult questions. Should state-owned enterprises (SOEs) pursue more extensive CSR strategies than their private counterparts? Should state share holders arrange their ownership function in accordance with heightened CSR considerations? Could human rights law provide a normative base for such requirements?

In this article, the issue is approached from the perspective of two international soft law instruments commenting on the proliferation of state ownership, the United Nations (UN) Protect, Respect and Remedy Framework (UN Framework) and its Guiding Principles (GPs) and the organization for Economic Co-operation and Development (OECD) Guidelines on Corporate Governance of State-Owned Enterprises (OECD SOE Guidelines). It is submitted that the

---

* Mikko Rajavuori, Doctoral candidate, University of Turku, Finland.

instruments' treatment of CSR reveals entrenched and conflicting notions about the rationales of regulating state ownership function.

The analysis is structured in four sections. Section 2 explains the increased significance of state ownership in the global economy. Section 3 discusses intersections between state ownership function and corporate social responsibility. Section 4 introduces the OECD SOEs and the UN Framework and the GPs, detailing their conflicting regulatory rationales regarding state ownership. Section 5 concludes.

1. The Fall and Rise of State Owner

Over the last century, the rationales for state ownership have varied among countries and industry sectors. At times, strong state ownership positions have been used to curb private enterprises amassing monopolistic market positions, as was the case in post-war Europe. [①] More recently, state ownership policies have greatly influenced Chinese " Go Global " strategies, which have attempted to internationalize Chinese economy. [②] In general, the important motivations behind strong state presence in markets through corporate ownership have included development, industrial and employment policies, the provision of public goods, the existence of natural monopolies and strategic national interests.

The last few decades have, however, witnessed major readjustments and restructurings of SOE sectors. Rooted in globalization, economic liberalization and deregulation, state ownership policies have primarily been characterized by waves of privatization since the late 1970s. States all over the world have sold major blocks of their ownership positions to the private sector. According to some estimates, privatization transactions between the late 1970s and the early 2000s amounted to US $ 1,230 billion globally, or roughly one-fifth of the total value of issues

---

[①]   See e. g. Erika Szyszczak, *The Regulation of the State in Competitive Markets in the EU* (Hart Publishing 2007) 1 – 3.

[②]   See e. g. Larry Catá Backer, 'Sovereign Investing in Times of Crisis: Global Regulation of Sovereign Wealth Funds, State-Owned Enterprises, and the Chinese Experience' (2010) 19 Transnational Law & Contemporary Problems 3, 100.

floated on public equity markets during that period. [1] The rationales behind the privatization policies are well documented. In brief, SOEs are considered less efficient than private corporations because of their perceived governance problems: the double role of state as a market participant and a regulator has been seen to lead to idiosyncrasies in setting corporate objectives; the political interventions can lead to severe agency problems; and the presence of a deep-pocketed shareholder can prompt reckless risk-taking among managers. [2] In the international setting, SOEs have been described as potential market irritants jeopardizing competitive markets and a level playing field. Consequently, the rationales skeptical of state ownership have been utilized in a number of regulatory initiatives aiming at reducing and controlling the scale of direct state involvement in corporations since the late 1970s. [3]

However, several recent developments have greatly challenged the prevailing narratives of the demise of state ownership and the proliferation of private enterprise. Most importantly, recent studies suggest the increasing significance of SOEs and the states in corporate ownership roles, especially with regard to ownership in foreign corporations. United Nations Conference on Trade and Development (UNCTAD) statistics, for example, reveal that the number of state-owned multinational corporations (MNCs) has actually increased between 2010 and 2012. [4] Currently, their market value corresponds to 11% of the market capitalization of all listed companies worldwide, and their overseas investments account for roughly 11% of global foreign direct investment (FDI) flows. [5] According to some calculations, nearly 20% of the world's top 100 and over 10%

---

[1] Bernardo Bortolotti and Mara Faccio, 'Government Control of Privatized Firms' (2008) 22 Review of Financial Studies 2907, 2907 – 2908.

[2] For a summary of these arguments, see Daniel Shapiro and Steven Globerman, 'The International Activities and Impacts of State-Owned Enterprises' in Karl P. Sauvant and others (eds), *Sovereign Investment: Concerns and Policy Reactions* (Oxford University Press 2012) 114 – 124.

[3] Przemyslaw Kowalski, Max Büge, Monika Sztajerowska, and Matias Egeland, 'State-Owned Enterprises: Trade Effects and Policy Implications' (*OECD Trade Policy Papers*, No. 147, 2013) < http://dx. doi. org/10. 1787/5k4869ckqk71 – en > accessed 15 May 2013, 13 – 17.

[4] UNCTAD, 'World Investment Report 2013' < http://unctad. org/en/PublicationsLibrary/wir 2013_ en. pdf > accessed 9 July 2013 xiv, 12 – 13.

[5] UNCTAD, 'World Investment Report 2012' < ://www. unctad-docs. org/files/UNCTAD-WIR2012-Full-en. pdf > accessed 10 April 2013, 99.

of the top 2000 publicly traded MNCs are SOEs. [1]

The surge of SOE sectors is often explained by the activation of emerging economies seeking to acquire technology, intellectual property, brand names and natural resources through ownership stakes in foreign corporations. True enough, SOEs have emerged strongly especially in developing countries. In recent years, the majority of SOEs acquiring foreign assets have emerged from developing countries and the absolute value of their M & As has steadily increased. [2] Further, emerging and transition economies are home to roughly 60% of state-owned multinationals. [3] As often pointed out, Chinese government is the largest shareholder in country's 150 largest corporations, holding up to 80% of the total stock market value. [4] Despite these numbers, the increased significance of state ownership cannot be explained only by strategic interests of emerging economies. Instead, two additional developments have revitalized attention to state ownerships policies and SOE trade effects globally. First, the rise of sovereign wealth funds (SWFs) has continued to accelerate as a number of states have sought to target revenues from commodity exports or from foreign-exchange reserves to financial assets. [5] Second, the magnitude of government interventions in addressing the global financial crisis has reopened the debate over state involvement in private enterprises in Western states since 2008. [6] Together, these developments suggest that SOEs have strengthened their positions as important economic actors in the global economy.

---

[1]　Kowalski, Büge, Sztajerowska, and Egeland, 'State-Owned Enterprises: Trade Effects and Policy Implications' 31.

[2]　UNCTAD, 'World Investment Report 2012' xiv, 13.

[3]　UNCTAD, 'World Investment Report 2011' < ://www. unctad-docs. org/files/UNCTAD-WIR2011-Full-en. pdf > accessed 1 September 2012 xiv.

[4]　UNCTAD, 'World Investment Report 2013' 12 - 13.

[5]　See e. g. Fabio Bassan, *The Law of Sovereign Wealth Funds* (Edward Elgar 2011).

[6]　For US experience, see e. g. Benjamin A Templin, 'The Government Shareholder: Regulating Public Ownership of Private Enterprise' (2010) 62 Administrative Law Review 1127 - 1216. For European perspective, see Ginka Borisova, Paul Brockman, Jesus Salas, and Andrey Zagorchev, 'Government ownership and corporate governance: Evidence from the EU' (2012) 36 Journal of Banking & Finance 2917 - 2934.

2. State Ownership and Corporate Social Responsibility

As discussed in the previous section, the increased significance of state ownership in international markets has taken a variety of forms. After three decades of privatization experiences, the number of SOEs has started to increase and, contrary to many estimates, the global economic footprint of SOEs has grown fast. Alternatively, many states have assumed significant minority shareholder positions in corporations that do not fit in the traditional perception of public policy-oriented and market failure-correcting SOEs. In particular, states often find themselves as minority shareholders in former SOEs or as equity investors in completely new enterprises. [1] Consequently, the active internalization of state ownership has led wholly or partly state-owned entities to assume similar roles with private MNCs in the global economy.

The strengthened state shareholder positions have been registered in several policy and regulatory spheres. In general, the proliferation of state ownership has been met with a plethora of regulatory interventions, mostly in accordance with a traditional Washington Consensus-type of policy set. Accordingly, the increased state activity in shareholder capacity has primarily been met with policy and regulatory interventions designed to control potential market distortions emanating from this relationship.

In Canada, for example, the Investment Canada Regulations have been augmented with guidelines directed specifically towards investment by foreign SOEs. [2] Similarly, the activation of Chinese SOEs' overseas acquisitions has prompted the European Commission's interest in the relationship between Chinese state and its corporate nationals in the light of European merger control. In particular, the Commission has emphasized dissemination of the power of the

---

[1] See e. g. Narjess Boubakri, Jean-Claude Cosset, Omrane Guedhami, and Walid Saffar, ' The political economy of residual state ownership in privatized firms: Evidence from emerging markets' (2011) 17 Journal of Corporate Finance 244 – 258.

[2] Industry Canada, 'Investment Canada Act Guidelines: Statement Regarding Investment by Foreign State-Owned Enterprise' < ://www. ic. gc. ca/eic/site/ica-lic. nsf/eng/lk00064. html#state-owned > accessed 7 October 2013.

central and regional holding companies to exercise decisive influence on Chinese SOEs. [1] Finally, in somewhat different context, the 2008 – 2009 bailouts in the automotive industry sector forced the US policy makers to assess their stance on the potential influence state shareholders were able to exercise over corporations. In the case of General Motors, the government communicated that "as a common shareholder, the government will only vote on core governance issues, including the selection of a company's board of directors and major corporate events or transactions". In general, the government planned "to be extremely disciplined as to how it intends to use even these limited rights". [2] In sum, the commonality between the regulatory approaches has emphasized the importance of countering the negative effects of state influence in corporations competing in international markets.

However, the issue of state influence can also be approached from a CSR standpoint. As a corollary to the increased significance of states in shareholder capacities, states increasingly find themselves in situations where corporations in their portfolios are subjected to severe criticism from CSR, sustainability and human rights perspectives. For example, increased SOE activity has been claimed to lead to corporate human rights violations ranging from resource development [3] and land ownership [4] issues to provision of surveillance technology to repressive governments [5]. Due to their ownership structures SOEs are often confronted in more critical tones than their wholly private counterparts. In popular discourse, state ownership is usually portrayed as extension of state power and SOEs as

---

[1]　'Commission Decision of Mar. 31, 2011, Case COMP/ M. 6082-China National Bluestar/Elkem', 2011 paras 10, 17.

[2]　The White House, 'Press Release: Obama Administration Auto Restructuring Initiative for General Motors (Mar. 30, 2009)' < ://www. whitehouse. gov/the _ press _ office/Fact-Sheet-on-Obama-Administration-Auto-Restructuring-Initiative-for-General-Motors > accessed 7 October 2013.

[3]　Decision Regarding Communication 155/96 (Social and Economic Rights Action Center/Center for Economic and Social Rights v. Nigeria), African Commission on Human and Peoples' Rights, Case No. ACHPR/COMM/A044. 1, 27 May 2002.

[4]　'NGO's look to United Nations for Addressing Stora Enso's Human Rights Violations in China' < :// globalforestcoalition. org/2623-ngos-look-to-united-nations-for-addressing-stora-ensos-human-rights-violations-in-china > accessed 3 April 2013.

[5]　'Teliasonera i hemligt samarbete med diktaturer' < ://www. svt. se/ug/teliasonera-i-hemligt-samarbete-med-diktaturer > accessed 30 July 2012.

emanations of the state. ① For this reason, the increased significance of states in shareholder capacities is often coupled with the idea of heightened economic, social and environmental responsibilities. SOEs may be expected to refrain from layoffs in spite of decreased profitability②, to cap directors' excessive remuneration③ or to promote equal hiring opportunities④. Against this backdrop it is surprising that SOEs and state ownership have remained conspicuously undertheorized in general CSR discourse. ⑤

Recent studies have, however, explored CSR dimensions of state ownership from a variety of angles. ⑥ Three distinct research patterns can be detected. First, the most common approach has emphasized the shortcomings of SOEs with regard to CSR issues. It has been argued that SOEs' CSR strategies are not always on par with other MNCs' commitments⑦; that SOEs are more likely to invest in countries with poor rule of law⑧; and that often SOEs operate beyond normal regulatory mechanisms, making their potential violations harder to discern,

---

① See e. g. May Tan-Mullins and Giles Mohan, 'The potential of corporate environmental responsibility of Chinese state-owned enterprises in Africa' [2012] Environment, Development and Sustainability.

② The Budapest Business Journal, 'Layoffs planned at state-owned mobile company' < ://www. bbj. hu/business/layoffs-planned-at-state-owned-mobile-company-_65493 > accessed 30 October 2013.

③ Stine Ludvigsen, 'State Ownership and Corporate Governance: Empirical Evidence from Norway and Sweden' (*PhD Thesis, BI Norwegian School of Management, Department of Public Governance*, 2010) < ://brage. bibsys. no/bi/bitstream/URN: NBN: no – bibsys_ brage_ 12105/1/2010 – 03 – Ludvigsen. pdf > accessed 11 December 2012.

④ Darren Rosenblum, 'Feminizing Capital: A Corporate Imperative' (2010) 6 Berkeley Business Law Journal 55 – 95.

⑤ Juliet Roper and Michèle Schoenberger-Orgad, 'State-Owned Enterprises: Issues of Accountability and Legitimacy' (2011) 25 Management Communication Quarterly 693, 694 – 700.

⑥ The Chinese experience has been identified as a key driver in revitalized research interest. Alessia A. Amighini, Roberta Rabellotti, and Marco Sanfilippo, 'Do Chinese state-owned and private enterprises differ in their internationalization strategies?' [2013] China Economic Review.

⑦ Rae Lindsay, Robert McCorquodale, Lara Blecher, Jonathan Bonnitcha, Antony Crockett, and Audley Sheppard, 'Human Rights Responsibilities in the Oil and Gas Sector: Applying the UN Guiding Principles' (2013) 6 The Journal of World Energy Law & Business 2 – 66.

⑧ Carl Henrik Knutsen, Asmund Rygh, and Helge Hveem, 'Does State Ownership Matter? Institutions' Effect on Foreign Direct Investment Revisited. ' (2011) 13 Business and Politics 1 – 31.

investigate and redress[1]. Second, others have drawn attention to states' enhanced abilities to exercise positive CSR influence over corporations. Some studies have posited that state ownership is usually associated with higher degree of CSR disclosures[2]; that states are particularly well suited for social investor activism due to their long investment horizons[3]; that the responsible investor activities pursued by states ripple throughout national firms, rendering their investments patterns more prone to societal and environmental considerations[4]; and that active state ownership facilitates agreement on businesses' role in development[5]. Third, SOEs are often presented as a special case of corporate human rights obligations in emerging business and human rights literature. In some conceptualizations, state-owned or controlled companies are considered parts of the state making them bearers of human rights obligations under international law like any other governmental entity. [6] While scholarship on the impacts of state ownership on CSR issues is mixed, emerging research patterns are clearly signaling that the relationship is increasingly relevant.

3. Regulating State Ownership Function: Two Tales

This section provides a concise reading of two international instruments commenting on the proliferation of state ownership from a CSR perspective. First, the OECD SOE Guidelines are used to illustrate the prevalent narrative of

---

[1] Michael Kelly, 'Ending Corporate Impunity for Genocide: The Case Against China's State-Owned Petroleum Company in Sudan' (2011) 90 Oregon Law Review 414 – 448.

[2] Nazli A. Mohd Ghazali, 'Ownership structure and corporate social responsibility disclosure: some Malaysian evidence' (2007) 7 Corporate Governance 251 – 266; Wenjing Li and Ran Zhang, 'Corporate Social Responsibility, Ownership Structure, and Political Interference: Evidence from China' (2010) 96 Journal of Business Ethics 631 – 645.

[3] Salar Ghahramani, 'Sovereign wealth funds and shareholder activism: applying the Ryan-Schneider antecedents to determine policy implications' (2013) 13 Corporate Governance 58 – 69.

[4] Gurneeta Vasudeva, 'Weaving Together the Normative and Regulative Roles of Government: How the Norwegian Sovereign Wealth Fund's Responsible Conduct Is Shaping Firms' Cross-Border Investments' (2013) 7039 Organization Science (Articles in Advance) 1 – 21.

[5] Anne Welle-Strand and Monica Vlaicu, 'Business and State Balancing International Development Agendas-The Case of Norwegian CSR' (2013) 6 Journal of Politics and Law 103 – 116.

[6] Surya Deva, *Regulating Corporate Human Rights Violations. Humanizing Business.* (Routledge 2012) 110 – 111.

embedding CSR considerations in state ownership function. Second, an emerging human rights reading of state ownership will be examined in the context of the UN Framework and the GPs. Ultimately, it is posited that the instruments portray conflicting notions on the rationales of regulating state ownership function.

3.1 The OECD Guidelines on Corporate Governance of State-Owned Enterprises

Issued in 2005, the OECD SOE Guidelines comprise a set of non-binding guidelines and best practices on corporate governance of SOEs. The instrument accompanies the OECD Principles of Corporate Governance[1]from state ownership perspective. Most fundamentally, the OECD SOE Guidelines focus on corporate governance issues that derive from a complex chain of agents involved in the management and performance of SOEs. Accordingly, the guidelines'main function is to ensure a level playing field between private corporations and those entities where state has significant control, either through full majority or significant minority ownership. [2] While non-binding, the instrument has been adopted and implemented in several jurisdictions. In Finland, for example, state ownership function has been remodeledto a large degree as per the OECD SOE Guidelines' suggestions. [3]

The core idea of the OECD SOE Guidelines is to develop a set of governance practices in order to avoid market distortions emanating from state-corporation-relationship. To this end, the instrument proposes a variety of measures ranging from transparent ownership policies and equitable treatment of shareholders to restructuring of ownership function in order to isolate commercial objectives from political objectives. According to the OECD SOE Guidelines, there should be a

[1]   OECD, 'Principles of Corporate Governance (2004)' < ://www. oecd-ilibrary. org/industry – and – services/oecd – principles – of – corporate – governance – 2004 _ 9789264015999 – en > accessed 19 December 2012.

[2]   OECD, 'Guidelines on Corporate Governance of State-Owned Enterprises (2005)' < ://www. oecd. org/corporate/ca/corporategovernanceofstate-ownedenterprises/34803211. pdf > accessed 11 June 2012 preamble.

[3]   See e. g. Pekka Timonen, 'Valtio omistajana ja yrittäjäriskin kantajana' (2006) 7 – 8 Lakimies 1312 – 1324.

clear separation between the state's ownership function and other state functions. ①
Instead of ad-hoc political interventions, state ownership function should be guided
by the owner state pursuing active ownership within the general legal framework
and the legal structure of each company. ② Ownership policies are expected to be
consistent, explicit and transparent to provide SOEs, the market and the general
public with predictability and a clear understanding of the state's objectives in the
long term. ③

As the OECD SOE Guidelines strive to recalibrate SOE governance to follow
broadly the example set by general corporate governance and to mitigate market
distortions, the instrument does not tackle CSR issues explicitly. Yet it is
recognized that SOEs are also employed also in fulfilling essentially special public
policy purposes. ④ Further, it has been noted that "state-owned enterprises are
often expected to operate at higher standards of corporate social responsibility than
their private counterparts". ⑤ This expectation is often grounded in the historical
position of SOEs as vehicles of social and industrial policy and as providers of public
goods. The OECD SOE Guidelines do not deny the practicality or importance of
such SOE roles. However, in the instrument's view, any obligations and
responsibilities that a SOE is required to undertake in terms of public services
beyond the generally accepted norm should be clearly mandated by laws or
regulations. ⑥ As per the instrument's transparency guidelines, the market and the
general public should be clearly informed about the nature and extent of these
obligations and their impact on the SOEs' resources and economic performance. ⑦
This is to balance the multiple and contradictory objectives of state ownership "that
lead to either a very passiveconduct of ownership functions or conversely results in
the state's excessive intervention in matters or decisions which should be left to the

---

① OECD, 'Guidelines on Corporate Governance of State-Owned Enterprises' I. A.

② Ibid. II. F.

③ Ibid. II. A commentary.

④ Ibid. preamble.

⑤ Hans Christiansen, 'Balancing Commercial and Non-Commercial Priorities of State-Owned
Enterprises' (*OECD Corporate Governance Working Papers*, No. 6, 2013) < ://dx. doi. org/
10. 1787/5k4dkhztkp9r – en > accessed 9 February 2013, 8.

⑥ OECD, 'Guidelines on Corporate Governance of State-Owned Enterprises' II. C.

⑦ Ibid. I. C commentary.

company and its governance organs" . ①

While the OECD SOE Guidelines do not refer explicitly to CSR issues, they have been included in the scope of the instrument in its interpretative practice. The instrument provides for two different options their inclusion. First, all additional "public service" obligations have to be clearly mandated and communicated. Here, CSR issues are understood as public service functions that go beyond what is required from wholly private corporations. Second, the instrument suggests that the boards of SOEs should be required to develop, implement and communicate compliance programs for internal codes of ethics in conformity with state'snational norms and international commitments. ② The OECD SOE Guidelines also acknowledge that SOEs may play an important role in setting the business tone of the country, making it vital for them to maintain high ethical standards. ③

Together, the OECD SOE Guidelines' interventions recognize that SOEs' CSR policies have general significance also on the corporate governance level as well. On the one hand, their significance is bound to historical foundations of SOEs as public policy instruments. On the other hand, they are viewed as potential market irritants whose negative effects have to be controlled through transparent ownership policies. In sum, CSR issues are situatedin a more complex framework aiming to secure a level playing field between SOEs and private corporations. While state owners are empowered to use their shareholder positions to integrate CSR considerations in SOE operations, the procedures in facilitating this behavior are limited. States are expected to separate commercial and policy functions, to establish clear and transparent communications and to employ traditional corporate governance mechanisms. In short, the function advancing CSR agenda is embedded in the overall notion of securing competitive markets.

3. 2 The UN Protect, Respect and Remedy Framework and the Guiding Principles

Unlike the OECD SOE Guidelines, the UN Framework and the GPs approach

---

① OECD, 'Guidelines on Corporate Governance of State-Owned Enterprises' II. A commentary.
② Ibid. IV. C.
③ Ibid. IV. C commentary.

SOEs and state ownership from a clear human rights perspective. Since their unanimous endorsement on 16 June 2011 by the UN Human Rights Council, the GPs, draftedby John Ruggie, the Special Representative of the Secretary-General (SRSG), have been heralded as one of the most important attempts to sketch a transnational regulatory framework to counter adverse human rights impacts caused by business enterprises. While not binding, the SRSG's instruments have enjoyed considerable traction in CSR sphere. For example, a number of international instruments and policy documents have recently been revised to correspond with the GPs. [1]

During the span of the six-year mandate, the SRSG positioned corporate conduct in the context of liberalized and globalized trade, addressed governance gaps that enabled corporate human rights abuses and deemed existing regulatory responses ineffective to contain alleged corporate human rights impacts. [2] The end result of the mandate, the UN Framework and the GPs, rested on three equally important policy sections, or pillars, according to which: (i) states had a duty to protect against human rights abuses committed by third parties, including business enterprises; (ii) business enterprises had a responsibility to respect human rights; (iii) victims of business-related human rights abuses needed greater access to effective remedies. [3]

SOEs were a part of the SRSG's efforts from the early days of the mandate. Originally, they were approached from a practical perspective. In the first reports the SRSG stressed that:

---

[1] Because of this cross-fertilization, this section uses "CSR" and "human rights" interchangeably even though CSR issues are usually understood in broader terms than the language of human rights obligations. See OECD, 'Guidelines for Multinational Enterprises (2011)' < ://www. oecd-ilibrary. org/ governance/oecd-guidelines-for-multinational-enterprises_ 9789264115415 – en > accessed 12 September 2012; IFC, 'Performance Standards on Environmental and Social Sustainability' < ://www1. ifc. org/ wps/wcm/connect/c8f524004a73daeca09afdf998895a12/IFC _ Performance _ Standards. pdf? MOD = AJPERES > accessed 11 December 2012; Commission, 'A renewed EU strategy 2011 – 14 for Corporate Social Responsibility' (Communication) COM (2011) 681 final 14.

[2] SRSG, 'Interim report of the Special-Representative of the Secterary General on the issue of human rights and transnational corporations and other business enterprises. UN Doc. E/CN. 4/2006/97', 2006 (2006 Interim Report).

[3] SRSG, 'Protect, Respect and Remedy: a Framework for Business and Human Rights. A/HRC/8/ 5', 2008 paras 17 – 26 (2008 Framework Report).

Ways must be found to engage State-owned enterprises in addressing human rights challenges in their spheres of operation. They are becoming increasingly important players in some of the most troubling industry sectors yet appear to operate beyond many of the external sources of scrutiny to which commercial firms are subject. [1]

The rationale was that certain SOEs' growing influence in some industry sectors should be reflected in the supervision regarding their human rights performance. Similar approach continued in the SRSG's following reports. In 2007, the SRSG claimed that "evidence suggests that firms operating in only one country and state-owned companies are often worse offenders than their highly visible private sector transnational counterparts". [2] Further, SOEs from emerging economies had not associated themselves with voluntary CSR initiatives. [3] For the SRSG, there was "mounting concern in the public space about human rights protection and State-owned enterprises". [4]

While SOEs were clearly singled out because of their significance and potential impunity, the SRSG's approaches changed as the mandate progressed. Most importantly, SOEs started to emerge as a group of corporations that showed the greatest promise in changing their behavior as per human rights considerations. The development was discernible already in the SRSG's 2008 report introducing the UN Framework. SOE issues were grouped under state's ability to influence corporate cultures and policy alignments. The SRSG suggested that engaging SOEs was different from privately owned companies. Specific sustainability reporting required from Swedish SOEs was one such example. [5] The SRSG's view was that "in principle, inducing a rights-respecting corporate culture should be easier to achieve in State-owned enterprises". This was because "senior management in SOEs is typically appointed by and reports to State entities". Further, SOEs

---

[1] SRSG, '2006 Interim Report' 79 – 80.

[2] SRSG, 'Business and Human Rights: Mapping International Standards of Responsibility and Accountability for Corporate Acts. A/HRC/4/035', 2007 para 3 (2007 Mapping Report).

[3] Ibid. 81.

[4] SRSG, 'Addendum. State responsibilities to regulate and adjudicate corporate activities under the United Nations core human rights treaties: an overview of treaty body commentaries. A/HRC/4/35/Add. 1', 2007 para 78 (2007 Addendum Report).

[5] SRSG, '2008 Framework Report' 30.

presented home states with difficult reputational dilemmas: "beyond any legal obligations, human rights harm caused by SOEs reflects directly on the State's reputation, providing it with an incentive in the national interest to exercise greater oversight". ①

In later reports, the SRSG continued to underline "strong policy reasons for home States to encourage their companies to respect rights abroad, especially if a State itself is involved in the business venture". ② Because states conducted various transactions with businesses they were also given unique opportunities to help prevent adverse corporate-related human rights impacts. Specifically, "the closer an entity is to the State, or the more it relies on statutory authority or taxpayer support, the stronger is the State's policy rationale for ensuring that the entity promotes respect for human rights". ③ The SRSG also noted that some states were starting to push policies for greater "respect for human rights" in SOE operations. ④

To counter the developments in states' international market activities and gaps in SOE supervision, the SRSG's initial response was to emphasize how human rights treaty bodies had already held states responsible for SOE conduct. The commentary referred to states' role as the primary duty-bearers under international human rights law and the proximity of a business enterprise to the state. Further, state ownership and control also brought about the necessary means to ensure that relevant policies, legislation and regulations regarding respect for human rights were implemented, including SOEs' senior management typically reporting to state agencies and associated government departments having greater scope for scrutiny and oversight. ⑤ Accordingly, the SRSG advocated that states had both the responsibility and the possibility to influence corporations operating with statutory authority, taxpayer support or in other cases where they were closely aligned with

---

① SRSG, '2008 Framework Report' 32.

② SRSG, "Business and human rights: Towards operationalizing the 'protect, respect and remedy' framework. A/HRC/11/13", 2009 para 16 (2009 Towards Report).

③ SRSG, "Business and Human Rights: Further steps towards the operationalization of the 'protect, respect and remedy' framework. A/HRC/14/27", 2010 para 26 (2010 Further steps Report).

④ Ibid. 28.

⑤ SRSG, "Guiding Principles on Business and Human Rights: Implementing the United Nations 'Protect, Respect and Remedy' Framework. A/HRC/17/31. ", 2011 Commentary to Principle 4.

state functions. Human rights commitments of states were to be made categorical when interacting with market through corporate ownership. ① Ultimately, states were advised to use corporate law structures in shareholder capacity to advance human rights sensitivity in SOEs.

In sum, the SRSG made three significant assertionsregardingthe relationship between states and SOEs. First, SOEs were considered special because of a combination of their increasing international significance and potential impunity because of protective national measures. Second, the SRSG emphasized greater possibilities of attributing SOEs' acts to states. Third, when positioned within the state duty to protect pillar, the SRSG emphasized a wide range of influence possibilities states had over SOEs. In the UN Framework and the GPs, states were again empowered to use their financial power to push for CSR-related improvements in SOEs and other corporations in which state was involved in shareholder capacity. However, unlike the OECD SOE Guidelines, the UN Framework and the GPs framed the rationale of corporate involvement in terms of states' human rights obligations. Here, the instruments suggest that when states act in shareholder capacities their ownership function is actually constricted by international obligations emanating from human rights law and not by international obligations stemming from various market initiatives. Shareholder engagement and state ownership function are embedded in states' human rights functions.

4. Conclusion

Revitalized state ownership of internationalized corporations has been making waves around the globe. Both emerging and developed economies have witnessed a surge in various SOE sectors and state investment. Calls have been made for tighter regulatory frameworks for state investment, state shareholding and the acts of SOEs. So far, CSR dimensions of international instruments have not been systemically examined even though various initiatives have registered the increased state activity in the market sphere. For this reason, the OECD SOE Guidelines and

---

① See e. g. Christine Parker and John Howe, 'Ruggie's Diplomatic Project and Its Missing Regulatory Infrastructure' in Radu Mares (ed), *The UN Guiding Principles on Business and Human Rights* (Martinus Nijhoff 2012) 283 – 291.

the UN Framework and the GPs provide important sites for discussing both CSR effects and general parameters of active state ownership of corporations.

While the OECD SOE Guidelines and the UN Framework and the GPs have originated in totally different contexts and their aims differ considerably, both instruments acknowledge "the new rise" of state ownership, particularly with respect to international SOE operations. Further, both instruments are interested in regulating states active in shareholder capacities. Ultimately, both instruments seek to restrict state ownership function. However, while the OECD SOE Guidelines position themselves within the traditional regulatory regime characterized by a level playing field and competitive markets, the UN Framework and the GPs posit that state ownership function is restricted by state's international human rights obligations.

The instruments view CSR-promoting state shareholders in a very different light. For the OECD SOE Guidelines, additional CSR considerations communicated by a state shareholder may jeopardize the instrument's core aims unless arranged in a market-friendly manner. Conversely, the UN Framework and the GPs seek to embed heightened CSR considerations in the overall structure of state's international human rights obligations. Clearly, the OECD SOE Guidelines and the UN Framework and the GPs portray conflicting and deeply entrenched visions of the intersections of state ownership and CSR that have significance beyond the scope of the instrument themselves. Therefore, the question that needs to be asked in the future is how market-driven and human rights-driven regulatory rationales could or should be reconciled.

国家所有制与国际文书中的企业社会责任日程：如何处理相互矛盾的规制理念？

米科·拉雅弗欧里[*]

【摘要】本文从企业社会责任的角度讨论了国家所有制。作者指出，以企业所有者身份行事的国家正在以前所未有的规模利用全球经济自由化所取得的成就及其发展不平衡的现状。这一发展趋势促使有关方面加强规制性干预，以减少国家对企业的过度影响，从而在全球市场中确保公平的竞争环境。这种干预不可避免地增加了国家所有制与企业社会责任问题之间的交集，从而引发了一些棘手的问题。例如，与私营企业相比，国有企业是否应该采取更为广泛的企业社会责任策略？国有股东在安排其所有权职能时是否应更多地考虑企业社会责任？人权法是否能够为以上这些要求提供一个规范基础？本文从两个国际软法文书——《联合国保护、尊重和救济框架》及其《指导原则》和《经济合作与发展组织国有公司治理指南》——的角度分析了这一问题，并提出：以上这两个文书对企业社会责任问题的处理方式揭示了有关国家所有权规制原则的各种根深蒂固的和相互矛盾的理念。本文的分析分为四个部分：第二节解释了国家所有制在全球经济中所起到的日益重要的作用；第三节讨论了国家所有权职能与企业社会责任之间的交集；第四节介绍了《联合国保护、尊重和救济框架》及其《指导原则》和《经济合作与发展组织国有公司治理指南》，特别是其有关国家所有权的相互冲突的规制原则；第五节为结论部分。

---

* 图尔库大学博士研究生。

中国环境法的实效为何不理想？

常纪文[*]

【摘要】 环境法属于改革开放后起步早的领域法，目前已体系化，但是大气和水等区域性问题突出，说明环境法的实效不理想。原因在于，应对式环境立法无法解决三十多年经济"倾泻"式发展所带来的环境问题；法律制定滞后，历史性环境债务越积越多；虚化规定过多，实在效应总体不高；利益疏导不够，应然作用发挥打了折扣；监督机制缺乏，限权功能彰显不足。应采取以下方法予以克服：摈弃环境法治实效操之过急的思想，协助公众树立环境法治长期性的理念；加强环境问题的预见性立法和苗头性立法，防止新的环境历史债务产生；加强执法检查，评估立法和执法的效果，提出针对性的环境法实效提高措施；转变环境问题的调控思维，建立健全正反两个方面的利益调整和疏导机制，使守法成为有制度化保障的自觉自愿合作行为；加强环境法律规则的实在性建设，减少虚化规则的设置；调整法律实施的力量格局，发挥公众参与、公众监督和司法审查的作用，限制行政权的过分膨胀。

【关键词】 环境法　实效　法治

法学界普遍认为，环境法是改革开放以来最早启动和体系化的一个部门法。环境法的很多制度是国际借鉴和国内创新的产物，不可谓不先进，不可谓不实际，理应在国家经济、社会的发展中发挥重要的作用，既解决严重的环境问题，也促进经济和社会的良性发展。事实证明，作用发挥了，但是在强大的经济发展规模、宏大的经济开发领域和快速的经济发展速度面前，环境法的总体作用在过去三十多年却不是那么理想。水系和近海水质至今未得到根本改善，土壤污染威胁食品安全，大气雾霾横行侵害国民

---

* 常纪文，国务院发展研究中心研究员，中国社会科学院法学研究所教授。

的健康，原因何在？应从环境法治的立法、执法、守法、司法、法律参与和监督几个环节中去寻找。总的来看，环境法的现实作用问题既有环境立法的制定和条款的设计问题，也有实施的问题。

作用发挥缓慢，法律难以短时解决经济长期快速增长带来的复杂环境问题。经济本身的属性是市场的，如果不加任何束缚，经济的增长是完全自由的市场经济的增长。如果我们用国家权力完全剥夺经济发展的自由性，用计划来替代市场，那么经济的市场性就遭到扼杀，经济就变成完全没有自由度的计划经济。基于这一点，可以说，改革开放以来的经济体制改革，不是我们创造市场活力，而是给市场松绑，废除无所不在的管制式规则，使潜在的市场规则上位为现实的市场规则，释放市场积蓄已久的活力。当然，完全自由的市场经济是不存在的，对于其失灵的部分，国家还应当适度发挥政府的契约与管制作用。也就是说，改革开放三十多年的历史是给经济逐渐松绑发挥其利润创造本性与活力的历史。经济本性的发挥，如果松绑的方式和尺度适当，发展速度是惊人的，可以发挥到极致。总的来说，中国的经济松绑改革是成功的。中国用短短的三十余年，就走过了西方发达国家几百年的经济发展路程。但是市场也是自私的，松绑后如不加以适当的引导和法律限制，其产生的负效应，如侵害他人和社会利益的环境污染和生态破坏，也是惊人的。因此，需要给"野蛮"的市场附加必要的公法管制规则限制，使其发展规模、速度和方式理性化。由于环境法律的制定和实施涉及利益调整，必然要遇到阻力，所以其发展，与经济发展相比，要慢得多。相比要得到各方重视遵守，难度很大，加上法治文化不足，要想短期发挥很大作用，很难。打个比方，中国市场经济的发展，好比打开了上游的大坝，水会因为动能的长时间蓄积沿河流奔泻而下，短时间就到达下游的目的地。而环境法律规则的遵守好比水由低处往高处流，如要到达上游的目的地，需要不断的倒灌式积累，水位到达一定高度才行。因此，在缺乏法治传统的条件下，要想通过三十多年的有阻力的应对式环境立法来解决三十多年经济"倾泻"式发展所带来的环境问题，是不可能的。

法律制定滞后，历史性环境债务越积越多。而法律规则的制定，由发现问题到制定规则需要一个过程，往往在现实的问题很严重时才立法，因此预见性不足。滞后性是世界各国立法的通病，只是滞后程度不同罢了。在现实中，一些学者和媒体对苗头性和可能出现的环境问题很敏感，披露具有预见性。但是对现实问题的预见要得到立法采纳，变成立法规范的预见性，往往需要立法机关的可行性论证。而可行性论证往往受到各方面力量的左右。在很多情况下，环境立法新问题的预见性往往被利益集团的强大力量所埋葬。即使立了法，法律规则的实施往往受到与利益集团有着千丝万缕关系的执法者的选择性或者漠视性对待，因此，环境法难以全部解决现行的环境问题，不可避免地留下历史债务。如果环境法律规则的设计适当，环境污染和生态破坏的历史债务就会得到后续的解决。但是如果旧债没有解决，快速的经济增长又不时催生新的环境体制和制度问题，就需要新的立法予以解决。这时又需要环境立法的立改废。而立法是有周期的，往往难以及时响应，就会产生新的问题。新的问题和老的问题堆加，像滚雪球一样，越滚越大，环境污染和生态破坏就越难以得到有效的遏制。

　　虚化规定过多，环境法的实在效应总体不高。环境法是环境法律规则的总称。法律规则须是能够发挥实在作用的准则，即能够判断是否合法以及如何评价并处理的准则。为了配合这些准则发挥作用，环境立法除了阐述国家的政策和工作方针外，基本上都设置一些不带法律后果的鼓励性和限制性条款，如鼓励干什么，支持干什么，限制干什么，引导干什么，等等，以营造法治氛围。这些条款，也被很多环境法学者纳入法律规则的范畴。但是其数量不能过多，如过多，从表面看来，涵盖面好像更广一些，但是由于缺乏法律后果的支撑，这些规定在实实在在的利益面前就难以发挥有效作用，形同虚设。这样就会淡化环境法姓"法"的特点。从实践来看，环境立法的奖励规定、促进科技发展的规定、促进公众参与和监督的规定，就是如此。一些法律，如《循环经济促进法》《清洁生产促进法》，虚化的规定太多，不仅解决不了什么问题，还对树立国家环境立法的威信不利，因此饱受环境法学界的诟病。法律是解决问题的实在工具，虚化的条款设置过多是与法律的实在性原则相违背的，必须加以解决。

　　利益疏导不够，环境法的应然作用发挥打了折扣。法律是为了解决现实的问题而制定，法律的实施就是为了解决现实问题而调整利益。现实的环境问题，是市场越轨带来的利益问题。要破解利益问题，往往比触及灵魂还难。因此，总的来说，法律的实施具有遵守被动和消极抵制两个特点。由遵守被动到遵守自觉，由消极抵制到理性支持，既需要法律文化的培育，还需要法律的利益双向调整，即对遵守的利益支持和对违犯的利益剥夺。环境法作为一个独立的部门法，利益支持规则应当与利益剥夺规则的建设并重。但是，遗憾的是，前者并没有得到应有的重视。如果单纯地通过管制的剥夺性方法来解决法律遵守问题，缺乏合情合理的利益支持机制，环境法律的实施阻力就会越来越大。阻力越大，违法的几率也越高。一些地方缺乏系统的思维，无穷无尽地给企业施加各种杂乱的环境保护工作指令，包括一些缺乏法律依据的指令，致使企业应接不暇。企业即使努力地实现了，也心里打鼓，不知政府下一步又有什么大的动作，担心自己能不能承受得起。因此，守法成本太高，企业的抵触心理越来越强。选择成本低的环境违法成为一些企业不得已的选择。一些地方为了促进本地的 GDP，防止企业大量倒闭，也不愿意完全按照环境法律的规定办事。因此，老的环境法律难以有效地解决长期存在的老问题，新的环境法律也难以解决新出现的问题。

监督机制缺乏，环境法的限权功能彰显不足。法治社会应当是一个充满监督的社会。按照法理，社会参与和监督及司法权力的监督设置缺位或者退位，行政权就会越位甚至替位；社会和市场的权利维护机制欠缺，行政权就会滥用、缺位或者不到位。只有加强社会和市场参与和监督的渠道建设，建立有序参与、表达、申诉和监督的制度和机制，吸纳公众共同操持国家事务，才能使他们身临其境地理解国家和社会建设的难处，提升国家的法治文化和氛围，化不满与不合作为积极的参与和合作。从现实能力上看，环境保护需要常态性监管，而政府监管力量的存在与出现是偶然的，具有视野有限的不足。对于环境违法行为，因为政府力量不足经常出现现场监管缺位的现象。对所发现的违法行为做出处罚，相对广泛的违法行为而言，具有个别性和偶然性的特点，不能全面、有效打击违法。而社会公众监督资源非常丰富，在绝大多数场合，他们的发现与监督力量是常态存在的。目前，中国的环境立法和法律实施，过分强调行政力量的掌控作用，公众的常态性发现与监督力量不被重视，导致环境保护钓鱼式执法、选择式执法、寻租式执法、非文明执法、限制式执法、运动式执法、疲软式执法、滞后式执法等执法不公、执法缺位问题层出不穷，使环境法律规范的实施走了调，变了样，环境法作为一个部门法所具有的独立功能也没有得到有效发挥。

基于以上分析，建议采取以下几个措施加强环境法的现实作用。一是摈弃环境法治实效操之过急的思想，协助公众树立环境法治长期性的理念。二是立法部门应当加强调查研究，加强环境问题的预见性立法和苗头性立法，防止新的环境历史债务产生；加强执法检查，评估立法和执法的效果，提出有针对性的环境法实效提高措施。三是转变环境问题的调控思维，建立健全正反两个方面的利益调整和疏导机制，增加企业义务施加和守法结果的可预见性，提高违法成本，减少企业守法的抵触心理，使守法成为有制度化保障的自觉自愿合作行为。四是结合现实需要和现实可行性，加强环境法律规则的实在性建设，减少虚化规则的设置。五是调整法律实施的力量格局，发挥公众参与、公众监督和司法审查的作用，限制行政权的过分膨胀，使环境保护工作在环境法治的文化中健康发展。

Causes of the Unsatisfactory Effect of Environmental Laws in China

Chang Jiwen *

【Abstract】 Although environmental law is a branch of law that has a relatively early start in China and has already been systematized today, many environmental problems, including regional atmospheric and water pollution, are still very prominent in China, indicating that the actual effect of the law is unsatisfactory. This is because the passive mode of environmental legislation in China has failed to cope with the environmental problems brought about by the "torrential" mode of development during the past thirty years. Because environmental legislation has been lagged behind social and economic development, historical environmental debts have accumulated over the years; too many empty provisions has led to the low overall effect of environmental law; the lack of coordination between different interests has weakened the role played by environmental law; and the lack of supervision mechanism has prevented the law from giving full play to its power-restraining function. The above problems can be dealt with through the adoption of the follow measures: avoiding over-hastiness in the pursuit of substantial results and cultivating among the general public the idea of long-term construction of environmental law system; strengthening predicative legislation and legislation targeted at emerging problems so as to prevent the accumulation of historical

* Professor, Development Research Center of the State Council; Professor, Institute of Law, Chinese Academy of Social Sciences.

environmental debts; strengthening law enforcement inspection, carrying out evaluation of the effect of legislation and law enforcement, and adopting targeted measures aimed at raising the effectiveness of environmental law; changing the way of thinking on the regulation of environmental problems, establishing and improving interest regulation and coordination mechanisms, so as to make observance of law an institutionally guaranteed voluntary and cooperative act; strengthening the substantiality of the rules of environmental law and reducing the number of empty provisions in the law; adjusting the power pattern of law enforcement and giving full play to the role of public participation and supervision and judicial review; and containing the excessive expansion of administrative power.

【Keywords】 Environmental Law; Practical Effect; Rule of Law

The Outlines of Energy Efficiency Legislation in Finland and in the European Union

Ari Ekroos, Inga-Liisa Paavola and Jenny Rontun *

【 Abstract 】 Climate change mitigation requires large changes in consuming energy. The European Union has taken action in order to mitigate climate change: the so-called EU 20 − 20 − 20 target consists of improving energy efficiency by 20% . The target is set to be accomplished by 2020. According to the Treaty on the Functioning of the European Union article 194 EU policy on the energy shall aim e. g. to promote energy efficiency and energy saving. The new energy Efficiency directive (2012) consists of two main aspects: energy efficiency in general and energy efficiency of buildings. The directive e. g. includes new obligation is that energy companies are requested to reduce their energy sales to industrial and household clients by at least 1. 5% each year. The Energy Performance of Buildings directive (2006) includes several obligations related to building sector and Eco-design directive (2005) sets frameworks for regulation energy use of products. Finland as a member of EU shares the ambitious goal in climate and energy policy.

---

* Ari Ekroos, Professor of Environmental and Energy Law, University of Helsinki and Professor of Economic Law, Aalto University; Inga-Liisa Paavola, Doctoral Candidate, University of Helsinki; Jenny Rontun, Doctoral Candidate, University of Helsinki.

1. Introduction

EU has very strong and broad consensual legislative position on climate change mitigation, which calls for global cooperation focused on energy efficiency objectives and developing guiding instruments. Climate change mitigation requires large changes in consuming energy. Mitigation of climate change is likely to be the most complex, long-term energy challenge that societies need to address and solve within the coming decades. With more than 80 percent of primary energy supplied by oil, coal and natural gas, and an increasing demand for energy, mostly in emerging economies, greenhouse gas emissions reach new record levels every year.

Finland as a member of EU shares the ambitious goal in climate and energy policy. New measures for increased energy efficiency are proposed by the European Commission which includes also obligations for energy performance of buildings. The European Union has taken action in order to mitigate climate change: the so-called EU $20-20-20$ target consists of decreasing emissions by 20%, improving energy efficiency by 20% and promoting the use of energy produced with renewable sources by 20%. The target is set to be accomplished by 2020. The new energy Efficiency Directive will replace the previous Directive. The Directive consists of two main aspects: energy efficiency in general and energy efficiency of buildings. The main changes to the existing Directive are: energy companies are requested to reduce their energy sales to industrial and household clients by at least 1.5% each year. A 3% renovation rate for public buildings which are central government-owned and occupied has been set. An obligation on each EU member state is to draw up a roadmap to make the entire buildings sector more energy efficient by 2050 (commercial, public and private households included). The new directive also includes additional measures on energy audits and energy management for large firms, cost-benefit analysis for the deployment of combined heat and power generation (CHP) and public procurement.

Energy efficiency's primary objective is the reduction of greenhouse gas emissions in a cost-effective way. Besides being part of climate policy, saving energy also remains important for traditional reasons, including securing the energy supply, reducing energy costs and from other environmental viewpoints. In many energy conservation measures and in terms of the efficiency of energy use, Finland is among the leading countries in the world. Cogeneration of heat and electricity, broad coverage of energy efficiency agreements, and the systematic implementation of energy audits are good examples of successful energy conservation measures[①].

According to the 2011 World Energy Outlook, published by the International Energy Agency, more than 70 percent of projected CO_2 emission reductions by 2020 can be delivered by energy efficiency. A combination of energy efficiency measures and renewable power generation could deliver almost 70 percent of the required emissions reduction over the next two decades. Energy efficiency contributes to resolve other major energy-related challenges such as energy poverty, resource depletion and security of supply.

2. Energy Efficiency Regulation Framework

2. 1 Background

At the EU level, the Treaty of Lisbon (2007/C 306/01) introduced new objectives, such as climate change and energy solidarity, to the scope of environmental law in the EU. The new provisions ensure that the energy market functions well, in particular with regard to energy supply, aiming at energy efficiency and savings and promotion of energy from new and renewable energy sources. The Article 194 of the Treaty on the Functioning of the European Union[②] regulates energy matters. In the context of the establishment and functioning of the internal market and with regard for the need to preserve and improve the environment, Union policy on energy shall aim, in a spirit of solidarity between member states, to ensure the functioning of the energy market, ensure security of energy supply in the Union, promote energy efficiency and energy saving and the development of new and renewable forms of energy and promote the interconnection of energy networks.

Additionally, promotion of measures at international level to deal with climate change is emphasized. The EU climate package is based on commitment of the EU

---

① Ministry of Employment and the Economy: Energy efficiency. See www. tem. fi. Visited 27. 12. 2013.

② Consolidated version of the Treaty on the Functioning of the European Union-Part three: Union policies and internal actions-Title XXI: Energy-Article 194. Official Journal 115, 09/05/2008 P. 0134 – 0134.

to reduce its overall emissions to at least 20% below 1990 levels by 2020 and to reduce energy consumption. The target of upraising the share of renewable energy up to 20 % of the total use of energy by the year 2020 is set in the Directive on the promotion of the use of energy from renewable sources (2009/28/EC). For Finland, the target according to the Directive is to upraise the use of renewal energy up to 38% which increases the use of renewal energy 9.5% compared to the level in 2005. Regarding to energy efficiency EU has adopted an Action Plan aimed at achieving a 20% reduction in energy consumption by 2020 (the Action Plan for Energy Efficiency: Realising the Potential (COM (2006) 545)).

There are numerous EU regulations regarding energy efficiency and the field is somewhat diverse, for instance the Directive 2010/31/EU on the energy performance of buildings, Directive 2006/32/EC on energy end-use efficiency and energy services, and the Eco-design Directive 2005/32/EC forenergy-using products. In addition, there is the policy of Energy Efficiency: delivering the 20% target (COM (2008) 772). The EU climate package is an essential basis in order to achieve a climate-friendly community structure but much more needs to be done in order to achieve long-term climate change mitigating targets.

2.2 General on Energy Efficiency Legislation

The Energy Efficiency Directive (EED) (2012/27/EU) entered into force on 4 December 2012. The EED replaces the Energy Services Directive (2006/32/EC) and the CHP Directive (Directive 2004/8/EC on the promotion of cogeneration based on a useful heat demand in the internal energy market) The national legislation required by the EED must be enforced by 5 June 2014.

The European Union's Directive on the Energy Performance of Buildings (2010/31/EU) was implemented in Finland through the Act on Energy Certification of Buildings and Ministry of the Environment Decree on Energy Certification of Buildings. The Act and Decree came into force on 1 January 2008. The national building regulations on energy efficiency were also made more precise with the implementation[1].

---

① Ministry of the Environment: Eco-efficiency and energy consumption in buildings. See www. environment. fi. Visited 27.12.2013.

When it comes to regulating energy efficiency of the products, Ecodesign Directive 2009/125/EY establishes a framework to set mandatory ecological requirements for energy-using and energy-related products sold in all 27 member states. Its scope currently covers more than 40 product groups (such as boilers, lightbulbs, TVs and fridges), which are responsible for around 40% of all EU greenhouse gas emissions[1].

Eco-labels are placed on certain products to enable consumers to choose those which have been recognised as less harmful to the environment. They are voluntary public schemes based on specific scientific environmental criteria, open to all businesses in a transparent and non-discriminatory manner. Eco-labelling Directive (2010/30/EU) has set the legal framework, while Commission Decisions establish the requirements that the products have to meet in order to be awarded with the EU eco-label[2].

There is the Finnish Government Decision on Energy Efficiency Measures as well. On 4 February 2010, the Finnish Government passed a resolution on energy saving and energy efficiency measures for implementation during the current decade. This government decision is based on a June 2009 report by a broad-based Energy Efficiency Committee, appointed by the Ministry of Employment and the Economy. The energy efficiency measures implement the objectives of the Long-Term Climate and Energy Strategy[3].

The new energy efficiency agreements for the period 2008 – 2016, for which the Ministry of Employment and the Economy holds the main responsibility, were signed by the House of the Estates on 4 December 2007.

As more voluntary based regulation mechanism, there have been introduced the New Energy Efficiency Agreement Scheme for the Promotion of Energy Efficiency and Use of Renewable Sources of Energy in 2008 − 2016. The purpose of the energy efficiency agreement scheme is to contribute, in accordance with the national energy and climate strategy, to the fulfilment of our international commitments in the fight against climate change. This new agreement scheme is

---

① European Commission: Enterprises and Industry: Sustainable and responsible business. http://ec. europa. eu. Visited 22. 12. 2013.

② European Commission: Enivronment: Ecolabel. http://ec. europa. eu. Visited 22. 12. 2013.

③ Government Decision on Energy Efficiency Measures 4. 10. 2010.

especially important to the implementation of the Energy Services Directive (ESD) that entered into force in May 2006. The Energy Services Directive conferred a 9% energy conservation target upon Finland for the period 2008 - 2016, which, translated into energy, amounts to 17.8 TWh. Under the new agreement scheme, efforts have been made to take the obligations of this Directive into account, and Finland succeeded in negotiating agreements on the implementation of these obligations as alternatives to regulatory steering. Where the implementation of the obligations pursuant to the Directive is not possible through these agreements, the necessary regulations will be prepared in early 2008[1].

In Finland, implementing the new Energy Efficiency Directive that replaces the previous Directive into national legislation is under work, the deadline of implementation is in year 2014. The new Directive consists of two main aspects: energy efficiency in general and energy efficiency of buildings. The main changes to the existing Directive are: energy companies are requested to reduce their energy sales to industrial and household clients by at least 1.5% each year. A 3% renovation rate for public buildings which are central government-owned and occupied has been set. An obligation on each EU member state to draw up a roadmap to make the entire buildings sector more energy efficient by 2050 (commercial, public and private households included). The new directive also includes additional measures on energy audits and energy management for large firms, cost-benefit analysis for the deployment of combined heat and power generation (CHP) and public procurement.

Finland as a member of EU shares the ambitious goal in climate and energy policy. New measures for increased energy efficiency are proposed by the European Commission which includes also obligations for energy performance of buildings. Common target in EU, set out in the directive on energy performance of buildings, is to achieve nearly zero energy buildings in the year 2020. Improving the energy performance of buildings is a cost-effective way of fighting against climate change and improving energy security[2].

---

[1]　Ministry of Employment and the Economy: Energy Efficiency Agreements and Audits. See www. tem. fi.

[2]　Energy Roadmap 2050, 2011, p. 9.

3. Energy Efficiency Directive Content in Brief

The Energy Efficiency Directive (EED) brings forward legally binding measures to step up Member States' efforts to use energy more efficiently at all stages of the energy chain from the transformation of energy and its distribution to its final consumption. Measures that are listed in article 1 include the legal obligation to establish energy efficiency obligations schemes or policy measures in all member states.

These will drive energy efficiency improvements in households, industries and transport sectors. Other measures include an exemplary role to be played by the public sector and a right for consumers to know how much energy they consume.

Targets of the EED are set in the article 3. Each member state shall set an indicative national energy efficiency target, based on either primary or final energy consumption, primary or final energy savings, or energy intensity. Member states shall notify those targets to the Commission.

Member States shall also express those targets in terms of an absolute level of primary energy consumption and final energy consumption in 2020 and shall explain how, and on the basis of which data, this has been calculated.

According to the article 3, when setting the energy efficiency targets, member states shall take into account:

(a) that the Union's 2020 energy consumption has to be no more than 1 474 Mtoe of primary energy or no more than 1 078 Mtoe of final energy;

(b) the measures provided for in this Directive;

(c) the measures adopted to reach the national energy saving targets adopted pursuant to article 4 (1) of Directive 2006/32/EC; and

(d) other measures to promote energy efficiency within member states and Union.

What is more, the member states may also take into account national circumstances affecting primary energy consumption, such as remaining cost-effective energy-saving potential, GDP evolution and forecast, changes of energy imports and exports, development of all sources of renewable energies, nuclear energy, carbon capture and storage and early action.

EED sets out some energy efficiency related obligations to the public bodies of the member states. Public bodies shall purchase only products, services and buildings with high energy-efficiency performance, insofar as that is consistent with cost-effectiveness, economical feasibility, wider sustainability, technical suitability, as well as sufficient competition. However, these obligations shall apply to the contracts of the armed forces only to the extent that its application does not cause any conflict with the nature and primary aim of the activities of the armed forces. Member states shall encourage public bodies to follow the exemplary role of their central governments to purchase only products, services and buildings with high energy-efficiency performance, too, and encourage public bodies to assess the possibility of concluding long-term energy performance contracts that provide long-term energy savings.

Article 7 of the EED regulates, that each member state shall set up an energy efficiency obligation scheme. Member states can also use alternative measures according to article 7 (9) of the EED. Finland has notified the Commission that it will use alternative measures. [1]

Energy efficiency obligation scheme shall ensure that energy distributors and/or retail energy sales companies that are designated as obligated parties operating in each member state's territory achieve a cumulative end-use energy savings target 2020.

That target shall be at least equivalent to achieving new savings each year from 2014 to 2020 of 1.5 % of the annual energy sales to final customers of all energy distributors or all retail energy sales companies by volume, averaged over the most recent three-year period prior to 2013. The sales of energy, by volume, used in transport may be partially or fully excluded from this calculation. Member states shall decide how the calculated quantity of new savings referred to in the second subparagraph is to be phased over the period.

Article 8 of the EED includes regulations about energy audits. Member states shall promote the availability to all final customers of high quality energy audits which are cost-effective and are carried out in an independent manner by qualified and/or accredited experts according to qualification criteria or are implemented and supervised by independent authorities under national legislation. The energy audits

---

[1] See http://ec.europa.eu/energy/efficiency/eed/article7_en.htm, visited 10.1.2014.

may be carried out by in-house experts or energy auditors . For the purpose of guaranteeing the high quality of the energy audits and energy management systems, transparent and non-discriminatory are minimum criteria for energy audits.

Article 9 goes on with the metering of the energy consumption. Member states shall ensure that, in so far as it is technically possible, financially reasonable and proportionate in relation to the potential energy savings, final customers for electricity, natural gas, district heating, district cooling and domestic hot water are provided with competitively priced individual meters that accurately reflect the final customer's actual energy consumption and that provide information on actual time of use.

Articles 10 and 11 deal with the cost of the metering and billing information. Where final customers do not have smart meters, member states shall ensure that billing information is accurate and based on actual consumption, including energy distributors, distribution system operators and retail energy sales companies, where this is technically possible and economically justified.

This obligation may be fulfilled by a system of regular self-reading by the final customers whereby they communicate readings from their meter to the energy supplier. Only when the final customer has not provided a meter reading for a given billing interval billing shall be based on estimated consumption or a flat rate.

Member states shall ensure that final customers receive all their bills and billing information for energy consumption free of charge and that final customers also have access to their consumption data in an appropriate way and free of charge.

4. Energy Performance of Buildings

4. 1 Background

Buildings account for 40 % of total energy consumption in the Union. The building sector is also continuously increasing, which necessarily means that the energy consumption of this sector is steadily rising. Therefore, the energy saving potential is prominent.

EU adopted on 19th of May 2010 the directive on the Energy Performance of Buildings (2010/31/EU). The directive is a recast of the previous Energy Performance of Buildings directive (2002/91/EN). The new directive plays a key role on the field of energy efficiency regulation. Simplified, it sets down four main requirements for the member states. Firstly, member states must establish and apply minimum energy performance requirements for both, new and existing buildings. Secondly, member states are required to ensure the certification of buildings energy performance. Thirdly, member states shall require inspection of boilers and air conditioning systems in buildings, and fourthly, member states must ensure that by 2021 all new buildings are so-called nearly zero-energy buildings.

The Energy Performance of Buildings Directive (EPBD) is a so-called minimum directive, which means that the requirements set down in the directive are minimum requirements and the member states may maintain or introduce more stringent measures. Still, all measures shall be compatible with Union law. The directive gives the general framework for the calculation of the energy performance of buildings in Annex I.

4. 2 The Main Requirements of EPBD in Brief

Under article 4 the member states shall take the necessary measures to ensure that minimum energy performance requirements for buildings or building units are set. Member states shall also take the necessary measures to ensure that minimum energy performance requirements are set for building elements that form part of the building envelope and that have a significant impact on the energy performance of the building envelope when they are replaced or retrofitted.

The aforementioned article underlines the importance of taking cost effectiveness into account when setting and applying the minimum requirements. Member states shall calculate cost-optimal levels in accordance with the so-called comparative methodology framework. The framework differentiates between new and existing buildings and between different categories of buildings. Cost-optimal level in the directive refers to the energy performance level, which leads to the lowest cost during the estimated economic lifecycle.

When setting the minimum requirements, member states may differentiate between new and existing buildings and different building types. The requirements shall also take into account the general indoor climate conditions, local conditions and the designated function and the age of the building. Article 4 gives the possibility not to apply the requirements to certain building types such as officially protected buildings and temporary buildings.

In accordance with article 6 member states shall take necessary measures to ensure that new buildings meet the minimum energy performance requirements. The directive also encourages the usage of alternative systems. Member states are required to ensure that before construction starts the technical, environmental and economic feasibility of the following systems are taken into account: decentralised energy supply systems based on energy from renewable sources; cogeneration; district or block heating or cooling; and heat pumps.

In addition to new buildings, the minimum requirements shall be met with already existing buildings. The requirements apply to existing buildings when they undergo major renovation. Major renovation refers to renovation of more than 25% of the surface of the building envelope or when the total cost of the renovation is higher than 25% of the value of the building. Depending on the scale of the renovation, the requirements apply to the building as whole or the renovated building elements. It should also be noted that the minimum energy performance requirements shall be met only when this is technically, functionally and economically feasible.

EPBD introduces the concept of nearly zero-energy building. The term refers to a building that has a very high energy performance. Furthermore, the very low amount of energy required should be covered to a very significant extent by energy from renewable sources. In accordance with article 9 all new buildings must be nearly zero-energy buildings by 31 December 2020. New buildings occupied and owned by public authorities must meet this requirement already by 31 December 2018.

Article 11 obligates the member states to establish a system of certification of the energy performance of buildings. It is essential that owners or tenants of the building or building unit are able to have information on the energy performance of the building with an energy performance certificate. Energy performance certificate indicates the energy performance of a building or building unit. The calculating methods are set out in Annex I. The directive also sets down requirements on displaying the energy performance certificate in public buildings.

Under articles 14 and 15 member states shall lay down necessary measures to establish a regular inspection of systems used for heating buildings and air-conditioning systems. The inspection requirements applies to heating systems with boilers of an effective rated output for space heating purposes of more than 20 kW and air-conditioning systems of an effective rated output more than 12 kW. Additionally, member states shall ensure that energy performance certification and the inspection of heating and air-conditioning systems are carried out by qualified and/or accredited experts.

4. 3 Implementation of EPBD in Finland

In Finland the requirements set down in EPBD are implemented by amendments of the Land Use and Building Act (132/1999) (LUBA) and by the Ministry of the Environment decrees, which are published in the National Building Code of Finland. According to Section 117g of LUBA, a building shall be built and designed so, that it spends as little energy and natural resources as possible. Fulfilment of the energy efficiency requirements shall be stated by calculations based on energy use, energy loss and form of energy. The energy performance shall be improved when renovating the existing buildings, if it's technically, financially and functionally possible.

Section D3 of the National Building Code sets regulations and guidelines concerning new buildings that use energy in heating of rooms and ventilations, and possibly cooling, to maintain appropriate indoor climate conditions. According to D3 building's total energy consumption (E-number) shall be calculated. E-number refers to the annually purchased amount of energy weighted by fuel-specific factors and divided by net heated area. The fuel specific factors are as follows: electricity 1, 7; district heating 0, 7; district cooling 0, 4; fossil fuels 1, 0; and renewable fuels used in the building 0, 5. The National Building Code section D3 also sets out the maximum values for E-numbers by the size and type of the building.

The Ministry of Environment gave a decree on improving buildings energy performance in renovations and modifications (4/13) on February 2013. The energy efficiency requirements shall be taken into account when renovations are subject to building or action permit or when the purpose of the building is changed. The decree gives three possible routes for improving the energy efficiency. The requirements may be met per building component, which U-values shall be in accordance with the requirements set forth in section 4 of the decree. The owner of the building may also lower the energy consumption based on standard use or alternatively lower the E-number of the building. The decree sets down specific requirements on energy consumption and E-number limits for different building types.

The Act on Energy Certificates for Buildings (50/2013) was used to implement the sections of EPBD that apply to energy certificates. Building owners must obtain an energy certificate in conjunction with the building permit proceedings for new buildings. A certificate must also be obtained when a building or part thereof is sold or rented out. The energy class must be also reported in sales and rental listings. In some public buildings, the certificate must be publicly displayed.

5. Overview Energy Efficiency Legislation of Products

5. 1 Background

The energy efficiency concerning products is regulated with two framework directives: the Eco-design Directive (2009/125/EC) and the Energy Labelling Directive (2010/30/EU). Eco-logical design requirements are specified for products under the Ecodesign Directive. A product may not be launched onto the market within EU if it fails to meet the requirements set for it. The Energy Labelling Directive, on the other hand, includes provisions on energy labels that must be attached to specific products. These labels help the end-users in selecting energy-efficient products.

The Ecod-esign Directive and the Energy Labelling Directive are so-called framework directives, which mean that binding product-group specific requirements are issued under the directives. Today, these requirements are issued in the form of European Commission Regulations, in force as such.

5. 2 Eco-design

The requirements considering eco-design are set forth to improve energy efficiency and to integrate environmental aspects and the life cycle approach to the design state of certain products. For the most part the requirements concern the energy consumption during the use of the product. The directive contributes to sustainable development by increasing energy efficiency and the level of protection of the environment, while at the same by time increasing security of the energy supply.

The Eco-design Directive, as a framework directive, sets obligations to producers and importers only after European Commission has set requirements for the product-group at hand. The directive sets the grounds for selecting the product-groups. It is required that the product is sold at least 200 000 units per year in the EU. The product must also have considerable environmental impact. In addition, the product shall present significant potential for improvement without entailing excessive costs.

The directive introduces products' CE marking. In accordance with article 5, CE marking shall be affixed onto the product before it is placed on the market and/ or put into service. The product also needs EC declaration of conformity whereby the manufacturer or its representative ensures and declares that the product complies with all relevant provisions of the applicable implementing measure.

The Eco-design Directive and Energy Labelling Directive have both been enforced in Finland through the Eco-design Act (1005/2008, amended 1009/ 2010). The requirements of the directives apply to the product groups for which the European Union has defined product-groups' specific requirements.

5. 3 Energy Labelling

Energy labelling aims to influence consumers so they would choose energy-efficient products. The products, which are subject to the product-group specific energy labelling regulation, must be affixed with the energy label. The label indicates the energy consumed during the use of the product on a scale of A – G. In some cases, classes higher than A is used (A +, A + + and A + + +).

Energy Labelling Directive sets the framework for the energy labelling. The European Commission gives binding product-group specific regulation under the directive. In accordance with article 10, the Commission may give a regulation concerning a product-group if: 1) according to most recently available figures and considering the quantities placed on the Union market, the products shall have a significant potential of saving energy and, where relevant, other essential resources; 2) products with equivalent functionality available on the market shall have wide disparity in the relevant performance levels; 3) the Commission shall take into account relevant Union legislation and self-regulation, such as voluntary agreements, which are expected to achieve the policy objectives more quickly or at lesser expense than mandatory requirements.

The Energy Labelling Directive does not apply to any means of transport for persons or goods. The EC adopted the directive relating to the availability of consumer information on fuel economy and CO_2 emissions in respect for marketing of new passenger cars (1999/94/EC) in 1999. The purpose of the directive is to ensure that information relating to the fuel economy and CO_2 emissions of new passenger cars offered for sale or lease in the Community is made available to consumers in order to enable consumers to make an informed choice. In accordance with article 3, the member states shall ensure that a label on fuel economy and CO_2 emissions is attached to or displayed in a clearly visible manner near each new passenger car model at the point of sale. The directive also sets down requirements on giving information of fuel economy and CO_2 emissions in posters, advertisements and brochures. In addition, there is a regulation on setting emission performance standards for new passenger cars as part of the Community's integrated approach to reduce CO_2 emissions from light-duty vehicles ((EC) No 443/2009). The regulation establishes CO_2 emissions requirements for new passenger cars in order to ensure the proper functioning of the internal market and to achieve the overall objective of the European Community of 120 g CO_2/km as average emissions for the new car fleet. Article 4 requires that each manufacturer of passenger cars shall ensure that its average specific emissions of CO_2 do not exceed its specific emissions target determined in accordance with Annex I of the regulation.

Tyres account for 20 to 30 percent of the fuel consumption of vehicles. Because of this a reduction of the rolling resistance may contribute significantly to the energy efficiency of road transport and thus to the reduction of emissions. Therefore the European Parliament and Council have given the regulation on the labelling of tyres with respect to fuel efficiency and other essential parameters ((EC) No 1222/2009). The regulation establishes a framework for the provision of harmonised information on tyre parameters through labelling, allowing end-users to make an informed choice when purchasing tyres.

6. Final Remarks

The link between energy efficiency and mitigating climate change is clear. In addition, energy efficiency is closely linked with development of regulating, e. g. renewable energy, CCS (Carbon Capture and Storage), CHP (Combined Heat and Power) and building and construction planning. For instance, the combination of energy efficiency measures and renewable power generation could deliver almost 70 percent of the required emissions reduction over the next two decades. Energy efficiency contributes to resolve other major energy-related challenges such as energy poverty, resource depletion and security of supply.

The building sector forms a significant part of the overall energy consumption and CO_2 emissions in European Union. The Energy Performance of Buildings Directive is therefore an important instrument in achieving the set goals on emission reduction. The directive gives frameworks on calculation of buildings energy performance and sets down binding requirements for the member states concerning both, new and existing buildings. One major goal of the directive is that all new buildings would be nearly zero-energy buildings in the future.

The targets to the period from 2020 to 2030 are now under consideration. There's an undeniable need for the new targets: improved energy efficiency makes an essential contribution to all of the major objectives of EU climate and energy policies; improved competitiveness, security of supply; sustainability, and the transition to a low carbon economy. There is broad political consensus about its importance. The EU target for energy efficiency is not binding and progress is being delivered by specific policy measures at Union and national levels including for domestic and industrial appliances, vehicles, and for the building stock. The Energy Efficiency Directive takes a more holistic approach to energy savings in the EU. While the transposition deadline is not until June 2014 (and not all member states have yet implemented it) an assessment was requested by the Council and European Parliament by mid −2014. This assessment will look at the progress made towards reaching the 2020 target. Currently, a shortfall against the 20% targets predicted. Once the review has been carried out, the Commission will consider whether it is necessary to propose amendments to the Energy Efficiency Directive. While this review will be necessary to establish the exact ambition of future energy savings policy and the measures necessary to deliver it, it will be built on the analysis underpinning this communication and the targets and objectives for greenhouse gas reductions and renewable energy. Energy savings should complement the deployment of renewable energy by the member states as part of their plans to deliver greenhouse gas savings which should also identify national measures to improve energy efficiency. The Commission's analysis shows that a greenhouse gas emissions reduction target of 40% would require an increased level of energy savings of approximately 25% in 2030.

In some sectors, such as industry and passenger vehicles, the improvements observed in recent years will have to continue; while in sectors such as housing, other transport modes, and electrical equipment there will be a need for a significant acceleration of current efforts to tap the significant unexploited potential. This will require large investments in the building sector (that lead to lower running costs), framework conditions and information that encourage consumers to take up innovative products and services and appropriate financial instruments to ensure that all energy consumers benefit from the resulting changes.

The EU needs to continue complementing national efforts with ambitious EU-wide energy efficiency standards for appliances, equipment, buildings and CO_2 standards for vehicles. Making use of the economies of scale of the internal market, this can benefit EU manufacturers and help them to maintain technological leadership. [1]

What is more, by 2050, the European Union could cut most of its greenhouse gas emissions. With its roadmap for moving to a competitive low-carbon economy in 2050[2], the European Commission has looked beyond these short-term objectives and set out a cost-effective pathway for achieving much deeper emission cuts by the middle of the century. All major economies will need to make deep emission reductions if global warming is to be held below 2℃ compared to the temperature in pre-industrial times. The roadmap suggests that, by 2050, the EU should cut its emissions to 80% below 1990 levels through domestic reductions alone. It sets out milestones which form a cost-effective pathway to this goal-reductions of the order of 40% by 2030 and 60% by 2040.

Energy efficiency will be a key driver of the transition. By moving to a low-carbon society, the EU could be using around 30% less energy in 2050 than in 2005. Households and businesses would enjoy more secure and efficient energy

---

① COM (2014) 15 final. A policy framework for climate and energy in the period from 2020 to 2030.

② COM (2011) 112 final. A roadmap for moving to a competitive low carbon economy in 2050.

services. On average, the EU could save 175 − 320 billion annually in fuel costs over the next 40 years[1].

Yet, legal research is still needed to analyze how developing all the energy efficiency legislation will impact climate change in Finland and EU's perspective and analyze insights for better understanding of the driving forces and climate policy in Finland and EU. Climate change impacts in Finland and EU will raise the need for energy efficiency and the energy performance of buildings. The need for energy efficiency affects the energy regulation structures and in turn, these energy regulation structures and mechanisms will have an impact on Finland and EU.

芬兰和欧盟能源效率立法概要

阿里·艾克鲁斯　因加－丽萨帕弗拉　燕妮·荣图[*]

【摘要】 为缓解气候变化，各国必须在很大程度上改变其能源消耗方式。欧盟已为缓解气候变化采取了行动：所谓的"欧盟20－20－20目标"就是在2020年将能源效率提高20%。根据《欧盟运作条约》第194条，欧盟有关能源的政策应该促进能源使用效率的提高和能源的节约。欧盟新发布的2012年《能源效率指令》主要有两个方面的内容：一般意义上的能源效率和建筑物的能源效率。它规定了一项新的义务，即能源公司必须每年将其提供给工业和家庭用户的能源总量减少至少1.5%。2006年《有关建筑物能效的指令》规定了有关建筑领域的一些义务；而2005年《生态设计指令》则建立了规制产品能源使用的框架。作为欧盟的一个成员国，芬兰也必须实现以上有关气候和能源的政策中确定的雄心勃勃的目标。

---

[1]　European Commission; Climate Action; Policies; Roadmap 2050. http://ec. europa. eu/clima/policies/roadmap/index_ en. htm. Visited 4. 2. 2014.

[*]　阿里·艾克鲁斯，赫尔辛基大学环境与能源法教授、阿尔托大学经济法教授；因加－丽萨帕弗拉，赫尔辛基大学博士研究生；燕妮·荣图，赫尔辛基大学博士研究生。

中国生态文明法律体系的
构建：问题及思路

刘洪岩[*]

【摘要】 生态文明作为人类文明的新形态，是应对传统工业文明不可持续的生产方式和消费方式，着眼于人类的长远发展，引导人类社会走人与自然和谐发展道路的新起点。自生态文明作为中国国家战略的总体布局之一提出，就意味着它必将引发中国现有法律体系价值理念的更新和制度设计的重构。中国生态文明社会之构建必须直面整个社会传统积习"经济优先"的落后观念、法律制度空洞教条的现实、生态教育投入不足和生态文化缺失的诸多弊端，并以务实的态度将对现有法律体系进行"生态化"改造作为生态文明顶层设计和制度保障的逻辑起点和实现路径。

【关键词】 生态文明　法律生态化　法制化　生态安全

生态文明作为人类文明的一种形态，以尊重和维护自然为前提，以人与人、人与自然、人与社会和谐共生为宗旨，以建立可持续的生产方式和消费方式为内涵，以引导人们走上持续、和谐的发展道路为着眼点。党的十七大报告提出"建设生态文明，基本形成节约能源资源和保护生态环境的产业结构、增长方式、消费模式"，并强调在全社会必须牢固树立生态文明观念，这其中蕴含了生态文明的科学内涵及其价值取向。党的十八大又将生态文明写入党章，并提出"建设生态文明，是关系人民福祉、关乎民族未来的长远大计"，首次提出努力建设"美丽中国"的目标，实现中华民族永续发展。同时将生态文明建设列入继经济建设、政治建设、文化建设、社会建设之后的国家五位一体总体布局。生态文明问题融社会、经济、生

---

* 刘洪岩，中国社会科学院法学研究所研究员。

态、制度于一体，具有全球性、综合性和复杂性的特点。生态文明建设的国家总体布局的确立，对中国的环境法治建设将产生极大的影响，标志着中国环境法治的发展经历基本国策、可持续发展战略、科学发展观三个发展时期，步入生态法治发展阶段。

（一）生态文明概念之考证

生态文明何时提出，哪个国家提出的，目前学界说法不一。何为生态文明，迄今并没有公认的学理定义。文明是人类社会发展的产物，是一切物质财富和精神成果的总和。生态文明涉及"生态"和"文明"两个层面。"生态"本质上属于自然科学研究的视域，而文明则属于文化发展的范畴。1866年，德国动物学家海克尔首创了以"有机体与环境相互关系"为研究对象的生态学，第一次将生物体与自然环境之间的存在状态、相互关系及演化规律作为一门科学加以关注。而将"生态"与"文明"结合到一起，日本民族和人类学学者梅棹忠夫做出了巨大贡献。20世纪中叶以来，生态危机频发严重威胁人类自身安全，盲目追求物质财富的科技理性弊病尽显，工业化无节制发展的恶果促使人类深刻反思现有的社会发展理念和制度安排，先前被忽视的生态文明价值受到前所未有的关注。1967年梅棹忠夫在其出版的《文明的生态史观：梅棹忠夫文集》中，以生态史观的视角研究人类文明的发展规律，用生态学方法认识人与自然关系、处理环境与发展问题，并得出自然环境、生态条件对文明史进程有着重要影响的崭新世界观和方法论。

"生态文明"一词的使用时间并不长，从公开的出版物来考证，苏联环境学家在《莫斯科大学学报·科学共产主义》1984年第2期发表的《在成熟社会主义条件下培养个人生态文明的途径》一文中首先采用，认为人类发展必须重视生态状况。1985年中国的《光明日报》将该文刊载于"国外研究动态"栏目，生态文明第一次以转载的形式出现于中国。

中国对生态文明的关注，始于20世纪80年代初生态经济学研究的兴起。生态文明的内涵不断丰富，中国学者对此做出了重要贡献。中国生态经济学的提出和建立始于1980年，比美国最先提出的生态经济学概念晚了10多年。20世纪80年代初，中国生态学会前理事长、世界环境与发展委员会委员马世骏先生提出，社会的发展不能只要经济，也不能只要环境，还应该有社会。1980年8月，经济学家许涤新首先提出了进行生态经济研究和建立生态经济学科的建议。同年9月，中国社会科学院经济研究所和《经济研究》编辑部联合召开了中国首次生态经济问题座谈会。在这次座谈会上，学者们对中国特色社会主义市场经济条件下的生态文明内涵进行了阐释，并提出中国特色社会主义市场经济条件下的生态文明应由"环境为体、经济为用、生态为纲、文化为常"四者共同组成。并于1980年出版了由许涤新、马世骏、刘思华主编的第一部以生态经济为研究对象的《生态经济学》专著。书中翔实论述了可持续发展的有关理论问题，以生态经济协调发展理论为核心的生态经济学在中国初步形成。随着生态经济理论的发展，人们对生态文明的认识越来越深刻。

在20世纪80年代后期至90年代初，生态经济协调发展理论成为中国生态经济理论的主流，并影响着中国学界对"生态文明"理论研究的不断深入。1987年，刘思华教授提出了"现代文明"是"物质文明、精神文明、生态文明的内在统一"的观点。叶谦吉教授从人与自然关系角度将生态文明解读为"人类既获利于自然，又还利于自然，在改造自然的同时又保护自然，人与自然之间保持和谐统一的关系"。1997年在中国科学技术出版社出版的《生态文明观与中国可持续发展走向》一书中提出"生态文明是继农业文明、工业文明之后的一种先进社会文明形态"。2000年王如松教授在《当代生态农业》第1期发表《论生态革命走向生态文明》一文，对生态学与文化学相互关系进行深入研究，提出了许多科学见解。潘岳从中华文明传承、社会主义生态伦理及生态价值观等方面对生态文明进行系统梳理，发表了一系列文章。国内已出版了多套"生态文明丛书"。

2005年12月，中国生态文明建设的社会实践得到了飞速的发展，《国务院关于落实科学发展观加强环境保护的决定》出台并强调："倡导生态文明，强化环境法治，完善监管体制，建立长效机制，建设资源节约型和环境友好型社会"；"弘扬环境文化，倡导生态文明"，"以环境文化丰富精神文化"。这一重大决定为中国建设生态文明打下了坚实的法制基础。2011年11月，中国生态文明研究与促进会成立，试图推进生态文明研究，并通过试点探索生态文明城市建设经验，把生态文明作为中国特色社会主义文明体系生成阶段性的组成要素，作为中国科学发展观理论体系密不可分的重要理论基础。"十二五"规划纲要也将"提高生态文明水平"作为未来五年中国发展的重要目标。

作为一种应对生态危机、反思人与自然关系的全新的社会发展的文明类型，生态文明以尊重和维护生态环境价值和秩序为主旨，以可持续发展为依据，以人与自然相和谐为出发点，突破了以往发展观只注重生产力发展的狭隘性，它注重将发展观与生态观相结合，主张既要遵循经济发展规律，也要尊重自然规律，力求达到生态效益与经济效益的最佳结合。为此，世界各国实现和促进社会发展与保护生态环境两者的统一，追求自然界与人类社会之间的和谐发展，早在 20 世纪 70 年代就开始了有关生态文明的立法尝试和实践。虽然有些国家并没有"生态文明"的提法，但其相关立法所体现的改变单一经济发展模式、促进人与自然相互和谐共生的价值理念与生态文明核心本质相吻合。

（二）中国生态法治存在的问题

生态文明建设客观上要求必须以法律手段约束人类的自由行动，在不违反自然规律的范围内利用自然，实现人与自然的和谐相处。在生态文明价值理念的实践中，人与自然关系的现代化理论的本质或者核心是实现人与自然之间的关系从"对立"到"和谐"的转变，此种现代化的主要任务是在实践中将"理性地处理人与自然关系"之基本理念贯穿于人类行为的方方面面，终极目标则是实现人与自然的和谐共生和持续发展。当前，中国在生态文明法治建设方面存在诸多与生态文明核心理念和价值追求不相适应的问题。

1. 生态文明立法理念落后

中国的一些涉及生态文明的重要法律法规在立法目的、原则及内容上并未遵循生态原理实现彻底的生态化转向，还没有根本改变"经济优先"的传统发展观，并没有把生态文明的价值理念在立法中充分体现和贯彻。如作为目前环境保护基本法的《环境保护法》，修改前缺少对可持续发展、代际公平、生态安全理念的贯彻，于 2014 年 4 月 24 日修订通过，自 2015 年 1 月 1 日起施行的新法修改草案也未能全面对涉及生态安全的自然资源保护、生态保育、生态灾害防治等基本领域做出回应。

2. 生态文明的法制化缺乏系统规划，就生态法治体系化而言存在诸多的立法空白

生态文明建设是一项系统工程，它需要各领域、各环节的支撑，因此其制度的构建在立法方面也应有一个总体的规划，如在推动生态政治方面需要哪些立法，为建设生态文明在经济及社会领域需要进行哪些立法，而为衔接和协调这些立法及制度又需要进行哪些补充性立法，为建设和维护生态文明在运行机制上需要哪些法律制度构建，等等。中国当前在生态文明立法上的空白主要体现在以下方面：（1）涉及生态安全的相关立法，如《生态安全法》、《原子能法》、《生态保险法》等；（2）生态政治及相关监督的立法，如涉及建立符合生态规律的政绩制度、生态责任追究制度、绿

色经济指标考核、公众参与决策与监督制度等方面的法律法规；（3）生态文明的相关经济立法，如涉及经济活动的产业政策与消费政策立法等；（4）生态文明的相关社会立法，如生态文化法以及涉及自然资源使用的公民参与立法等。上述立法的缺失使生态文明的制度构建难以形成一个系统的、相互促进发展的有机链条，严重阻碍了生态文明建设进程的顺利推进。

3. 生态立法架构失衡

中国前期生态立法由于缺乏系统的规划与统筹而存在两方面问题：一是相关立法侧重于"转"（转变经济发展方式）、"节"（全面促进资源节约）、"保"（加大自然生态系统和环境保护力度）三个方面，对"调"（优化国土空间开发格局）、"建"（加强生态文明制度建设）过于忽视，但是这五个方面是一个有机联系的整体，"转""节""保"由于缺乏"调""建"的配合与协调而难以取得预期的成效，甚至出现了环境状况愈治愈恶化的尴尬局面；二是由于立法缺乏生态规划和指向，导致了"转""节""保"相关立法也存在一系列的空白和缺陷，如中国在生态安全保障方面的立法严重缺乏，并未形成有效运行的法律制度体系。同时，相关法律制度运行机制的不配套和脱节问题也相当严重，执法缺、漏长期难以得到有效弥补，西方国家那种以严密法律制度体系和运行机制促进生态文明立法、执法和守法的模式在当前中国法制不健全情况下行不通。

4. 法律的"生态化"程度不足

涉及与可持续发展相关的经济立法中的生态保护措施不健全，且缺乏可操作性和公众监督保障；相关环境保护法律法规也尚未明确规定国家及其职能机关在保障生态安全方面的具体职责以及公民在生态安全方面的权利内容；在《刑法》中没有将生态利益确定为相关条款的保护客体。在制度构建方面，相关立法尚未建立国家生态环境安全监测预警机制，以此对一些严重的自然灾害和人为的环境破坏事件迅速做出警示和反应，从而减少对国家生态环境的破坏。

5. 生态法律制度及生态教育缺失

时至今日环境损害的生态补偿机制和环境公益诉讼制度尚未建立，难以从经济的角度对生态资源进行合理的价值评估和司法救济，很难实现生态安全保障与经济发展的良性互动。此外，中国还缺乏一套全面完善的以生态安全培训为主体的生态教育制度，公民环保意识淡薄，社会生态文化缺失，难以对公民在接受生态安全教育活动方面提供现实的保障。

上述制度的缺失说明了中国在生态文明立法上的准备不足，缺少统一协调生态文明法律保障的制度体系。

（三）推进中国生态文明法制化的路径与对策

鉴于当前中国环境立法中存在的诸多问题，同时结合中国经济和社会发展的客观实际，本人认为，中国生态文明法制化的建设不可能一蹴而就，应结合中国的实际国情稳步推进。中国特色社会主义市场经济条件下的生态文明应是"环境为体、经济为用、生态为纲、文化为常"的基本架构。当务之急，应该对生态文明的法律体系及制度架构进行系统规划和设计，借助"法律生态化"的改造手段，建构以维护生态安全为目标的法律制度系统，并以此作为助推中国生态文明法制化发展的动力之源和制度保障。

1. 生态文明法制化的基本目标的确立

生态安全是生态文明基本的建构目标和底线保障。自人类步入风险社会之后，特别是全球化时代以来，各种生态安全问题日益受到各国和各界人士的关注和重视，其中生态安全立法在环境法治和生态文明社会构建中的核心作用越发显得重要。生态安全通常应具备如下标准：（1）生态系统的平衡得到维护，自然界的自然过程保持一种和谐状态；（2）可再生自然资源的再生条件得到保护；（3）不可再生的资源备受珍惜和得到节约利用；（4）自然界的环境容量受到尊重；（5）环境的自然净化能力得到维护；（6）整体自然环境处于良好状态；（7）维持人的生命活动和健康所需要的正常条件得到保障；（8）人的环境权利受到尊重和保护。"生态安全是指人的环境权利及其实现受到保护，自然环境和人的健康及生命活动处于无生态危险或不受生态危险威胁的状态。"[1]为维护生态安全，应积极改善人与自然的关系，建立良性的生态运行机制，同时在物质、精神与制度方面提供相应的保障。从这一方面来看，生态安全与生态文明的要求与内涵产生了高度契合，生态安全法律体系构建应成为生态文明社会构建进程中的法制路径和基本方向。

2. 生态安全法律体系的建构

俄罗斯及日本的生态文明的立法经验启示我们，中国生态文明的法制化发展路径当务之急就是构建以生态安全保障为基本目标的生态法律体系，这是建设生态文明的最基本路径和保障。

新型的生态法律体系以生态安全作为宗旨和目标，是一种融合环境、

---

① 王树义：《生态安全及其立法问题探讨》，《法学评论》2006 年第 3 期。

资源和生态观的大环境法体系。它既要在宏观上加强协调性、整体性的生态文明立法，特别是要加强立法的规划性，以适应生态文明和可持续发展战略思想的要求；也要在微观上从宪政层面、经济层面、社会层面和涉外领域进行一系列立法与制度重构，尤其要填补环境法领域的一些立法空白。

3. 法律的生态化改造

鉴于中国已经宣布社会主义法律体系已经建成的客观现实，理论上来讲，对现有法律体系做大规模的修正已不可能。唯一现实的做法就是对中国现有的法律体系进行系统的"生态化"改造，以使现有的法律体系能够与生态文明的法治目标相契合。

法律的生态化与生态文明的发展具有密不可分的联系，在生态文明思想理念的实践中，人与自然之间的关系从"对立"到"和谐"转变的终极目标则是实现可持续发展；从法律的角度探究，人与自然关系的现代化必然要求法律逐渐迈向生态化趋势。[1] 显然，"法律作为人类的社会规律的理性总结，必须符合自然生态系统的整体要求，顺应自然生态系统的需要"，[2]"法律必须接受生态规律的约束，只能在自然法则许可的范围内编制"。[3] 生态文明是一种全新的文明，它使评价物质文明和精神文明的标准发生了改变，使建立文明的基础和目标发生了改变，上述变化体现了生态文明的核心观念和要求——人与自然和谐相处，要达到这一目标则要求法律的生态化。[4] 生态文明是资源节约型社会和环境友好型社会的文明形态和文化形式，它的价值诉求多样化，强调多样性、可持续性、整体性、和谐性、民主性，人与自然和谐相处是最能体现生态文明特点的核心观念和核心内容。生态文明建设是一种从物质生产方式到政治、法律及社会文化观念的整体转变，从这个意义上讲，生态文明必然要求包括环境法治文化，生态文明的特点要求和决定了环境法律生态化的发展走向。[5] 可见，法律生态化是建设生态文明的内在要求和主要路径，这是一种无法规避的必然选择。

---

① 刘芳、李娟：《法律生态化：生态文明下中国法制建设的路径选择》，《生态文明与环境资源法——2009 年全国环境资源法学研讨会论文集》，第 116 - 125 页。

② 陈泉声等：《科学发展观与法律发展：法学方法论的生态化》，法律出版社，2008，第 55 页。

③ 徐祥民：《被决定的法理——法学理论在生态文明中的革命》，《法学论坛》2007 年第 1 期。

④ 李爱年：《生态文明建设呼唤环境法的生态化》，《生态文明与环境资源法——2009 年全国环境资源法学研讨会论文集》，第 98 - 111 页。

⑤ 蔡守秋：《以生态文明观为指导，实现环境法律的生态化》，见《"生态文明与环境法制建设"笔谈（三篇）》，《中州学刊》2008 年第 2 期。

4. 生态法治的制度革新与重构

以宪法为起点，通过一系列的法律修订实现中国生态立法理念与立法目的的革新。域外的生态文明的立法经验表明，"人类中心主义"的立法理念已不能适应生态文明发展的客观需要，确立"人与自然共同利益"的价值理念是未来法治现代化的基本发展趋向，这必将引发法律价值观的深刻调整：从法的"规范主义"占主导地位向"自然权利至上"传承与转换；从"利用刑事惩罚手段与生态犯罪作斗争"向"预防生态犯罪"这一国家政治的首要任务转变。受此启示，中国应考虑专门进行一系列的法律修订活动，使生态文明的价值理念贯彻到国家的整个法律体系中，从而彰显生态文明在国家治理中的突出地位，尤为重要的是应在国家根本法——宪法中明确生态文明、生态安全对国家、社会及公民的价值。

5. 以制度的系统化构建为目标填补生态文明的立法空白

在生态文明法律体系建构方面，应进行一系列推进生态文化建设的制度设计，如政绩绿色考评制度、生态责任追究制度、绿色经济指标考核制度、公众参与决策与监督制度，以上立法的目的在于促进政治决策的生态理性，通过确立合理的决策机制，使决策者能够以理性的方式进行决策，进一步完善生态保护与发展综合决策制度；参照域外立法经验，对涉及生态文明、生态安全的相关问题与领域进行立法，如制定生态安全法、原子能法、生态保险法、居民辐射安全法、生态损害责任法、保障汽车运输生态安全法、生态文化法、规划设计预防法、绿色产业法以及涉及宏观政策性问题和公民参与内容的法律法规；通过单独立法对生态安全保障进行大胆的制度创新，建立譬如生态审计、生态认证、生态许可、生态税征收、生态警察、生态安全预警等经济和行政的调节制度，一定程度上可为中国"资源节约型、环境友好型社会"的构建和"节能减排"目标的实现、清洁生产制度的整合与创新提供制度上的保障。同时为促进各领域生态文明法律制度之间的协调和系统化运行，应以立法形式建立相应的匹配制度，如符合生态价值观的立法制度（立法法）、类似《生态安全法律信息使用的分类方法》的规则制度等。

6. 强化公民生态教育立法，营造社会生态文化

以推动生态文明建设为主旨的生态教育的法制改革是实现社会生态文化发展的必要途径。凡是生态保护状况好和生态法治发展水平比较高的国家，公民的环保意识通常比照其他国家公民而言都相对高。生态文明如果离开了公众参与，生态法治就得不到社会的响应，其实效无法想象。为此，

加强公民生态教育、制定教育大纲和加强相关生态保护的培训投入，通过法制的力量贯彻执行生态文明对于当下严重缺失生态文化的中国社会不仅必要，而且应当。

生态文明的法治化是一个系统而全面的人文工程，在短期内不可能一蹴而就，要求立法者既深刻领会生态文明的价值底蕴和要求，又需要有所甄别地吸纳先进国家的相关立法成果，需要历经一段时期的摸索才能真正建立全面、系统、进步而又契合中国本土文化和国情的法律生态文化，从而使之在推动中国生态文明建设的历史进程中发挥卓有成效的历史作用。

The Construction of the Legal System of Eco-civilization in China: Problems and Approaches

Liu Hongyan [*]

【Abstract】Eco-civilization, as a new form of human civilization, marks a new beginning in the process of coping with the unsustainable modes of production and consumption of traditional industrial civilization and guiding the human society onto a road of development based on the harmonious relationship between men and the nature. The establishment of the goal of constructing eco-civilization as part of China's national strategy will inevitably lead to the renewal of the values system and restructuring of institutional design of the current system of law in China. In constructing eco-civilization, China must face up to the numerous problems currently existing in the country, including traditional concepts and old habits, the backward idea of "giving priority to economic development", the hollowness and dogmatism of the system of law, the insufficient investment in eco-education, and the absence of a eco-culture, and carry out "ecological reform" of the current system of law, so as make it the logical starting point of and the path to the top-level design and institutional guarantee of eco-civilization.

【Keywords】Eco-civilization; Ecologization of Law; Bringing into the Orbit of Law; Eco-safety

---

[*] Professor, Institute of Law, Chinese Academy of Social Sciences.

中国的民间环保组织与环境法治发展

——以新《民事诉讼法》的实施为视角

徐　卉*

【摘要】 本文回顾了中国民间环保组织在过去三十多年间的发展进程，阐释了民间环保组织在中国环境法治发展中所起的独特作用，其具体表现为：提高环保法律意识，推动公众参与；影响环保公共决策，监督社会主体行为；促进环保法律的执行；参与立法及政府决策；提起环境公益诉讼，维护公众环境权益。目前影响中国民间环保组织发挥作用的障碍主要包括：社团管理模式的限制，民间组织的自身建设不足，以及财政税收制度等方面的限制。本文着重分析了在新《民事诉讼法》的实施过程中，民间环保组织在环境公益诉讼中的主体地位问题。指出中国的环境法治发展应当立足于大力扶持以民间环保组织为主体的公益诉讼，赋予更多的民间环保组织以诉讼权，并建立关于环境公益诉讼的诉权行使规则、证据规则、鉴定规则和诉讼费用规则等实施机制。

【关键词】 民间环保组织　环境法治发展　公益诉讼

民间环保组织，亦即环保 NGO，是指主要从事环境与资源保护的非政府组织，围绕着生态环境保护和维护人为的环境利益而开展活动的环境保护团体。自 1978 年中国第一个环保 NGO——中国环境科学学会成立后，中国的环保 NGO 发展迅速，迄今已有 7000 多家。环保 NGO 在推动中国的环境法治发展中，发挥了非常重要的作用。

---

* 徐卉，中国社会科学院法学研究所研究员。

一　中国环保 NGO 概况

近年间，中国的环保 NGO 数量增长很快，据中华环保联合会 2008 年发布的《2008 中国环保民间组织发展状况报告》，截至 2008 年 10 月，中国的环保 NGO 已逾 3500 家，其中由政府发起成立的环保 NGO 1309 家，学校环保社团 1382 家，草根环保 NGO 508 家，国际环保组织驻中国机构 90 家。这个数字与 2005 年相比，环保 NGO 的数量增加了 700 余家，其中草根环保 NGO 增加较为明显，增加了近 300 家，约为一倍多。而截至 2012 年底，环保 NGO 总计达 7881 家，其中全国生态环境类社会团体已有 6816 家，生态环境类民办非企业单位 1065 家。随着全社会环境意识的提高，环保 NGO 织的数量在过去 5 年间有了大幅增长，从 2007 年到 2012 年增长了 38.8%。①

（一）环保 NGO 的组织形式

从组织形式上来看，中国的环保 NGO 目前主要存在四种类型。

1. 注册的环保 NGO

注册的环保 NGO 是指依照现行相关法律注册，被政府认可、具有较严格的组织性和较明确法律地位的非政府组织。主要是指按照 1998 年国务院颁布的《社会团体登记管理条例》的相关规定进行登记管理的社会团体，如自然之友、绿色江河；以及按照 2004 年国务院颁布的《基金会管理条例》的相关规定成立的基金会，如中华环境保护基金会、中国绿化基金会、北京环保基金会等；还包括一些按照 1998 年颁布的《民办非企业单位登记管理条例》注册成为民办非企业单位的环保组织，以及国际环保组织驻中国大陆机构。

2. 非营利企业

非营利企业是在工商部门登记获得企业法人资格，但开展公益性活动，执行非营利组织功能的一类环保组织。这种非营利企业开展的是非营利活动，但是因为具有法人身份并且又要履行法人的相关纳税义务，因此这类环保 NGO 属于公司法人型的环保 NGO，如"北京地球村""北京环境与发展研究所"。它们都是以公司法人身份注册的环保 NGO，主要是因为申请设立时没有找到业务主管单位（即挂靠单位），不符合社会团体设立的条件，为了成立该组织故注册为公司。

---

① 该数据来自 2013 年 12 月 2 – 3 日在北京举行的 2013 中华环保民间组织可持续发展年会。

3. 未注册的志愿团体

该类环保 NGO 是未经任何注册，也没有挂靠在任何单位或者合法登记团体之下，而是通过采取多种变通的方式生存和活动。目前在中国这类组织的数量不少，它们虽然未经注册，但因其内部良好的自治能力，已经在社会中产生了一定的影响。例如发展比较好的有"绿家园志愿者""绿色知音"，还有通过网络运行的未注册的"绿网""绿色北京"等，这些组织都为环境保护的推进做出了很大的贡献。

4. 高校社团和研究机构

注册为学生社团的高校环保社团是以在校大学生为主体发起成立的从事环保公益事业的组织，它们是按照团中央以及各高校出台的关于学校社团管理的规章制度进行管理，如"四川大学环保志愿者协会"。目前，中国各省份都有相应的高校环保社团成立，仅中国大陆地区已经有 200 多所高校组织成立了学生环保社团。但高校环保社团分布却呈现出极大的不平衡性：北京、上海、天津、武汉、西安、成都、广州等地高校较多的城市拥有为数众多的高校环保社团；而海南、西藏、贵州等地却仅有个别学生环保社团存在。[①] 研究机构是指那些具有大学或研究机构背景的环保 NGO，其中最为有名的是"中国政法大学污染受害者法律帮助中心"。该中心参与了多个与环境污染相关的案件，为受害人一方免费提供法律援助，帮助受害者挽回经济损失。

从地域分布上看，20 世纪 90 年代初期，中国的环保 NGO 主要集中在北京，数量也非常有限。20 世纪末 21 世纪初，中国的大部分省份都出现了环保 NGO，均形成一定规模。规模较大的环保 NGO 现在主要集中在北京、上海、天津、四川、重庆、云南、内蒙古、湖南、湖北等地，草根环保 NGO 主要分布在有草地、湿地、山地、林地的省份及长江、黄河流域，多为自然资源丰富和生态脆弱的地区。值得关注的是，近年来，中国虚拟性的网络环保 NGO 出现了快速发展的势头。仅北京地区就出现了"绿色北京""绿网""瀚海沙"等一批有影响的网络环保 NGO。[②]

---

① 王名主编《中国 NGOs 研究——以个案为中心》，联合国区域发展中心、清华大学 NGO 研究中心，2001，第 47 页。
② 张雷：《我国网络草根 NGO 发展现状与管理论析》，《政治学研究》2009 年第 4 期。

二　环保 NGO 在环境法治发展中的作用

（一）提高环保法律意识

在这方面，环保 NGO 通过动员、组织等方式，有效地聚集民间的环保力量。环保 NGO 通过举行环境保护集会、演讲、报告、展览、演出、情报交流、学术研究、义务活动、反污染抗议活动等各种群众性活动，在公众中宣传环境保护法律，提高公民的环保法律意识，并且在一定程度上指导了公众的环保行为。统计表明，仅 2005 年，79% 的环保 NGO 发起过志愿活动，共动员志愿者 857 万人次，平均每个环保 NGO 吸引 2500 多万人次。[①]

（二）推动公众参与，影响环保公共决策

近年来，环保 NGO 通过自己的非政府身份和环保志愿主义的精神，赢得了社会各界的信任，整合社会资金和资源，形成一股强大的社会力量，有组织地参与到环境保护中去。环保 NGO 汇集了相当数量的专家资源，吸纳了社会各界人士，形成的专业化支持体系与良好的社会公信基础，给政府的环保决策做出了较为正确的导向，从而在一定程度上减少了政府决策的盲目性和不适当性。以重庆市绿色志愿者联合会为例，该组织积极参与环境决策的制定，进行了一系列的活动，主要有：参与长江上游川西天然林保护的调查、监督，解决川西洪雅滥伐天然林事件，促成四川省做出全面禁伐天然林的决定，推动了全国天然林保护工程的实施；为解决重庆电荒问题，重庆市政府决定在主城区建 30 万千瓦燃煤发电机组，这将严重影响主城区环境，在重庆市绿色志愿者联合会的积极参与下，重庆市政府顺应民意，撤销了该建设项目。[②]

（三）监督社会主体行为，促进环保法律的执行

政府、企业和其他社会机构在各项活动中存在着各种各样的不环保行为，监督环节至关重要。在中国每年受理的近 60 万件环境信访举报中，有 1/10 是环保 NGO 提供的。[③] 此外，环保 NGO 在动员社会资源形成舆论压力方面具有优势，如 2002 年，环保 NGO "绿网"成功阻止了北京顺义湿地开发高尔夫球场的商业计划，使得北京平原地区唯一的一处湿地得以保护。[④]

[①]　中华环保联合会：《中国环保民间组织发展状况报告》（2008 年），来源：中华环保联合会。

[②]　刘培峰：《非政府组织参与的几个问题》，《学海》2005 年第 5 期。

[③]　《民间组织成为中国公众参与环保重要途径》，《华声报》2003 年 12 月 10 日。

[④]　中华环保联合会：《中国环保民间组织发展状况报告》（2005 年），《环境保护》2006 年第 10 期。

2008 年 3 月至 9 月，中华环保联合会对重庆大足碳酸铬污染环境问题进行了持续调研，通过递送建议书、上报内参和媒体曝光等形式督促当地整改，引起了较大反响。温家宝总理对此做了重要批示，指示有关部门严肃处理，并首次在重庆启用区域限制。① 2008 年 8 月底，著名造纸企业印尼金光集团旗下公司——金东纸业股份有限公司寻求股票上市被包括自然之友、绿家园及国际环保组织绿色和平在内的多家环保 NGO 阻挠，联名上书国家环境保护部，呈报金东纸业及其数家控股公司的多起环境违法和违规记录，建议"暂缓批准"其上市，对其进行环保核查。其声势及社会影响均属空前。② 环保 NGO 通过发挥自己的监督权和表达权保证了环境法律政策的实施，同时让社会公众更加了解和支持国家"绿色证券"的环境政策，给环保上市"把了关"。

（四）参与立法及政府决策

在中国，环保 NGO 常常利用制度性渠道进入立法和政府决策过程。例如"自然之友"在每年的全国人大和政协会议上都会提交立法议案和政策提案。又如 2007 年 1 月至 6 月，中华环保联合会四次赴湖南调研洞庭湖周边小造纸企业关停情况，对推动当地落实温家宝总理的相关批示起到了积极的促进作用。③ 2008 年 7 月，中华环保联合会对太湖周边两省三市进行了实地调研，并先后与江苏省环保厅、浙江省环保厅以及湖州市、无锡市和苏州市的环保、水利、农林、公用事务等部门进行了座谈，广泛研究了综合治理太湖水污染的问题。④ 此外，对领导干部实行环保考核，每月少开一天车等，均是由环保 NGO 首倡进而推广开来的。⑤

同时，环保 NGO 还积极参与中国政府在国际事务方面的决策。如 2002

① 中华环保联合会：《关于商请妥善解决重庆铜梁县、大足县有关地区碳酸锶生产企业环境污染投诉的函》《重庆市环保局迅速落实市领导批示精神抓紧碳酸锶企业污染整治工作》，中华人民共和国国境保护部网站，http://www.zhb.gov.cn/zhxx/gzdt/200807/t20080723_126043.htm。
② 吕斌：《"绿色证券"或成企业上市门票》，《法人》2008 年 10 月 9 日。
③ 《2007 年：科学发展看环保》，中国网，http://www.china.com.cn/aboutchina/zhuanti/08zgshxs/2008-03/31/content_13957123_2.htm。
④ 2009 年 11 月 8 日，中华环保联合会副主席兼秘书长曾晓东在江苏无锡市举办的"湖泊水环境治理与生态文明城市建设国际论坛"上的发言。
⑤ 《绿色 GDP 北京试点　领导干部将实行环保政绩考核》，《新京报》2005 年 3 月 1 日；2006 年 5 月 15 日，北京环保宣教中心和 79 家车友会及环保 NGO、新闻媒体共 112 家单位发起"为首都多一个蓝天，我们每月少开一天车"的环保公益活动，详见《京华时报》2006 年 5 月 16 日，第 8 版。

年，30 多家中国 NGO 参与了在南非约翰内斯堡举行的世界可持续发展首脑会议，这是它们首次以一个整体的形象亮相于国际舞台。1993 年北京申办 2000 年奥运会时，当国际奥委会官员询问中国有无环保 NGO 时，中方代表团还不知如何作答。而 2001 年 2 月，当国际奥委会评委们来到北京考察时，自然之友、北京地球村环境文化中心等三家环保 NGO 的负责人已被聘为北京市奥申委的环保顾问。我国环保 NGO 的理念之先进，实践之深入，给评委们留下了很深的印象。① 在 2008 年北京奥运会提出绿色奥运的口号后，环保 NGO 为办好绿色奥运更是提供了大量的帮助。②

（五）提起环境公益诉讼，维护公众环境权益

由环保 NGO 对有关环境污染受害者提供法律援助、开展环境维权的做法非常普遍，如中华环保联合会为帮助污染受害者特别是弱势群体进行环境法律维权，专门设立了"环境法律服务中心"，该中心的宗旨是通过环境法律维权，协调和配合政府落实环境保护目标，组织开展维护环境权益和立法，动员社会力量运用法律手段对环境权益受到侵害的公民、法人和其他组织，尤其是弱势群体进行环境权益的维护。

在这方面，非常著名的案件如福建省南屏县 1721 人诉榕屏化工厂案，这个案件曾被中华全国律师协会评为 2005 年十大影响性诉讼之一。中国政法大学污染受害者法律帮助中心用三年多的时间，最终不仅帮助 1721 位村民获得了胜诉判决，并且推动了环境公益诉讼在中国的发展。③ 2005 年，在中国国务院发布的《国务院关于落实科学发展观加强环境保护的决定》中，就第一次明确提出"发挥社会团体的作用，鼓励检举和揭发各种环境违法行为，推动环境公益诉讼"，从国家政策的层面提出了环境公益诉讼的概念，同时也强调了社会团体（包括环保 NGO）推动环境公益诉讼的作用。

2009 年 7 月 6 日，中华环保联合会以公益诉讼人身份状告江苏江阴港集装箱有限公司环境污染侵权纠纷一案被江苏省无锡市中级人民法院受理，此案被称为中国环保 NGO 公益诉讼"破冰"第一案。2009 年 7 月 29 日，贵州省清镇市法院对中华环保联合会再次以公益诉讼原告人的身份状告贵州省清镇市国土资源管理局一案也予以立案，这标志着中国环境公益诉讼

---

① 《催生绿色文明——我国公众参与环境保护纪实》，《人民日报》2001 年 12 月 7 日；《中国支持非政府组织参与环保事业》，《人民日报》（海外版）2004 年 3 月 13 日。

② 《民间环保组织积极实践绿色奥运》，《人民日报》（海外版）2008 年 3 月 13 日。

③ 《2005 中国十大影响性诉讼评选揭晓》，国务院法制办网站，http://www.chinalaw.gov.cn/article/xwzx/fzxw/200601/20060100022557.shtml。

实践又有了重要突破——环保 NGO 作为环境公益诉讼原告的资格已在司法实践中被认可。2010 年，中华环保联合会又在贵阳市清镇环保法院起诉贵阳市乌当区定扒造纸厂，要求被告立即停止向河道排放污水，承担原告律师费和诉讼费用，该案也获得了胜诉判决，法院判决支持原告的全部诉讼请求。[①]

此外，如 2009 年 8 月重庆市绿色志愿者联合会向武汉海事法院提起诉讼请求金沙江中游水电开发商停止违法建设，2010 年 5 月重庆市绿色志愿者联合会向昆明中院提起诉讼请求国电阳宗海发电有限公司减少二氧化硫排放并赔偿损失等，均为环保 NGO 提起环境公益诉讼的典型案例。[②]

环保 NGO 环境公益诉讼的开展，有力地推动了地方环保法律的执行。为此，云南、贵州、广东、江西等省份的司法机关成立了专门的"环保法庭"，先后受理、审理了一些环境公益诉讼案件。并且在地方立法层面上，明确了环保 NGO 的环境公益诉讼原告资格。

2012 年，环保 NGO 的公益诉讼实践最终获得了立法上的确认，2012 年8 月 31 日第十一届全国人民代表大会常务委员会第二十八次会议审议通过了《关于修改〈中华人民共和国民事诉讼法〉的决定》，修改后的《民事诉讼法》增设了公益诉讼制度，其中明确规定："对污染环境、侵害众多消费者合法权益等损害社会公共利益的行为，法律规定的机关和有关组织可以向人民法院提起诉讼。"

三　影响中国环保 NGO 发挥作用的障碍

1. 社团管理模式的限制

目前的社团管理模式不利于环保 NGO 的发展，间接地限制了其环境公益诉讼作用的发挥。这主要缘于《社会团体登记管理条例》和《民办非企业单位登记管理暂行条例》，确立了 NGO 的登记注册管理及日常性管理实行登记管理部门和业务主管单位双重负责的体制，这样的规定使得环保NGO 作为社会团体在登记与管理方面受到许多限制。[③] 目前，在加强和创新社会管理的要求下，中国的立法机关已着手研究完善这方面的法律规范。

---

① 中华环保联合会：《中华环保联合会开展环境公益诉讼情况的通报》，来源：中华环保联合会。
② 见重庆市绿色志愿者联合会网站主页，http://www.greenu.org.cn。
③ 刘太刚：《非营利组织及其法律规制》，中国法制出版社，2009，第 35 页。

2. 环保 NGO 自身建设不足

这主要体现在环保 NGO 在制度化、规范化建设方面存在的问题。中国现行的管理条例对 NGO 的内部治理有一些规定，但是这些规定过于笼统，在实践中缺乏可操作性。因此，迫切需要一部包容性的法律规定，对环保 NGO 内部事务的管理、管理人员的组成、活动情况报告、信息公开等方面做出规定，这有利于环保 NGO 的自律和社会监督。

3. 财政税收制度方面的限制

现阶段中国的 NGO 面临的主要难题就是资金匮乏，根据 2008 年《中国环保民间组织发展状况报告》：中国 74% 的 NGO 没有固定的资金来源，44.8% 的 NGO 没有自己的办公场所，很多草根环保 NGO 为了节省资金，通常是两个组织共同租用一套民宅作为办公场所。中国的相关法律在 NGO 的财政、税收待遇方面的规定不够明确，公益捐助方面的规定也过于粗糙，应在制度上予以明确对 NGO 的财政支持及税收优惠，并且在社会对 NGO 的公益捐助方面，有必要适当加大对捐助者的优惠力度，提高社会捐助的积极性。

四　环保 NGO 作为环境公益诉讼主体的问题

2012 年 8 月 31 日，全国人大常委会通过了《关于修改〈中华人民共和国民事诉讼法〉的决定》，修改后的《民事诉讼法》明确规定："对污染环境、侵害众多消费者合法权益等损害社会公共利益的行为，法律规定的机关和有关组织可以向人民法院提起诉讼。"该规定普遍被认为开启了中国环境公益诉讼的法制之门，有媒体甚至乐观预判，环境公益诉讼的春天就要来了。[①]

但是，自新《民事诉讼法》实施以来，在司法实践中，由环保 NGO 提起环境公益诉讼的状况并不乐观。据报道，2013 年，中华环保联合会共开展 8 起环境公益诉讼，均被法院以"原告主体不适合"为由未予立案。[②]

究其原因，环保 NGO 在环境公益诉讼中的地位问题仍是目前制约环境公益诉讼发展的瓶颈问题。

（一）环保 NGO 作为环境公益诉讼原告的适用范围

根据《民事诉讼法》第 55 条的规定，有权作为原告提起环境公益诉讼

① 王琳：《环境公益诉讼之春为何迟迟不来》，《广州日报》2013 年 6 月 26 日。
② 《环保法修订破例四审　代表建议加大环境违法惩罚》，中国网，http://finance.china.com.cn/news/special/lianghui2014/20140311/2249172.shtml。

的应当是"法律规定的机关和有关组织"。对于何者为"法律规定的机关和有关组织",2014 年 4 月 24 日第十二届全国人民代表大会常务委员会第八次会议修订的《环境保护法》对此做出了规定,修订后的《环境保护法》规定:"对污染环境、破坏生态,损害社会公共利益的行为,符合下列条件的社会组织可以向人民法院提起诉讼:(一)依法在设区的市级以上人民政府民政部门登记;(二)专门从事环境保护公益活动连续五年以上且无违法记录。符合前款规定的社会组织向人民法院提起诉讼,人民法院应当依法受理。提起诉讼的社会组织不得通过诉讼牟取经济利益。"

事实上,《环境保护法》对于环境公益诉讼主体规定的出台可谓一波三折、饱受争议。自全国人大启动了对于《环境保护法》的修订工作以来,对于环境公益诉讼主体的认定一直是草案审议过程中的一个焦点。由于《环境保护法》自 1989 年正式颁行以来,至今已经有 25 年没有实质修改,而这期间正是我国环境急速恶化的 30 年。因此,在《环境保护法》草案送审之前,有环保人士和专家学者即公开呼吁放开公益诉讼主体资格限制,建立环境信息统一公开平台,完善环境影响评价制度,加强行政部门履职监督。①

2011 年,《环境保护法》正式进入修订计划,当时环保部提交的建议稿将环境公益诉讼主体的范围规定为"经依法登记的环境保护社会团体、县级以上地方人民政府环境保护行政主管部门"。民间环保组织是主体之一。但是 2012 年 8 月,《环境保护法》修正案草案首次审议时,与"环境公益诉讼"有关的条款并未出现。结果这一草案遭到了业内专家和多部门的普遍反对。② 为此,在 2013 年 6 月提交全国人大常委会二次审议的《环境保护法》修正案草案中,规定了环境公益诉讼制度,二审草案规定:"对污染环境、破坏生态,损害社会公共利益的行为,中华环保联合会以及在省、自治区、直辖市设立的环保联合会可以向人民法院提起诉讼。"该规定将环境公益诉讼主体限定为中华环保联合会,这一规定引发社会广泛争议,普遍认为环境公益诉讼的主体范围过窄。对此,有参与立法的权威人士表示,

---

① 陈媛媛:《环境公益诉讼主体资格限制过严遭质疑　应赋予更多民间组织诉讼权》,《中国环境报》2013 年 11 月 1 日。

② 2012 年 9 月 26 日,由马骧聪、汪劲、王灿发、王树义、吕忠梅等 12 名国内环境学界知名学者代表中国法学会环境资源法学研究会提交了一份专家联名意见,对《环境保护法》的修订草案公开表示反对,认为草案在有关环保的法律原则和法律制度,如公益诉讼制度方面存在认识上的谬误。

二审稿"中华环保联合会及地方省级联合会"，是因误会环保联合会职能，以为类似于消协。[①]

　　此后，在征求了社会各方的意见后，《环境保护法》修正案三审草案改为："对污染环境、破坏生态、损害社会公共利益的行为，依法在国务院民政部门登记，专门从事环境保护公益活动连续五年以上且信誉良好的全国性社会组织可以向人民法院提起诉讼。"对于这一改动，众多环保组织和法学专家认为，该规定依然在理论上无依据，立法上不科学，实践中难操作。比如，"信誉良好"的评判标准是什么？由谁来评判？这样弹性极强的规定很容易导致自由裁量权的滥用。另外，"全国性社会组织"的限定也缺乏合理的依据。由于环境问题具有区域性，因此往往是当地的公众和环保组织更关心当地的环境，当地的环境问题也更大程度上关乎当地人的环境权益，所以，草案的这一规定将当地的公众和环保组织排除在环境公益诉讼主体之外，是有失公允的。有专家甚至直言："从（环境公益诉讼主体）范围来讲，三审稿比二审稿收得更紧。"有专家用带"环保"字样的关键词检索，发现全国性社会组织只有三家，除了中华环保联合会外，只剩下中国环保机械行业协会、中国化工环保协会，而这两家作为环保行业协会，并没有从事公益诉讼等活动。[②] 而据环保部统计，按照三审稿的要求，民政部登记的全国环保组织就 24 家，刨去植树造林等不相关的，剩下的就是环保部下属的，如环保基金会等，但其中只有环保联合会提起过诉讼。[③]

　　另外，从环保 NGO 的实际状况上看，由于它们具有公益性和非营利性，因此很少有单位愿意担任其业务主管部门并承担责任。由此带来的结果就是，我国环保 NGO 在各级民政部门的正式注册登记率非常低，有一大批环保 NGO 不得不在当地工商部门登记。所以按照三审草案的规定，实际上符合提起环境公益诉讼的主体就只有环保部下属的几家环保组织了，即中华环保联合会、中华环保基金会和中国环境科学学会。

　　当然，最终通过的《环境保护法》修订案规定的环境公益诉讼主体范围比三审稿有所扩大，根据修订后的规定，目前全国符合条件能够提起环境公益诉讼的环保 NGO，国内有 300 家左右。不过对于这一规定，仍有环

────────────

① 《环境公益诉讼主体范围或将扩大》，《北京青年报》2014 年 4 月 17 日。
② 章柯：《环保法修订草案三审　公益诉讼主体被指"过度限定"》，《第一财经日报》2013 年 10 月 23 日。
③ 《环境公益诉讼主体范围或将扩大》，《北京青年报》2014 年 4 月 17 日。

保 NGO 表示了不同的看法，如"自然之友"认为，该规定还是没有考虑到直辖市这一特殊情况，希望后续的司法解释能够对此做出说明。而且在司法实践中，即使对于符合条件的环保 NGO 提起的环境公益诉讼，人民法院不受理环保相关诉讼的情况依然很多。[1]

　　至于为何要对环境公益诉讼主体进行限定，立法者的意见是：环境公益诉讼是一项新规定，宜积极稳妥地推进，而且确定环境公益诉讼主体范围需要考虑诉讼主体的专业能力、社会信誉等因素，防止滥诉。但是，从鼓励公众参与、促进中国环境法治发展的角度来看，应当规定依法设立的环保 NGO 对污染环境、破坏生态、损害公共利益的行为可以向法院提起诉讼。[2] 而且，从世界上其他国家的环境公益诉讼实践来看，让 NGO 甚至公民提起环境公益诉讼，并不会造成滥诉现象的发生。[3]

（二）环保 NGO 与其他机关行使环境公益诉讼的诉权问题

　　根据《民事诉讼法》的规定，有权行使环境公益诉讼诉权的，是"法律规定的机关和有关组织"。对于该条规定的适用，通常认为，这里法律规定的机关和有关组织主要是环保行政机关、检察机关和环保 NGO。[4] 但是，同样作为行使环境公益诉讼的诉权主体，这三者之间究竟应当是怎样的关系，目前仍然是一个在立法和司法解释中都没有明晰的问题。

　　就环保行政机关而言，它们作为负有管理责任的环境监管部门，隶属于地方政府。而通常，在环境公益诉讼中的被告往往是一些实力雄厚的排污企业或个体经营者，地方政府基于经济发展的需要，往往对当地污染企业的存在和发展采取不同程度的放纵态度，也存在一些所谓的"潜规则"问题，即地方政府为了提高自己的政绩或当地的 GDP，而对污染企业的环境污染行为不问、不顾。[5] 在这种情形下，以环境监管与处罚为主要手段的行政行为往往在政府部门追求经济发展的强大压力下显得无能为力。环保

---

①　金煜：《新环保法亮点：社会组织可提环保公益诉讼》，《新京报》2014 年 4 月 25 日。

②　2013 年 10 月 21 日，全国人大法律委员会副主任委员张鸣起在向十二届全国人大常委会第五次会议做关于环保法草案修改情况汇报时的发言。

③　Hudson P. Henry, "Annual Review of Environmental and Resources Law: Constitutional Law Standing, a Shift in Citizen Suit Standing Doctrine", 28 *Ecology Law Quarterly* 23.

④　郭少青：《环境公益诉讼在摸索中前进》，《检察风云》2013 年 6 月 6 日；李爱年、龙海燕：《关于我国环境公益诉讼的立法思考——兼评〈民事诉讼法修正案〉第九条》，《江西理工大学学报》2012 年第 6 期；别涛：《环境公益诉讼》，法律出版社，2007。

⑤　王曦委员：《地方政府 GDP 优先思想导致环境污染》，人民网，2012 年 3 月 6 日，http://lianghui.people.com.cn/2012cppcc/GB/239430/17307163.html。

行政机关的性质决定了它应当依职权主动或依申请被动地做出相关的处罚、惩治决定，但是环保行政机关往往怠于或疏于行使职权，这也是至今环境公益诉讼发展缓慢的一个重要因素。

关于检察机关提起环境公益诉讼问题，在我国，检察机关是依法实行法律监督、维护司法工作的国家公权力机关，是社会利益的维护者与维护我国最高法律秩序的代表机关。检察机关作为国家公共利益的代表，在环境公共利益受到侵害而无人起诉或不愿起诉的情况下，可以依其职权履行原告的职责。因此我国很多学者都主张借鉴西方国家的检察机关提起环境公益诉讼的做法，并且在我国实践中也存在这种做法。[①] 如 2003 年山东省乐陵市人民检察院诉范某非法小炼油项目案，2004 年四川省资阳市雁江区人民检察院诉清水河流域 8 家石材厂违规加工石材案，2008 年湖南省望城县人民检察院代表 49 户村民诉水泥厂污染案，2012 年广州市番禺区检察院起诉食品公司大气污染案，等等。并且，很多地方检察机关也都出台了办理环境公益诉讼的适用意见和办法，如 2008 年 11 月，由昆明市委政法委牵头，昆明市中级人民法院与昆明市检察院、昆明市公安局、昆明市环境保护局共同出台了《关于建立环境保护执法协调机制的实施意见》，建立了环境保护执法协调机制。该实施意见对环境公益诉讼的主要问题做了初步规范：关于诉讼主体的确定，将起诉主体限定为检察机关、环保行政机关和环保社团组织。

但是另一方面，检察机关作为环境公益诉讼的主体，存在着检察机关民事公益诉权的行使可能对环境受害人民事诉权行使构成威胁或侵犯，以及检察机关与环境侵害人之间的调解是否会贬损此类环境案件的公益性问题。[②] 特别是，尽管检察机关具有大量的法律专业人才，对法律很了解，对案件如何提起和进行很熟悉，这样可以节省法律成本，提高效率，但是由于检察机关在人员、编制、财政收入方面与地方政府皆有关系，面对涉及地方政府的公益诉讼案件，检察机关在起诉还是不起诉的问题上显然会陷入两难境地。而且由于检察机关并没有专门机构和人员负责公益诉讼方面的工作，也不具备搜集公益诉讼证据的专业能力，这一点在对专业要求很高的环保公益诉讼中表现得尤为突出，这不仅使得大多数检察机关作为原

---

① 徐卉：《通向社会正义之路——公益诉讼理论研究》，法律出版社，2009，第 180 – 196 页。

② 蔡彦敏：《中国环境民事公益诉讼的检察担当》，《中外法学》2011 年第 1 期。

告发起环境诉讼"没有太多积极性"，也使检察机关提起公益诉讼在专业性方面存在较大的不足。同时，检察机关的法律监督地位与检察机关在公益诉讼中所担任的基本职能是冲突的，检察机关作为法律监督者的身份提起公益诉讼，不但可以监督对方当事人，甚至可以监督法院的审判活动，这就会破坏原告、被告、法院三方所形成的平衡构造关系。①

在这方面，环保 NGO 的先天性优势决定了它在环境公益诉讼中有着举足轻重的作用。环保 NGO 无论是与环保行政机关相比，还是与检察机关相比，它们更能体现受污染损害群体的公共利益诉求。其民间性、中立性的特征也决定了 NGO 在公益诉讼过程中，在诉讼意志上很少会受到干扰，既能有效地帮助政府和国家起诉环境污染者，也能帮助民众和弱势群体起诉污染肇事者，从而更真实地表达受害群体的公共利益诉求，使环境违法者承担法律责任，对环境进行修复补偿。同时，由于环保 NGO 拥有更加专业的人员和更强的技术支持，能够克服检察机关在提起环境公益诉讼中面临的各种问题，环保 NGO 积极提起环境公益诉讼，能够有效地避免政府机构在执行公务中的不作为和变相纵容环境违法行为的问题，这样有利于实行依法治理环境，实现生态和谐。

（三）　基于环境公益诉讼主体而展开的程序规则建构问题

由于环境问题事关全社会的共同利益，环境问题的复杂程度也远超人们的想象。因此，关于环境公益诉讼的问题远非《民事诉讼法》第 55 条这一简单的授权性规定所能够予以调整、规范的，必然需要建构相关配套的诉讼机制，如证据规则、调解规则、诉讼费用规则等。

在此，一个前提性的问题是，这些诉讼规则的确立，究竟应当以何者为主体而建构。事实上，在我国法学界普遍存在着一种无主体的制度观与法律规则观。在中国的社会转型中，制度与立法常常被当作产生一切问题的根源和解决一切问题的万灵药，对制度的考察和对法律法规的探讨与解释充斥于谈论各种问题的话语中。但我们对于制度的理解，似乎是认为存在着那样一个客观的制度，它与人无关，仿佛只要你在电脑里设计出来，然后把它放在社会中就可以发挥效用了。我们在制定制度与确立规则时，实际很少认真关注过主体性问题，它们不过是分析中的一个变量，甚至有时连参数都不是，而只是一个被各种结构性力量操纵、控制的"客体"。然

---

① 王健：《检察院公益诉讼　困惑中前行》，《民主与法制》2013 年第 2 期。

而另一方面，在转型的社会现实中，制度、法律与规则的有效性又是一个极其突出的问题。这表现为中国当下的一个特有现象，那就是制度与法律越立越多、越来越复杂，秩序却越来越混乱。导致这一状况的产生，与这种去主体化的制度观与法律观有着很大的关系。①

从环境公益诉讼的主体来看，环保行政机关、检察机关和环保 NGO 都是有权行使环境公益诉讼诉权的主体，但很显然，此三者在提起诉讼的积极性、有效性和专业性等方面均存在着较大的差异。从有效推动中国环境法治发展建设的角度看，应当立足于大力扶持以环保 NGO 为主体的公益诉讼，这样才能真正使环境公益诉讼的制度落到实处。因此，在相应的诉讼规则和程序机制的设置上，应当主要围绕着环保 NGO 实施公益诉讼来展开，从而达到激励和保障环保 NGO 参与环境公益诉讼的目的和作用。

据此，首先应当扩大原告资格的范围，赋予更多的环保 NGO 以提起环境公益诉讼的诉权。在这方面，应采取一个较为开放的标准来规定环保 NGO 的诉讼地位，即凡依法设立的环保 NGO，针对污染环境、破坏生态、损害公共利益的行为，都有权向法院提起诉讼。依法设立是对环保 NGO 的登记注册要求，而这里的"环保 NGO"的界定，则是指环保团体的设立宗旨或其活动范围只要与环境破坏行为或政府有关环境问题的决策存在某种联系，就可以享有提起环境公益诉讼的权利。只有这样设定原告的资格范围，才能够达到鼓励更多的群体参与环境保护行动的立法目的。

同时，在起诉要件上应当规定，对污染环境的行为，环保 NGO 有权要求环境保护管理机构及时进行查处，环境保护管理机构未在合理期限内对环保 NGO 举报的涉及公共环境利益的污染问题做出答复或处理的，该环保 NGO 可以依照法律提起环境公益诉讼，要求有关责任主体承担立即停止侵害、排除妨碍、消除危险、恢复原状等责任。概言之，即在诉权行使规则上，行政机关的诉权是第一顺位的，环保 NGO 是第二顺位的，只有在第一顺位的诉权主体不行使诉权时，第二顺位的诉权主体才可以起诉。

在证据规则的设定上，环境污染侵权诉讼在举证责任的分配上，应当适用举证责任倒置，即环境公益诉讼中被告的危害行为、损害事实、损害后果由公益诉讼人承担举证责任，而被告侵权行为与损害后果之间不存在因果关系则由被告承担举证责任。基于无过错责任原则，原告需要对被告

---

① 　徐卉：《通向社会正义之路——公益诉讼理论研究》，法律出版社，2009，第 336 - 337 页。

的加害行为、损害结果承担举证责任，而由加害人就法律规定的免责事由及其行为与损害后果之间不存在因果关系承担举证责任。同时必要时，人民法院应当依职权调查收集相关证据。

环境公益诉讼中，被告的加害行为、损害后果以及两者的因果关系往往涉及复杂的科学技术问题，原被告双方可能都不具备相应的举证能力，因此具有专业知识背景的鉴定机构的存在就显得尤为必要。然而，在我国目前的司法鉴定体系中，并无专门的环境损害鉴定机构，这导致环境公益诉讼中当事人举证、法院采证都存在一定的困惑和困难。① 环境污染的成因非常复杂，检测又需要各种专业仪器设备，因此应当对环境保护行政机关的鉴定义务做出规定，环境保护行政机关应对环境污染事故进行鉴定，并委托有资质的机构对造成的损害后果进行评估，对环境公益诉讼提供必要的技术支持。

由于环境公益诉讼过程中涉及环境影响评价、环境污染评估等高技术含量的问题，环境公益诉讼的诉讼成本较一般的诉讼要大得多，因此关于诉讼费用规则，应实行有利于原告的方式。原告起诉时可缓缴诉讼费，若判决原告败诉，则应免缴诉讼费，若判决被告败诉，则应判决由被告承担，建立相应的诉讼保障和激励机制。

总之，新《民事诉讼法》关于公益诉讼的规定，为环保 NGO 推进中国的环境法治发展开启了一扇制度的大门。但是，良好的制度需要有保障的、切实可行的实施机制，这方面的配套规范建设仍然任重道远。

---

① 王社坤：《我国环境公益诉讼司法实践与制度构建调查报告》，《中国环境法治》（2011 年卷上），法律出版社，2011。

Environmental NGOs and the Development of the Environmental Legal System in China: from the Perspective of the Implementation of the New Civil Procedure Law

Xu Hui[*]

【Abstract】 This article reviews the development of environmental NGOs (ENGOs) in China during the past 30 years and explains the unique roles played by ENGOs in the development of the environmental legal system in China, including enhancing people's consciousness of environmental law, promoting public participation, influencing public decision-making, supervising over the acts of various social subjects, promoting the implementation of environmental law, participating in legislation and government decision-making, initiating environmental public interests litigation, and upholding people's environmental rights and interests. Currently the main factors preventing ENGOs from giving full play to their roles in China include: the defective NGO administration mode, the lack of self-construction on the part of NGOs themselves, and restrictive financial and tax systems. This article focuses on the analysis of the legal standing of ENGOs in environmental public interest litigation, and points out that, in developing the environmental legal system, China should vigorously support public interest litigation initiated by ENGOs, give more litigious rights to NGOs, and establish corresponding implementation mechanisms, such as rules on the exercise of litigious rights by ENGOs, on the producing of evidence, on expert witness, and on court costs.

【Keywords】 ENGO; Development of the Environmental Legal System; Public Interest Litigation

---

[*] Professor, Institute of Law, Chinese Academy of Social Sciences.

第二部分

人权的法治保障

保障人权的重大意义

李步云　张秋航[*]

【摘要】 中国政府 1991 年的《中国的人权状况》白皮书提出,人权是个"伟大的名词"。人权保障具有重大意义,即人权保障是社会主义的崇高理想,是实现"为人民服务"宗旨的切实保障,是制定和实施社会主义法律的根本目的,是推进科学发展的出发点和最终归宿,是全人类的共同价值追求。

【关键词】 人权　社会主义　人民　科学发展

1991 年 11 月,中国国务院授权国务院新闻办公室发布《中国的人权状况》白皮书。这是新中国成立以来,中国政府发布的有关人权问题的第一个专门的重要文件。该白皮书开宗明义指出:"享有充分的人权,是长期以来人类追求的理想。从第一次提出'人权'这个伟大的名词后,多少世纪以来,各国人民为争取人权作出了不懈的努力,取得了重大的成果。"这是中国政府对保障人权重大意义的高度评价。

"人权"为什么伟大?笔者认为可以概括为以下五条。

一　享有充分的人权,是社会主义的崇高理想

什么是社会主义?邓小平同志曾做过如下概括:解放和发展生产力,以公有制为主体,最终实现共同富裕。这是对以往有关什么是社会主义理念的重大发展。因为"贫穷不是社会主义",社会主义必须代表那个时代最先进的生产力,从而纠正了"以阶级斗争为纲"的错误思想和路线。"以公有制为主体"意味着除公有制外还应允许私有和多种所有制并存,但是小

---

* 李步云,广州大学人权研究与教育中心主任;张秋航,湖南大学法学院副教授。

平同志提出的前两条，本质上是手段而不是终极目的。依据马克思、恩格斯等马克思主义的创始人以及国际共产主义和建设中国特色社会主义的成功实践经验，社会主义社会的本质特征可以概括为，那是一个"人人自由、人人平等、人人富裕、人人享有宪政文明"的社会。

自由是人的本性和本质，人的自由、自觉活动是人区别于动物的基本特点；人的思想与行为自由，是人能动地认识世界和创造世界的力量源泉。马克思曾多次提出，我们所追求的理想社会是一个"每个人的自由发展是一切人的自由发展的条件"的联合体。①新民主主义革命时期毛泽东同志明确提出，未来社会主义的新中国将是一个"自由民主的中国"。他说，"'自由民主的中国'将是这样一个国家，它的各级政府直至中央政府都由普遍、平等、无记名的选举所产生，并向选举它的人民负责。它将实现孙中山先生的三民主义，林肯的民有、民治、民享的原则与罗斯福的四大自由。"②中国自 1978 年党的十一届三中全会以来实行的改革开放政策可以用两个字概括——"松绑"，即扩大地方、社会组织、企事业单位和劳动者个人的自由度，以调动起方方面面的主动性、积极性、创造性。这正是 30 多年我们能够取得经济发展世界奇迹和政治文化发展巨大进步的根本原因所在。

关于平等，马克思指出，平等"是共产主义的政治的论据"。其意思是说，共产党人闹"革命"就是因为工人阶级和广大劳动人民太贫困，社会财富分配与占有太不平等，这是违背社会正义的。现在世界上有些社会主义国家，尽管人们对其政治体制会有这样那样的不同评价，但其政党在实现社会平等上是诚心诚意的，成就是显著的，这是任何人都不能否认的。在各国社会主义运动的实践中，尽管其经济制度模式有不同取舍，有过失误也有过成功，但其初衷、动机和根本宗旨是解放和发展生产力，使广大劳动群众摆脱贫困，以实现全社会的共同富裕，这是毋庸置疑的。笔者所理解的宪政，包括"人民民主、依法治国、人权保障、宪法至上"。

民主、法治、人权是宪政的实体内容，宪法具有至高无上的权威，是宪政的形式要件。这是对"政治文明"最高度、最具体、最鲜明的概括。因为，民主是文明的，专制、独裁、凡事领导者个人说了算是不文明的；法治是文明的，无法可依、有法不依、一切大事都由领导者靠个人的看法与好恶来处理是不文明的；人民有权是文明的，他们的各种权利得不到保

---

① 《马克思恩格斯选集》第 1 卷，人民出版社，1995，第 294 页。
② 中共中央文献研究室编《毛泽东文集》第 4 卷，人民出版社，1996，第 27 页。

障或肆意遭受侵犯是不文明的；宪法作为集中体现人民的利益、意志和治国安邦的总章程具有崇高的权威是文明的，不依法治国和依宪执政，对种种违宪行为熟视无睹是不文明的。

党的十七大报告指出，"人民民主是社会主义的生命"；依法治国已被执政党和国家机构确立为"治国基本方略"；"国家尊重和保障人权"已被庄严地记载在我国的《宪法》中。因此，自由、平等、富裕、宪政，乃是社会主义的本质要求和基本特征。正是出于以上考虑，笔者认为，社会主义者应当是最进步的人道主义者，社会主义者也应当是最彻底的人权主义者。

二 享有充分的人权，是实现为人民服务宗旨的切实保障

"为人民服务"是我们立党立国的根本宗旨。但"人民"是一个抽象的集合名词，中国"人民"包括13亿多个活生生的，各有自己的喜怒哀乐和七情六欲，有自己的各种需求、利益、幸福和追求的老百姓。所有这些，在民主法治社会里，都表现为"人权"，即个人的各种权益。如果我们仅仅强调要为人民服务，而不重视尊重和保障个人的权益即人权，"为人民服务"就只能成为一句空话，甚至有可能将"为人民服务"作为幌子来肆意侵犯具体个人的各种权益。一个例子是现在有些地方搞的"面子工程"。为官一方，在任期间多出政绩是无可厚非的，也是应当的，但是，如果只是为了自己的"乌纱帽"或"钱袋子"而搞一些没有多大必要的、劳民伤财的"面子工程"，就是应当加以反对、防止和纠正的。如某省某县曾发生一万多农民到县委和县委书记家里打砸的事件。事件起因是"集资修公路"，当时农民实在出不起所摊派的钱财。更为典型的例子是十年"文化大革命"。当时很多国家机关、企事业单位都搞所谓"早请示，晚汇报"，即全体员工排队站在毛主席像前举着"红宝书"（"老三篇"）做"请示"或"汇报"。"老三篇"中有一篇就是《为人民服务》，而这十年浩劫却使千千万万的老干部、老专家和广大人民的人权遭受到了肆意践踏，达到了无以复加的地步。为什么会出现这种情况？根本原因，是长期以来我们在观念上、政策上没有处理好国家、集体和个人的关系。其具体表现是长期流行的一句口头禅："大河有水小河满，大河无水小河干。"其实，这是违背自然和社会发展规律的。这句话应当完全倒过来："小河有水大河满，小河无水大河干。"滚滚长江与黄河的水是从哪里来？是来自千万条支流与小河。

而小河的水不是来自大河，而是来自天上落下的雨和地下水。这种错误观念导致了国家、集体与个人利益彼此之间的失衡，并出现某种"国家主义"倾向，即国家的利益高于一切，忽视了个人的价值和利益；国家权力大于一切，轻视了个人的权力与权利；国家的职能包罗一切，以致人们的"吃喝拉撒睡"什么都要管。这种状况的出现有多种原因。一是由于几千年封建专制主义的文化传统。中国古代的民本思想、和谐理念，是其民主性的精华；而重义轻利、重宗族、重整体，轻视个人的价值和利益，则从某种程度上限制了个人对自由和权益的追求。二是中国革命的胜利，是枪杆子里出政权，革命战争环境要求个人利益绝对服从集体利益，权力与权利必须高度集中，要求集中优位于民主、纪律优位于自由，但进入和平建设年代，情况应有很大不同。三是在新中国成立后一度实行的经济、政治、文化体制的权力过度集中，而市场经济的实行和民主法治目标的确立，自然要求国家尊重和保障人权。未来，我们必须世世代代保持"为人民服务"的立党、立国的根本宗旨，但在经济上必须正确与合理地调整好国家、集体与个人利益之间的关系，切实保障公民个人的经济、社会、文化权利。在意识形态上必须正确与合理地处理好群体与个体的关系，切实保障公民个人的人身人格权利，包括生命权、人身安全权、人身自由权、思想自由权、人格尊严权、个人隐私权等，在伦理上必须进一步树立人道、正义、博爱精神，切实保障社会弱势群体包括妇女、儿童、老人、残疾人、少数民族、灾民等的权利，切实保障社会特殊群体，包括服刑人员、战俘、难民等的权利。在政治上必须正确与合理地处理好社会政治稳定同逐步加强对公民个人政治权利与自由的保护的关系，逐步使公民的选举与被选举权、参政议政权、监督权、知情权以及结社、言论、出版自由等权利进一步得到保障。总之，只有切实实现我国《宪法》中已庄严记载的"国家尊重和保障人权"的原则，使13亿中国公民个人和若干社会群体的权利逐步得到切实保障，各阶层人民包括精英阶层和广大劳动群众对执政党和政府"为人民服务"宗旨的认知度才能逐步得到扩大、加强与巩固。

三　充分实现人权，是制定和实施社会主义法律的根本目的

法律有私法公法之分。私法是以权利与义务的形式来调整自然人与自然人之间、法人与法人之间、自然人与法人之间的利益关系。权利是利益的获取，义务则是利益的付出。公法是以职权与职责的形式来调整国家机

关及国家机关工作人员相互之间的关系，以及以权力与权利为形式来调整国家机关和国家机关工作人员同自然人、法人和其他社会组织之间的关系，但是国家机关和工作人员的权力，是公民（即自然人）通过行使权利所赋予的，而权力是手段，权利是目的，国家机关及其工作人员存在的意义和价值就是为公民谋利益，就是为保障与实现全体公民以及社会团体和企事业单位的各种权利服务，否则它就没有存在的意义和价值。在现代民主法治社会里，人们的各种需求与利益，包括物质的、精神的、人身人格的及思想与行为自由等，都可概括为"人权"二字。我们的法律具有社会主义的性质，充分实现人权就更应当是制定和实施法律的根本目的。正如马克思所说："我们的目的是要建立社会主义制度，这种制度将给所有的人提供健康而有益的工作，给所有的人提供充裕的生活和闲暇时间，给所有的人提供真正的充分的自由。"① 列宁也指出："一切'民主制'就在于宣布和实现在资本主义制度下只能实现得很少和附带条件很多的'权利'；不宣布这些权利，不立即为实现这些权利而斗争，不用这种斗争精神教育群众，社会主义是不可能实现的。"②

中国共产党的著名法学家张友渔教授早在抗日战争时期就曾指出："保障人民的权利实为宪法最重要的任务……而宪法便是人民权利保障书。"③ 这同列宁所说"宪法就是一张写着人民权利的纸"④ 一脉相承。现在中国国内有关宪法的各种教科书几乎都采纳了"宪法是人权保障书"这一定义。之所以能够用"保障人权"来定义宪法、宪法的本质属性和根本任务，是基于以下原理。

一是"人民主权"原理。"人民主权"是现代民主的理论基础和根本原则。"主权在民"是"主权在君"的对立物。中外历史上的封建主义信仰与实行的是"君权神授"。近代资产阶级民主革命，依据唯物主义和人本主义原理，推翻了封建专制主义的一套原则，建立起"主权在民"的民主共和国。但是实现"人民是国家的主人"以后，任何国家又都不能由全体人民去直接管理国家，而必须由有选举权的公民行使选举权，产生国家机关，代表人民去管理国家，这就是现代的"代议制"。西方多数国家称其为议会，我们叫"人民代表大会"制度。然而，人民选出的政府有可能权力无

① 《马克思恩格斯全集》第21卷，人民出版社，1965，第570页。
② 《列宁全集》第28卷，人民出版社，1990，第167页。
③ 《宪政论丛》上册，群众出版社，1986，第98页。
④ 《列宁全集》第12卷，人民出版社，1987，第50页。

限和滥用权力，甚至肆意侵犯公民应有的各种权利，这就需要制定一部以前封建专制制度下没有过的根本大法来规制政府的权力，使其不致越权或失职，不致不按程序办事而乱来；同时全面详尽地明确列举公民的种种应有的权利，要求政府不得侵犯并保证其实现。这就是近代以来的宪法。近代宪法的产生是实现人民主权原理与原则的必然的客观要求和产物。宪法不是"阶级斗争"的产物，资产阶级领导人民反封建的斗争，只是出现近代宪法的手段和条件。

二是国家权力与公民权利互相关系原理。此即前面所述，宪法的主要内容是规制国家权力与保障公民权利，而在终极的意义上，国家权力只是手段，保障公民权利才是目的。国家权力存在的意义与价值，是"为人民服务"，即保障公民应有的各项权利即人权。

三是宪政实体内容相互之间关系原理。宪政的科学内涵，包括人民民主、依法治国、人权保障、宪法至上。民主、法治、人权，是现代宪法的三大原则，亦即宪政的实体内容；而宪法具有至高无上的权威，任何政党和国家领导人都要依宪法办事，是宪政的形式要件。胡锦涛同志曾多次强调，依法治国首先要依宪治国，依法执政首先要依宪执政。而"依宪治国"，"依宪执政"，就是"宪政"。就宪法的三大原则——民主、法治、人权的相互关系而言，在终极的意义上，人权是目的，民主和法治则既是目的又是手段。"国家的一切权利属于人民"，"人民应当成为国家的主人"，这是目的。民主既具有这样的伦理性价值，又具有自己的工具性价值，即民主能集中广大人民群众或多数人的智慧、才干和能力，能更好地认识与改造世界，包括更好地保障人权。法治的伦理性价值表现在它是人类社会文明的重要标志。因为，法的出现不是阶级斗争的产物，而是人类社会自始至终存在三大基本矛盾的客观要求。三大基本矛盾，一是社会秩序与个人自由的矛盾；二是人的两大需求即物质的与精神的利益，在人与人之间产生的矛盾冲突；三是任何社会都要有组织，都要有管理者与被管理者，要有权威与服从，两者之间也必然产生矛盾。这三大矛盾在客观上要求有一种共同制定或认可的社会规则去调整，这就是"法"。如果没有法去调整这三大矛盾，社会就会出现只有自由，没有秩序，或相反；就会出现要么无政府主义，要么专制主义；或出现侵犯他人权利。社会就不会有文明。同时，法治是人类社会文明的主要标志，这是由法自身的属性所决定的。法具有一般性，它不是为某些人而是为全体人民所制定，因此要求所有社会成员都要遵守。法具有平等性，如果有人在法律面前享有特权，法就不会有权威，而损坏其应有的属性和功能。法具有公开性，内部规定不是法，用人们无法知道的规矩去处罚人们的行为，是不公平的。法还具有不溯及既往性，即用现今新的规定去处理人们过去的行为，也是不正义的。这些也是决定法之成为公平正义象征的根本原因。其工具性价值则表现在它具有规范、指引、预测、评价、教育、警诫人们行为的社会功能；而通过法律将人应当享有的权利变为具体、明确的法定权利，进而通过法律的权威，能更好地保障人们享有的人权。

四　充分实现人权，是推进科学发展的出发点和最后归宿

科学发展观是实现科学发展的世界观和方法论。发展是科学发展的第一要义。这里所说的"发展"同"发展权"是两个不同而又紧密联系的概念。根据1986年制定的国际人权文书《发展权利宣言》的规定，"发展权"有广义和狭义之分。广义的发展权是指"人人都有参与发展和享有发展成果"的权利。这对任何国家的任何人都适用。狭义的发展权是该宣言的序言第16自然段所说的："确认发展权利是一项不可剥夺的人权，发展机会均等是国家和组成国家的个人的一项特有权利。"它是特指存在于不合理国际经济秩序下的"发展中国家"的人民应当有"发展机会均等的权利"，而前面所说的"发展"是指生产力的提高和社会的全面进步。"发展"的第一要务首先是指应以经济建设为中心，因为人活着，首先要吃饭穿衣，而经济的发展又是社会政治、文化、生态发展的基础；其次，"发展"也要求社会的全面发展。

然而，"发展"从终极意义上讲，它本身不是目的，不是"为发展而发展"，而是为了增进人民的福祉，为了全体人民过上更幸福的生活，即所谓"发展为了人民"。同时，科学发展观又要求"发展依靠人民"，即各方面的发展都要调动广大人民群众的积极性、主动性、创造性，以使物质文明、政治文明、精神文明、社会文明、生态文明建设取得又好又快的发展。这实际上也是一个民主问题，是涉及公民"参与权"的实现问题。此外，"科学发展观"还特别强调，"发展成果由人民共享"。这实际上是一个平等问题，是涉及社会主义的一个本质要求，即实现人民的"共同富裕"。

对此，党的十八大报告做出了十分明确的论述和要求，指出：我们要在2020年实现国内生产总值和城乡居民人均收入比2010年翻一番，全面建成小康社会。它有五个基本指标，第二个指标就是"人民民主不断扩大"，

包括："民主制度更加完善，民主形式更加丰富，人民积极性、主动性、创造性进一步发挥。依法治国基本方略全面落实，法治政府基本建成，司法公信力不断提高，人权得到切实尊重和保障。"为了实现这一目标，"报告"提出了推进政治体制改革的主要措施："必须继续积极稳妥推进政治体制改革，发展更加广泛、更加充分、更加健全的人民民主。必须坚持党的领导、人民当家作主、依法治国有机统一，以保证人民当家作主为根本，以增强党和国家活力、调动人民积极性为目标，扩大社会主义民主，加快建设社会主义法治国家，发展社会主义政治文明。要更加注重改进党的领导方式和执政方式，保证党领导人民有效治理国家；更加注重健全民主制度、丰富民主形式，保证人民依法实行民主选举、民主决策、民主管理、民主监督；更加注重发挥法治在国家治理和社会管理中的重要作用，维护国家法制统一、尊严、权威，保证人民依法享有广泛权利和自由。"这里强调的民主、法治、人权，即具有伦理性价值，即它们是"政治文明"的主要内容，是科学发展的重要目标；民主与法治又具有工具性价值，能保证经济的发展以及社会、文化、生态的发展。所有这些，都同人民享有广泛的人权息息相关。

五　享有充分的人权，是全人类的共同价值追求

人权的普适价值，是由全人类具有共同的人性、共同的道德、共同的利益所决定的。有人说，只有具体的人性，没有抽象的人性，这种观点是不对的。如果人没有共同的人性，就会和动物没有区别，就不会存在"人类"这一伟大的称谓。世界上的万事万物，都是抽象和具体、一般与个别、共性与个性的辩证统一。如果民主、法治、人权、自由、平等、博爱不具有"普适价值"，那么在北京举办的奥运会的口号"同一个世界，同一个梦想"就不可能打动与激励那么多的中国人与世界各国人民的心；而我们常说的"毛泽东思想""邓小平理论"是马克思主义的普遍真理同中国革命的具体实践相结合，那也不对了。我国《宪法》规定，每个公民都应遵守"社会公德"，这同人类具有共同道德准则的理论是完全相通的。全人类具有正义、平等、博爱等道德价值追求，是任何人都应当享有人权的伦理基础。包括《世界人权宣言》、《经济、社会及文化权利国际公约》及《公民权利和政治权利国际公约》在内的"世界人权宪章"以及所有主要国际文书，都一致宣称：人权享有者即人权主体是"人人"，即只要你是人，就应当和可以享有人权。如《世界人权宣言》第 2 条庄严宣告："人人有资格享有本

宣言所载的一切权利和自由，不分种族、肤色、性别、语言、宗教、政治或其他见解、国籍或社会出身、财产、出生或其他身份等任何区别。"这也正是人权的一个"伟大"之处。

21 世纪是一个人权受到空前尊重的世纪。原属于联合国经社理事会管辖的"人权委员会"已升格为"人权理事会"，与"安全理事会"和"经社理事会"并列。安全理事会和经社理事会分别担负解决全人类的和平安全问题和经济社会发展问题，实际上这就是全人类最大的人权问题。我国作为安理会五个常任理事国之一，作为人权理事会的理事国，一贯重视参与国际人权保护，并做出了自己的重大贡献。我国已批准了 25 个国际人权公约，并认真履行自己的义务；我国积极参与了一系列重要国际人权文书的制定，包括第二次世界人权大会制定的《维也纳宣言和行动纲领》和《残疾人权利公约》等。我国也参与了国际对某些严重侵犯人权行为的国家的制裁，如对前南非种族主义政权的制裁。我国的维和部队经常受到国际有关机构的表彰；原中国残联主席邓朴方曾获联合国的"人权奖"，卫生部原部长钱信忠因中国的计划生育成效突出而获国际奖。2012 年 10 月温家宝总理也因执政党和政府实行"三农问题是工作重中之重"，保证了粮食连续九年增长而获国际隆重嘉奖。这一切都说明，保障人权是全人类的共同价值和伟大事业。

The Significance of Human Rights Protection

Li Buyun [*] , *Zhang Qiuhang* [**]

【**Abstract**】 It is stated in the white paper of Human Rights in China (1991) that Human Right is "a great term". This article analyzes the significance of human rights protection from the following five perspectives: human rights protection is a lofty ideal of socialism; human rights protection is the practical guarantee for realizing the objective of "serving the people"; human rights protection is the

*　Director, Research and Education Center for Human Rights, Guangzhou University.

**　Associate Professor, Law School of Hunan University.

fundamental objective of the adoption and implementation of socialist laws; human rights protection is the starting point as well as the ultimate goal of scientific developments; and human rights protection is the common value pursuit of all mankind.

【**Keywords**】Human Rights; Socialism; the People; Scientific Development

The European Convention on Human Rights: Minimum Standards for European Criminal Justice Policies

Merita Huomo-Kettunen [*]

【Abstract】 This article describes how the European Convention on Human Rights affects criminal justice policies and the foundations of criminal law throughout Europe. The article asks whether the Convention regime has a criminal justice policy of its own, and finds that even though the European Court of Human Rights has stated that the Convention does not support any particular type of criminal justice system or policy, the Convention regime affects the foundations of national criminal justice systems greatly, as well as criminal justice cooperation in the European Union framework.

1. Introduction

The Council of Europe is a human rights organization which has 47 member states, including all Member States of the European Union. The most important human rights instrument of the Council of Europe is the European Convention on Human Rights (henceforth the ECHR or the Convention) , which has been ratified by all of the member states of the Council of Europe. The purpose of the Convention is to protect human rights, democracy and the rule of law. The

---

* Merita Huomo-Kettunen, Doctoral Candidate, University of Helsinki.

European Convention on Human Rights consists of several human rights provisions as well as provisions on the establishment of the European Court of Human Rights (henceforth the ECtHR or the Court). The Court has the competence to interpret and apply the Convention and its protocols in inter-state cases, in which a contracting party claims that another contracting party to the Convention has breached the Convention rights, and in cases brought to it by individuals claiming to be victims of a violation by one of the state parties.

The European Convention on Human Rights regime (henceforth the ECHR regime) affects criminal justice systems. The Convention system influences the criminal procedure, investigation measures, criminalization and the use of sanctions. The ECHR regime affects criminal law in two ways. Firstly, penal provisions must fulfil the requirements stemming from the Convention. It is of primary importance that the national legislators exercise abstract *ex ante* human rights control in the legislative process. Secondly, the interpretation of penal provisions needs to follow the Convention and the case law of the European Court of Human Rights. National courts in the member states of the Council of Europe ought to evaluate criminal provisions in the light of the requirements stemming from the Convention. It is not sufficient that human rights issues are taken into account during the legislative processes, since the protection of human rights cannot be limited simply to the legislative process. The dynamic and evolutive human rights protection requires that the Convention is seen and interpreted as a living instrument. This means that the protection of human rights is also a task of the authorities applying the law case by case. Dynamic and evolutive interpretation is a task of both the national courts and the European courts (the ECtHR and the Court of Justice of European Union).

Negotiations concerning the accession of the European Union (henceforth the EU) to the European Convention on Human Rights are in progress. According to the EU's basic Treaties,① the EU shall accede to the ECHR. This means that the two European legal orders, the European Union and the Council of Europe, will be connected and in interaction with each other more than ever. The two courts,

---

①　Treaty on European Union and Treaty on the Functioning of the European Union, 2012/C 326, 26 October 2012.

the European Court of Human Rights and the EU's European Court of Justice, have already made references in their judgments to each other's case law. The EU also takes the requirements stemming from the ECHR into account; for example, in its own Charter of fundamental rights,① in which it is explicitly mentioned that in so far as the Charter contains rights which correspond to rights guaranteed by the ECHR, the meaning and scope of those rights shall be the same as those laid down by the said Convention (article 52. 3 of the Charter) and that the EU Charter shall not be interpreted as restricting or adversely affecting human rights as recognized in the Convention (article 53). Once the EU has acceded to the Convention, the Convention and the ECtHR case law will become binding upon the EU and its institutions.②

2. Layers of Criminal Justice Policy in the European Legal Space

The primary EU law, the basic Treaties of the EU, the Charter and the Member States' accession treaties, and the ECHR regime are often seen to be constitutional by nature. The various European legal orders, the EU, the ECHR regime, and the national legal orders, can be described as having a pluralistic interrelationship. Heterarchical constitutional structures pertaining between the national and European legal orders enable flexible but close cooperation between the orders.③ The pluralistic perspective is that in a single social realm (here in Europe) more than one legal order can be identified,④ but it does not seek to suggest hierarchical structures between them.⑤ As more than one constitutional actor can be identified in Europe, different

---

①   Charter of Fundamental Rights of the European Union, 2012/C 326, 26 October 2012.

②   On the current interrelationship of EU law and the ECHR regime and on the relationship after the EU's accession to the ECHR, see Merita Huomo-Kettunen, 'Heterarchical Constitutional Structures in the European Legal Space' (2013) Vol. 6 Issue 1 *European Journal of Legal Studies*, pp. 59 – 62. Available on the internet http://www. ejls. eu/12/Full. pdf.

③   Huomo-Kettunen, 'Heterarchical Constitutional Structures in the European Legal Space'.

④   John Griffiths, 'What is Legal Pluralism?' (1986) 24 *J L Pluralism & Unofficial L* 1, 12; Gunther Teubner, 'The Two Faces of Janus: Rethinking Legal Pluralism' (1991 – 1992) 13 *Cardozo L Rev* 1443, 1457, 1448.

⑤   Paul Schiff Berman, 'Global Legal Pluralism' (2006 – 2007) 80 *Southern California L Rev* 1155, 1166.

influences from these European legal orders affect criminal justice policy at the domestic level.

The European Union law and the ECHR regime affect national criminal justice policy in their own unique ways. Whereas the ECHR regime emphasizes the effective realization of human rights, the EU law strives towards effective implementation of Union law and policies. EU criminal law itself is suggested to derive from the so-called spill-over of power. ① The need for EU competence to tackle crime stems from the disappearance of internal borders in the EU and from the unwanted cross-border criminal activities deriving from it. ② The EU criminal law framework takes human rights protection into account, but its primary aim seems to be the effective realization of other EU policies, such as the functioning of the internal market. We see that there is some tension between the aims of criminal justice policy that these two European legal orders propose.

Here, it is useful to make a distinction between a decisional top-down perspective and an action-oriented bottom-up perspective on policy, because policy can also be seen as an unintended outcome of action by actors who might not have intended to influence policy-making. ③ Thus even though an actor might claim it does not have policy-making aims, its actions might actually create policy. This leads to the first question addressed in this article.

3. Does the ECHR Regime Have a Criminal Justice Policy of Its Own?

Even though it is obvious that the ECHR regime affects national criminal justice systems greatly both substantive criminal law and criminal procedural law – the ECtHR has found that the Convention does not support any particular kind of criminal justice system. What matters is that the national criminal justice systems do

---

① On the concept of spill-over, see Leon N. Lindberg, *The political Dynamics of European Economic Integration* (Stanford University Press, Stanford, 1963), pp. 10 – 11.

② Maria Fletcher and Robin Lööf with Bill Gilmore, *EU Criminal Law and Justice* (Edward Elgar Publishing, 2008), pp. 21 – 23.

③ Michael Hill, *The Public Policy Process* (Pearson, Harlow, Sixth Edition, 2013), p. 17.

not contravene the principles set out in the ECHR. ① The Court has also stated that the member states of the Convention have the right to determine their own criminal policy. ② In other words, the Court finds that the contracting parties of the Convention have a wide margin of appreciation in choosing the best criminal justice policy option for their own country. The only restriction on this is that the system chosen does not infringe the Convention rights and principles.

The Court does not have competence to review the criminal justice systems or criminal policy choices of the Member States in the abstract. It can only review the conformity between elements of criminal justice systems and the Convention in relation to a specific case and a question to hand. Still, it is possible that some sort of basic choices concerning the criminal justice system made at national level could infringe the Convention rights.

The Court can make rulings in which it refers to a more *general incompatibility* with the Convention or to *systemic or structural* problems. If there is a violation that had "originated in a systemic problem affecting a large number of people *general measures at national level could be called for in the execution* of its judgments". This is called a "pilot-judgment procedure" and is designed to help the contracting parties to fulfil their obligations and to resolve problems at the domestic level. ③ The pilot judgment procedure is a technique that is used to tackle structural problems revealed through repetitive cases that stem from common dysfunction at domestic level. The Court can guide the governments to resolve the structural or systemic problem. The member states can decide how they will fulfil their obligations deriving from pilot judgments. The Council of Ministers supervises the execution of the judgments. ④ The examination of the other related cases can be adjourned for a set period of time on the condition that the respondent state fulfils its obligations

---

① Case of *Kafkaris v. Cyprus* App no 21906/04 (ECHR, 12 February 2008), para. 99; case of *Archour v. France* App no 67335/01 (ECHR 29 March 2006), para. 51.

② Case of *Kafkaris v. Cyprus* App no 21906/04 (ECHR, 12 February 2008), paras. 126, 151.

③ Case of *Sejdovic v. Italy* App no 56581/00 (ECHR, 1 March 2006), para. 120; Case of *Broniowski v. Poland* App no 31443/96 (ECHR 22 June 2004), paras. 188 – 194; Case of *Broniowski v. Poland* App no 31443/96 (ECHR, 28 September 2005), paras. 34 – 35.

④ European Court of Human Rights, *Factsheet-Pilot Judgments* (July 2013), http://www. echr. coe. int/Documents/FS_ Pilot_ judgments_ ENG. pdf (accessed 5 September 2013).

based on the pilot judgment. ①

The ECHR regime has an impact on the choices of the contracting parties in regard to their criminal justice systems even if the judgments do not require systemic changes or if the judgment is technically directed to another state. One could say therefore that the ECHR regime affects the criminal justice policy of the contracting parties indirectly and implicitly. The case law of the ECtHR inevitably and unavoidably shapes the criminal policy of the contracting parties and brings their criminal justice systems closer to each other at some level.

One reason why the Convention regime does not support any specific type of criminal policy or criminal justice system stems from the Convention's founding values. These are respect for human rights, the rule of law, and pluralistic democracy. The pluralistic view of democracy requires a respect for different kinds of choices made in the member states on their social and criminal policy. Even though pluralism entails an acceptance of different views, it also requires that the states respect the basic values of the Convention in their criminal justice systems. This means, for example, that discriminatory criminal legislation is prohibited.

Even though the ECHR regime and the ECtHR do not support any particular type of criminal justice policy or criminal justice system, the Convention system and the Court's case law actually constitute some sort of scattered combination of choices concerning the foundations of criminal law throughout Europe. These choices include broader principles enshrined in the Convention and its protocols, such as Protocol No. 13 of the Convention on the abolition of death penalty, and in the Council of Europe criminal justice conventions, such as the Criminal Law Convention on Corruption, the Convention on Cybercrime, the European Convention on Extradition etc. , and more specific positions stated by the Court in its case law. The next section illustrates these choice sat an abstract level.

4. The dual role of human rights

Human rights have a dual role – a defensive role and an offensive role in the

---

① European Court of Human Rights, *The Pilot Judgment Procedure* – Information note issued by the Registrar, http://www. echr. coe. int/Documents/Pilot_judgment_procedure_ENG. pdf (accessed 5 September 2013).

framework of criminal law. The role which protects individuals from the use of criminal law is the defensive role, which is especially articulated in the procedural safeguards, such as the principle of legality. The offensive role of human rights means that the human rights protection can sometimes prove to be the driving force for the use of criminal law measures. Sometimes, in extreme situations, only the use of criminal law is seen to be a satisfactory means to protect the fundamental values of the society − fundamental and human rights. ① Human rights affect criminal policy in two ways that direct the policy choices in two different directions.

The human rights-oriented view on criminal policy is often described as defensive criminal policy. According to Nils Jareborg, the defensive criminal law policy supports a restrained approach to the use of criminal law and emphasizes the need to protect individuals against the state's use of power and excessive repression in particular. Legal certainty and procedural safeguards are essential in fulfilling this task. Because defensive criminal law aims to calmconflicts, the respect for the values of legal certainty and justice is paramount for it; the defensive approach is built upon the *Rechtssta at* ideology. ② Several elements of the ECHR regime express the defensive role of human rights in criminal policy.

Article 6 and the requirements of due process need to be taken into account during the criminal process. The prohibition of torture is a founding principle that covers situations starting from investigation and stretching to enforcement of the sentence. During imprisonment and detention, the treatment of prisoners and prison conditions should be taken into account to the extent the Convention requires. The abolition of the death penalty is also a criminal justice policy choice that is widely supported in Europe. ③ Of the 47 member states of the Council of Europe and of the contracting parties to the Convention but one have ratified Protocol No. 6 concerning the abolition of the death penalty and abolished the use

---

① Françoise Tulkens, 'The Paradoxical Relationship between Criminal Law and Human Rights' (2011) 9 *Journal of International Criminal Justice.*

② Nils Jareborg, *Scraps of Penal Theory* (Iustus Förlag, Uppsala 2002), pp. 92, 94 – 95.

③ Els Dumortier, Serge Gutwirth, Sonja Snacken and paul De Hert, 'The Rise of the Penal State: What Can Human Rights Do About It?' in Sonja Snacken and Els Dumortier (eds.) *Resisting Punitiveness in Europe? Welfare, human rights and democracy* (Routledge 2012), pp. 114 – 117.

of the death penalty in peace time. A great majority of the member states, 43 in all, have ratified Protocol No. 13 concerning the abolition of the death penalty in all circumstances, including in time of war. The Court has found that due to these Protocol ratifications the second sentence of Article 2 ECHR, which contains a limitation clause on the right to life and allows the use of the death penalty, has been amended to prohibit the death penalty in all circumstances. In addition to this, the death penalty can be considered inhuman and degrading and thus contrary to Article 3 of the Convention. [1]

The ECHR regime also limits substantive criminal law by limiting the state actors from criminalizing certain types of conduct or using certain types of sanctions and sanctioning practices in relation to certain types of offence. [2] In the case of Goktepe v. Belgium, the applicant claimed that his right to a fair criminal trial had been violated since he was found guilty not only of theft, but also of assault and homicide in which he claimed he had no part and which constituted aggravating circumstances for his sentencing. The sentencing was based on the theory of shared criminal liability (*emprunt matériel criminalité*) which derives from the idea that aggravating circumstances would automatically apply to all participants in the offence even though one of the offenders had not participated in the behaviour that is considered as the aggravating circumstance. The Court found that this was not compatible with the adversarial principle which is the heart of the fair trial guaranteed in Article 6 ECHR, since the national court did not have to consider the arguments concerning essential points that affected the sentencing. [3]

In relation to freedom of expression and defamation cases, the Court has restricted the use of imprisonment as the form of sanctioning only to cases of hate speech, incitement to violence and promotion of negationism. [4] The use of

---

[1] Case of *Al-Saadoon and Mufdhi v. the United Kingdom* App no 61498/08 (ECtHR, 2 March 2010).

[2] Els Dumortier, Serge Gutwirth, Sonja Snacken and Ppaul De Hert, 'The Rise of the Penal State: What Can Human Rights Do About It?' In Sonja Snacken and Els Dumortier (eds.) *Resisting Punitiveness in Europe? Welfare, human rights and democracy* (Routledge 2012), pp. 117 – 120.

[3] Affaire *Goktepe c. Belgique* Requete no 50372/99 (ECtHR, 2 juin 2005), paras. 26 and 29.

[4] See for example the case of *Cumpănă and Mazăre v. Romania* App no 33348/96 (ECtHR 17 December 2004), paras. 37, 48, 50, 112, 115 – 119; the case of *Mariapori v. Finland* App no 37751/07 (ECtHR, 6 July2010), para. 67.

sanctions in relation to offences concerning freedom of expression is limited because heavy sanctions, as well as heavy damages, might negatively influence the media's willingness to fulfil its functions, especially its role in the democratic processes in society (the so-called chilling effect). ①

The Convention system also sets limits on criminalizing certain types of conduct. For example, the Court has established that criminal law should not in principle be applied in the case of consensual sexual practices which fall under the protection of Article 8 ECHR on the right to private and family life. ② More specifically, the Court has found that criminalization of homosexual acts infringes the right to private life as guaranteed in Article 8. According to the Court, penal provisions criminalizing homosexual acts between consenting adults capable of valid consent cannot be justified asnecessary in a democratic society or as being proportionate. ③

Human rights not only set limitations on the national legislators and authorities applying the law, but also require active realization from national authorities. In other words, states also have positive obligations to protect human rights in addition to their negative obligations to restrict themselves from infringing human rights. Criminal law measures can be expected to be used in order to protect individuals from others infringing their rights. Human rights can thus legitimize the use of criminal law and its punitive logic. ④ Many penal provisions protect human and fundamental rights and the protected interests may derive from these

---

① For example, Parliamentary Assembly Recommendation 1506 (2001) Freedom of expression and information in the media in Europe, paras. 1, 5, 12. See also Parliamentary Assembly Resolution 1535 (2007) Threats to the lives and freedom of expression of journalists, paras. 3, 6. See also Parliamentary Assembly Resolution 1577 (2007) Towards decriminalization of defamation, paras. 1, 4 – 7, 11 – 14, 17. On the chilling effect, for example Case of *Cumpănă and Mazăre v. Romania* App no 33348/96 (ECtHR 17 December 2004), para. 119.

② Case of *K. A. and A. D. v. Belgium* App nos 42758/98 and 455558/99 (ECtHR, 17 February 2005).

③ Case of *Dudgeon v. the United Kingdom* App no 7525/76 (ECtHR, 22 October 1981), para. 60; the case of *Norris v. Ireland* App no 10581/83 (ECtHR, 26 October 1988), paras. 38, 46; Case of *A. D. T. v. the United Kingdom* App no 35765/97 (ECtHR, 31 July 2000), para. 38.

④ Françoise Tulkens, 'Human Rights as the Good and the Bad Conscience of Criminal Law' in Sonja Snacken and Els Dumortier (eds.) *Resisting Punitiveness in Europe? Welfare, human rights and democracy* (Routledge 2012), p. 156.

rights. Decriminalization of conduct such as rape or murder would clearly then violate fundamental and human rights.

The ECtHR has sometimes required the use of criminal law measures in its case law. In the case of Öneryildiz v. Turkey, the Court found that life-endangering offences should not go unpunished and that judicial systems must ensure that criminal penalties are applied when lives are lost as a result of dangerous activity and when the use of the criminal penalties is justified because of the states' positive obligation to protect lives as enshrined in Article 2 ECHR. ① The Court has also stated that as required by Article 2, effective judicial systems "may, and in under some circumstances must, include recourse to the criminal law". As a limitation to this main rule, when "the infringement to the right to life or physical integrity is not caused intentionally, the positive obligation imposed by Article 2 to set up an effective judicial system does not necessarily require the provision of a criminal-law remedy in every case". ② These cases aptly demonstrate that the ECHR regime requires that criminal law measures are adopted in relation to serious human rights violations. This also means that the ECHR regime requires that the member states of the Council of Europe have effective criminal justice systems. A more specific norm can also be deduced: intentional infringements of the right to life or personal integrity ought to be criminalized in the Council of Europe member states.

The Court has emphasised the deterrent effect of the criminal justice system as a means to protect human rights. According to the Court,

> The national courts should not under any circumstances be prepared to allow life-endangering offences to go unpunished. *This is essential for maintaining public confidence and ensuring adherence to the rule of law and for preventing any appearance of tolerance of or collusion in unlawful acts.* — The Court's task therefore consists in reviewing whether and to what extent the courts, in reaching their conclusion, may be deemed to have submitted the case to the careful scrutiny required by Article 2 of the Convention, so that *the deterrent effect of the judicial system in*

---

① Case of *Öneryildiz v. Turkey* App no 48939/99 (ECtHR, 30 November 2004), paras. 94 – 96.

② Case of *Vo v. France* App no 53924/00 (ECtHR, 8 July 2004), para. 90; the case of *Calvelli and Ciglio v. Italy* App no 32967/96 (ECtHR, 17 January 2002), para. 51.

place and the significance of *the role it is required to play in preventing violations of the right to life* are not undermined. [1] (emphasis added)

Effective criminal law measures must also be used, at least in certain situations, where Convention right is seriously violated. In the case of M. C. v. Bulgaria, the ECtHR found that " effective protection against rape and sexual abuse requires measures of a criminal-law nature". [2] This judgment is unique in the sense that the Court implicitly outlined how the penal provision on rape ought to be formulated in the member states since the ECtHR concluded that criminal prosecution and imputation ought to be possible in matters of sexual violence, including situations which are based on the lack of consent. In other words, rape could not be defined in penal provisions based on the existence of physical resistance. [3] This judgment is a good example in illustrating that the ECtHR case law may and does contain explicit instructions for the member states to use effective criminal law measures to tackle a particular type of crime.

5. Conclusions

The ECHR regime brings national criminal justice systems closer to each other. In a way it sets minimum standards for the national criminal justice policy. Even though the ECHR regime does not support any particular type of criminal policy or criminal justice system, the Convention system and the ECtHR case law affect the national criminal justice systems significantly in an indirect way. Since the Court has required that the member states provide criminal law protection for certain values, however, one specific criminal justice system, abolition ism, is excluded from the choices. The ECHR regime not only supports defensive criminal policy but also an offensive approach in what amounts to protecting human rights and the fundamental values of the Convention.

---

① Case of *Öneryildiz v. Turkey* App no 48939/99 (ECtHR, 30 November 2004), para. 96.

② Case of M. C. v. *Bulgaria* App no 39272/98 (ECtHR, 4 December 2003), para. 186.

③ See for example Els Dumortier, Serge Gutwirth, Sonja Snacken and paul De Hert, ' The Rise of the Penal State: What Can Human Rights Do About It?' in Sonja Snacken and Els Dumortier (eds.) *Resisting Punitiveness in Europe? Welfare, human rights and democracy* (Routledge 2012), p. 126.

欧洲人权公约：欧洲刑事司法
政策的最低标准

梅丽塔·霍莫–凯图宁[*]

【摘要】 本文介绍了《欧洲人权公约》影响整个欧洲刑事司法政策和刑法基础的方式，就《欧洲人权公约》制度是否具有其自己的刑事政策这一问题进行了考察，并得出结论：虽然欧洲人权法院声称《公约》不支持任何特定的刑事司法制度或政策，《公约》制度对欧洲各国国内刑事司法制度以及欧盟框架内的刑事司法合作都产生了很大的影响。

＊ 梅丽塔·霍莫–凯图宁，赫尔辛基大学博士研究生。

人权视野下的环境保护

柳华文[*]

【摘要】 虽然国际人权法中缺少对于发展权的正式的条约规定，但是联合国的相关文件有重要的规定和阐发。中国政府重视发展权，并以以人为本的科学发展观为指导，尊重和促进人权。在中国政府通过的两个《国家人权行动计划》中，环境保护都是重要内容，既有措施和任务，又有具体、可衡量的指标；既回应社会和民众热切关注的问题，又强调付诸实施和监督。环境权和发展权一样，在国际法上也是重要的软法主题。完善包括环境保护在内的可持续发展方面的全球治理，应当遵循整体应对的原则和共同但有区别的责任原则。中国与欧盟的联系日益紧密，双方在环境保护等领域的国际协调与合作具有广阔前景和重要意义。

【关键词】 人权　发展权　环境保护　软法　国家人权行动计划

环境保护是当下国内外共同关注的一个焦点，是保障人权特别是发展权的重要内容。

笔者拟概括中国政府关于发展权的认识和理解，阐述中国从政策到实践层面所倡导的以人为本的科学发展观的内涵，以及在环境保护和发展权领域的新发展，并对在国际社会开展的可持续发展领域的全球治理提出看法。

一　发展权概述

发展权概念受到重视的背景是，自 20 世纪 60 年代以来，广大发展中国

---

* 柳华文，中国社会科学院国际法研究所所长助理、研究员，中国社会科学院人权研究中心副主任、秘书长。

家着手打破旧的国际政治经济秩序，争取政治、经济、社会和文化的全面
发展。1970 年，联合国人权委员会委员卡巴·穆巴耶在一篇题为"作为一
项人权的发展权"的演讲中，明确提出了"发展权"的概念。

1979 年，第三十四届联合国大会在第 34/46 号决议中指出，发展权是
一项人权，平等发展的机会是各个国家的天赋权利，也是个人的天赋权利。
1986 年，联合国大会第 41/128 号决议通过了《发展权利宣言》，对发展权
的主体、内涵、地位、保护方式和实现途径等基本问题做了全面的阐释。
它在第 3 条第 2 款中还特别提到，对于该宣言要按照有关国家间友好关系与
合作的国际法原则来理解。与此密切相关的是 1970 年 10 月联合国大会通过
的《联合国关于国家间友好关系与合作的决议》。1993 年世界人权大会通过
的《维也纳宣言和行动纲领》重申发展权是一项不可剥夺的人权。①

《发展权利宣言》的第 1 条将发展权定义为：发展权是一项不可剥夺的
人权，由于这种权利，每个人和所有各国人民均有权参与、促进并享受经
济、社会、文化和政治发展，在这种发展中，所有人权和基本自由都能获
得充分实现。

可见，发展权包括对个人权利和集体权利的认可。关于发展权的目标，
学者们认为，它的首要目标必须是根除贫困和采用能够有效地维持后世发
展的方式满足所有人的基本需要。②

关于中国对于发展权的理解，可以从中国人权研究会 2005 年所做的人
权知识普及资料中得到典型的反映，它对发展权的特点做了如下的概括：③

第一，发展权是一项个人人权，同时也是一项国家或民族的集体人权。
这两个方面是相辅相成、不可分割的。在一国范围内，发展权首先是一项
个人人权。个人只有作为发展权的主体，才能充分地、自由地参与政治、
经济、社会和文化的发展，并公平享有发展所带来的利益。但是，个人和
集体是相互依赖的，没有国家或民族的发展，也就很难谈到个人的发展。
因而，发展权也是一项不可否认的集体人权。

第二，个人发展权，其诉求主要指向国家，集体发展权则主要针对整
个国际社会。在一国范围内，实现个人的发展权主要依靠国家。在国际范
围内，实现国家或民族的发展权则主要依靠国际社会的共同努力。各国均

---

① 《维也纳宣言和行动纲领》第 10、11 段。
② 国际人权法教程项目组编写《国际人权法教程》，中国政法大学出版社，2002，第 456 页。
③ 中国人权研究会：《什么是发展权》，《人民日报》2005 年 5 月 20 日，第 9 版。

有促进本国发展的责任。为保障发展权，必须建立国际政治经济新秩序，消除妨碍发展中国家发展的各种障碍。

第三，根据《发展权利宣言》的定义，发展权是实现各项人权的必要条件。

据此，实现发展权的条件包括两方面：

首先，对国家而言，一是创造有利于发展的稳定的政治和社会环境；二是每个国家对本国的自然资源和财富享有永久主权，并制定适合本国国情的发展政策；三是每个人和全民族积极、自由和有意义地参与发展进程、决策和管理，并公平分享由此带来的利益。

其次，对国际社会而言，一是坚持各国主权平等、相互依存、互利与友好合作的原则；二是建立公正合理的国际政治经济新秩序，使发展中国家能够民主、平等、自由地参与国际事务，真正享有均等的发展机会；三是消除发展的各种国际性障碍。发达国家应采取行动，为发展中国家提供全面发展的便利条件。

和平、发展和人权是并列的联合国改革和发展的三大支柱。发展与人权的关系密切相关。发展权可以说是发展主题与人权主题的交集，也是社会问题和人类挑战的核心。

但是，与其重要性相比，上述这些与发展权直接相关的文件所规定的条款本身并不具有严格的法律约束力。学者们认为，它们具有特殊的国际法上的法律意义，至少指明了国际法发展的方向。① 笔者宁愿将它们称为"软法"文件，虽然它们不像条约和国际习惯那样具有法律约束力，但是在实践中发挥着重要作用，是承载国际社会的法律期待，解释和实施既有国际法规则，引导新国际法规则生成的重要文件。

在笔者看来，软法盛行，可以说是当代国际法的一个特点，其原因是：首先，国家之间达成共识，完成烦琐的国际立法和国内批约等法律规则形成程序时间长、工作多，并不容易，甚至在环境法等一些领域现在看还不太可能，所以只能软法先行或者软法单行。其次，不论政府间国际组织还是非政府组织，它们都希望在创设和实施国际法方面发挥自己的主动性、建设性和创造性，单单依靠、依附于主权国家及其政府显然不能达到这样

---

① 关于国际组织决议在国际法法律渊源上的意义以及诸如《维也纳宣言和行动纲领》一类的"准条约"文件的效力和使用，参见白桂梅《国际法》，北京大学出版社，2010，第52-60页。

的目的。最后，已形成的国际法本身具有抽象性、稳定性、长期性以及不容易修正的特点，而软法可以满足具体化、灵活性、阶段性和适应性的特点，所以越来越广泛地受到重视并得到使用。

可见，尽管联合国与发展权直接相关的这些文件对发展权非常重视，其具体内容也体现在《公民权利和政治权利国际公约》和《经济、社会和文化权利国际公约》、《消除针对妇女歧视公约》、《儿童权利公约》、《残疾人权利公约》等一系列国际公约当中，但是对于发展权的全面、系统和专门的条约规定和立法还存在欠缺。这也许是将来国际人权法发展的一个新的方向。

在国内层面来看，发展权同样具有纲领性和原则性的特点。发展权的具体内容以及实现方式，随着经济与社会的发展，具有与时俱进的特点，也会面临许多新的机遇和挑战。

在笔者看来，实现发展权，即使不是一个新课题，也有许多新的因素、新的发展，值得我们给予重视。其中颇为核心的一点就是，发展必须是环境友好型、资源节约型的发展，发展权与环境权密切联系在一起。

二　中国：科学发展观和《国家人权行动计划》

在中国的传统价值观中，蕴含着可持续发展的精神。早在两千多年前，中国古代哲学家就提出"天人合一""道法自然"的思想，倡导人与自然和谐相处，这是可持续发展追求的最高境界。

中国政府把节约资源、保护环境确立为基本国策，把可持续发展战略上升为国家战略。进入新世纪，我们将科学发展观确立为经济社会发展的重要指导方针，环境保护是其中的重要内容。

在世界各国经历国际金融危机广泛而深刻的影响的大背景下，虽然面临诸多挑战和困难，中国经济发展速度之快仍然令人瞩目。不过，中国的发展是全面的发展，它超出了经济发展的范畴。在这方面，科学发展观的概念是我们这个发展中大国治国理政的一个核心理念。

什么是科学发展？笔者认为，它的内涵非常丰富。简单地说，其基本要求是坚持以人为本、实现全面协调可持续发展。具体来看，在经济领域，它意味着不是个别区域的局部发展，不是简单的数量的增长，不是资源高消耗、破坏环境的发展，而是区域平衡、结构优化、质量提高、资源利用效率提升、环境友好的发展；在社会领域，它的含义同样丰富，包括减少区域、阶层之间的贫富差距，促进分配公平，实现人的有尊严的发展等，这些正是人权原则和规则的重要内容。可见，人权保障和环境保护同是科学发展的重要内容，而且存在着密切联系，是新时期和未来中国实现个人和集体的发展权的重要内容。

中国历来重视环境保护，但是经济快速发展所面临的环境保护的压力是很大的，在个案中产生环境破坏的教训也是深刻的。因此，用科学发展观来指导经济发展特别是环境保护工作，特别是基于科学发展观来思考发展权的实现在中国具有特别的意义。

2004 年我国修订《宪法》，规定"国家尊重和保障人权"，为人权事业的进一步发展奠定了坚实的根本法基础。其实在新中国成立以来制定的宪法及历次修订当中，均载有人权内容，只是没有使用"人权"这一词语。所以，"人权入宪"指的是人权概念第一次写入《宪法》，特别是它表明了国家对于人权的一般性态度。①

近年来，我国政府倡导的以人为本的科学发展观又为该计划的制定提供了重要的政策依据。保护人权的内容已经写进了《中华人民共和国国民经济和社会发展第十一个五年规划纲要》和《中华人民共和国国民经济和社会发展第十二个五年规划纲要》，也写进了执政党中国共产党的章程和党的第十五次、第十六次、第十七次和第十八次全国代表大会的报告当中。

1993 年维也纳世界人权大会通过了《维也纳宣言和行动纲领》，建议每个会员国考虑拟订国家人权行动计划，明确该国为促进和保护人权所应采取的步骤。根据联合国人权事务高级专员办公室的统计，包括中国在内，世界上只有 29 个国家开展了制定国家人权行动计划的实践，其中只有 8 个国家制定两次以上的国家人权行动计划。

2009 年 4 月 13 日，经国务院授权，国务院新闻办公室发布《国家人权行动计划（2009 – 2010 年）》。这是我国第一次制定以人权为主题的国家规划，是一个历史性的突破，堪称我国人权事业发展过程中的一个里程碑。笔者认为，该计划是人权主流化在政府层面的重要标志。它意味着政府的各个部门的工作都要接受人权视角的审查，从人权保障的角度进行必要的整合和协调。换句话说，政府部门的各项工作不仅仅是与人权有关，而且是要自觉地纳入人权的视角，自觉地为促进人权目标而努力。

----

① 徐显明：《宪法修正条款修正了什么》，载中国人权研究会编《"人权入宪"与人权法制保障》，团结出版社，2006，第 47 页。

在首个《国家人权行动计划》当中，就有一部分专门讲环境保护的内容。在规定具体的举措和任务指标之前，该计划一般性地指出："坚持人与自然和谐发展的方针，合理开发利用自然资源，积极参与国际合作，创造有益于人类生存和持续发展的环境，努力建设资源节约型、环境友好型社会，保障公众环境权益。"计划详细列举了各项要求，内容包括：控制二氧化硫和化学需氧量排放、确保核与辐射环境安全，改善地表水水质和空气质量，减少环境相关性疾病发生，严厉查处环境违法行为和案件，发展可再生能源，减缓温室气体排放，提高森林覆盖率，治理退化、沙化和碱化草地，促进水土流失综合治理等多项措施和内容。

2011 年 7 月，国务院新闻办公室发布了《国家人权行动计划（2009 - 2010 年）评估报告》，其中指出：

"环境质量进一步改善，……截至 2010 年底，单位国内生产总值能耗、全国化学需氧量（COD）和二氧化硫的排放量均实现或超过《行动计划》的目标。重点城市空气质量优良天数比例平均为 91.5%，95.6% 的重点城市空气质量优良天数超过 292 天。两年来，各地共出动执法人员 508 万余人次，检查企业 204 万余家次。开展各类重金属排放企业和造纸企业的专项检查。全面排查沿江沿河化工石化企业，特别是距离饮用水水源地较近的企业存在的环境污染隐患。截至 2010 年底，全国已有 80% 的地市级环保部门和 70% 的县级环保部门开通了'12369'环保举报热线，30% 的县级以上环保部门成立了环境投诉受理中心。2009 年，国家修订了可再生能源法。到 2010 年，新增水电装机容量、风电装机容量、太阳能光伏电池产量、太阳能热水器集热面积均居世界第一。"

"实施《全国林地保护利用规划纲要》。目前，中国森林面积达 29.32 亿亩，森林覆盖率从 20 世纪 90 年代初期的 13.92% 提高到 20.36%；人工林保存面积达 9.26 亿亩，居世界首位。截至 2010 年底，在森林覆盖率、改良草地、治理退化、沙化和碱化草地、灌溉水有效利用、典型森林生态系统和国家重点野生动植物保护、自然湿地保护以及水土流失综合治理等方面均完成或超额完成《行动计划》的目标。"

2012 年 6 月 12 日经国务院授权国务院新闻办公室新发布的《国家人权行动计划（2012 - 2015 年）》。它在导言中指出："近年来，中国政府坚持以人为本，妥善应对国际金融危机的巨大冲击和重大自然灾害的严峻挑战，积极解决发展中存在的矛盾和问题，坚定不移地推进人权事业，人权状况持续改善。"特别是"坚持将保障人权与推动科学发展、促进社会和谐结合起来"。制定和实施该行动计划的指导思想就包括："深入贯彻落实科学发展观","将人权事业与经济建设、政治建设、文化建设、社会建设以及生态文明建设结合起来,顺应各族人民过上更好生活的新期待,继续把保障人民的生存权、发展权放在首位,着力保障和改善民生,着力解决人民群众最关心、最直接、最现实的权利和利益问题,切实保障公民的经济、政治、社会和文化权利,促进社会更加公正、和谐,努力使每一个社会成员生活得更有尊严、更加幸福"。

第二个国家人权行动计划明确规定了"环境权利"的内容。它要求"加强环境保护,着力解决重金属、饮用水源、大气、土壤、海洋污染等关系民生的突出环境问题,保障环境权利"。其具体规定如下:

"——修改环境保护法。保护和改善生活环境和生态环境,防治环境污染和其他公害。

"——有效防治重金属污染。完善重金属污染防治体系、事故应急体系和环境与健康风险评估体系。

"——加大水污染防治力度。改善跨省界断面、污染严重的城市水体和支流水环境质量,减轻重点湖泊富营养化,进一步提高水功能区达标率,逐步恢复部分水域水生态。加大生态良好湖泊保护力度。持续削减主要水污染物排放总量。建立地下水环境监管体系,基本掌握地下水污染状况,初步控制地下水污染源,启动地下水污染修复试点。

"——改善大气质量。到 2015 年,化学需氧量、二氧化硫、氨氮、氮氧化物排放总量分别控制在 2347.6 万吨、2086.4 万吨、238.0 万吨、2046.2 万吨。重点区域可吸入颗粒物年平均浓度逐年降低。到 2015 年将细颗粒物（PM2.5）项目监测覆盖地级以上城市。

"——推进生态建设。到 2015 年,陆地自然保护区总面积占陆地国土面积的比例保持在 15% 左右,使 90% 的国家重点保护物种和典型生态系统类型得到保护。全国森林覆盖率达到 21.66%,新增沙化土地治理面积达到 1000 万公顷以上。新增水土流失综合治理面积 20 万平方公里。城市建成区绿化覆盖率达到 39%,村屯建成区绿化覆盖率达到 25%。

"——加强海洋生态保护,推进海洋保护区建设,强化对海洋工程、海洋倾废等的环境监管。

"——加强放射性污染防治。推进早期核设施退役和放射性污染治理。开展民用辐射照射装置退役和废源回收工作。加快放射性废物贮存、处理和处置能力建设,基本消除历史遗留的中低放废液的安全风险。加快铀矿、伴生放射性矿污染治理，关停不符合安全要求的铀矿冶设施，建立铀矿冶退役治理工程长期监护机制。

"——严格监管危险化学品。依法淘汰高毒、难降解、高环境危害的化学品，严格限制生产和使用高环境风险化学品。

"——完善环境监察体制机制。建立跨行政区环境执法合作机制和部门联动执法机制，健全重大环境事件和污染事故责任追究制度。"

其中，关于PM2.5的有关规定是一个备受关注的亮点，是对社会焦点问题的一个积极回应。

第二个《国家人权行动计划》的另一个特点是，强化计划的监督和实施。任何工作规划，重在执行。为了增强计划的可操作性和实效性，特别新增"实施和监督"一章，其中强调中央和国家机关各有关部门、各级地方政府应高度重视，结合各部门工作职责和各地区特点，采取切实有效的措施完成《国家人权行动计划》确定的各项目标任务；专门成立的国家人权行动计划联席会议机制还将开展阶段性调研、检查和终期评估，并且公布评估报告。

为了促进计划的实施，明确要求将《国家人权行动计划》纳入人权教育和培训的内容，并鼓励新闻媒体发挥实施、宣传和监督作用。

特别值得一提的是，计划提出，要尊重和发挥人民群众的主动性、积极性和创造性，创新社会管理机制，发挥社会组织在人权保障中的建设性作用。可见，该计划也与全社会密切联系。在政府的领导和主导下，全社会的共同参与和贡献将是《国家人权行动计划》有效落实的基本保障。

而对于《国家人权行动计划》以及相关文件的法律地位和性质特别是它们与法律实施关系的认识，引起了关于"软法之治"作为依法治国和保障人权新趋势的讨论。[①] 笔者认为，在中国，《国家人权行动计划》对环境保护的重视值得肯定。计划的落实必将推动中国人权事业的进步，特别是发展权的实现。

三　国际社会：公平责任和共促发展

在国际层面，1972年6月，联合国在瑞典斯德哥尔摩召开了首次人类环境会议，发表了具有划时代意义的历史性文献《人类环境宣言》，形成了人类环境行动计划，提出了一个响遍世界的口号："只有一个地球！"它还

---

① 参见柳华文《软法与人权和社会建设》，《人权》2012年第2期。

表达了明确的有关环境的个人人权："人人拥有自由、平等和为保障健康生活足够的环境条件的基本权利，并且承担一项为现在和未来的人们保护和改进环境的神圣义务。"

1992 年召开的环境与发展里约热内卢会议通过的《里约热内卢宣言》并没有重申或者扩展这一概念。它只是规定："人类在关注可持续发展方面处于中心的地位。他们有权获得与自然和谐统一的健康和富足的生活。"

1994 年联合国人权委员会特别报告员凡特曼·左拉·森蒂尼在她起草的最后报告中包括一个《人权和环境原则草案》，其中包括这样的语句："所有人拥有享受一个安全、健康的生态环境的权利。"但是，该草案并未获得有法律约束力的后续文件的跟进。

因此，环境权只是在"软法"层面获得明确规定，在《经济、社会和文化权利国际公约》等人权条约中有相关条款，但是尚未在人权条约中获得明确确认。笔者认为，环境保护是与人权特别是发展权密切相关的重要内容，是可持续发展的必然要求，因此，环境保护的规则可以置于发展权之下予以规定和讨论。虽然国际环境法与国际人权法是国际法中两个相对独立的法律部门，但是它们之间存在着密切的联系。一方面，环境保护不是单纯人权视角的问题，它涉及更为广泛的经济、政治和社会议题和领域；另一方面，环境保护直接牵涉可持续发展，影响人权特别是发展权的实现和享有。①

几十年来，中国参加了可持续发展理念形成和发展中具有里程碑意义的历次国际大会，对于环境保护的国际事业持非常积极和建设性的态度。

目前可持续发展的全球共识已经达成，但共同行动还有欠缺，还不平衡，加强国际合作、完善全球治理势在必行。完善可持续发展全球治理，应当遵循两个基本原则。

首先是整体应对的原则。必须统筹兼顾经济增长、社会进步和环境保护这三大支柱，而不是仅仅局限于环境治理。

其次是共同但有区别的责任原则。该原则是 1992 年环境与发展大会的重要成果之一，也是国际发展合作的指导原则。促进发展中国家获得公平的发展权，承担与自身能力相适应的责任。要尊重各国可持续发展自主权，增加发展中国家在可持续发展全球治理机制中的代表性和话语权，而不是

---

① 关于以人权为出发点探讨环境问题的有关争议，参见 Anderson, Michael R., "Human Rights Approaches to Environmental Protection: An Overview", in Boyle, Alan E., Anderson, Michael R. (eds.), *Human Rights Approaches to Environmental Protection* (Clarendon Press, 1966), pp. 1-23。

构筑绿色壁垒。发达国家应切实履行官方发展援助承诺，提供充足的资金和先进的技术，增强发展中国家的环境保护和可持续发展能力。

2012年9月20日，时任国务院总理温家宝在比利时布鲁塞尔同欧洲理事会主席范龙佩、欧盟委员会主席巴罗佐共同出席第十五次中欧领导人会晤，并发表了联合新闻公报。①

公报中说，双方领导人"就重大全球和国际问题交换看法，并一致认为，中欧互动与相互依存日益紧密。中欧关系已超越双边范畴，具有全球影响。中欧在21世纪的国际舞台上具有重要影响，都是推动世界和平、繁荣与稳定的关键力量，都强调多边主义和联合国在国际事务中的核心作用。双方将进一步共同努力应对国际金融和经济危机、可持续发展、环境保护、气候变化、粮食和水安全、能源安全以及核安全等全球性挑战"。

在"全球问题"部分，有大量篇幅涉及环境保护问题：

"四十三、强调'里约 + 20'会议成果具有重要意义，有必要尽快落实包括建立可持续发展目标政府间进程等决定。双方重申实行绿色经济政策的重要性。

"四十四、强调水资源、粮食安全与营养安全的重要性，这是双方环境和农业方面的共同利益所在，也是重大全球性问题。双方注意到，粮食安全与水资源安全密切相关。领导人承诺继续通过多双边努力解决粮食安全、营养安全及水资源安全关切。双方欢迎中欧水资源交流平台的建立，这将成为未来中欧开展综合水资源管理合作的良好机制。

"四十五、欢迎中欧环境政策对话以及林业执法与施政对话取得的进步，并同意加强双边合作，包括水污染防治、废弃物管理政策及重金属污染防治合作。

"四十六、强调有必要开展国际合作应对气候变化问题，并重申致力于继续合作推动《联合国气候变化框架公约》、《京都议定书》及相关缔约方大会的决定得到全面、有效和可持续的执行，包括去年德班会议达成的所有决定，并期待确保多哈会议取得成功。

"四十七、强调应对国际民用航空排放问题的重要性，同意共同推动在《联合国气候变化框架公约》和国际民航组织等多边机制下采取行动。

"四十八、同意在中欧气候变化伙伴关系框架下，就应对气候变化和推进低碳发展进一步深化政策对话和务实合作。双方同意在此领域达成的具

---

① 引自外交部网站，http://www.gov.cn/jrzg/2012 - 09/21/content_2229701.htm，最后访问日期：2012年10月10日。

体合作倡议基础上加强碳排放交易体系的务实合作。

"四十九、认识到北极地区的日益重要性，尤其是在气候变化、科学研究、环境保护、可持续发展、海洋运输等相关方面，同意就北极事务交换意见。"

可以看出，中欧双方在政府层面，已经达成了大量关于环境保护和科学发展的共识，并有广泛的合作空间。而中欧合作也是中国广泛开展国际双边或者多边合作的一个实例。

的确，环境保护不仅是一国国内的大事，也是整个国际社会的焦点。共识也好，合作也好，离不开对问题的客观和正确的认识。在这方面，历史地看待发达国家、发展中国家和欠发达国家在发展阶段上的差异和历史上遭受殖民主义压迫和剥削的事实以及发达国家在消耗能源和资源以及对环境造成的压力以及破坏，公平对待发展中国家和欠发达国家，倡导共同而有区别的责任，加强环保领域的国际协调与合作是非常重要的，也是国际环境保护取得成效的关键。

中国是一个人口大国，一个发展中的新兴国家。我们的经济规模巨大，但是人均国民生产总值不高，人均消耗资源和能源的量远低于其他国家，而且因为我们被称为"世界工厂"，处于国际市场分工中最苦最累、最消耗资源和能源的生产环节，在为世界经济发展和各国人民日常生活做出贡献的同时，承担了大量的环境保护压力和资源与能源压力。

而不平等的国际经济秩序，在某种程度上固化了国家间在经济链上的分工环节，在定价、贸易和金融规则及其实践方面，发展中国家常常处于劣势。在国际环境立法当中，共同而有区别的责任原则正是体现对历史和现实的真切关照的产物。

我们追求平等和公平，可是这个世界仍然存在许多不平等和不公平，令人遗憾的事情时常发生。近年来中国与其他国家之间的稀土之争即是一例。多年来，中国以世界23%的稀土资源储量承担了世界90%以上的市场供应。稀土属于不可再生资源，中国长期低价出口稀土，而提高定价就招致其他国家的不满，它们通过多种方式加以阻挠和施加压力，美、日、欧等许多稀土进口国声称中国政府制定管理政策属于出口限制行为，违反了世界贸易组织规则。① 但是就是这些进口国，许多国家自己国内有丰厚的稀土储藏却并不开发，只是希望进口来自中国的稀土。稀土的不当和无序开采和生产严重破坏

---

① 有关反驳意见，可参见刘敬东《中国管理稀土资源并不违反 WTO 规则》，引自中国法学网，http://www.iolaw.org.cn/showArticle.asp? id=2862，最后访问日期：2012 年 10 月 10 日。

矿区环境，有损当地的环境质量和民众的身体健康，也对中国的自然资源造成了浪费和破坏，中国政府有权利依法控制稀土的开采、生产和出口。这也是环境保护和促进可持续发展、保障中国人人权的要求。

可以看出，国际层面的环境事业需要政治、经济、贸易、科技等各个方面的善意合作和努力，而且其最终目标也不仅仅是保护和改善环境本身，更涉及人权特别是发展权的享有和实现。

总之，我们希望中国能与世界各国及其人民一道，既加强国内环境保护和人权保障领域的交流与合作，又为促进国际政治、经济新秩序的建立，完善以可持续发展为目标的全球治理，促进国际环境保护和人权事业的发展共同合作，做出应有的贡献。

Environmental Protection from the
Human Rights Perspective

Liu Huawen [*]

【 Abstract 】 Although there is no formal treaty provision on the right to development in international human rights law, the relevant UN instruments contain important provisions and elaborations on this right. The Chinese government, taking people-oriented scientific outlook of development as its guidance, attaches great important to the right to development, and respects and promotes human rights. Environmental protection is an important content of the two national human rights action plans adopted by the Chinese government, which contain not only relevant measures and tasks, but also concrete measurable indices, and not only responses to issues of social and public concerns, but also emphasis on implementation and supervision. Like the right to development, the right to environment is also an important soft law issue under international law. The principle of " global response " and the principle of " common but differentiated

* Professor and Assistant Director, Institute of International Law, Chinese Academy of Social Sciences; Deputy Director and Secretary-General, Center for Human Rights Studies.

responsibilities" should be adhered to in improving the global governance relating to sustainable development, including environmental protection. China and EU are becoming more connected to each other than ever before and the coordination and cooperation between them in the field of environmental protection has broad prospective and great significance.

【Keywords】Human Rights; Right to Development; Environmental Protection; Soft Law; National Human Rights Action Plan

中国儿童妇女权利的家庭法保障

——以国际人权公约为视角

薛宁兰[*]

【摘要】家庭是人们生息繁衍、感情交流的重要场所，也是构成社会的基本单元和细胞。中国家庭法对儿童、妇女权利的保障体现在权利的享有和实现两方面。以中国加入的联合国《消除对妇女一切形式歧视公约》和《儿童权利公约》为标准，中国儿童、妇女普遍享有平等的家庭权利，但在儿童姓氏权、知晓父母权、免受家庭暴力权、离婚妇女财产权实现方面还存有障碍，需以国际公约确立的儿童最佳利益原则、实质平等理念，检审现行法律、法规和司法解释，推动制定家庭暴力专门法并修改现行相关规定。

【关键词】儿童家庭权　妇女家庭权　儿童公约　妇女公约　家庭法

一　家庭法的特性与地位

当今社会，所有人，无论老幼、男女、已婚未婚、贫穷富有，都生活在家庭之中。家庭是人们生息繁衍、感情交流的重要场所，也是构成社会的基本单元和细胞。家庭对于儿童和老人尤其重要，他们因为年幼或年老，需要得到父母、成年子女的关爱与供养；家庭又是儿童生存和走向社会的第一学校。中国实行计划生育政策已有 30 多年，在城市，核心家庭普遍存

---

* 薛宁兰，中国社会科学院法学研究所研究员。

在①，亲子关系因此成为与夫妻关系并重的一类家庭关系。由此不难理解，家庭法在一国法律体系中的基础地位和对于人类生存发展的重要性。

按照中国学者的通常解释，所谓"家庭法"（中国大陆地区习惯称"婚姻家庭法"）是调整一定范围的亲属之间的人身关系和财产关系的法律规范的总称。中华人民共和国在成立的 60 年间，先后颁行了两部调整婚姻家庭关系的基本法：1950 年婚姻法和 1980 年婚姻法。从婚姻法在法律体系中的地位看，新中国成立头 30 年，婚姻家庭法是独立的法律部门。这是新中国成立之初，政府宣布彻底废除"旧的法统"，全面照搬苏联法律部门划分的结果。1978 年中国实行"改革开放"政策之后，重提民法典制定，今天对于婚姻家庭法在法律体系中的定位已达成共识：它是民法典的一部分。60 年来，中国婚姻家庭法经历了从独立法律部门到回归民法部门的历史性变迁。

在一国法律体系中，家庭法无论是独立法律部门还是隶属民法，其特性是不会发生改变的。中国学者通常认为，习俗性（民族性）和伦理性是家庭法的两个基本特性。所谓习俗性，是指家庭法与某一民族世代延续的婚姻家庭习俗有密切关系，是具有强烈民族传统特色的法律，是固有法而不是继受法。因此，婚姻家庭法中"与'国情'不相符合的规定，鲜能发挥其效用"。② 所谓伦理性，是指由婚姻、血缘和法律拟制连接而成的诸如夫妻、父母子女、兄弟姊妹、祖孙等亲属关系，以人类社会客观存在的人伦秩序为基础，具有浓厚的人伦感情色彩。即便是亲属间的财产关系，其性质和社会功能与其他财产关系也有很大不同。亲属之间的财产关系是实现家庭经济职能和亲属共同生活的需要，它与亲属人身关系同样具有伦理性。而其他民事财产关系如物权关系、债权关系，是民事主体为满足商品交换的需求而产生的，具有等价有偿的特点。

因此，回归民法之后的中国家庭法在调整对象、立法目标、价值取向等方面应区别于民法财产法，是民法体系中相对独立的部分③，需要一些特

---

① 中国第六次人口普查显示，截至 2010 年 11 月 1 日零时，全国有 401517330 个家庭，平均每个家庭户的人口为 3.10 人，比 2000 年第五次全国人口普查的 3.44 人减少 0.34 人。其中，0－14 岁人口约 222459737 人，占总人口的 16.60%。女性人口为 652872280 人，占 48.73%。总人口性别比（以女性为 100，男性对女性的比例）由 2000 年第五次全国人口普查的 106.74 下降为 105.20。国家统计局：《2010 年第六次全国人口普查主要数据公报（第 1 号）》，资料来源：http://baike.baidu.com/view/5643934.htm。

② 史尚宽：《亲属法论》，中国政法大学出版社，2000，第 1 页。

③ 杨大文：《婚姻家庭立法的思考》，《中国妇女报》2010 年 4 月 30 日。

殊的、不同于民法财产法的调整方法和规则。①

整体而言，儿童、妇女、老人因其年龄、性别，更因父权制的历史文化传统，在家庭中处于相对的弱势地位。家庭法以维护家庭成员的平等地位和基本权益，实现家庭社会功能为目标；在价值取向上，它除了以平等、自由为追求外，还具有保护弱者功能，通过给予家庭中的弱者以特别保护，实现家庭成员间实质的公平与正义。② 故此，中国婚姻法除"实行婚姻自由、一夫一妻、男女平等的婚姻制度"外，还将"保护妇女、儿童和老人的合法权益"作为一项基本原则（《婚姻法》第 2 条）。

基于本文题目，以下就中国儿童、妇女家庭权利的法律确认与实现，以及未来法律改革展开论述。

二　儿童、妇女的家庭权

家庭权，是基于婚姻关系、血缘关系、收养关系或其他亲缘关系，在亲属之间依法产生的权利。儿童、妇女的家庭权，是她/他们基于婚姻家庭成员特定身份关系依法产生的，以身份权为基础的权利总称。③ 从民法角度看，该项权利可细分为人身权和财产权两部分。

（一）国际人权公约确认的儿童、妇女的家庭权

中国是联合国《消除对妇女一切形式歧视公约》（1979）、《儿童权利公约》（1989）的缔约国。1998 年中国签署了联合国《公民权利和政治权利国际公约》（1966），对该公约的批准已经进入议程。

上述国际法律文件，对儿童、妇女的家庭权利有明确规定。例如，《消除对妇女一切形式歧视公约》第 16 条要求，"缔约各国应采取一切适当措施，消除在有关婚姻和家庭关系的一切事务上对妇女的歧视，并特别应保证她们在男女平等的基础上"，享有相同的结婚和离婚的自由（即婚姻自主权）、生育权、抚养教育子女的监护权、夫妻之间相同的个人权利（包括选择姓氏、专业和职业的权利），以及夫妻双方在财产的所有、取得、经营、管理、享有、处置方面同等的权利。《儿童权利公约》序言强调家庭对于儿童的重要性，认为家庭是"作为家庭所有成员、特别是儿童的成长和幸福的自然环境"，"为了充分而和谐地发展其个性，应让儿童在家庭环境里，

---

① 薛宁兰：《婚姻家庭法需要不同于财产法的调整规则》，《中国妇女报》2010 年 5 月 13 日。

② 马忆南：《婚姻家庭法的弱者保护功能》，《法商研究》1999 年第 4 期，第 19 页。

③ 参见班文战、夏吟兰主编《人权知识　妇女权利读本》，湖南大学出版社，2012，第 152 页。

在幸福、亲爱和谅解的气氛中成长"。根据该公约，儿童享有的家庭权利主要有：自出生起获得姓名的权利、尽可能知晓父母并受父母照料的权利（第7条）；必要时不与父母分离的权利（第9条）；获得相当生活水准的权利（第27条）；受监护人保护的权利（第18条）；免受家庭暴力的权利（第19条）；等等。

联合国一系列法律文件为缔约国在本国法律中确认儿童、妇女家庭权利内容确立了国际标准。中国法律对儿童、妇女家庭权利的确认主要体现在《宪法》、《民法通则》、《婚姻法》、《未成年人保护法》和《妇女权益保障法》等法律中。目前，中国已经形成以《宪法》和《民法通则》为依据，以《婚姻法》为主干，由《收养法》、《继承法》、《妇女权益保障法》、《未成年人保护法》、《老年人权益保障法》和《婚姻登记条例》等相配套，以其他部门法相关规定和最高人民法院司法解释为补充的婚姻家庭法律规范体系。

（二）中国儿童的家庭权利

依照国际标准和中国法律，家庭法中的儿童是指不满18周岁的未成年人。① 中国《婚姻法》《未成年人保护法》对儿童权利的保护主要体现在亲子关系中。《未成年人保护法》突出了对儿童家庭保护的重要地位，其第二章专门规定父母或其他监护人对未成年人的保护义务。上述法律赋予儿童的家庭权主要有以下几种。

1. 平等/不受歧视权

中国法律规定，非婚生子女、婚生子女、养子女、继子女法律地位平等，他们享有同等权利，任何人不得加以危害和歧视；不得歧视女性未成年人或者有残疾的未成年人。

2. 姓名权

《儿童权利公约》第7条规定："儿童出生后应立即登记，并有自出生起获得姓名的权利，……"中国法律确认儿童享有上述基本权利。《婚姻法》对于儿童出生后的姓氏选择做出授权性规定："子女可以随父姓，可以随母姓。"（第22条）

3. 受父母抚养教育的权利

未成年子女享有接受父母抚养教育的权利；父母或者其他监护人应当创造良好、和睦的家庭环境，依法履行对未成年人的监护职责和抚养义务。

---

① 参见联合国《儿童权利公约》第1条、中国《未成年人保护法》第2条。

4. 免遭家庭暴力权

法律规定，禁止溺婴、弃婴和其他残害婴儿的行为；禁止对未成年人实施家庭暴力，禁止虐待、遗弃未成年人。

5. 对父母遗产的继承权

法律规定，子女是父母遗产的第一顺序的法定继承人；父母立遗嘱时，应为无劳动能力和无生活来源的未成年子女保留必要份额。

（三）中国妇女的家庭权利

依照中国《宪法》、《民法通则》、《婚姻法》和《妇女权益保障法》，妇女的家庭权利主要有以下几种。

1. 婚姻自由权

婚姻自由包括结婚自由和离婚自由。妇女享有选择配偶和自由缔结婚姻的权利。中国《婚姻法》将婚姻自由作为一项基本原则，是对达到成婚年龄的男女基本人权的保障。为保障妇女婚姻自由权，针对现实生活中干涉婚姻自由的主要表现形式，法律规定："公民享有婚姻自主权，禁止买卖、包办婚姻和其他干涉婚姻自由的行为。"（《民法通则》第103条）"禁止包办、买卖婚姻和其他干涉婚姻自由的行为。禁止借婚姻索取财物。"（《婚姻法》第3条）

为保障妇女婚姻自由权的实现，中国法律确立了若干特别保护措施，规定："女方在怀孕期间、分娩后一年内或中止妊娠后六个月内，男方不得提出离婚。女方提出离婚的，或人民法院认为确有必要受理男方离婚请求的，不在此限。"① 2001年修改后的《婚姻法》新增离婚家务劳动补偿制度和离婚损害赔偿制度，完善了离婚救济制度，以消除妇女因离婚后生活无着落而不愿离婚的顾虑。为保证男女平等享有婚姻自由权，中国《刑法》还规定了暴力干涉婚姻自由罪（第257条）。

2. 生育权

生育权是妇女享有的生育自由权和生殖健康权。《妇女权益保障法》第51条指出："妇女有按照国家有关规定生育子女的权利，也有不生育的自由。"《人口与计划生育法》进一步明确了生育问题上权利与义务的一致性，第17条指出："公民有生育的权利，也有依法实行计划生育的义务，夫妻双方在实行计划生育中负有共同的责任。"

---

① 参见中国《婚姻法》第34条、《妇女权益保障法》第45条。

2011 年实施的《最高人民法院关于适用〈婚姻法〉若干问题的解释（三）》（以下简称《婚姻法司法解释（三）》）第一次明确了夫妻生育权冲突的解决方式。《婚姻法司法解释（三）》第 9 条规定："夫以妻擅自中止妊娠侵犯其生育权为由请求损害赔偿的，人民法院不予支持；夫妻双方因是否生育发生纠纷，致使感情确已破裂，一方请求离婚的，人民法院经调解无效，应依照婚姻法第三十二条第三款第（五）项的规定处理。"这表明：妻方以自己的意愿中止妊娠的行为是合法行为，不构成对丈夫生育权的侵犯；夫妻双方因是否生育发生纠纷，致使夫妻感情确已破裂，可以通过离婚程序解除婚姻关系。再者，丈夫虽可因妻子单方中止妊娠为由起诉离婚，但要遵守《妇女权益保障法》和《婚姻法》关于女方"中止妊娠后六个月内，男方不得提出离婚"的规定。这也是法律对女性的特殊保护。

此外，中国妇女享有的家庭权利还包括：对未成年子女的监护权、免受家庭暴力权、对夫妻共同财产的所有权、夫妻相互扶养权、遗产继承权等。

三　儿童、妇女家庭权的实现

中国已经进入经济社会快速发展的时期。社会学调查表明[①]，频繁的人口流动、急剧的城镇化，以及人们婚姻家庭观念的变化，使中国婚姻家庭经历着全球化和市场化的洗礼，正步入现代化的过程。当前，儿童、妇女家庭权利实现中存在的问题突出表现在以下四方面。

（一）儿童姓氏权

中国法律允许"子女可以随父姓，可以随母姓"，然而，中国千百年来的文化传统却是要子女出生后随父姓。

司法实践中，儿童姓氏权出现的主要问题是父母离婚后，直接抚养子女一方变更子女姓氏所产生的纠纷。对此，中国最高人民法院 1993 年发布的《关于人民法院审理离婚案件处理子女抚养问题的若干具体意见》第 19 条规定："父母不得因子女变更姓氏而拒付子女抚育费。父或母一方擅自将子女姓氏改为继父或继母姓氏而引起纠纷的，应责令恢复原姓氏。"这是否符合联合国《儿童权利公约》确立的未成年子女最大利益原则，是否关照

---

① 中国社会科学院五城市家庭调查课题组：《五城市家庭结构与家庭关系调查报告》（李银河执笔），资料来源：www. sociology. cass. cn/shxw/shgz/shgz，2011 年 1 月 7 日。

到子女本人的意愿，愈来愈受到学者和法官的质疑，出现了法官审理此类案件时有的依照这一规定，判令被告恢复子女原来姓氏，有的则从子女利益出发做出相反判决。（案情从略）①

从这些判例可见，中国司法对子女姓氏权的保护理念在不断进步，但如何实现儿童利益最大化还面临挑战。这种挑战既来自司法者对儿童保护的认识水平，也与立法和司法解释中对该项原则贯彻和体现的程度有关。

（二）知晓父母权

联合国《儿童权利公约》为保障儿童身份的确定和健康成长，第7条指出儿童有尽可能知道谁是其父母并受其父母照料的权利。可见，子女享有获知自己血统来源的权利，这是一项受宪法保护的基本人格权。为保障儿童能够行使这一权利，各国家庭法大都设立了子女亲生的推定、否认与认领制度，简称"亲子关系确认制度"。②

中国现行《婚姻法》中还没有这一制度。近些年，随着人口流动的频繁、离婚率的上升，以及人们婚姻家庭观念的变化，司法实务中有关亲子关系否认之诉和子女认领之诉日渐增多。为确立解决这些关涉儿童基本权益纠纷的判案标准，2011年《婚姻法司法解释（三）》专条（第2条）对此做出解释，将夫妻，即父母，作为有权提起否认之诉的权利人。父母作为亲子关系的一方当事人当然享有该权利，然而，将子女排除在外，却有不当，也不代表世界立法趋势。子女是亲子关系的一方当事人，亲子关系的否认之诉直接关涉其利益。如果否认之诉成立，将由此改变该子女的亲属关系和生活环境，这对于儿童的影响尤其重大。随着亲子关系立法从"父母本位"向"子女本位"的转变，近年来各国及地区相继修改民法典，将否认权人范围由父母扩大到子女。例如，中国台湾地区2007年修改民法典第1063条，将否认权人的范围从夫妻之一方扩大到子女，规定"子女在未成年时知悉的，可在成年后二年内提起"。其中，两年是否认权的有效期间。

作为联合国《儿童权利公约》的缔约国，儿童最大利益原则已为我国《未成年人保护法》《中国儿童发展纲要（2011－2020年）》所肯定，上述司法解释在子女亲生否认之诉的否认权人中将子女排除在外，是对子女法

---

① 相关案例参见中国法院网，hppt://www.chinacourt.org.cn/html/article/200709/19/265509.shtml；《母亲再婚后，儿子改姓继父姓氏》，《新京报》2009年3月5日。

② 薛宁兰、解燕芳：《亲子关系确认制度的反思与重构——基于婚姻法司法解释（三）的讨论》，《中华女子学院学报》2011年第2期。

律主体地位的忽视，与《儿童权利公约》的精神不符合。

（三）免受家庭暴力权

家庭暴力是对儿童、妇女基本人权和尊严的侵害。《儿童权利公约》第19条确认，针对儿童的家庭暴力，是指儿童在受父母、法定监护人或其他任何负责照管儿童的人的照料时，受到的"任何形式的身心摧残、伤害或凌辱，忽视或照料不周，虐待或剥削，包括性侵犯"。

由于受时代的局限，《消除对妇女一切形式歧视公约》并没有明确涉及对妇女的暴力问题。消除对妇女歧视委员会1989年发布的"第12号一般建议"要求缔约各国关注本国的对妇女暴力问题。1992年，委员会再次就"对妇女的暴力行为"发布更加综合全面的"第19号一般建议"。建议明确了对妇女的"基于性别的暴力是严重阻碍妇女与男子平等享受权利和自由的一种歧视形式"。其中，"家庭暴力是对妇女的最有害的暴力形式之一。它在所有的社会都普遍存在。在家庭关系中，各个年龄的子女都会遭受各种各样的暴力，包括殴打、强奸、其他形式的性攻击、精神方面的暴力以及由于传统观念而长期存在的其他形式的暴力。因缺乏经济独立，许多妇女被迫处在暴力关系之中。男子不承担其家庭责任的行为，也是一种形式的暴力和胁迫。这些形式的暴力置妇女的健康于危险之中，并损及她们平等地参与家庭生活及公共生活的能力"。

中国法律明确禁止家庭暴力，对家庭中的弱势群体——妇女、儿童和老人给予必要法律救济，始于2001年修改后的《婚姻法》。2005年修订的《妇女权益保障法》规定禁止对妇女实施家庭暴力，确立多机构合作预防和制止家庭暴力的干预模式；2006年修订的《未成年人保护法》增加"禁止对未成年人实施家庭暴力"的原则规定；2012年修订后的《老年人权益保障法》也增加规定"禁止对老年人实施家庭暴力"。这些规定宣誓性强、操作性弱。为此，相关学术研究一直致力于推动国家立法机关制定防治家庭暴力的专门法律，妇女NGO组织也坚持不懈地推动反家庭暴力的国家立法。中华全国妇女联合会连续四年在中国全国人大和政协会议期间提交议案和提案，推动将反家庭暴力专项立法纳入国家立法计划。目前，家庭暴力专项立法已列入2012年中国全国人大立法规划。①

---

① 夏吟兰：《制定家庭暴力防治法　促进社会和谐》，《妇女研究论丛》2012年第3期，第28页。

各种调查数据表明，妇女、儿童和老人是家庭暴力的主要受害人。他们基于性别、年龄，以及社会历史文化传统等原因，在家庭中是易受到暴力侵害的劣势一方。[①] 因此，在人权保障理念下，制定中的中国家庭暴力防治法应当具有儿童视角和性别视角。

家庭暴力立法的儿童视角体现在许多方面。首先，需将儿童作为具有独立人格的权利个体，确立对未成年受害人予以优先和特殊保护的原则，以实现反家庭暴力的儿童利益最大化。其次，在家庭暴力的定义中增加列举对儿童家庭暴力的特有形式，例如，父母及其他法定监护人对儿童的体罚、其他残忍的或有辱人格的惩罚；监护人等其他近亲属对儿童的性侵害与忽视；等等。因为，基于社会观念和历史文化背景，这些对儿童的家庭暴力常常被成人社会忽略或合理化。因此，在界定家庭暴力时，应当将在中国社会一定程度存在的上述对儿童家庭暴力的形式进行列举。再次，反对家庭暴力应当"预防优先"。在有关家庭教育的倡导性条款中，可规定鼓励父母采取积极的、非暴力的、参与性的抚育子女方式，并且通过父母培训等方式，宣传非暴力的价值观。这种积极的、预防性措施较之暴力发生后起诉施暴父母或其他监护人，会更有利于子女最大利益的实现。最后，规定有效的对未成年受害人救助与服务措施，如规定强制报告制度、设立紧急救助和庇护场所、开展多专业的社会服务，帮助受害儿童康复，设立专项救助基金，等等。

家庭暴力立法的性别视角也体现在许多方面：立法目的应当突出对受害人权益的保护，而不是泛泛而言"保障家庭成员合法权益"。在界定家庭暴力时，应突破现有司法解释的局限，将家庭暴力的侵害客体，扩大到受害人的身体、性、精神等方面的人身权利，以便在列举其形式时不只限于身体暴力，还包括精神和性的侵害；在行为的程度上，只要对受害人造成损害，都应构成家庭暴力，而不以"一定伤害后果"为要件。再者，应加强刑事法律规范在惩治和预防亲密或可信赖关系中针对妇女暴力的作用。例如，为减少妇女因长期受虐而伤害或杀害施暴丈夫或伴侣的恶性事件发生，在刑事责任中可专条规定："被认定为存在受虐妇女综合征的家庭暴力

[①] 具体数据参见 2011 年《第三期中国妇女社会地位调查主要数据报告》，http://www.wsic. ac.cn/academicnews/78621.htm；国务院妇女儿童工作委员会、国家统计局社会和科技统计司、联合国儿童基金会：《中国儿童发展指标图集 2010》，第 120 - 123 页；张雪梅：《未成年人遭受家庭暴力案件调查分析与研究报告》，http://www.chinachild.org/zhi/1qglx/show. asp? id = 2421。

受害人，故意杀害、伤害施暴人构成犯罪的，应当免除或者减轻处罚。"①

（四）离婚妇女财产权

离婚妇女财产权是婚姻财产权的有机组成部分，它以离婚时依法分割夫妻共有财产为核心。中国实行婚后所得共同共有的法定夫妻财产制。这一财产制的基本含义是：婚姻关系存续期间夫妻双方或一方所得的财产，除法律另有规定或夫妻另有约定外，均为夫妻共同所有。它要求夫妻双方在婚姻关系存续期间，对共同财产平等地享有占有、使用、受益和处分的权利（第17条）。中国《婚姻法》对夫妻离婚时共有财产的分割确定了基本原则，即"离婚时，夫妻的共同财产由双方协议处理；协议不成时，由人民法院根据财产的具体情况，照顾子女和女方权益的原则判决"（第39条）。

然而，《婚姻法司法解释（三）》第7条、第10条有关夫妻婚后所得房产归属的认定，不以财产取得（指所有权）的时间点为准，而以夫妻及其他利益相关人出资的多少，依照民法财产法规则认定房屋权属。这样的规则对婚姻家庭关系的特殊性，对夫妻财产关系与一般民事财产关系不同特点的重视和区分不够。这种侧重保护夫妻一方个人所有权的价值取向，使得法定夫妻财产制下双方共有财产的空间受到较大挤压。在婚后所得共同制下，夫妻共有财产的法定空间过于狭小，并不利于婚姻家庭社会功能的发挥。因此，司法解释对《婚姻法》条文中未具体列举为夫妻双方共有或一方所有的财产，应根据夫妻共同生活的需要，从维护婚姻家庭的稳定，发挥家庭养老育幼社会功能的角度出发，做出偏向于夫妻共有的认定。

四　未来法律改革之面向

（一）儿童主体资格的确认与儿童利益最大化

近期，中国儿童权利保护出现新趋势。2009年《国家人权行动计划（2009 - 2010年）》明确提出："根据儿童最大利益原则，努力保障儿童的生存、发展和参与的权利。"2011年7月30日国务院颁布的《中国儿童发展纲要（2011 - 2020年）》，将儿童优先原则与儿童最大利益原则并列作为儿童保护工作的两项基本原则：在制定法律法规、政策规划和配置公共资源等方面优先考虑儿童的利益和需求；从儿童身心发展特点和利益出发处

---

① 参见中国法学会家庭暴力网络2010年《中华人民共和国家庭暴力防治法（项目建议稿）》第108条，载夏吟兰主编《家庭暴力防治法制度性建构研究》，中国社会科学出版社，2011，第31页。

理与儿童相关的具体事务，保障儿童利益最大化。

在中国《婚姻法》中，"保护儿童合法权益"是与保护妇女、老人合法权益相并列的一项原则。现行《婚姻法》的有些规定体现了子女最大利益原则的精神，有些规定却将未成年子女的利益与母亲利益或父母利益并列同等保护，甚至个别司法解释条文以父母利益或愿望作为确立离婚后何方享有子女监护权的依据。未来修改婚姻法或制定民法典婚姻家庭编时，应将"未成年子女最大利益"作为一项独立原则，同时，在离婚确立子女直接抚养方时以符合子女最大利益为唯一依据；在离婚诉讼中设立代表未成年子女利益的"诉讼代理人制度"；规定探望权不只是父母的权利，也是未成年子女的权利和父母双方的义务；等等。

（二）性别平等：从形式到实质

《消除对妇女一切形式歧视公约》确立的性别平等观是实质平等观。为此，公约第 4 条第 1 款指出："缔约各国为加速实现男女事实上的平等而采取的暂行特别措施，不得视为本公约所指的歧视，亦不得因此导致维持不平等或分别的标准；这些措施应在男女机会和待遇平等的目的达到之后，停止采用。"消除对妇女歧视委员会"第 25 号一般性建议"对妇女公约第 4 条第 1 款含义给出了详尽阐述，指出"仅仅保证男女待遇相同是不够的。必须考虑到妇女和男子的生理差异以及社会和文化造成的差别。在某些情况下，必须给予男女不同待遇，以纠正这些差别"（第 8 款）。可见，暂行特别措施并非不歧视准则的例外，而是一种强调，是"缔约国的一项必要战略的组成部分，其目的是在享受人权和基本自由方面实现事实上或实际的男女平等"（第 18 款）。实质平等模式是一种纠偏式方法。它在衡量是否存在歧视时，不是与男性的"相同经历"对照，而是以男女之间持续和实际存在的差异为依据。它强调妇女与男子平等享有利用本国资源方面的机会平等，同时关注结果平等，要求应有法律和政策框架以及使法律和政策得以运作的体制和机制的支持。① 中国家庭法对于妇女家庭权益的保障，既要坚持男女平等基本原则，又要针对传统社会文化习俗对妇女家庭权享有存在的偏见与歧视，结合男女两性社会经济地位和家庭劳动分工的差别，为实现两性在家庭关系中的实质平等，采取对妇女特别保护的措施。

---

① 参见黄列《社会性别与国际人权法》、〔芬〕卡塔琳娜·佛罗斯特尔《实质平等和非歧视法》，《环球法律评论》2005 年第 1 期。

Family Law Protection of the Rights of Children and Women in China: from the Perspective of International Human Rights Conventions

Xue Ninglan *

【Abstract】 Family is the basic unit of society, in which people live, procreate, and make emotional contact. The protection by the Chinese family law of the rights of children and women is embodied in the enjoyment and realization of rights. An assessment based on the Convention on the Elimination of All Forms of Discrimination against Women and the Convention on the Rights of the Child, to both of which China is a state party, shows that currently children and women in China generally are able to enjoy equal family rights. However, China is still faced with many obstacles in realizing some rights of women and children, including children's rights to a family name and to know their parents, the right to be free from domestic violence, and the property right of divorced women. The Chinese government needs to review its current laws, administrative regulations and judicial interpretations to see whether they conform to the principle of the best interest of the child, the principle of substantive equality, and other principles established by international conventions and promote the adoption of the Law against Domestic Violence and the revision of other relevant laws and regulations.

【Keywords】 Children's Family Rights; Women's Family Rights; Convention on the Right of the Child; Convention on the Elimination of All Forms of Discrimination against Women; Family Law

---

* Professor, Institute of Law, Chinese Academy of Social Sciences.

谁为妇女的家务劳动买单

——国际人权法的视角

戴瑞君[*]

【摘要】关于男女社会角色的定型观念致使妇女成为家务劳动的主要承担者。此外,一些"保护妇女"的法律本身也在强化这种角色定型。长期形成的带有性别偏见和性别歧视的社会观念和社会制度将妇女束缚在了家庭领域。但是长期以来,妇女家务劳动所创造的价值并没有得到应有的肯定。妇女承担大量家务劳动,直接导致她们在许多方面与男子相比处于劣势地位,妇女的多项基本人权,如受教育权、就业权、社会保障权、财产权以及政治权利等也因此得不到充分的享有或行使。为此,一些国际公约开始确认家务劳动的价值,并强调男女平等分担家务的义务。而国家作为保障人权的主要义务主体,应当为妇女因家务劳动而付出的代价买单,应当采取各种适当措施为妇女的全面发展,为妇女平等享有各项基本人权创造条件。

【关键词】妇女　家务劳动　平等　人权

一　妇女"适合"做家务?

家务劳动通常包括洗衣、做饭、清洁、整理房间、购物、日常修理、照顾家庭成员等活动。在全球范围内,家务劳动的主要承担者是女性。

"重男轻女""男主外、女主内"等一些关于男女社会角色的定型观念

---

* 戴瑞君,中国社会科学院国际法研究所助理研究员。

致使妇女成为家务劳动的主要承担者。这些定型观念根深蒂固，而且在世界范围内普遍存在。尽管政府、民间团体等力量已经在宣传性别平等方面做了大量工作，但是时至今日，妇女承担主要家务劳动的格局并没有明显改变。而且，随着女性正规就业比例的提高，女性将承担有偿工作和家务劳动的双重负担。联合国的一项报告指出，各地区的调查，包括从时间使用研究中得出的数据显示，男女之间在有偿就业、家庭责任分工和照料工作方面存在很大的差别和不平等状况。[①] 在大多数国家，虽然妇女从事有偿工作的比例有所增加，但与此同时男性从事无偿工作的比例并未因此而增加。[②] 一些国家的现有数据表明，妇女比男性花费更多的时间做饭、清洁和照顾子女。如果把有偿和无偿工作的时间相加，妇女每周工作时间往往比男子更长，而休闲或睡眠的时间更少。[③]

　　长期形成的带有性别偏见和性别歧视的社会观念将妇女束缚在了家庭领域。而一些"保护妇女"的法律本身也在强化着这种角色定型的观念。例如，国际劳工组织 1935 年通过的关于《妇女在各类矿山井下作业公约》，其第 2 条规定"任何妇女，不论其年龄如何，一概不得受雇从事矿山井下作业"。劳工组织 1948 年修订后的关于《妇女夜间工作公约》则禁止任何公共或私人企业（industrial undertakings）于晚上 10 点至次日早上 7 点之间雇用女工。[④] 批评者认为，这些公约虽然表面上是保护妇女的，实际上却是歧视性的，因为它们强化了妇女的角色定型。以禁止妇女夜间工作为例，隐含在这一规定背后的考虑实际上是将妇女看作家务的承担者、照顾者而不是养家糊口者的角色。

　　国内立法中这样的例子也显而易见。以我国的《妇女权益保障法》为例，该法第 26 条第 1 款规定："任何单位均应根据妇女的特点，依法保护妇女在工作和劳动时的安全和健康，不得安排不适合妇女从事的工作和劳动。"何谓"不适合妇女从事的工作和劳动"，这是一个非常笼统、模糊的概念。适合或不适合通常由用人单位、用人者主观判断。这一模糊的规定

①　联合国妇女发展基金：《世界妇女进展情况：妇女、工作与贫穷》，纽约，2005。

②　UN Commission on Status of Women, *2009 World Survey on the Role of Women in Development*: *Women's control over Economic Resources and Access to Financial Resources, including Microfinance*, UN publication, Sales No. E. 09. Ⅳ. 7, 2009, p. 31.

③　UN Doc. E/CN. 6/2009/2，秘书长的报告：《男女平等分担责任，包括艾滋病毒/艾滋病患者有关护理》，2008 年 12 月 18 日，第 16 段。

④　ILO, *Night Work (Women) Convention* (Revised), 1948 (No. 89), article 2 & 3.

极有可能成为用人单位不雇用妇女的挡箭牌。正如有的学者所指出的，"过度的保护性措施已经成为女性广泛就业的障碍"，"我们需要谨防陷入一种把性别歧视合法化的陷阱"，① 因此，要关注女性职业禁忌所带来的负面影响。②

一些政策，虽然表面上看起来是性别中立的，却助长了性别的陈规定型。例如捷克曾开设"家务管理"学校，虽然学校没有正式的性别选择，但基本上专为女学生而设，培养她们担当传统的陈规定型的角色。

这些陈规定型的观念是限制妇女与男性平等参加就业及公共生活的主要原因，同时也限制了男性公平分担家庭责任。

二　家务劳动与"次等"公民

尽管妇女花费了大量的体力和精力，经年累月地重复着操持家务的劳动，使家庭生活正常运转，使家庭其他成员有更多的体力和精力投入学习、工作和自我发展当中。但是长期以来，妇女家务劳动所创造的价值并没有得到应有的肯定。传统的经济学认为这些劳动不具有直接的交换价值，不应纳入国民生产总值中加以计算，家务劳动的社会价值由此长期得不到肯定。③ 发生在 20 世纪 90 年代的关于将无偿劳动纳入国民收入核算的大讨论并未让这一结论有所改变，④ 2009 年国际劳工组织的报告仍遗憾地指出，大部分照料工作仍然是无偿的，并且仍然被归入非经济活动。⑤

妇女由于承担大量家务劳动，直接导致在许多方面与男子相比处于次等地位，成为"次等"公民，妇女的多项基本人权因此得不到应有的保障。

1. 家务劳动限制妇女和女童受教育权的平等享有

在有女孩的家庭，女孩往往比男孩更早接触家务，并承担更多的家务。特别是在农村地区，早婚和家务致使女孩的辍学率高于男孩。许多女童因为承担较多家务，比如照顾弟弟妹妹，而提早退学，不能充分接受教育。

成年妇女面临同样的问题。妇女因为结婚、承担家务而中断、放弃学业的例子也屡见不鲜。男子于结婚之后继续求学的比例明显高于妇女。妇

---

① 马忆南：《"女性禁忌从事的劳动"再思考》，《妇女研究论丛》2009 年第 2 期。

② 刘明辉：《关注女职工职业禁忌的负面影响》，《妇女研究论丛》2009 年第 2 期。

③ 参见冉启玉《成本与收益：夫妻家务劳动价值的法经济学分析》，《北方论丛》2009 年第 5 期。

④ UNDP, "Gender and Human Development", *Human Development Report*, New York, 1995.

⑤ ILO, *Global Employment Trends for Women*, Geneva, 2009.

女为支持丈夫，承担更多家务，并牺牲个人的发展；而能够做出同样牺牲的男子并不多见。联合国消除对妇女歧视委员会 2003 年收到的第一份个人申诉是"B. J. 女士诉德国"的案子。申诉人原来学习的是护士专业，结婚后同意留在家中承担家务，为了丈夫的事业而不再继续求学。在此期间，她养育了三个子女。申诉人曾经提出希望继续被中断的学业，但是丈夫由于自己在职业中遇到困难而不愿她去求学。在子女均已成人之后，申诉人再次提出求学的愿望，丈夫却提出离婚要求。这时，申诉人已经 52 岁。①虽然这一申诉的诉求并不是受教育权问题，但也具有这方面的说服力。

2. 家务劳动限制妇女就业权的平等享有

研究已经表明，男女在无偿工作，特别是照料工作中的不平等，影响女性在劳动力市场的就业选择。② 承担家务劳动的妇女，根据其家务劳动量的大小以及自身的体力、精力等因素，面对就业时，可能做出不同的选择：要么干脆不就业，做全职的家庭妇女；要么参与一些临时性的非全时的工作；要么选择全时工作。无论是哪一种情况，妇女的就业权都会受到不同程度的限制。

做全职家庭妇女的原因，一部分可能是其他家庭成员的收入足以支付生活费用而没有必要再就业；而很多时候是家务劳动耗费了妇女大量的体力、精力，客观上导致妇女不能够选择就业。既然无法迈入职场，也就无法享受因为就业带来的各种福利，比如退休金、各种社会保险等。

另一种情况是家务劳动量不是特别大，在完成家务之余，妇女还有部分精力，可以选择一些临时性的、非全时的工作。但是这类工作往往不稳定，工资很低，雇主和国家也不会为其提供全面的社会保障。因此，这一类工作只能换取一定的现金收入，而无法像全职工作那样得到比较全面的社会保障。③ 另外，选择兼职工作的同时还面临着更加严重的同工不同酬问题。调查显示，全职工作的妇女的工资是承担同样工作男性工资的 82%，而兼职工作的妇女的工资却只有同样从事兼职工作的男性的 59%。④

---

① UN Doc. CEDAW/C/36/D/1/2003, Ms. B. J. v. Germany.

② UN Commission on Status of Women, *2009 World Survey on the Role of Women in Development*: *Women's control over Economic Resources and Access to Financial Resources*, *including Microfinance*, UN publication, Sales No. E. 09. Ⅳ. 7, 2009.

③ Chant, S., and C. Pedwell (2008), "Women, Gender and the Informal Economy: An Assessment of the International Labour Organization (ILO) Research and Suggested Ways Forward," Geneva: *International Labour Organization* (ILO).

④ ILO, *Breaking the Glass Ceiling*: *Women in Management*, Geneva, 2004 update.

　　还有一种情况是，其他家庭成员的收入不足以负担生活费用，或者妇女自身希望实现社会价值的愿望比较强烈，虽然需要承担家务，但是妇女仍然选择全职工作。这也是许多城市妇女的生活状态。此时，表面上看，妇女的就业权得到了满足，但是由于她需要肩负家务劳动与全职工作的双重负担，而这是绝大部分男性不会面临的境遇，限于体力、精力，妇女自然会在同无须承担家务的男性同事进行竞争时处于劣势，进而影响到其升迁、评优以及由此带来的利益。而且在这种情况下，由于妇女长期透支体力，其健康也会受到损害。

　　以上各种情况可能恰好为职场中的性别隔离做了一个注脚。横向的，妇女只能从事需要体力、精力较少的行业，而这些行业往往是不稳定、低工资、不被劳动法和社会保障体系所涵盖的"非典型"或非正规就业，远未达到国际劳工组织所界定的"体面工作"的标准。而没有体面的工作，被认为是造成贫困的主要原因。① 纵向的，妇女家务劳动使妇女没有更好的精力和经验优势去竞争更高的职位，绝大部分处于初级或中级岗位，女性担任高级管理岗位的比例明显少于男性。

　　3. 家务劳动影响妇女平等享有社会保障权

　　家务劳动通常被视为不创造价值的无偿劳动，家务劳动的承担者不能像其他劳动者一样，享受与劳动相关联的社会福利与保障。而选择同时承担家务劳动和就业的双重责任的妇女，如前文所分析的，由于在职场中的竞争力低下，与职场地位和能力相关联的社会保障会受到影响。

　　"因生育子女造成的职业中断、不平等地承担没有工钱的照顾责任、从事不规范的工作以及较低的收入水平，致使许多妇女无法确保自己有能力应对年老、疾病、残疾、失业和其他生活危机带来的挑战。"②

　　4. 家务劳动有损妇女对财产权的享有

　　因为家务劳动的价值得不到肯定，家务劳动对家庭的贡献也不被承认，从而在很大程度上抹杀了妇女，尤其是那些以承担家务劳动为主要工作的妇女对家庭的贡献。这样一来，妇女对婚姻、家庭财产的管理、支配以及处置权利均受到很大程度的制约。

　　此外，家务劳动的无偿性导致家务劳动的承担者在离婚财产分割中处

---

① ILO, *Gender Equality at the Heart of Decent Work*, Geneva, 2009.

② UN Commission on Status of Women, *2009 World Survey on the Role of Women in Development*: *Women's control over Economic Resources and Access to Financial Resources, including Microfinance*, UN publication, Sales No. E. 09. Ⅳ. 7, 2009.

于相当不利的地位。我国现行法律在离婚财产分割的相关规定中考虑了家务劳动的因素。例如，2001 年修订的《婚姻法》第 40 条规定："夫妻书面约定婚姻关系存续期间所得的财产归各自所有，一方因抚育子女、照料老人、协助另一方工作等付出较多义务的，离婚时有权向另一方请求补偿，另一方应当予以补偿。"2005 年修订的《妇女权益保障法》做出了类似的规定。相关规定以法律的形式在一定程度上确认了家务劳动的价值及其对家庭的贡献，这一点值得肯定。但是，相关规定又设置了许多前置条件，使得真正能从中受益的家务劳动承担者非常之少。首先，规定只适用于书面约定分别财产制的婚姻关系，而我国绝大部分婚姻适用的是夫妻共同财产制，对于后者，没有明确的法律依据支持主要承担家务劳动的一方去寻求获得补偿。其次，对于可要求补偿的家务劳动的范围，法律也做了明确的列举，包括抚养子女、照料老人、协助另一方工作等，而我们通常所说的洗衣、做饭、清洁、整理等工作是得不到补偿的。最后，要求补偿是家务劳动承担者的一项权利，她可以自由决定是否行使，而实践中很少有妇女主动提出补偿要求。这些因素都严重降低了相关规定的价值，使得绝大部分承担大量家务劳动的妇女并不能从中受益。

在前述 B. J. 女士诉德国的案例中，申诉者的真正诉求是要求判令其前夫支付其赡养费，同时质疑德国的社会结构和法律规定，认为德国的社会结构经常是确保男方在婚姻关系中事业有所发展，而女方则由于承担着家务和养育子女的主要责任而不得不中断事业，使她们处于极端不利的地位，在分居或离婚之后更是如此。消除对妇女歧视委员会的两位委员在审理本案的个别意见中也指出："申请人除了家庭之外没有工作经验，社会上视之为年老妇女，没有多少机会进入劳动力市场，在财政上自我维持。经过一生的家务劳动，养大了三个子女，而在违背她意愿离婚的五年之后，她却生活在一个没有经常性可靠收入的环境中，这是可悲的。"①

消除对妇女歧视委员会的第 21 号一般性建议已经明确指出："在一些国家，在分配婚姻财产时，更多地强调婚姻期间对所获财产的经济贡献，而轻视其他贡献，诸如哺育子女、照顾老年亲属以及从事家务职责等。通常，正是由于妻子的这种非经济贡献，才使得丈夫得以挣取收入，增加资

---

① UN Doc. CEDAW/C/36/D/1/2003, Ms. B. J. v. Germany, Decision of the Committee on the Elimination of Discrimination against Women, Appendix, *Individual opinion of Committee members Krisztina Morvai and Meriem Belmihoub-Zerdani* (*Dissenting*).

产。对经济贡献和非经济贡献应同等看重。"①

5. 家务劳动限制了妇女行使政治权利

除了上述各项权利的限制，妇女因为承担家务劳动而受到严重束缚的还有其政治权利以及参加公共生活的权利。消除对妇女歧视委员会的第 23 号一般性建议深刻地指出了造成这一局面的原因。"妇女一般从事私人或家庭领域活动，负责生育和抚养子女，所有社会都将这些活动视为次一级。相比之下，公共生活受到尊重和尊敬……而男子历来既支配公共生活，且掌有权力将妇女限制并制约在私人领域之内。尽管妇女在支撑家庭和社会方面起着核心作用，并对发展做出贡献，但她们被排斥在政治生活和决策进程之外，而决策进程却决定她们日常生活的模式和社会前途。""妇女在经济上依靠男子，往往阻碍她们做出重要的政治决定，并阻碍她们积极参与公共生活。妇女承受双重工作负担，经济上的依赖性，加上公共及政治生活工作时间长而且不具灵活性，使妇女无法更加积极地参与。"②

三　国际社会的平权努力

妇女被束缚在私领域，被束缚在家庭里，承担主要家务劳动而使其处于相当不利的处境。这一现象引起了国际社会的重视，并逐步采取措施予以纠正。

1979 年，联合国通过了《消除对妇女一切形式歧视公约》，该公约在宣言部分就特别指出"妇女对家庭的福利和社会的发展所做出的巨大贡献至今没有充分受到公认"。该公约一再强调，养育子女是父母共同的责任；为实现男女完全平等需要同时改变男子和妇女在社会上和家庭中的传统任务。为监督缔约国执行该公约，缔约国根据公约成立了消除对妇女歧视委员会。委员会通过一般性建议指导缔约国如何消除因为家务劳动而导致的歧视妇女现象。委员会在第 17 号一般性建议中建议缔约国鼓励和支持调查和试验，研究衡量妇女无偿家务活动的价值；并且定量计算妇女的无偿家务活动并将其列入国民生产总值。③

除了《消除对妇女一切形式歧视公约》的规定之外，消除对妇女歧视

① 联合国消除对妇女歧视委员会第 21 号一般性建议：《婚姻和家庭关系中的平等》，第 32 段。
② 联合国消除对妇女歧视委员会第 23 号一般性建议：《政治和公共生活》，第 8～9 段，第 11 段。
③ 联合国消除对妇女歧视委员会第 17 号一般性建议：《妇女无偿家务活动的衡量和定量及其在国民生产总值中的确认》。

委员会在审议缔约国提交的定期履约报告时，也一直关注家务劳动给妇女带来的不利影响问题，并不断敦促缔约国采取措施以消除这些问题。作为对委员会的回应，一些国家表示将计算无偿家务劳动对国家总产值的贡献。有的国家，比如委内瑞拉、厄瓜多尔等，已经在宪法中确认了家务的经济和社会价值。而哥伦比亚的宪法法院已确认家务劳动应有报酬，建立了判例。还有一些国家通过法律促进男女平等承担无偿的家务劳动。例如，瑞典2006年通过的一项政府法案要求"妇女和男子应当为家务劳动承担同等的责任"；吉尔吉斯斯坦2003年的《就业中的性别平等法》中明确"就业领域的性别平等原则也适用于家务劳动"，并规定无论男女在家务劳动上应当承担平等的义务。

在联合国之外，国际劳工组织也在确认家务劳动的价值方面有所贡献，这集中体现在其第156号关于《负有家庭责任的劳工公约》之中。制定于1981年的该公约直言不讳地指出，1958年的《就业和职业歧视公约》没有涵盖基于家庭责任的歧视，现在有必要予以补充。该公约要求缔约国制定国家政策，使负有家庭责任但有就业意愿的人不致因家庭责任而受到歧视，此外国家还应提供或保障必要的社区服务，例如照顾婴儿服务，家庭服务的设施等。①

四　为妇女的家务劳动买单

国际社会的努力只是一种外部的力量，只能起到一种促进作用。鉴于家务劳动已经成为歧视妇女的一个重要原因，妇女各项基本人权的享有因此受到严重限制，又鉴于保护基本人权最主要的责任在国家，因此，国家应当担负起消除妇女因为承担大部分家庭劳动而带来的不利后果的主要责任。然而，要逐步扭转主要根源于根深蒂固的社会观念而造成的不利局面不是一蹴而就的，它是一个系统工程。在这一过程中，用人单位、社会组织和个人的作用同样举足轻重。

首先，国家有义务采取措施消除社会广泛存在的"男主外、女主内"等对性别角色的陈规定型观念，倡导男女平等分担家务的理念。国家应当确认养育子女是父母、妇女与男子以及整个社会的共同责任，绝不应以妇女孕产、生养子女以及妇女在生育方面的角色为由歧视她们或限制其全面参与社会生活；应当通过设计、实施和推动有利于家庭的立法、政策和服

---

① ILO, *Workers with Family Responsibilities Convention*, 1981（No. 156）.

务，促进妇女和男子兼顾工作及家庭责任，并平等分担就业和家庭责任；应当开展宣传活动，强调男子在家务劳动方面的平等责任，并促使舆论和其他相关行为体认识到这些问题。

教育界、传媒界在此方面也有较大的作为空间。这些领域应当具备足够的性别敏感度，避免通过教科书或者各种媒介进一步强化陈规定型观念。

其次，国家应将性别主流化政策贯彻到立法、政策制定以及执行的过程中，为妇女谋求全面发展创造法律空间和政策条件；应当定期对法律和政策进行性别盲点检审，既要避免直接歧视妇女，也要避免表面中立的法律、政策实际上产生歧视妇女的后果。消除直接歧视和间接歧视也是国家根据国际人权条约所承担的义务。一些国家和地区的法律较好地呼应了这一点。例如，中国香港特别行政区的《家庭岗位歧视条例》就将家庭岗位歧视行为分为直接歧视和间接歧视两种。直接歧视是某人基于其家庭岗位而受到的待遇比另一人差；间接歧视是向所有人一律施以同样的条件或要求，但实际上并无充分理由施加此类要求，结果对有家庭岗位的人不利。① 这些较好的实践值得借鉴和推广。

再次，国家负有义务提供必要的设施，使妇女有条件从家庭劳动中解放出来。当前一些因素甚至增加了家务劳动的负担。随着社会的急剧老龄化以及诸如艾滋病等疾病的增加，照料对象已经从孩童扩展到了老年人和应处于工作年龄的成年人；城市化和移民浪潮则进一步弱化了传统的家庭支撑体系，单户主家庭的增加进一步加重了照料工作的负担。对此，国家有义务提供负担得起的、方便的和高质量的托幼、托老等护理服务，减轻家务劳动负担。② 中国台湾地区的《性别工作平等法》就要求县级主管机关为妇女就业的需要编列经费，办理各种职业训练、就业服务及再就业训练，并于该期间提供或设置托儿、托老及相关福利设施；上级主管机关应为此提供经费补助。③

最后，家务劳动社会化，即家务劳动由社会化服务承担，也有利于妇女从家务劳动中解放出来。它一方面使家务劳动的社会价值得到了肯定，另一方面也为妇女减轻家务劳动负担，有更多的时间和精力发展自我创造了条件。

---

① 香港特别行政区法例第 527 章：《家庭岗位歧视条例》，第Ⅱ部。
② 联合国妇女地位委员会第 55 届会议商定结论：《关于妇女和儿童接受和参与教育、培训、科学技术，包括促进妇女平等获得充分就业机会和体面工作的商定结论》，第（gg）段。
③ 中国台湾地区《性别就业平等法》第 6 条。

Who Should Pay for the Housework Done by Women: an International Human Rights Law Perspective

Dai Ruijun *

【Abstract】 As a result of stereotyped social roles of men and women, housework has become women's main responsibility. Besides, some laws aimed at "protecting women" have also reinforced such stereotyped role of women. Long-standing gender-biased social ideas and institutions have confined women to the realm of family. However, for a long period of time, the value of women's housework has not been recognized. Women's housework responsibility has directly led to their disadvantaged position in family and affected their full enjoyment or exercise of many fundamental human rights, including the right to education, the right to employment, the right to social security, property right and political rights. To deal with this problem, some international conventions begin to recognize the value of housework and emphasize the equal sharing of housework between men and women. The state, as the main subject of the obligation to safeguard human rights, should pay for the cost incurred by women in doing housework and adopt appropriate measures to create conditions for the comprehensive development of women and the enjoyment by women of various fundamental human rights on an equal basis with men.

【Keywords】 Women; Housework; Equality; Human Rights

---

* Assistant Professor, Institute of International Law, Chinese Academy of Social Sciences.

《公民权利和政治权利国际公约》的实施：限制与克减

——国际法委员会与人权委员会对条约保留意见的相关比较

余少祥*

【摘要】 根据《维也纳条约法公约》及有关规定，国际法上的"保留"通常是指"一国于签署、批准、接受、赞同或加入条约时所做之片面声明，不论措词或名称为何，其目的在摒除或更改条约中若干规定对该国适用时之法律效果"。由于《公民权利和政治权利国际公约》本身对保留并未做任何规定，实践中曾引发大量问题。长期以来，联合国国际法委员会和人权委员会在该公约的保留问题上做过大量工作，并在其草案、文件中提出了很多关于保留的指导性意见。总体说来，两委员会承认各缔约国对于公约的保留，但认为保留应有一定限度。其中，国际法委员会主张采取积极措施，包括成立专门审查机构、转变登记保存机关职能等，以达到对各国提具保留的实际限制，并对撤销保留采取比较宽松的做法；人权委员会则更倾向于推动各国国内立法，以"内求"的方式减少缔约国对人权公约的保留，并希望成员国接受全部义务。两种意见并不矛盾，在某种程度上是一个问题的两个方面，可以相互促进，相互影响。

【关键词】 国际法委员会 人权委员会 保留 限制

保留作为国际法中的一项权利，最早是在 18 世纪末 19 世纪初出现的。1815 年，在签署《维也纳公会最后文件》时，瑞典暨挪威的全权代表罗文

---

* 余少祥，中国社会科学院法学研究所副研究员。

汉姆提出一项正式声明，声称瑞典政府将不会接受有关卢卡地区主权和承认斐迪南四世为西西里国王的第 101、102 和 104 条。这被称为历史上第一个对多边条约提具保留的事例。[①]

　　国际法上的保留一般包括两层含义：（1）一国的保留声明是该国为了维护有关条约的特殊利益而单方提出的，不能认为这种声明一经提出就直接具有对抗他国或拘束他国的效果，必须至少有一个缔约国接受才能产生效果；（2）保留是各个国家的单独行为，即使一些国家提出了内容相同的保留，也不能将这些保留归结为一个保留，因为其他国家完全可以对一个国家的保留提出反对，而对另一个国家相同的保留不予表态或表示接受。

　　保留概念及其发展有相对完整的历程。1935 年《哈佛条约法》草案认为，保留是指"一个国家在签署、批准或加入条约时做出的正式声明，目的是限制该条约适用和其他国家或可能成为当事国的国家之间关系的效果"。佩特·马兰科组克则提出，保留是"一国可愿意接受条约大部分条款，但也由于种种原因反对该条约的其他条款"。[②] 1948 年，由于各国围绕《防止及惩治灭绝种族罪公约》保留问题展开了激烈的争论，因而国际法委员会开始准备在条约法公约草案中对"保留"给予一个权威定义。经过布莱尔利、劳特派特、菲茨莫里斯和沃尔多克等人的努力，国际法委员会实现了这一目的。1969 年《维也纳条约法公约》明确规定，保留是"一国于签署、批准、接受、赞同或加入条约时所做之片面声明，不论措词或名称为何，其目的在摒除或更改条约中若干规定对该国适用时之法律效果"。1986 年《关于国家和国际组织间或国际组织相互间条约法的维也纳公约》对于保留的阐述也基本沿袭了这一定义。

　　在国际法领域，允许条约保留通常使该条约更具普遍性，而不加限制地保留则毫无疑问破坏条约的目的和宗旨，因此，如何在保存条约的价值和争取条约的普遍参加之间维持一种平衡，一直是国际法理论和实践中一个引起很大争论的问题。

　　《公民权利和政治权利国际公约》（Civil and Political Rights）（以下简称《公约》）于 1966 年 12 月 16 日由联合国大会第 2200A 号决议通过并开放给各国签字、批准和加入，1976 年 3 月 23 日生效。据统计，截至 1994 年 11

---

① 石磊：《试论条约保留的概念及与解释性声明的区别》，《信阳师范学院学报》（哲学社会科学版）2003 年第 4 期。

② Peter Malanczuk, *Akehurst's Modern Introduction to International Law* (seventh revised edition) Routledge, 1997, p. 135.

月，该《公约》的 127 个成员国有 46 个国家就公约义务提具了意义不同的 150 项保留。① 如美国对《公约》的第 6 条和第 7 条做出了保留。美国的这一保留曾遭到许多欧洲国家反对，它们认为这些保留与条约的目的和宗旨是不相容的。1995 年 3 月，人权委员会在审查美国依《公约》提交的报告时也批评了这些保留，并建议撤回。

根据国际惯例及相关规定，保留一般有如下几种：② （1）全面禁止保留，即不允许对条约提具任何形式的保留。如《废止奴隶制、奴隶贩卖及类似奴隶制的制度与习俗补充公约》和《取缔教育歧视公约》明确规定，禁止国家对条约做出任何形式的保留。（2）默认保留。如 1954 年生效的《妇女政治权利公约》第 7 条规定，一国可以对该公约的任何条款做出保留，任何国家对该保留可以提出反对，不反对即视为默认，但在反对国与保留国之间，条约不发生效力。（3）明示保留，即不允许条约禁止或准许的特定保留之外的保留。如《关于难民地位的公约》第 42 条规定，禁止对公约第 1、3、4 条，第 16 条第 1 款，第 33、36 和 46 条的保留，并且对该公约不得做出任何其他保留。（4）多数规则，即由条约的多数当事国来决定一项保留能否被接受。如《消除一切形式种族歧视国际公约》第 20 条第 2 款规定，如果至少三分之二的国家反对一项保留，则该保留应被认为与该公约的目的和宗旨不相符而不被准许。（5）排除规则，即与条约目的及宗旨不符合的，不得保留。

由于《公民权利和政治权利国际公约》对保留本身并未做任何规定，实践中各国一般都依据《维也纳条约法公约》第 19 条第 3 款之规定做出保留。③ 由此引发的一系列问题是：（1）各国都是从国内法或国内政策角度考虑是否提具保留；（2）由于缺乏明确标准，确定一项保留是否符合公约的目的和宗旨不可避免带有一定的主观性；（3）即使委员会确定某一项保留与条约的目的和宗旨相违背，对其如何处理或处理结果如何还需解决或尚待检验。这就使得对《公民权利和政治权利国际公约》的保留呈现出一种"无限"的局面和趋势，同时使得《公民权利和政治权利国际公约》的实施不免陷入尴尬境地。

---

① 朱晓青：《〈公民权利和政治权利国际公约〉的实施机制》，《法学研究》2000 年第 2 期。

② 参阅万鄂湘、郑曦林《论国际人权条约的保留》，《武汉大学学报》（哲学社会科学版）1995 年第 6 期。

③ 我国于 1997 年 5 月 9 日经全国人大常委会批准加入《维也纳条约法公约》，并就第 66 条做出保留。

　　有学者提出，《公民权利和政治权利国际公约》属国际人权条约范畴，国际人权条约所包含的规范是强行性规范，国家对国际人权条约所承担的义务是普遍性义务，体现在一般性多边条约关系中的相互性原则不能适用于国际人权条约，因此，对于国际人权条约的任何保留都是无效的。尽管如此，实践中，在人权公约允许保留或不禁止保留的情况下，国家一般会充分利用这种机会。

　　国际法学者卢达认为，《维也纳条约法公约》第 19 条第 3 款与第 20 条第 4 款规定前后矛盾，前者指一国不得做出与公约目的和宗旨相违背的保留，而根据后者，一项保留对于所有接受该保留的国家、没有提出反对的国家以及只是提出"相对性"反对的国家，效果都是一样的。柯西亚则将一国不得做出与条约的目的和宗旨相违背的保留看作一个习惯法规范，他认为一项保留只要不违反强行法规定，即使与条约的目的和宗旨相违背，也可以因为被接受而有效。① 根据卢达的结论，国家在做出保留和接受保留时实际上不受任何法律限制，而根据柯西亚的理论，国家除受强行法的限制外，可以对条约做出任何保留。

　　对此，国际法委员会认为，保留是否符合《公民权利和政治权利国际公约》的目的和宗旨，完全属于国际法上的条约解释问题。在《维也纳条约法公约》缔约之初，起草者曾提议设置一个一般性程序以对该问题做出权威判断。大会讨论了好几种方案，比如沃尔多克提出的由一个专门机关进行判断的方案，日本、韩国、印度等国提出的多数决定的方案，都没有获得广泛支持。最后，《维也纳条约法公约》仍将这一判断权赋予各国自身。

　　其实，国际保留不能适用于人权公约。如 1965 年《消除一切形式种族歧视国际公约》第 20 条第 2 款规定："凡与本公约的目标及宗旨抵触的保留不得容许，其效果足以阻碍本公约所设任何机关之业务者，亦不得准许。凡经至少三分之二本公约缔约国反对者，应视为抵触性或阻碍性之保留。"1984 年《禁止酷刑和其他残忍、不人道或有辱人格的待遇或处罚公约》第 28 条第 1 款、1979 年《消除对妇女一切形式歧视公约》第 28 条第 2 款以及 1989 年的《儿童权利公约》第 51 条第 2 款都做了类似规定。②

---

① 万鄂湘、郑曦林：《论国际人权条约的保留》，《武汉大学学报》（哲学社会科学版）1995 年第 6 期。

② 朱晓青：《〈公民权利和政治权利国际公约〉的实施机制》，《法学研究》2000 年第 2 期。

关于《公民权利和政治权利国际公约》及人权条约的保留问题，国际法委员会（International Law Commition）与人权委员会（Commition on Human Right）做过大量工作，并且在其草案、决议等文件中提出了大量的、关于条约保留的指导性意见。国际法委员会是根据《国际法委员会规约》成立的联合国辅助机构，1947年成立，宗旨是促进国际法的逐渐发展与编纂。① 委员会主要负责处理国际公法方面的问题，有时也涉及国际私法方面的问题。人权委员会是联合国经济及社会理事会根据《联合国宪章》第68条的规定设立的人权机构，其宗旨是：将保障人权与保卫和平联系起来，不但欲免后世再遭战祸，而且重申基本人权、人格尊严与价值之信念，促成国际合作，且不分种族、性别、语言和宗教，增进对于全体人类之人权及基本自由之尊重。②

国际法委员会和人权委员会在《公民权利和政治权利国际公约》保留上一个共同意见是，尽管该《公约》对保留没有做任何规定，但并不意味着允许对公约的任何保留。它们在形式上都承认各缔约国对《公约》的保留权利，但认为应尽量减少保留，并对各国的保留予以必要的限制。

对于保留如何认定问题，国际法委员会认为，保留与解释性声明是不同的。菲茨莫里斯和沃尔多克曾分别在他们的1956年和1962年第一次条约法报告中都认为，解释性声明不是保留，不适用保留规则。但是在1962年国际法委员会通过的条约法公约草案报告中，委员会的释义又指出："国家在签署、批准、加入、接受、赞同一个条约时，经常会声明他们对于某一特定条款的解释，这种声明可能只不过是对该国立场的澄清，也可能等于是保留，这需要根据它是否更改或排除条约条款的适用来决定。"③ 该释义实际上是承认，某些更改或排除条约适用效果的解释性声明可能是保留。

在保留提出的时间上，国际法委员会认为，保留一般须在缔约国表示同意承受条约拘束时提出。根据《维也纳条约法公约》的定义，保留是指一国在签署、批准、接受、赞同或加入时所做的声明，如果在上述时间之后做出保留，应该是无效的。因为保留必然会给条约关系带来一定的不确定因素，如果对保留提出时间没有限制，这种不确定因素就会持续增加。

2000年，国际法委员会第54届会议在"条约保留"议题下，讨论了有

---

① 王家福、刘海年主编《人权百科全书》，中国大百科全书出版社，1998，第333页。
② 王家福、刘海年主编《人权百科全书》，中国大百科全书出版社，1998，第496页。
③ 石磊：《试论条约保留的概念及与解释性声明的区别》，《信阳师范学院学报》（哲学社会科学版）2003年第4期。

关保留的程序和撤销保留的准则草案，并临时通过了 11 条准则。① 具体内容有：（1）设立条约监督机构对提具保留予以审查。准则草案规定，如果条约监督机构审定有关的保留是不可接受的，保留国必须根据有关机构的决定采取措施，如部分或全部撤销保留。（2）关于部分撤销保留问题，特别报告员就部分撤销保留问题单独起草了准则条款，对撤销保留采取较为宽松的做法。（3）关于条约保留机关的职能。准则草案规定，在保存机关认为保留明显不可接受时，可以提请保留国注意，如果保留国坚持己见，保存人则应将有关保留转送其他缔约方并附上他和保留国之间交换的意见。（4）关于用电子邮件和传真等形式通知条约保留的方式，委员会认为应该承认其效力。

由此可见，国际法委员会在公约的保留问题上主张实行更为严格的限制，并提议设立专门的监督机构以对各国提具之保留进行审查，这在人权公约实施的草案中还是第一次。在公约保存机关职能方面，国际法委员会认为应赋予其异议提请权，而不是仅仅被动的接受权。当然，这一意见遭到包括中国在内的许多国家的反对。一些国家认为，由于该准则草案对于"条约监督机构"的概念没有明确界定，这类机构可以是司法机构，也可以是监督条约执行的委员会，它们的决定或审查结论可以是对当事方有拘束力的，也可以只是建议。另外，是否撤销保留是缔约国的权利，条约监督机构的审查并不能改变缔约国之间的条约关系，其结论也不能当然导致条约保留的撤销。由于种种原因，最后国际法委员会决定不将该准则草案提交起草委员会。有关人士认为，这一决定可能是国际法委员会慎重考查的结果，这样做对条约监督机构本身的正常工作并不会产生不利影响，同时也确保了条约制度的有效性。

关于赋予条约保存机关对保留提出异议的职能问题，一些国家提出，条约保存机关是条约约文的保管者，行使《维也纳条约法公约》第 77 条所赋予的职责。具体到条约保留而言，条约保存机关可以根据第 77 条第 1 款（丁）和（戊）项的规定审查各国提具的保留在形式方面是否妥善，是否符合《公约》有关条款的规定，必要时提请有关国家注意。至于一项保留是否可以被接受，应当由缔约国自行决定。由于条约保存机关不是条约约文的解释者，也不是一项保留在实质内容上的可接受性的评判者，它只能对

---

① 中国代表关键先生在第五十七届联大第六委员会关于"国际法委员会第 54 届会议的报告"议题（条约保留和国家单方面行为）的发言，http://www.un.org。

保留做形式上的审查。因此，一些国家主张，关于条约保留的有关准则草案，应当尊重条约法有关规定的文字和精神，维护条约法体系的稳定。

在《公民权利和政治权利国际公约》保留的合法性问题上，人权委员会认为，按照1969年《维也纳条约法公约》关于保留的规定，保留的生效并不以所有其他缔约国的同意为原则。因此，在《公民权利和政治权利国际公约》未对保留做明文规定的情况下，一个缔约国所做的保留是否有效，遵循的依然是"依其是否符合条约的目的和宗旨的标准，由其他缔约国各自决定"的规则。但《维也纳条约法公约》关于保留的规定的实际结果就是，一方面使该《公约》的缔约国数量增多，另一方面也使保留难以受到实际限制，这就不能不对其的完整性以及《公约》义务的履行产生一定的消极影响。

为了规范和限制各国对该《公民权利和政治权利国际公约》的保留，1994年人权委员会提出"关于批准或加入《公约》及其《任意议定书》时提具保留或依《公约》第四十一条发表声明的问题的一般性意见"，该意见主要内容有：（1）《公约》"未作禁止保留的规定并不意味着允许任何保留"，对此，《维也纳条约法公约》第19条第3款规定了相关标准，即允许与条约的目的和宗旨相符合的保留。人权委员会还对"与《公约》的目的和宗旨相违背"做了具体的阐释，如保留违反了强制规则或国际习惯法，或者保留使缔约国不履行其对侵犯人权的行为提供补救的保证，或者意欲逃脱委员会监督作用的保留就都是与《公约》的目的和宗旨相违背的。（2）尽管提具保留的可能性可以鼓励缔约国加入，并且"保留在能使缔约国将其法律中的特定因素与公约所阐明的每个人所固有的权利相适应方面起着有益的作用"，委员会原则上还是希望成员国接受全部义务，因为"人权标准是每个人作为人应该享有的基本权利的法律表述"。（3）在已做出的150项保留中，一些保留排斥了规定和保障公约所载的特殊权利的责任，另一些保留则力图确保某些国内法律规定的至上地位，还有一些保留是针对委员会的权限，因此"保留的数量、内容和范围可能会逐渐损害公约的有效实施，并趋于削弱缔约国义务的遵守"。

相比之下，人权委员会对《公民权利和政治权利国际公约》的实施和保留现象的反应是深层的担忧，不像国际法委员会直接提议采取各种措施以防止对《公约》实施危害之产生。在《公约》的实施机制上，人权委员会更倾向于通过国内立法而不是直接制定规则以确保有关人权条约的实施。这主要是囿于国际法中国际主权原则，人权委员会决议拘束力十分有限。

虽然国际法委员会的决议一样不能对各国产生直接拘束力，但人权问题更有特殊性，如人权委员会在报告的提交和审议方面均依赖缔约国政府的合作，对于违反人权的现象和事情，委员会只是将其列入名单，并发出提醒函，不能采取任何制裁措施，这在一定程度上制约了人权委员会维护国际人权的效用与力度。

总之，国际法委员会与人权委员会在《公民权利与政治权利国际公约》的保留问题上，既有共同之处又有不同意见。共同之处是允许各缔约国对《公约》的保留，但不是没有限度的保留。不同之处是，国际法委员会主张采取积极措施，包括成立专门审查机构、转变登记保存机关职能等，以达到对各国提具保留的实际限制，并对撤销保留采取比较宽松的做法；人权委员会则更倾向于推动各国国内立法，以"内求"的方式减少缔约国对人权公约保留，并希望成员国接受全部义务。笔者认为，两种方式并不矛盾，从某种意义上说是一个问题的两个方面，可以相互促进、相互影响。无论如何，只有各国真正遵循"条约必须信守"原则，《公民权利与政治权利国际公约》才能得以有效实施。

A Comparative Study on the Opinions of UN International Law Commission and of UN Human Rights Commission on Treaty Reservations

Yu Shaoxiang *

【 Abstract 】 According to Vienna Convention on the Law of Treaties, "reservation" in international law means "a unilateral statement, however phrased or named, made by a State, when signing, ratifying, accepting, approving or acceding to a treaty, whereby it purports to exclude or to modify the legal effect of certain provisions of the treaty in their application to that State". The absence of any provision on reservation in the International Covenant on Civil and Political Rights (ICCPR) has led to many problems. Over a long period of time, the UN

* Associate Professor, Institute of Law, Chinese Academy of Social Sciences.

International Law Commission and the UN Human Rights Commission have done lot of work on the reservation to the ICCPR and provided guiding opinions on this issue in many documents adopted by them. Generally speaking, both commissions recognize the reservations made by state parties to the ICCPR, but hold that such reservations should have a limit. The International Law Commission advocates positive measures, such as the establishment of special review organs and the change of the functions of the reservation registration and deposition body, aimed at limiting reservations to the Covenant, and a less strict approach towards the withdrawal of reservations, whereas the Human Rights Commission is more inclined to promote the adoption of relevant domestic laws aimed at reducing the need for reservations to human rights conventions and the acceptance by state parties of all the obligations under the Covenant without any reservation. The different approaches adopted by the two commissions are not contradictory. Rather, they deal with different aspects of the same problem and are mutually supportive.

【Keywords】UN International Law Commission; UN Human Rights Commission; Reservation; Restriction

中国少数民族语言法律保护事例分析

吴　峻[*]

【摘要】 中国民族语言保护框架基于宪法规定所确立，为少数民族使用自己语言从事活动的权利提供了充分的保障。其中，需要建立保护少数民族使用自己语言与使用国家通用语言之间的平衡，这是对少数民族语言进行法律保护的基础。彝族是中国文化历史悠久的民族之一，人口众多，语言差异性大。中国对彝族语言进行保护的制度及政策的演进与发展，充分说明了中国在立法及实践中对少数民族语言的重视及其与中国经济发展要求的平衡。

【关键词】 少数民族语言保护　彝族语言保护　少数民族文化保护

中国是个多民族的国家，少数民族语言文化资源丰富。在全国55个少数民族中，54个民族有自己的语言（回、满两个民族通用汉语言）；新中国成立前，21个民族有自己的文字。20世纪50年代，国家帮助10个少数民族创制了文字，帮助一些少数民族改革或改进了文字。目前，大多数少数民族的多数人以本民族语言为主要交际工具。彝族语言的保护现状及其发展，充分说明了中国对少数民族语言的重视。

一　中国民族语言法律保护框架

《宪法》第4条第3款规定："各民族都有使用和发展自己语言文字的自由。"以该宪法条文规定为基础，确定了中国民族语言的基本法律架构。其中，使用和发展自己民族语言文字的自由包含两方面的内容：一方面，中国各民族有权决定自己的语言如何使用、如何发展，其他人不得干

---

* 吴峻，中国社会科学院法学研究所助理研究员。

涉和歧视；另一方面，对于各民族使用和发展自己语言及文字的权利，政府须予以保障。基于这两方面，中国采用了一系列具体的民族语言法律保护措施。

另外，《宪法》第 134 条规定："各民族公民都有用本民族语言文字进行诉讼的权利。人民法院和人民检察院对于不通晓当地通用的语言文字的诉讼参与人，应当为他们翻译。在少数民族聚居或者多民族共同居住的地区，应当用当地通用的语言进行审理；起诉书、判决书、布告和其他文书应当根据实际需要使用当地通用的一种或者几种文字。"对于少数民族使用自己语言文字的权利而言，这一条规定更是一种强化的保障。

（一）民族区域自治法

1984 年 5 月 31 日第六届全国人民代表大会第二次会议通过，并根据 2001 年 2 月 28 日第九届全国人民代表大会常务委员会第二十次会议《关于修改〈中华人民共和国民族区域自治法〉的决定》修正了《中华人民共和国民族区域自治法》（以下简称《民族区域自治法》）。根据《宪法》的规定，在民族语言文字方面，对民族区域自治地区使用少数民族语言的问题，《民族区域自治法》做了如下方面的规定。

1. 保障使用少数民族语言的自由

民族自治地方的自治机关保障本地方各民族都有使用和发展自己的语言文字的自由，都有保持或者改革自己的风俗习惯的自由。[①] 这一规定是对《宪法》规定的确认，并进一步明确了民族自治地区自治机关的职责。

2. 自治机关职务语言

民族自治地方的自治机关在执行职务的时候，依照本民族自治地方自治条例的规定，使用当地通用的一种或者几种语言文字；同时使用几种通用的语言文字执行职务的，可以以实行区域自治的民族的语言文字为主。[②] 这种规定确定了两条原则。一是，民族自治地方自己制定的自治条例可以确定当地通用的语言文字，这其中就包括少数民族使用的通用文字。二是，在确定多个通用文字的前提下，可以将区域自治民族的语言文字作为主要文字。这两条原则在语言文字的官方使用方面尊重了少数民族自治地区的文字使用，也有力促进了民族自治地方的语言自治。

---

① 《民族区域自治法》第 10 条。
② 《民族区域自治法》第 21 条。

3. 语言教育

招收少数民族学生为主的学校（班级）和其他教育机构，有条件的应当采用少数民族文字的课本，并用少数民族语言讲课。① 各级人民政府要在财政方面扶持少数民族文字的教材和出版物的编译和出版工作。② 这种规定从教育角度对使用少数民族文字和语言进行了保护和传承。但是，教育本身的目的不仅仅局限于少数民族语言，还应该为该民族在整个社会中的发展及融合创造条件，因此，《民族区域自治法》规定，根据情况从小学低年级或者高年级起开设汉语文课程，推广全国通用的普通话和规范汉字。③

为了在保护少数民族使用自己语言的权利与推广使用全国通用语言之间达至平衡，《民族区域自治法》进一步规定：民族自治地方的自治机关教育和鼓励各民族的干部互相学习语言文字。汉族干部要学习当地少数民族的语言文字，少数民族干部在学习、使用本民族语言文字的同时，也要学习全国通用的普通话和规范文字。民族自治地方的国家工作人员，能够熟练使用两种以上当地通用的语言文字的，应当予以奖励。④ 这样，通过不同民族之间的语言使用促进交流，并在保护少数民族使用自己通用语言文字的基础上，推广全国通用语言，以推进整体社会建设及少数民族文化、经济的发展。

4. 对使用民族语言进行诉讼的权利予以保障

民族自治地方的人民法院和人民检察院应当用当地通用的语言审理和检察案件，并合理配备通晓当地通用的少数民族语言文字的人员。对于不通晓当地通用的语言文字的诉讼参与人，应当为他们提供翻译。法律文书应当根据实际需要，使用当地通用的一种或者几种文字。保障各民族公民都有使用本民族语言文字进行诉讼的权利。⑤ 该条规定实际上是对《宪法》相关规定的落实和细化，进一步明确了少数民族使用本民族通用文字进行诉讼的权利。

《民族区域自治法》作为保护少数民族权利及促进各民族和谐发展的一部重要法律，其有关民族语言的规定落实了少数民族使用自己本民族语言

---

① 《民族区域自治法》第 37 条第 3 款。
② 《民族区域自治法》第 37 条第 4 款。
③ 《民族区域自治法》第 37 条第 3 款。
④ 《民族区域自治法》第 49 条。
⑤ 《民族区域自治法》第 47 条。

的宪法权利，确保了少数民族语言文化的发展；同时，《民族区域自治法》也注意全国通用语言的推广，以在保障少数民族使用本民族通用语言权利的基础上，促进少数民族经济的发展和繁荣，从而在确保使用少数民族语言与使用全国通用语言之间达至必要的平衡。

（二）少数民族语言的具体政策和措施

在《宪法》相关规定基础上，中国采取了一系列政策和措施来保障少数民族的语言权利，并在此基础上促进其语言、文化、经济的发展。

首先，由于许多少数民族没有自己的文字，有的少数民族虽然有自己的文字却存在着各种各样的不足，因此，中国少数民族语言保护的第一步就是帮助少数民族创制、改进和改革自己的文字。1956 年，国务院下发了《关于各少数民族创立和改革文字方案的批准程序和实验推行分工的通知》，其中明确规定："中国科学院少数民族语言研究所负责作出创立和改革文字方案的初步设计，由省、自治区人民委员会审核，并广泛征求本民族各界人士的意见，经过充分协商讨论取得同意以后，提出意见，报民族事务委员会审查。经确定后，由省、自治区人民委员会公布作为实验推行的方案。"从 1951 年起，中国开始对部分地区的少数民族语言进行调查。1956 年，中央组织了 700 多人的中国科学院语言调查工作队，分为七组，赴全国 17 个省、自治区进行少数民族语言普查。在 1956 年至 1958 年间，七个调查组基本摸清了中国少数民族大多数语言的分布、使用人口和使用状况、与周围民族语言的关系；调查了 42 个民族共 50 多种语言；收集了超过 1500 个调查点的资料；了解了中国少数民族使用自己语言文字的情况。

其次，为了保护和发展少数民族语言，中国大力培养少数民族语言人才。1950 年，政务院批准了《筹办中央民族学院试行方案》，在中央民族学院（现中央民族大学）建立语文系，招收高中毕业以上志愿做少数民族工作的汉族学生以及有相当学历的少数民族学生，专修各少数民族语文。中央民族学院为此开设了蒙古、藏、哈萨克、朝鲜、彝、苗、傣、景颇、傈僳、拉祜等数十种语言专业，培养了大批少数民族语言人才。

最后，《民族区域自治法》颁布后，中国少数民族语言文字工作的法制化体系基本搭建完成，为各少数民族因地制宜推行少数民族语言文字工作提供了法律依据。1991 年 4 月，国家民族事务委员会（以下简称"国家民委"）向国务院呈报《关于进一步做好少数民族语言文字工作的报告》。该报告是在国家民委协同有关部门广泛深入调查研究中国少数民族语言问题、充分听取各种不同意见的基础上形成的。同年 6 月，国务院以国发〔1991〕

32 号文件批转了这项报告（以下简称"32 号文件"），对中国少数民族语言工作具有指导意义。32 号文件总结了 40 多年以来中国民族语言工作的成绩和现存问题，提出了贯彻国家的民族语言政策、加强民族语言法制建设、推进民族语言学术研究、推进民族语言人才培养等方针。在 32 号文件出台后的 20 年内，其制定的方针任务得到了很好的贯彻落实，少数民族语言文字在社会生活诸多领域得到了应用，并根据 32 号文件制定了许多少数民族语言保护的地方法规。

二　彝族语言文化

彝族是中国西南地区历史悠久的少数民族之一，主要分布于四川、云南、贵州和广西四个省份。在东南亚、南亚等与中国接壤的一些国家与地区，也有部分彝族分布。根据中国 2010 年第六次全国人口普查的数据，彝族有 8714394 人，位列回、壮、满、维吾尔、苗族之后，超过之前少数民族人口排名第六的土家族，成为全国人口数排名第六的少数民族。[①]

（一）　彝族语言文字具有悠久的历史

彝族具有悠久的历史，是南下氐羌族群与南方土著部落长期文化交融的结合体，至少有两千多年文字记载的历史。其文字多系毕摩掌握。在彝族文献中，许多史实均靠这些成为毕摩的巫师录载。[②]

彝族文字的传播及推广深刻地影响了彝族的风俗习惯。例如：传说洪水泛滥后，毁灭了彝文，天宫派遣三个毕摩携带彝文经书降临，拯救人民，三个毕摩各骑一头黄牛，将经书系在牛角上，但牛角经书被海水浸湿，遂在青树枝上曝晒，但被树叶粘破了一半，也有传说称系被老鹰叼去一半。因此，现在彝族毕摩在祭祀时，必须在祭祀场地插些青树枝，意即补抵已损失的一半经书;[③] 或者毕摩在诵经时须头戴法帽，帽沿上系一对老鹰爪，也是以鹰爪补充所损失一半经书的意思。因此传说，后来的彝族毕摩为了追念其祖师下凡时运送彝文经书的伴侣——牛，都不吃牛肉。

（二）　彝族语言概况与现状

彝文是一种已经发展得比较完善的单音节表意兼表音的方块文字。彝文在彝族历史上曾经有过比较统一或约定俗成的通用语言时期。但随着古

[①] 国家统计局：《中国 2010 年人口普查资料》，资料来源：http://www.stats.gov.cn/tjsj/pcsj/rkpc/6rp/indexch.htm，最后访问日期：2012 年 9 月 17 日。

[②] 马锦卫：《彝文起源及其发展考论》，民族出版社，2011，第 128 - 133 页。

[③] 马锦卫：《彝文起源及其发展考论》，民族出版社，2011，第 100 页

代彝族氏族部落的分化、分支和各自的迁徙，相互距离越来越远，因山川阻隔造成了彼此之间的交流日益不畅；但同时，语言却是不断发展的。这种情形就使得彝族语言产生了不同的方言和土语。随着时间的推移，方言、土语日益发展，终于形成了现今彝族语言的六大方言区：东部、东南部、南部、西部、中部、北部。这六大方言区中间又形成了彝族语言的次方言和土语的次土语。作为记录彝族语言符号的彝文，随着彝族各方言、土语的产生及之间差异化的发展，彼此之间也出现了差异性，这种差异性的发展就形成了各具土语和方言特色的彝文"流派"。①

在这六大方言区中，彝文现在仍被流传使用的有东部、东南部、南部、北部四大方言区。西部和中部的彝文方言基本失传。不同方言区之间彝文的互通比较困难，不同流派之间阅读彼此的彝文古籍也比较困难。即使在同一方言区，不同的土语和次方言之间也有差异。这种流派及土语和次方言之间的差异并非文字性质的差别，而仅仅是彝文作为记录彝族语言的符号的差别，反映了彝族语言在不同方言区、在不同土语间及在不同次方言间的差异。这种彝文的差异性使得通晓所有彝族语言变得十分困难，使得彝文文献难以通读和互相理解。即使是彝文水平很高的毕摩或现代彝文研究人员，也很难做到通晓所有流派及种类的彝文。

三　对彝族语言的保护

中国对彝族语言的保护分为语言的改进及改革、彝文古典文献保护及通用彝文推广诸方面。

（一）　彝族语言的改进及改革

新中国成立初期，中国科学院语言研究所派遣川康工作队深入四川凉山地区调查彝语。截至1955年底，共调查了超过90个点。1956年1月，中国少数民族语言调查第四工作队组成，先后派出96人次全面调查彝语，用11个月的时间，对分布在四省、自治区的125个县市的彝语进行调查，记录了254个点的资料。以此为基础，进行了彝语的比较研究，提出了将彝语划分为前述六大方言区的主张。1956年12月，在四川成都召开了彝族语言文字科学讨论会，各地彝族代表参加。与会代表一致同意先解决四川凉山地区的语言文字问题。对于原有的凉山彝文，认为是宗教界使用的

---

① 参见王成有《略论彝语方言的划分》，《中央民族大学学报》（哲学社会科学版）1998年第6期。

不科学的音节文字，在群众中没有基础，因此需要另行设计一套拉丁字母的彝文。会议讨论并一致通过了早在 20 世纪 50 年代初期就已经在凉山部分地区实验教学并在此次会议期间进行修订的《凉山彝族拼音文字方案（草案）》。因为彝族原有文字系音节表义文字，故凉山彝族拼音文字又被称"新彝文"。

在彝族小聚居大分散、支系繁多、方言分歧、差异较大的背景下，"新彝文"的出现是为了创建彝族之间通用的文字，帮助彝族创制以拉丁字母为基础的彝文，于是就出台了彝文拼音文字方案。这种拼音方案是以北部方言为基础的一种新文字。这种新彝文的创制方式符合少数民族文字方案中设计字母的原则："少数民族创制文字应当以拉丁字母为基础"；"少数民族语言和汉语相同、相近的音，尽可能用汉语拼音方案里相当的字母表示"。这种原则的制定，符合中国的实际情况。作为一个以汉族为主体的多民族国家，少数民族新创文字与汉语拼音方案取得一致，有利于少数民族在掌握本民族语言的同时学习汉语，有利于各民族互相学习语言文字。规定以拉丁字母为基础，符合世界文字发展的趋势。

但是，对彝语进行改革和创设时，仅仅看到了彝语方言差异大的不足，对原有彝文的潜力认识不足，对新彝文的可行性及民众的接受程度估计过于乐观。由于新彝文实际上否定了原来彝文的体系，属于新创语言，所以彝族民众对它的接受度并不高。同时，在彝族内部统一所有地区的方言和文字可能并不必要，统一的文字并不是识别一个民族的前提条件。[1] 因此，新彝文出台后，由于彝族群众对它并不接受，所以使用了一些时候就停止了。1974 年 9 月，四川省委决定采用原有彝文，在整理、规范的基础上予以推行。据此，四川省民委和凉山彝族自治州政府对原有彝文进行了整理规范，在原有彝文的基础上，以四川凉山喜德语音为标准音、以圣乍话为基础方言，从近万个原有彝文中选出 819 个原字加上高调符号及一个替音符号共 1165 个规范彝文，并引入现代标点符号等新成分，制定出了《彝文规范方案》。1976 年 1 月，四川省彝族地区开始试行规范彝文。

1980 年 1 月，在北京召开了国家民委和中国社会科学院联合主办的"第三次全国民族语文科学讨论会"。讨论会上确认《凉山彝族拼音文字方案》停止试行。同月召开全国彝族文字工作会议，通过了《全国彝族文字

---

① 孔祥卿：《彝文规范的前景》，《中央民族大学学报》（哲学社会科学版）2004 年第 4 期。

工作会议纪要》。在 1976 年整理和规范四川凉山传统彝文和试行四川彝文规范方案的基础上，国务院于 1980 年 12 月批准了《彝文规范方案》，并在《四川日报》上公布推行。在 20 世纪 80 年代，对于彝文这样虽然有传统文字但是不能在本民族所有地区通用的少数民族语言，侧重于母语教学和在非官方民间活动中的大量使用。

（二）通过地方条例推行的彝族语言

正是由于彝族"大杂居、小聚居"的人口分布特点及彝族语言内部方言、土语及次方言差异大的特点，通过一刀切的方式推行整个彝族统一适用的彝族语言比较困难。因此，《彝文规范方案》是通过地方条例，在成熟的地方逐渐推广使用的。四川地区就有三个地方通过了彝族语言文字工作条例；而云南的彝族语言工作是通过自治地方的自治条例加以分别规定的。

1.《凉山彝族自治州彝族语言文字工作条例》

四川是一个彝族分布较多的省份。其凉山彝族自治州、马边彝族自治县及峨边彝族自治县分别于 1992、1994 及 1995 年通过了各自的彝族语言文字工作条例，对彝族语言在当地的使用和推广进行了规定。其中，《凉山彝族自治州彝族语言文字工作条例》（以下简称《凉山彝族语言条例》）是比较典型的。

凉山彝族自治州从 1989 年就开始着手制定自己的彝族语言工作条例。在广泛征求和采纳各方意见的基础上，其草案于 1992 年为凉山彝族自治州人民代表大会通过并被四川省人民代表大会批准，《凉山彝族语言条例》自此正式生效。

《凉山彝族语言条例》的原则可概括为两方面。一方面，《凉山彝族语言条例》根据中国《宪法》和《民族区域自治法》的相关规定而制定，反映中国民族语言法律保护框架的相关要求和内容，并从中确定了彝文同全国通用语言的关系，规定自治州内通用彝语文和汉语文。① 另一方面，《凉山彝族语言条例》"要为促进各民族平等、团结、互助和共同繁荣，促进自治州的经济发展和社会进步服务"。② 《凉山彝族语言条例》在规定彝文法律地位的同时，注重发挥彝文的交际沟通功能。"自治州内一切单位和个人，

---

① 《凉山彝族语言条例》第 4 条第 1 款。
② 《凉山彝族语言条例》第 6 条。

使用彝文应当遵守国务院批准的《彝文规范方案》。"① 其中体现了在条件成熟的凉山推行规范彝文的原则。这符合自治州经济发展、社会进步的要求，也兼顾了彝文保护的需要。

《凉山彝族语言条例》共分为七章三十条，这七章分别规定了自治州国家机关执行职务时使用彝语文的要求，规定了彝语文在民族文化教育事业中的地位和任务，规定了各种公开标志要适用彝、汉两种文字，规定了交通运输和邮电业务中适用彝语文的要求，并对彝语文工作的自身建设做了规定。

《凉山彝族语言条例》进一步尊重和保障了学习、使用和发展彝族语言文字的自由，推动建立了彝语文的翻译、出版和新闻、传媒系统；通过推行规范彝文，扫除了农村、厂矿的文盲，开展了彝文、汉语的双语教学；使得凉山行政、司法程序及服务行业始终重视彝语文的适用；彝文学术研究取得很大成绩，并出版了诸如《凉山文艺》等彝文杂志和报刊；将学习、使用和发展彝文的工作纳入法制轨道，进一步推动了彝文在凉山的广泛适用；加强了彝语文教育事业，逐步建立和完善了双语教学体系。《凉山彝族语言条例》的出台，对彝族语言的规范化、标准化、信息化，提供了法律保障。

2. 云南等地各自治地方在自治条例中对彝族语言工作进行规定

在云南，彝族是人口最多的一个少数民族，在 2005 年共有 416 万余人，占全国彝族总人口的 62.1%。云南彝族主要分布于澜沧江以西的绝大多数县（自治县）、市。其中，楚雄彝族自治州、红河哈尼族彝族自治州、玉溪市是彝族分布最集中的三个地区。

《云南省楚雄彝族自治州自治条例》于 1986 年 4 月经州人民代表大会通过，同年 7 月经云南省人民代表大会常务委员会批准后生效。该自治条例有四条规定了彝族语言文字。其中，该条例第 14 条重申了《宪法》中"使用和发展自己的语言文字的自由"；第 21 条规定了自治机关使用彝语、汉语和汉文执行职务的义务，并规定了使用规范彝文的可能；第 26 条重申了《宪法》规定的用本民族语言进行诉讼的权利；第 72 条则鼓励各民族干部、教师、专业人员互相学习、使用各自的民族语言。《云南省红河哈尼族彝族自治州自治条例》也有相似的规定。

---

① 《凉山彝族语言条例》第 5 条。

由于云南省彝族及其他各民族"小聚居、大杂居"的现象尤为突出，且云南多为高原、高山地貌，交通不便，彝族语言之间的差异性也尤为明显。虽然国务院在 1980 年 12 月批准了《彝文规范方案》，但在这种背景下只能因地制宜，尊重本地彝族民众的语言习惯，而不能硬性推行彝族语言的规范化。但是，以《云南省楚雄彝族自治州自治条例》为代表的地方自治法规也规定"要积极研究和规范彝文……"，[①] 为进一步的彝文规范化留下了空间，有利于形成彝族本民族内部通用语言。

（三）对彝族古籍的保护

彝族语言具有悠久的历史，在发展演变中形成了丰富的典籍，记载了彝族民众的生活，反映了彝族民众的思想，具有极高的文献和文化价值。但是，由于彝族语言内部差异化大，而掌握传统彝族语言的毕摩又重视口语传承，因而使得彝族丰富的古籍得不到体系化的研究，且随着时间的流逝有泯灭的危险。毕摩文献构成了彝族古籍的主体，被彝族民众视为民族之根。

1983 年 11 月，云南省民族工作部和云南省民族事务委员会在昆明召开云南、四川、贵州、广西四省区彝文古籍整理出版工作协作会议。会议根据现存的彝文古籍目录、类别和内容，确定了彝文金石图录文集等七个协作项目。会议并且商定成立四省区彝文古籍整理出版协作组，下设办事组，机构设在昆明。

除此之外，中国积极建立了《国家珍贵古籍名录》，对包括彝文古籍在内的古籍进行保护。目前，国务院已经公布了第一、第二批国家珍贵古籍名录，第一批共入选 209 个单位和个人的 2392 部古籍。其中汉文古籍 2282 部，民族文字古籍 110 部，其中包括 10 部彝族古籍。第二批共入选 280 个单位和个人的 4478 部古籍，其中 33 部彝族古籍入选。[②] 这些措施为彝族古籍保护提供了具体的法律依据，有利于彝族古籍的收集保护。

结　语

彝族语言作为彝族文化的基础性组成部分，对彝族文化的发展及经济社会发展都有着重要的意义。中国对彝族语言进行保护，经历了比较长时

---

① 《云南省楚雄彝族自治州自治条例》第 21 条第 2 款。

② 普梅笑：《彝族古籍的数字化保护和开发》，《河池学院学报》2009 年第 6 期。

间的探索过程，从创设拉丁语文字到在旧彝文的基础上规范彝文，从一刀切地规范彝文推行到因地制宜地推行规范彝文，体现了中国对彝族语言文化的重视和对少数民族文化习惯的尊重。彝文体现了中国语言文化资源的多样性，对于中国的文化建设和发展也具有重要的意义。

2007 年 7 - 8 月，中央民族大学组成"里山彝语的现状及其演变"调查组，在云南省通海县里山彝族民族乡进行了为期 1 个月的田野调查。过去，里山彝族村相对封闭，彝语世代相传，天天使用，所以能被较好保留。如今，里山彝族村已对外开放，彝语面临外来语的冲击，但仍然在大部分彝语地区中得到稳定使用，没有出现明显的衰退。调查组认为，这固然是因为里山彝族相对聚居、具有相对较强的民族内部凝聚力从而使得家庭与社区都有使用保留彝族母语的坚实基础，但中国的民族语言政策保障里山彝族彝语的使用也是一个重要的原因：在政府机构执行公务、教育机构进行教学等方面，对彝语地位予以充分尊重。虽然经济的发展使得彝语受到冲击，但在和彝族进行交易的场合，彝语也得到了广泛的使用。① 这充分说明，彝族的社会经济发展与彝语的发展并不矛盾，中国因地制宜的彝族语言政策取得了初步效果。

同时也应当看到，外来语言的冲击的确对彝语的发展产生了一定影响。"里山彝语的现状及其演变"调查组发现：里山彝族青少年母语能力的确存在着一定程度的下降。这里边有多重因素在综合作用。一方面，彝族自身对汉语的期望值要高于彝语；另外一方面，囿于其语言本身的局限，彝语承载的信息量少，很多场合不得不借助汉语来表达。② 这就对彝语文化的保护和发展提出了新的课题。但是，作为交流的语言虽然有可能受到冲击，但在中国保护少数民族非物质文化遗产政策暨其他法律措施之下，可以着重对语言文化本身进行保护，从而可以超越语言交流层面，在不妨碍彝族地区经济发展的前提下，对彝族语言为代表的彝族文化给予更有效的保护。笔者认为这也许是彝族语言保护的解决方式，也是少数民族语言保护的出路。

---

① 戴庆厦主编《云南里山乡彝族语言使用现状及其演变》，商务印书馆，2009，第 9 - 30 页。
② 戴庆厦主编《云南里山乡彝族语言使用现状及其演变》，商务印书馆，2009，第 73 - 74 页。

Case Study on the Legal Protection of Minority Languages in China

*Wu Jun**

【Abstract】 China has established a framework of legal protection of minority languages based on the Constitution, which provides sufficient protection to the right of ethnic minorities to use their own languages. The legal protection of minority languages should be based on the establishment of a balance between the need to protect the right of ethnic minorities to use their own language and the need to promote the use of the standard Chinese language. The Yi nationality is an ethnic minority in China that has a long history, a large population, and a language very different from that of the standard Chinese language. The development of the institutions and policies protecting the language of the Yi nationality fully demonstrates the importance attached by the Chinese government to the protection of minority languages in both legislation and practice and the balance between such protection and the need for economic development in minority areas.

【Keywords】 Protection of Minority Languages; Protection of the Language of the Yi Nationality; Protection of the Cultures of Ethnic Minorities

---

＊ Assistant Professor, Institute of Law, Chinese Academy of Social Sciences.

第三部分

法治政府建设与司法体制改革

Open, Efficient, Independent

—An Evolving Doctrine of European Administrative Law

Olli Mäenpää[*]

【 Abstract 】 The considerable expansion of European administration and the concurrent increase of its powers have made it necessary to lay down the legal basis of its functioning. The objective of this presentation is to analyze the evolution of the doctrine of European administrative law and the attempts to codify the basic rules of European administrative procedure and decision-making.

Introduction

The evolution of European administrative law can quite sketchily and for the sake of elucidation be divided into three stages. The first two stages are the elementary stage and the contemporary stage which I will describe rather briefly. What is perhaps most interesting in this context is that there appears to be also a third stage, a future stage of European administrative law. My presentation will focus on its future challenges, the possibility of the progress of the European legal doctrine and the eventual normative codification of its central tenets.

Why is this topic of significance? I would like to offer two parallel answers. First, the European administration has gradually developed into a large transnational and multi-level executive with increased powers and specific procedures. It is important to bear in mind that European administration does not necessarily refer

---

[*] Professor of the Faculty of Law of the University of Helsinki.

only to the transnational administration of the European Union (EU). Also the national administrations of the Member States of the EU can be considered as elements or tools of the European administration when they apply, implement and execute EU law. Since some 60 –80 % of the national legislation derives, at least to a significant extent, from EU law, it is easy to see that the public administration of each Member State is a quite closely interconnected element of the European administration. There remains, however, a certain degree of national autonomy with regard to procedures, structures and judicial review.

Second, European administrative law as a regulatory framework is, somewhat belatedly, trying to catch up with this development. The Treaty of Lisbon (2007)① initiated a significant new phase in the gradual evolution of a European administrative law by emphasizing the qualitative characteristics of an open, efficient and independent European administration. In addition, the Treaty created both a clear legal basis and a mandate for the codification of European administrative law to regulate the functioning of the European administration. Yet, whether law in treaties can be put into action and implemented in reality, still remains an open question. So far the harmonization on this basis has only had scant, mainly formal and procedural results. The pace of reform has also been strikingly slow.

Elementary stages

Instead of the legislator, judicial organs have largely played the role of the Founding Fathers of European administrative law. The EU has been a project leaning on judge-made law from the very start. On the one hand, The EU Court has functioned as the first and foremost harmonizer of European administrative law since the 1960s. Its case law has gradually come to define the basic requirements of an administrative law based on the rule of law. They include the requirements of hearing the concerned parties before administrative decision-making, providing reasons to administrative decisions, effective judicial protection, as well as accountability in administrative action.

---

① The Treaty of Lisbon consists of two separate treaties: the Treaty on European Union and the Treaty on the Functioning of the European Union. The Charter of Fundamental Rights of the European Union, proclaimed in 2007, has the same legal value as the Treaties.

On the other hand, another judicial body, the European Court of Human Rights, has also been active in harmonizing national administrative laws through its case law. The focus of its judicial activity has been on issues such as access to justice in cases concerning executive application of the law, the quality of legal protection afforded to subjects of administrative decision-making, and the effectiveness of judicial protection. One may note that at the inception, this role was fairly unlikely since Article 6 (1) of the European Convention on Human Rights formally limits the access to justice only to legal disputes concerning "civil" rights and obligations. Gradually, however, the interpretation of that term has been extended to include nearly all legal disputes between the public authorities and citizens or other private parties.

Contemporary stage

The contemporary stage in the development of European Administrative Law is predominantly characterized by a top-level, general harmonization and codification of the centralelements of European administrative law. The EU Charter of Fundamental Rights has already for a number of years augured this stage although the Charter did not become legally binding until December 2010. After the entry into force of the Lisbon treaty, both codification and harmonization are slowly gaining momentum with respect to administrative law.

The principal qualitative and constitutional elements of European administrative law are laid down, albeit in a simplified form, in Article 41 defining the basic requirements of good administration. According to Article 41 of the EU Charter of Fundamental Rights on the Right to Good Administration:

1. Every person has the right to have his or her affairs handled impartially, fairly and within a reasonable time by the institutions, bodies, offices and agencies of the Union.

2. This right includes:

(a) the right of every person to be heard, before any individual measure which would affect him or her adversely is taken;

(b) the right of every person to have access to his or her file, while respecting the legitimate interests of confidentiality and of professional and business secrecy;

(c) the obligation of the administration to give reasons for its decisions.

3. Every person has the right to have the Union make good any damage caused by its institutions or by its servants in the performance of their duties, in accordance with the general principles common to the laws of the Member States.

4. Every person may write to the institutions of the Union in one of the languages of the Treaties and must have an answer in the same language.

As a concomitant, access to public information held by the EU can be seen as an inseparable component of the right to good administration. Article 42 of the EU Charter of Fundamental Rights is defining the Right of Access to Documents: "Any citizen of the Union, and any natural or legal person residing or having its registered office in a Member State, has a right of access to documents of the institutions, bodies, offices and agencies of the Union, whatever their medium." The right to good and open administration is supplemented and supported by the right to an effective remedy and to a fair trial (Art. 47), and the right to submit a complaint to the European Ombudsman (Art. 43). An important function of these rights is to strengthen the accountability and legality of European administration.

Without downplaying the significance of fundamental rights focusing on the European administration, these rights are formulated at a general level. Therefore they need further implementation to achieve their full force. In this respect, European administrative law and particularly legislation regulating European administrative procedure, discretion and decision-making are needed to supply the requisite concretization of the fundamental rights.

Future prospects

The Treaty of Lisbon contains a number of new legal provisions and new legal bases for further rule-making. The new provisions bring about significant amendments and they will also expand the powers of EU organs. A specific new article regulates the basic features of European administration and administrative law thus making it possible to implement and concretize the right to good, open and accountable European administration. Article 298 of the Treaty on the Functioning of the European Union (TFEU) reads as follows:

1. In carrying out their missions, the institutions, bodies, offices and agencies of the Union shall have the support of an open, efficient and independent European administration.

2. In compliance with the Staff Regulations and the Conditions of Employment adopted on the basis of Article 336, the European Parliament and the Council, acting by means of regulations in accordance with the ordinary legislative procedure, shall establish provisions to that end.

Article 298 TFEU makes it possible to harmonize the basic qualitative requirements of European administration. It also provides an unequivocal legal basis for new legislation governing the functioning of European administration. What is more, the Article also lays down an obligation: Pursuant to the Article regulations shall be adopted to define how the qualitative objectives will be accomplished.

Qualitative attributes of European Administration:

Openness is one of the central conceptualizations of accessibility and accountability of public governance. It partly realizes in terms of law the requirement of transparency and access to information held by European administrators. In this respect, openness is also based on the right of access to documents laid down in Article 42 of the EU Charter of Fundamental Rights. In addition, openness functions as a prerequisite for the supervision of administrative practices and therefore it may be used as a preventive guarantee against maladministration.

Effectiveness connects with a number of potentially conflicting ideas and goals. Consequently, it is also a contested concept. It may suggest the high performance, efficiency and functionality of administration. On the one hand, The objective of effectiveness may be to reduce friction and undue delay in acomposite administrative structure. These objectives by no means exclude an emphasis on the quality of administrative procedure consisting of a responsive, service-minded administration putting the citizen first. Good administration may actually serve as an indispensable condition for achieving effectively the goals of European administration. On the other hand, effectiveness may be construed on the basis of financial efficiency and immediate outcomes. Understood and implemented solely on this basis, the objective of effectiveness could lead to the marginalization of legitimacy, legal diversity and even rights and legal protection which in turn could jeopardize the right to good administration.

Independence can also be understood in different ways. It may denote independence of undue influence and detachment of interests compromising the general good. Independence is also a significant prerequisite for guaranteeing the integrity, objectivity and impartiality of administrative decision-making. At the same time, the independence of public administration is challenged by new mechanisms of governance, especially influenced by New Public Management, contractualism and contracting out of public functions. These and similar developments invite to consider, what "independence" really signifies and entails. If the borderline between the public and the private domains becomes more diffuse, will this development inevitably strengthen the inter-dependence between these domains? And if the exercise of public power scatters into network, will this undermine the integrity of administrative authorities participating in the network?

European administration

The scope of application of the new Treaty provision is also open for different interpretations. Article 298 TFEU focuses directly on "*European administration*" the duty of which is to "support" the EU authorities when they carry out their duties. The concept of a European administration is so flexible and vague that its scope leaves room for various interpretations. One can argue that the concept of European administration refers merely to EU authorities but a broader construction of the concept is equally justified.

In my view, a narrow understanding of the term "European administration" would be both less justified and less practical. Since the execution and application of EU law is mainly the duty of national administrations, a broader construction of the term would include both the EU level administration (especially the Commission and the EU agencies and institutes) and the Member States' administrations when they engage in the implementation of EU law and otherwise function in tasks falling under the scope of EU law. Similarly, the Right to Good Administration is also applicable not only to the EU but also to the Member States when they are implementing Union law (Article 51 (1) of the EU Charter of

Fundamental Rights).

The new legal basis laid down in Article 298 TFEU provides the basis for a regulation (or regulations) governing not only the Union's administrative procedure but also European administration functioning in between the Union and Member States. This intermediate administrative level has as its basic task to carry out common European administration based on EU committees, networks consisting of officials of the Union and the Member States, companionship and other forms of cooperation with the Member States, such as the functioning of structural funds.

As a whole, the multi-layered character of European administration implies that it may be impossible to exclude the Member States' authorities from the scope of the European administration. It can be argued therefore, that Article 298 TFEU also provides the legal basis for a normative harmonization of administrative law regulating the activities of national executive bodies, at least to the extent that national administrative authorities and officials implement and apply EU law. The objective of such a harmonization is to bring about a European administration that is open, efficient and independent in its functioning.

A Draft European Law of Administrative Procedure

A draft of a new regulation based on the general mandate in Article 298 TFEU has recently been discussed in the European Parliament. The European Parliament adopted a resolution on 15 January 2013 in which it requests that the EU Commission should draft a proposal for a regulation on a European Law of Administrative Procedure. [1] Such a draft should comply with the recommendations of the European Parliament.

The recommendations are of relatively detailed nature. The objective of the new regulation should be to guarantee the right to good administration based on a European Law of Administrative Procedure. The regulation should apply only to the EU administration in their relations with the public. Its scope would therefore

---

[1] European Parliament resolution of 15 January 2013 with recommendations to the Commission on a Law of Administrative Procedure of the European Union. http://www.europarl.europa.eu/sides/getDoc.do? pubRef = - //EP//TEXT + TA + P7 - TA - 2013 - 0004 + 0 + DOC + XML + V0// EN.

be limited to direct EU administration. The national administrations would in other words be excluded from the scope of its direct application. Although this limitation seems to be based on an unnecessarily narrow construction of Article 298 TFEU, one can envisage that at least indirectly the European law could still have a significant harmonizing effect on national administrative laws.

According to the Parliament's resolution, the regulation should include a universal set of principles and should lay down a procedure applicable as a minimum requirement where no sector specific EU legislation exists. With respect to special rules, the guarantees afforded to persons in sectoral legislation must never provide less protection than those provided for in the general regulation on administrative procedure.

Principles of Administrative Law

The Parliament resolution lists nine principles that should be incorporated in the new regulation. They include the principles of legality, transparency, fairness, equality proportionality and impartiality. Also respect for privacy and legitimate interests are mentioned.

Principle of lawfulness: The Union administration shall act in accordance with the law and apply the rules and procedures laid down in the Union legislation. Administrative powers shall be based on, and their content shall comply with, the law. Decisions taken or measures adopted shall never be arbitrary or driven by purposes which are not based on the law or motivated by the public interest.

Principle of non-discrimination and equal treatment: The Union administration shall avoid any unjustified discrimination between persons based on nationality, gender, race, colour, ethnic or social origin, language, religion or beliefs, political or any other opinion, disability, age, or sexual orientation. Persons who are in a similar situation shall be treated in the same manner. Differences in treatment shall only be justified by objective characteristics of the matter in question.

Principle of proportionality: The Union administration shall take decisions affecting the rights and interests of persons only when necessary and to the extent required to achieve the aim pursued. When taking decisions, officials shall ensure a fair balance between the interests of private persons and the general interest. In particular, they shall not impose administrative or economic burdens which are excessive in relation to the expected benefit.

Principle of impartiality: The Union administration shall be impartial and independent. It shall abstain from any arbitrary action adversely affecting persons, and from any preferential treatment on any grounds. The Union's administration shall always act in the Union's interest and for the public good. No action shall be guided by any personal (including financial), family or national interest or by political pressure. The Union's administration shall guarantee a fair balance between different types of citizens' interests (business, consumers and other).

Principle of consistency and legitimate expectations: The Union administration shall be consistent in its own behaviour and shall follow its normal administrative practice, which shall be made public. In the event that there are legitimate grounds for departing from such normal administrative practice in individual cases, a valid statement of reasons should be given for such departure. Legitimate and reasonable expectations that persons might have in the light of the way in which the Union's administration has acted in the past shall be respected.

Principle of respect for privacy: The Union administration shall respect the privacy of persons. It shall refrain from processing personal data for non-legitimate purposes or transmitting such data to unauthorized third parties.

Principle of fairness: Fairness must be respected as a basic legal principle indispensable in creating a climate of confidence and predictability in relations between individuals and the administration;

Principle of transparency: The Union administration shall be open. It shall document the administrative procedures and keep adequate records of incoming and outgoing mail, documents received and the decisions and measures taken. All contributions from advisory bodies and interested parties should be made available in the public domain. Requests for access to documents shall be dealt with in accordance with the general principles and limits laid down in Access Regulation of 2001.

Principle of efficiency and service: Actions on the part of the Union administration shall be governed by the criteria of efficiency and public service. Members of the staff shall advise the public on the way in which a matter coming within their remit is to be pursued. Upon receiving a request in a matter for which they are not responsible, they shall direct the person making the request to the competent service.

Procedural rules

In addition to outlining the nine leading legal principles binding in the application and enforcement of European legislation, the Resolution also focuses on the procedural rules governing the functioning of European administration. Thus, the future regulationon administrative procedure should also define the basic procedural requirements of good administration.

The draft rules identify ten principal stages of administrative procedure and provide brief indications for the contents of the future legal provisions. The most significant recommendations concern the guarantees of impartiality and objectivity of administrative decision-making, the right to be heard and have access to one's own file as well as the form and contents of administrative decisions. In addition, correction of administrative decisions should also be provided for.

The impartiality of administrative decisions will necessarily be compromised if any kind of conflict of interests could affect the procedure or the outcome of the procedure. Therefore an official must be excluded from taking part in the decision-making if he or she has a particular interest in the decision. The official concerned must report any potential conflict of interest to his or her immediate superior, who may disqualify the official, having regard to the particular circumstances of the case.

The right to be heard is a cornerstone of a fair and equitable administrative procedure. Hearing is also an integral part of the rights of the defence that must be respected at every stage of the administrative procedure. In order to guarantee the right to be heard, the persons concerned must be given the opportunity to express their views in writing or orally prior to making a decision that would directly affect their rights or interests.

In order for the hearing to be conclusive the concerned party must also be informed of the pertinent documents, public or confidential, which may be used as a basis for the administrative decision. The party must also be granted full access to the case file. It should be up to the party to determine which non-confidential documents are relevant.

The basic *requirements for administrative decision-making* are both procedural and substantive in character. Administrative decisions must be made within a reasonable time-limit and without delay. However, the complexity of the matters raised, the obligation to suspend the procedure pending the decision of a third party and similar reasons may be taken into account in defining the reasonableness of the possible delay. Decisions must be made in writing and they must be formulated in a clear, simple and understandable manner.

As to the contents of the administrative decisions, they must clearly state the reasons on which they are based and indicate the relevant facts and their legal basis. The decision must also contain an individual statement of reasons. If the decision affects the rights and interests of individuals it must be notified in writing as soon as it is adopted. They must also include information of the possibility of appeal and the procedure to be followed for the submission of such an appeal.

The regulation on administrative procedure should also provide a possibility for the authority to correct a clerical, arithmetic or similar error at any time on its own initiative or following a request by the person concerned. The rectification of the administrative decision should also be possible on other, clearly specified grounds.

The Future of European administrative law

The harmonization and codification process of European administrative law is by no means without problems. On the one side it is confronted with a variety of national administrations and well-founded traditions of national administrative law doctrines. On the other side there is a much newer structure of the complicated multi-faceted European administration and the highly fragmented and diffuse body of European legislation governing its functioning. All administrations have their vested interests including the demand for sufficient freedom of legal constraints. Yet, the legal processes, most significantly judicial activity, have slowly but surely made possible the evolution of a body of European administrative law. The new Article 298 may be conceived of as a new stage in this process and also as a factor strengthening the process.

The drafting of a general law on European Law of Administrative Procedure would be a step forward in codifying a variety of existing administrative law rules in the EU legislation. However, it can be argued that the drafting process should not be confined merely to systematizing the existing rules and bringing more coherence into fragmented legal regimes in existing EU legislation. The European Law of Administrative Procedure should also guarantee good administration based on – among other things – openness, efficiency and independence in the administrative decision-making. This would require also a strong qualitative approach to the codification process.

Given the rather clear mandate in Article 298 TFEU for the codification of European administrative law it is interesting to note that so far the drafting process of the new regulations foreseen in the Article has been conspicuously sluggish. The European Parliament has shown decisive activity and individual scholars in the field of European administrative law have given their independent contribution to the drafting of the new provisions. A more comprehensive and hands-on approach would be needed.

Literature

Busuioc, Madalina: *European Agencies: Law and Practices of Accountability.* Oxford 2013.

Craig, Paul: *EU Administrative Law.* Oxford 2012.

Craig, Paul: *A General Law on Administrative Procedure, Legislative Competence and Judicial Competence.* European Public Law 2013, pp. 503 –524.

Curtin, Deirdre: *Executive Power of the European Union. Law, Practices, and the Living Constitution.* Oxford 2009.

Hofmann, Herwig, Rowe, Gerard & Türk, Alexander: *Administrative Law and Policy of the European Union.* Oxford 2011.

Jans, J. H. & de Lange, R. & Prechal, S. & Widdershoven, R. J. G. M. : *Europeanisation of Public Law.* Groningen 2007.

Jansen, O. and Schöndorf-Haubold, B. (eds.): *The European Composite Administration.* Antwerp 2011.

Mir-Puigpelat, Oriol: *Arguments in favour of a general codification of the procedure applicable to EU administration.* European Parliament Directorate-general for internal policies, 2011. (http://www. europarl. europa. eu/studies)

Mäenpää, Olli: *Eurooppalainen hallinto-oikeus.* (European Administrative Law). Helsinki 2011.

Eva Nieto-Garridos, Eva & Martin Delgado, Isaac：*European Administrative Law in the Constitutional Treaty.* Oxford 2007.

Ziller, Jacques：*Towards Restatements and Best Practice Guidelines on EU Administrative Procedural Law.* European Parliament. Directorate-general for internal policies, 2011. （http://www. europarl. europa. eu/studies）

公开、高效和独立：欧洲行政法的
一项不断发展的原则

奥利·马恩帕[*]

【摘要】随着欧洲行政机构的大幅扩张及其权力的增长，有必要对其运作的法律基础做出规定。本文分析了欧洲行政法原则的发展过程以及将有关欧洲行政程序和决策的基本规则法典化的努力。

---

* 赫尔辛基大学法学院教授。

论互联网的规制体制

——在政府规制与自我规制之间

李洪雷*

【摘要】伴随着互联网的迅速发展，对于网络空间中秩序的维持和公民权益的保护，规制的重要性日益凸显。但这并不意味着政府应成为互联网的唯一规制主体，自我规制组织在网络空间中也应发挥重要作用。互联网法制建设的关键问题之一，是建立一个能够充分发挥政府规制和自我规制各自比较优势的规制体制。本文以互联网规制的比较研究为基础，描述了中国当下的互联网规制体制，分析了其缺陷与不足，并对其未来发展提出了若干设想。文章认为，要完善我国未来互联网规制体制，一方面应提高互联网政府规制的法治化、规范化和公开化水平，增强其效能和正当性；另一方面应根据社会优先的理念，更多地放权于社会，让互联网行业团体在更大范围和程度上发挥作用。此外，在政府规制过程中应促进行业团体对规制决策的参与，而对于自我规制，政府也应发挥激励与监督作用。迈向政府规制与自我规制互相补充、互为支持的合作式规制体制，应成为我国互联网规制的发展方向。

【关键词】互联网　规制体制　政府规制　自我规制

一　引言

互联网作为一个对于人类社会具有革命性影响的新生事物，自 20 世纪

---

* 李洪雷，中国社会科学院法学研究所副研究员。

末叶在全球范围内迅猛发展，到 2012 年全球互联网用户已达 24 亿。在我国，截至 2013 年 9 月底，网民数量已达到 6.04 亿，互联网普及率达到 45%。互联网的出现深刻地改变了人们的工作、学习、消费和生活方式，"数字化生存"已然成为现实。但是，互联网在给人们带来诸多便捷的同时，也成为形形色色社会问题的温床。诸如网络谣言、信息泄漏、不正当竞争、金融诈骗、侵犯知识产权、网络色情和赌博、网络病毒传播等等，在互联网中屡见不鲜，有的还有愈演愈烈之势。这些问题中既有虚拟世界所独有的，如网络病毒传播，也有在物理空间中早已存在的，但因为网络传播的快捷、无国界、匿名等特征，而危害尤剧，如网络谣言。如果说在互联网发展的最初阶段，有一些人还对互联网抱有许多玫瑰色的幻想，以为其能带来一个无须规制的新世界的话，① 伴随互联网发展而日益暴露出来的各种社会问题，已经彻底粉碎了这种幻想。完全依赖于网络参与者的个人自律不可能保障网络世界的安全和良性运作，"网络无政府"（cyberanarchy）② 状态和现实世界的无政府状态一样会导致弱肉强食的"丛林状态"，虚拟世界与现实物理世界同样需要规制，已渐渐成为人们的共识。但是互联网具有高度的技术性、动态性、国际性和融合性，其发展日新月异，对于自由有着特别的需求，如何建构适合互联网特征的规制体制机制，在保障公共秩序、安全和福祉的同时又能维护互联网的自由创新精神，保证互联网发挥作为生机勃勃的社交平台和经济发展的动力引擎的角色，对此仍没有太多成熟的经验或先例可循。本文聚焦于互联网的规制体制问题，其核心是政府和行业组织在互联网规制中的角色地位与职能分配，也即政府规制和（行业）自我规制的关系问题。

---

① "电子边疆基金会"（EFF）的创始人之一——美国的约翰·佩里·巴洛（John Perry Barlow）1996 年在网上发布的《赛博空间独立宣言》是这方面的典型代表。其中宣布："工业世界的政府，你们这些令人生厌的铁血巨人，我来自赛博空间——一个崭新的心灵家园。我代表未来，要求属于过去的你们不要干涉我们。我们不欢迎你们。在我们聚集的地方，你们没有主权。"中译文可参见李旭、李小武译《网络独立宣言》（引用时有改动），载高鸿钧主编《清华法治论衡》第四辑，清华大学出版社，2004。英文版见 https://homes.eff.org/~barlow/Declaration-Final.html（2013 年 10 月 2 日最后访问）。EFF 的前主席 David Johnson 和研究员 David Post 还提出了"虚拟空间主权"（cyberspace sovereignty）的概念。David R. Johnson & David Post, Law and Borders—The Rise of Law in Cyberspace, *48 Stan. L. Rev.* 1367 (1996).

② Jack L. Goldsmith, Against Cyberanarchy, *65 U. Chicago L. Rev.* 1199 (1998).

二 影响互联网规制体制的因素

在互联网规制中政府和行业组织的角色，因规制对象、国别和互联网发展阶段的不同而有差异。

（一） 对象因素

对互联网的规制，涉及互联网物理设施、互联网基础结构和互联网的使用等。规制对象或领域的不同，对规制权力的配置有很大的影响。[①]

1. 互联网物理设施

这是互联网的物理层面，包括电信网、广电网、无线宽带网等。相关法律问题包括物理网络的运行和维护、网络接入和互联互通等。由于这一领域在传统上即受到法律的调整，因此其中的法律问题往往是新老问题的叠加，并且政府规制和行业自我规制均可能发挥重要作用。

2. 互联网基础结构[②]

这是互联网的代码（code）或协议（protocol）层面，是保证互联网运行的一系列技术模型、协议、方式和标准，包括互联网的架构（architecture）、根服务器系统、域名和 IP 地址系统、网页制作的技术标准等等，它们对于互联网这一"万网之网"（network of networks）的正常运行具有基础性作用。在这一领域中，到目前为止，非政府、非营利的自我规制机构仍占据主导地位，其中较为重要的有：（1）互联网名址分配公司（Internet Corporation for Assigned Names and Numbers，ICANN）。这是一个非营利公司，其受美国政府的委托，分配 IP 地址空间和协议参数（protocol parameter），管理国际域名系统和根服务器系统。互联网名址分配公司相当于互联网上的"交通警察"。（2）互联网工程工作组（Internet Engineering Task Force，IETF）。这是一个大型的、开放的、国际性的共同体，由网络设计者、运行者、商家和研究者所组成，向所有感兴趣的人开放，致力于推动互联网架构的发展。（3）万维网联盟（World Wide Web Consortium，

---

① Benkler 和 Zittrain 均将互联网区分为三个层面，但具体分类有所不同。Benkler 的三个层面分别是物理（如电缆）、代码（如浏览器和 IP）与内容，见 Benkler，*The Wealth of Networks, How Social Production Transforms Markets and Freedom*，Yale University Press，2006，pp. 383 – 459；Zittrain 的三个层面则是物理、协议（protocol）和应用，见 Zittrain，*The Future of Internet and How Stop it*，Yale University Press，2008，pp. 63 – 71。

② 互联网的基础结构也被称为"基础设施"（infrastructure）。但是考虑到在汉语中基础设施主要用来指称物理性的设施，容易与前述互联网物理设施混淆，因而这里称之为基础结构。

W3C）。联盟由互联网的发明者蒂姆·伯纳斯－李于 1994 年发起创立，作为其成员的有约 400 家组织，均为互联网行业的公司以及相关研究和教育机构。万维网联盟是互联网标准方面权威的机构，在有关标准和协议问题上，联盟所说的话就是互联网上的法。为解决网页应用中不同平台、技术和开发者带来的不兼容问题，保障网页信息的顺利和完整流通，万维网联盟制定了一系列标准并督促网络应用开发者和内容提供者遵循这些标准，其中包括可扩展标记语言（XML）和层叠样式表（CSS）等众多对互联网发展影响深远的标准规范。

3. 互联网的使用

这是互联网的应用层面，所涉及的是各类主体，包括政府、企业和普通网民对互联网的使用，包括媒体应用、即时通信、电子商务、电子政务、网络娱乐等。其中所涉及的法律问题包括言论自由限制、网络安全和国家安全、个人隐私保护、反垃圾邮件、知识产权保护等，焦点是互联网的内容。因互联网的使用而产生的法律问题是互联网规制讨论的重点。在这一领域中政府规制与行业规制均发挥着重要作用，但具体比重在不同国家有很大差别。

应当注意的是互联网的发展在很大程度上打破了网络载体（conduit）和内容（content）之间的界限，网络载体的运营商也往往同时提供与网络内容有关的服务，这导致互联网传输设施规制和内容规制之间的界限，有时变得模糊。[①] 此外，互联网作为一个新兴的、综合性媒体，其应用形式与传统媒介存在一定的相似之处但又不完全相同，例如其 email 功能与传统的邮政，网络通话与传统通讯，电子报纸与纸质媒体，网络广告与传统广告产业，等等，都是同中有异。这对各国如何进行有效的互联网规制提出了挑战。

（二）空间因素

在互联网的规制领域，根据各国对政府规制态度的差异，可以区分为不同的模式。[②]

---

① Rob Frieden, Adjusting the Horizontal and Vertical in Telecommunications Regulation: A Comparison of the Traditional and a New Layered Approach, *55 Fed. Comm. L. J.* 213 (2003).

② 美国缅因大学的 LyombeEko 将当今各国的互联网规制划分为 5 种模式，即国际主义者（Internationalist）模式、新重商主义者（Neo-merchantilist）模式、文化主义者（Culturist）模式、网关（Gateway）模式和发展主义者（Developmentalist）模式。LyombeEko, Many Spiders, One Worldwide Web: Towards a Typology of Internet Regulation, *6 Comm. L. & Pol'y* 445 (2001). 本文的模式划分借鉴了这一分类，但在类型和表述上均做了很大的调整。

1. 自由至上模式

美国对互联网规制采取的自由至上模式，强调行业自我规制（industrial self-regulation），最大限度地减少政府规制。这集中体现在克林顿和戈尔于 1997 年 7 月 1 日发布的"全球电子商务框架"（A Framework For Global Electronic Commerce）报告中。该报告提出："私人部门应当发挥引领作用。……政府应尽最大可能地鼓励行业自我规制，而且当私人部门发展以促进互联网成功运行为目标的机制时，为其提供支持。甚至当确实需要集体性的协议或者标准时，也应尽可能地让私人机构对此类事务的组织发挥领导作用。就是在需要政府行动或者政府间协议时，例如在有关税收问题上，私人部门的参与也应该成为政策制定过程中的一个正式部分。"① 除了电子商务之外，对于网上言论自由的保护，美国法的标准也是全球最高的。

美国之所以特别强调互联网的行业自我规制，首先是基于对互联网特性的把握。在美国人看来，互联网的发展，需要持续的创新技术、不断的拓展服务、吸引广泛的参与和提供低廉的价格，而这些都只有通过"市场驱动的竞技场"才能实现，其中必须由作为市场主体的私人部门而非政府发挥领导作用。但美国的立场也有其特殊的国情背景。一是美国具有根深蒂固的重视企业经营自由和个人言论自由、怀疑政府干预的传统。② 二是美国互联网行业发展较早，实力雄厚，游说能力也很强，对于美国政府的干预企图可以进行强有力的抵御。三是美国互联网技术和产业的遥遥领先，使其在国际竞争中具有显著的优势地位，提倡行业自我规制、反对国家过度干预，可以限制其他国家的政府对其本国互联网企业发展采取保护性的措施，最终有利于美国互联网企业在国际范围内的竞争。当然，这并不意味着在美国没有互联网的政府规制，只是其范围较为有限，主要目标是通过打击垄断和不公平竞争保证自由市场的顺利运行，保护公民免受侵犯隐私、剥削、欺诈等非法网络活动的侵害。

2. 互联网规制的其他模式

在美国之外的其他国家，对政府规制作用之重视均远超美国，可以将

---

① http://clinton4.nara.gov/WH/New/Commerce/read.html，2013 年 10 月 19 日最后访问。

② See LyombeEko, Many Spiders, One Worldwide Web: Towards a Typology of Internet Regulation, *6 Comm. L. & Pol'y* 445 （2001）.

这些国家纳入三类模式。其一是文化保护模式，强调维持本国文明或文化的独特性，张扬友爱、平等等社群主义理念，对保护个人隐私和自尊极为敏感，努力抵御以美国式的将互联网过度商业化的趋势，法国、加拿大、澳大利亚等国为其代表。例如，法国人认为，互联网并不是价值中立的，由于美国在互联网发展中的主导作用以及英语的强势地位，互联网实际上成为美国文化传播的最佳平台，为了保护法兰西的独特语言、文化和价值观，法国必须对互联网予以特别规制。[①] 为此，法国要求设在法国的网站必须要有一定数量的法语内容。其二是社会控制模式，强调政府对互联网尤其是网上信息传播的严格控制，以防止西方意识形态的泛滥，或者维护社会的道德伦理。这一模式以越南、伊朗、新加坡等国家为代表。其三是经济发展模式。这一模式以亚非拉的多数发展中国家为代表，它们将互联网作为促进经济发展的工具。这里应当指出的是，一个国家的互联网规制政策，从不同的角度观察可能会符合不同模式的特点。特别是采取经济发展模式的国家，因大多具有长期的权威主义和严格限制媒体的传统，它们往往限制互联网在经济发展之外的功能，从而也符合社会控制模式的特点。

（三）时间因素

从时间上来说，在 20 世纪 90 年代，互联网法更强调互联网成长的自发性和无边界性，高度重视自我规制，这被称为"第 1 版的赛博法"（Cyberlaw 1.0）。从 21 世纪初开始，随着互联网发展日新月异，政府规制开始扮演日益重要的角色，"第 1 版的赛博法"为"第 2 版的赛博法"（Cyberlaw 2.0）所取代。[②] 这是因为，一方面，因为网民数量曾几何级数的增加，作为早期互联网一大特点的网民同质性丧失，滥用互联网的现象日益普遍，公众的不满情绪被催生，对政府规制的社会需求增加；另一方面，政府也从原先对互联网的茫然无措中开始觉醒，在对互联网更多地了解之后也开始有信心和技术对其加以规制。但这并不意味着行业自我规制被抛弃，而是日益强调政府规制和行业自我规制的协调。

三　对互联网的政府规制

（一）政府规制的利弊

根据规制的一般理论，政府规制相较于行业自我规制具有如下优势：

---

① 这是所谓法国例外论的一个表现。Sophie Meunier, The French Exception, *79 Foreign Affair.* 104 (2000).

② 详见 Michael Geist, Cyberlaw 2.0, *44 B. C. L. Rev.* 323 (2003)。

首先，政府比自我规制组织具有更高程度的代表性和民主正当性。行业自我规制往往缺乏对行业团体成员之外群体利益的关注，而政府规制可以扩大消费者等主体的参与，从而增强规制体系的正当性。其次，政府规制因为受公法的约束，往往比行业自我规制具有更高的公开性和透明度。再次，与行业自我规制相比，政府具有强有力的执行手段，这有利于克服集体行动难题并对相互冲突的利益进行协调。最后，因为政府具有代表性和权威性，有时其相较于行业团体更容易参与全球合作。

但另一方面，政府规制也有其自身缺陷。首先，政府规制的行政成本高，会增加国家财政支出和纳税人的负担。其次，政府对行业发展缺乏必要的专业知识和充分的信息，对其未来发展趋势不能进行准确的把握。再次，政府的官僚体制导致决策僵化、缓慢，往往不能适应经济社会发展对规制弹性、灵活性和动态性的要求。最后，政府规制受到国家主权范围的限制，在处理某些跨国性或全球性事务时会遇到障碍。

（二）国外互联网领域的政府规制

在互联网领域，有一些学者基于互联网的匿名性、虚拟性、交互性、迅捷性、全球性等特性，认为政府不可能或者不应当对互联网进行规制。关于政府没有能力对互联网进行规制的论点，已经被各国的实践所证伪，也即各国都在实际上对互联网进行规制，尽管其效果不一。[1] 关于政府不应当对互联网进行规制的论点，也由于互联网中出现的大量反社会行为而日益衰落。目前在世界各国，互联网运行和发展中的诸多问题都对政府构成了巨大压力。欧盟将互联网给政府带来的挑战进行了较为全面的概括：国家安全（对炸弹制作的指导，非法毒品的制造，恐怖主义行动）；对青少年的保护（滥用的市场交易形式，暴力，色情）；对人性尊严的保护（激发种族仇恨或者种族歧视）；经济安全（诈骗，窃取信用卡）；信息安全（黑客攻击）；隐私保护（未经授权传播个人数据，电子骚扰）；名誉保护（非法的竞争性广告）；知识产权（未经授权传播具有版权的著作、软件或音乐）；等等。[2] 不同的国家基于其政治体制、文化传统等也有各自不同的关切，例如，法国对互联网上法语内容的比重，社会主义国家对政治意识形态，韩

---

[1]   理论上的论证，参见 Timothy S. Wu, Cyberspace Sovereignty? The Internet and the International System, *10 Harv. J. L. & Tech.* 647（1997）。

[2]   见欧洲议会和欧盟理事会于 1999 年通过的《关于采取通过打击全球互联网上的非法和有害内容以促进更安全使用互联网的多年度共同体行动计划的第 276/1999/EC 号决定》。

国对与朝鲜关系，德国对纳粹和反犹言论，等等。

纵观各国尤其是发达国家的互联网政府规制，大致可以发现如下特点。

其一，各国均未设立全方位规制网络空间的专门性政府机构。各国一般认为，网络空间无法与现实物理世界全然分离，对网络空间的规制涉及经济、社会、文化和政治等多个方面，设立一个专门的政府机构来对网络空间进行全方位的规制不具有可行性。

其二，关于互联网物理设施的规制。在很多国家中电信规制机构，如英国的通信管理局（Ofcom）和韩国的通信委员会（KCC）等，在其中发挥着重要作用。这一方面反映了互联网是通过传统电信网络平台发展起来的这一历史背景，另一方面是因为电信规制部门作为网络传输设施和平台的管理者，自然而然地参与到对互联网的规制中。但对于是否应当由电信规制机构来规制互联网并非没有争议。例如在美国，对于联邦通信委员会（FCC）是否有权管辖互联网服务也存在很大的争议。这其中既有对法律解释的问题，[①] 也涉及对联邦通信委员会这种特定部门型政府规制机构的怀疑，一种较为普遍的担心是这种规制机构会采取针对电信产业的传统模式，过度限制互联网产业的自主性。

其三，关于互联网基础结构的规制。这一部分目前主要是由自我规制机构进行规制，但已经有很多国家与国际组织对此表达了不满，它们希望有更多的机会参与这一过程，尤其是国际域名与 IP 地址的分配。[②] 例如欧洲联盟建议互联网名址分配公司（ICANN）在政策议题上应当征求政府的意见，并且只有董事会的三分之二多数不同意或推翻政府的意见时，该意见才能被否决。2001 年联合国法律顾问办公室的一名代表提出，将域名管

---

① 一种观点认为，互联网服务属于"信息服务"（information service），而非"电信服务"（telecommunication service），因此 FCC 不能根据 1996 年联邦通信法第 2 条对公共运营商（common carriers）的规制权规定（其仅适用于电信服务）来规制互联网运营商。反对意见则认为，即使 FCC 没有根据通信法第 2 条对互联网运营商进行规制的权力，仍可根据第 1 条的一般性权力进行规制，因其第 1 条规定，"为了规制在有线和广播通信领域的州际和对外贸易"，设立 FCC；其第 2（a）条规定，"本章规定应适用于有线和广播通信领域的州际和对外贸易"。参见 James B. Speta, FCC Authority To Regulate the Internet: Creating It and Limiting it, 35 *Loy. U. Chi. L. J.* 15 (2003)。

② 有些学者将这两项事务合称为互联网治理（internet governance），Volker Leib, ICANN-EU can't: Internet governance and Europe's role in the formation of the Internet Corporation for Assigned Names and Numbers (ICANN), *19 Telematics and Informatics* 159 (2002)。

理交给一个私人组织而非一个国际代表性组织，是不正常的。他认为，互联网要求多个层面的国际合作，而只有全球性的政府组织这样的合作才能实现。国际电信联盟（International Telecommunications Union，是联合国的一个专门机构）也主张，政府应在包括国际域名在内的互联网治理过程中发挥更大的作用。① 此外，对于 ICANN 所行使的职能，到底属于公共规制还是"技术管理"性质的私人职能，也存在很大的争议。②

其四，关于互联网内容规制。各国对于互联网内容规制引起政治、文化等背景的差异而各有其特色。多数国家将互联网内容规制职能交由广播电视规制机构来行使，如新加坡和澳大利亚等，但这并不意味着其采取与广播电视规制相同的规制方式，而是采用更加节制的方法。即使有些国家的法律初看起来非常严格，但这有时其实只是一种政治上的姿态，在执行上要缓和得多。多数国家原则上不要求互联网服务提供商对网上的非法材料负责，以符合互联网的开放性和即时性等特征，并防止对互联网的发展产生阻碍作用。例如德国 1997 年《信息和通信服务法》中规定："如果所提供的内容是他人的，那么只有在服务提供者了解这些内容并且在技术上有可能阻止，而且进行阻止并不超过其承受能力的情况下才负有责任。"

在一些国家，由于法律对互联网内容规制的管辖权主体没有明确规定，导致管辖权冲突现象时常发生。例如在英国对于互联网广告的规制就有多个机构主张拥有管辖权。另外，对于某些活动是否要由现存的政府规制机构进行规制也可能存在争议，其结果可能导致管理真空。

（三） 我国互联网的政府规制

针对我国互联网发展中出现的诸多问题，例如信息安全、网络谣言、侵犯知识产权、不正当竞争等等，我国政府已采取了多种措施，有的取得了较好的社会效果，有的则引起了很大的争议。总体而言，我国互联网领域的政府规制在诸多方面尚存在进一步完善的空间。

1. 关于互联网规制机构的职能

我国和各国相同，截至 2013 年并无一个负责对互联网领域进行全方位规制的专门机构。这或许也是互联网发展之福，因为一个既能控制互联网

---

① 关于对 ICANN 管理体制的批评，参见 Michael Geist, Cyberlaw 2.0, *44 B. C. L. Rev.* 353 (2003)。

② Jonathan Weinberg, ICANN and the Problem of Legitimacy, *50 Duke L. J.* 187 (2000).

技术层面、又能控制互联网内容层面的巨无霸型规制机构，对互联网上信息的自由传播可能构成很大的威胁，在法治尚不健全的社会中更是如此。

对于互联网物理设施的规制，主要由被称为互联网行业主管部门的工业和信息化部负责，其规制的重点是互联网的网络运营、接入及安全问题。因为互联网作为继电信网之后崛起的信息基础设施，二者长期相互交织、相辅相成，例如中国最为重要的三家商业性骨干互联网服务商（ISPs），即中国电信、中国联通和中国移动，同时也是中国最为重要的电信网络运营商；而且近年来伴随着移动互联网的迅猛发展，二者的应用融合步伐不断加快，因此由信息产业主管部门统一对互联网物理设施和电信网进行规制，有利于整合规制资源、实现信息共享、发挥专业优势。但由信息产业行业主管部门进行规制亦存在缺陷。一是不能适应有线电视网、电信网和互联网三网融合的需要，有线电视网的规制仍未纳入整个信息网络产业规制体系之中。二是由行业主管部门来进行规制，实行政策制定职能和规制职能的合一，由于行业主管部门可能出于行业发展的考虑而放松必要的规制，因此不利于保证规制的独立性和消费者权益的保护。三是在 2008 年机构改革中撤销信息产业部、成立工业和信息化部所导致的一个消极后果，是信息产业方面的行政职能受到工业行业管理的挤压而被相对弱化，目前在工业和信息化部中直接与互联网相关的司局只有信息化司和信息安全司。未来可考虑建立与宏观决策部分相分离的独立规制机构，统一规制电信、广电和互联网等领域的网络设施。

在互联网的基础结构规制方面，除了具有全球性的标准设定、国际域名管理等事务以外，信息产业部的规章《中国互联网络域名管理办法》和《互联网 IP 地址备案管理办法》，对互联网络域名和 IP 地址的管理做了详细规定，各级信息产业主管部门依据这些规定承担相关的规制职能。此外，中国互联网络信息中心（China Internet Network Information Center，简称 CNNIC）在这一领域中扮演着重要角色。它是经国家主管部门批准于 1997年 6 月 3 日组建的互联网管理和服务机构，其作为我国域名注册管理机构，负责运行和管理中国顶级域名 . CN、中文域名系统及通用网址系统。中国互联网络信息中心制定的《中国互联网络信息中心域名注册实施细则》和《中国互联网络信息中心域名争议解决办法》是域名管理方面的重要规范。中国互联网络信息中心的运行和管理工作，由中国科学院计算机网络信息中心承担。对于中国互联网络信息中心行使的互联网管理职能的性质，目前存在争议。有人认为属于行政职能，但也有人认为属于民事职能。目前法院判决倾向于后者。①

　　在互联网使用或内容规制方面，国家互联网信息办公室主要负责互联网信息管理的相关事务，国家新闻出版广电总局负责监管视听节目的网络传播，以及监督管理全国互联网出版工作和版权（著作权）行政管理工作，工商行政管理总局负责监管电子商务，公安部负责全国计算机信息系统安全保护工作以及对网络上有害的信息、网络犯罪、网络安全的规制，工业和信息化部负责网站和电子公告服务等的规制。根据国务院发布的《互联网信息服务管理办法》，除了对互联网具有规制职能的机构以外，教育、卫生、药品监督管理等有关主管部门在各自的职责范围内依法对互联网信息内容实施监督管理。而党的宣传部门也发挥着重要的领导作用。由于互联网所涉业务、事务的复杂性和融合性，对互联网规制主体各国均存在一定程度的管辖权冲突（包括积极冲突和消极冲突）等问题，但我国这一问题尤为严重。我国互联网实践中的一个常见现象是，大量的规制决策或行动由多个党政机构联合做出，这表面上体现了对相关问题的重视，但有时却可能恰恰暴露了没有哪一个部门能够真正对该问题负责，这显然会影响相关规制措施的科学性和实效性。造成这一现象的原因，首先在于行政组织法不完善，我国政府组织的权力往往没有明确的法律规定，而主要依据国务院的"三定"规定。"三定"规定作为政策文件，表述上往往比较含糊，做不同解释的余地很大。此外，我国各政府机构协调性差，本位主义严重，难于通过机构协商的方式寻求解决职能冲突的最优方案；② 而相关的议事协调机构也往往采取和稀泥的立场，希望两边不得罪，不能及时做出决断，以至于贻误最佳的规制时机。要解决这一问题，需要完善我国行政组织法的框架，贯彻职权法定的法治原则，同时加强规制机构之间的信息共享和沟通协调机制。

　　国家互联网信息办公室作为国家互联网信息内容的主管部门，自2011年成立以来在我国互联网内容规制体系中地位日益凸显，但其职能行使的

① 在"赵磊诉中国互联网络信息中心等计算机网络域名纠纷案"［北京市海淀区人民法院民事判决书（2007）海民初字第22111号］中，法院将中国互联网络信息中心有关网络域名的决定视为民事（违约）行为。另可参见李燕蓉《中国互联网络信息中心的法律地位和法律责任——关于以中国互联网络信息中心作为被告的域名案件的调查报告》，《知识产权审判实务》第2辑，法律出版社，2005。

② 美国行政机构的组织法尽管极为健全，仍然难以完全避免管辖权的冲突问题，这类问题很多是由相关机构通过协议来解决的。司法部和FTC在反垄断案件管辖权上的冲突即是如此。

依据是中央的内部文件（到目前还未向社会公开），这对其有效行使规制职能构成了很大的障碍，在正当性上也有欠缺。不仅如此，从行政法原理的角度，国家互联网信息办公室作为国务院的办公办事机构，是为国务院总理办理某一方面事务的内部机构，本不应具有对社会事务的管理职能。因此，未来在修订《互联网信息服务管理办法》将"国家互联网信息内容主管部门"载入其中并明确其职权的同时，应当将国家互联网信息办公室明确为国务院的直属机构，改名为国家互联网信息管理局，改变其办公办事机构的性质。

在我国互联网内容规制方面，公安机关的职能范围非常宽泛。为了维护互联网的安全，公安机关的作用确实是无可取代的。但公安机关因为其特有的组织文化、对秩序问题的高度关注、对互联网发展所要求的公民自由的不甚敏感，导致其规制手段往往过于简单，不利于维护互联网的合作、自由的精神，尤其是在内容管理方面，公安机关承担过多的规制职能是不合适的。我国未来互联网规制体系的重塑，需要慎重考虑哪些规制任务或事项适合交由公安机关，哪些规制任务或事项适合交由专业的规制机构，以更好地平衡互联网秩序和自由的需要。

2. 关于互联网政府规制的理念

在互联网政府规制领域，规制节制或者谦抑的理念极为重要。一方面，随着技术发展的日新月异，很多问题实际上可通过技术的发展或者市场竞争来解决，并不需要政府的直接干预，政府介入既增加成本，有时甚至还适得其反，使得问题最终无法得到合理解决，阻碍互联网的健康发展。互联网上的很多问题，例如一些网络谣言的存在和广泛传播，有着复杂的社会背景和根源，其改变非一朝一夕之功，试图在一定时间内通过行政和法律的手段，"毕其功于一役"地加以治理或者解决，这样的目标是难以实现的。正如桑斯坦教授所言："治疗可能比疾病更糟糕。明智的决策者都知道一些难题是无解的。"① 因此，规制者对一些问题和现象，在缺乏深入了解之前，更多地采取宽容的态度有时是必要的。因此，《行政许可法》所确立的个人自治优先、市场优先、自律机制优先等理念，② 不应仅仅适用于行政

---

① Cass R. Sunstein, Republic. com, Princeton University Press, 2002, p. 210.

② 我国《行政许可法》第 13 条规定："本法第十二条所列事项，通过下列方式能够予以规范的，可以不设行政许可：（一）公民、法人或者其他组织能够自主决定的；（二）市场竞争机制能够有效调节的；（三）行业组织或者中介机构能够自律管理的；（四）行政机关采用事后监督等其他行政管理方式能够解决的。"

许可领域，而应成为中国规制体系改革的一个方向。在判断是否确有必要就互联网领域中某一问题进行规制时，应当进行规制的成本收益分析，保证规制收益大于规制成本，包括行政机关的执行成本和被规制者的履行成本等。此外，即使需要规制，也应优先采取对相关主体干预较小的措施。我国政府机构所习惯采取的规制工具和策略比较单一和僵化，主要是命令控制型与事先审批等传统的规制手段，对于信息披露、激励性规制等新型、柔性的规制手段比较陌生。在互联网规制领域中这一点也得到体现。此外，中国政府机构仍惯于采取直接干预的措施，不善于利用民间组织如行业协会的力量，进行间接干预。这一问题在下文关于行业自我规制的部分再做进一步的讨论。

　　另一方面，尤其就网络内容的规制而言，因其直接涉及公民的表达自由这一宪法基本权利，如果干预范围过宽、用力过猛，会导致"寒蝉效应"（chilling effect），影响社会活力，弱化公民对公共人物与公共事务的监督。在我国，公民借助互联网参与公共事务、发表意见，涉及我国《宪法》第35条规定的言论自由和第41条规定的监督权，这两项权利是我国民主政治建设健康发展不可或缺的前提条件。特别是《宪法》第41条规定的监督权，不仅承载着意见表达的功能，而且承载着政治功能。基于言论自由和监督权所具有的特殊宪治价值，国家对非法网络言论（特别是与公共事务有关的言论）的干预不能过度，从而为人们监督政府、表达思想在制度上留下空间。对非法网络言论过于宽泛的界定或严格的干预，势必会限制或剥夺公民的言论自由和监督权。在此应当适用公法上的比例原则，即国家为实现公益目的所采取的公权力措施，其给私人权益所造成的损害与该公共利益之间，应当保持均衡，不应过度干预私人的权益。

　　在规制理念方面另一个需要关注的议题是互联网政府规制资源的配置。网络世界极为复杂，以有限的政府资源不可能完全解决网络世界的问题，因此政府规制的配置应重点针对那些社会危险性大的行为。目前我国政府规制资源过多地向政治问题倾斜，而导致其他同样重要的网络空间中的问题被忽略。这不是说政治问题不重要，而是在实践中，存在泛政治化或者泛意识形态化的弊病，对于很多经济、社会和宗教政策层面的讨论也视为政治问题，过于敏感，同时对于网民凡是涉及政治的一般牢骚或者理性谈论容忍度偏低。另一方面对网络色情、虚假网络广告、病毒防范等具有严重社会危险性的行为，所投入的规制资源过少，效果不明显。我国政府需要慎重、均衡、合理分配互联网规制资源，全面保障社会公共利益。

3. 关于互联网政府规制的法治化

政府规制的法治化，对于保护互联网的自由创新精神、增强公权力行为的可预见性和确定性，具有特别重要的意义。近年来我国互联网政府规制的法治化水平有了很大的提升，但离法治国家、法治政府的要求还有一定的距离。（1）我国互联网规制所依据的大多是层级较低的规章和其他规范性文件，其中许多规定有较大的模糊性与不确定性，在互联网内容规制领域有时候所依据的是不公开的内部政策性文件甚至口头指示，具有很大程度的随意性和不可预测性，在合法性和正当性上都有很大欠缺。《全国人民代表大会常务委员会关于维护互联网安全的决定》和《全国人民代表大会常务委员会关于加强网络信息保护的决定》为我国互联网规制的法治化发挥了重要的推动作用，但因为其以"决定"的形式出台，规定的内容在明确性方面仍有很大不足。未来互联网规制领域的法治建设，需要提升立法层级，并提高立法质量。（2）习惯于采取"运动式治理"模式，例如"打击网络色情的专项整治行动""打击网络侵权盗版专项行动""严打网络谣言专项整治行动"等等。这种模式的特点是以垂直命令、政治动员的方式，在某些特定的时期集中调动力量、配置资源，用以解决一些比较尖锐、比较突出的矛盾和冲突。这种模式往往具有行政主导、不计成本、"一刀切""一阵风"等特点，[1] 与法治对规制所要求的稳定性、常规性和可预测性不符。应尽量减少这种运动式治理模式，建立互联网治理的长效机制。（3）缺乏有效的专家咨询和公众参与的渠道。互联网规制很多具有很强的技术性，政府需要咨询专家意见；另外往往涉及数量众多的网民，社会关注度高，政府做出决定之前应当倾听公众的意见。目前中国政府规制机构还惯于"关门"决策，这尤其不适合互联网规制的要求。未来政府在互联网决策方面应更多地听取专家和公众意见，以保证决策符合互联网技术，并有效回应社会需求。（4）由于将互联网规制过度政治化，导致对于很多规制措施缺乏有效的司法救济渠道。因此，我国在互联网政府规制方面，需要完善相关立法，健全行政程序，强化专家和公众参与，畅通救济渠道。

4. 关于互联网政府规制的国际化

由于互联网的跨国界性，在规制时必须要有国际的视角，国际治理是互联网规制的一个重要特色。在域名系统、数据保护、减少通信成本、提

---

[1] 清华大学社会学系社会发展研究课题组：《以利益表达制度化实现长治久安》，《领导者》总第 33 期（2010 年 4 月）。

供税收的确定性、电子认证、知识产权保护、儿童保护等等方面，都需要国际合作和协调。目前中国政府在进行互联网规制领域的国际合作和协调方面尚缺乏主动性，未来一方面要通过中国在相关国际组织，如世界贸易组织（WTO）、国际知识产权组织（WIPO）、联合国国际贸易法委员会和国际劳工组织等的代表，另一方面要通过多边或双边协定等，更高程度地参与互联网的国际治理。

四　对互联网的自我规制

（一）　自我规制的利弊

在关于互联网规制讨论中，自我规制（self-regulation）是一个出现频率颇高的词汇，但自我规制是一个多义的概念。（1）自我规制有时是指企业等经济主体出于社会责任感、建立声誉或声望或自律（self-discipline）等动机，对于自己行为的自我约束和规范，这种意义上的自我规制与心理学上对自我规制的运用相似，是主体对自身行为的控制。（2）自我规制有时是指一个集体组织（collective group）对其成员或者其他接受其权威的相关人员进行的约束和规范，即自我规制组织或者协会（self-regulatory associations，SRAs；或者 self-regulatory organizations，SROs）进行的规制。第一种意义上的自我规制在现代规制国家中也非常重要，但不应将其作为整个规制体制的一部分。[①] 本文采用其第二种含义，强调自我规制的集体性，认为自我规制的本质是一种集体治理过程。[②]

对于自我规制可以从不同角度对其进行类型划分。英国伦敦政治经济学院（LSE）的布莱克教授，将自我规制划分为四种类型，对于我们理解自我规制和国家的关系很有帮助。一是委任型自我规制（mandated self-regulation），这是指政府要求或指派一个集体组织，例如一个产业或职业，在政府通常以笼统的方式所确立的框架内设计并执行规范。二是认可型自我规制（sanctioned self-regulation），这是指集体组织自身对规制进行设计，但其要经过政府的批准。三是被迫型自我规制（coerced self-regulation），这是指产业界自身设计并推行规制，但这是对政府压力的一种回应，如果它不进行自我规制，政府就会推行法定的规制。四是自愿性自我规制

[①]　Alan C. Page, Self-Regulation: The Constitutional Dimension, *49 The Modern Law Review* 141 (1986). 也可参见 Angela Cambell, Self-Regulation and the Media, *51 Fed. Comm. L. J.* 715 (1999)。

[②]　不过前述克林顿和戈尔报告中的产业自我规制，同时包含了自我规制的这两种含义。

（voluntary self-regulation），这是指政府对自我规制没有直接或者间接的积极介入。①

自我规制有着悠久的历史，传统上主要存在于手工业、媒体、法律服务等自由职业领域，近年来在技术标准、金融服务和产业安全等领域也得到日益广泛的运用。自我规制有如下优势。② 第一，自我规制主体拥有较高的专业技术水平、充分的"内部知识"和产业信息，这使得规制能够针对该领域中确实存在的突出问题，其手段也往往较为有效。第二，可以依靠伦理标准、同行压力或自愿性的行为准则（code of conduct）运作，这有利于促进规范事项的广泛性，并且在维持更高行为标准的同时获得业界的自愿接受。第三，自我规制主体作为私人组织，其在制定规则时不需要遵循严格正式的法定程序，这样，一方面规则制定的成本相对较低，另一方面也更加快捷，能够及时回应技术发展或经济形势变化的需要。同样，规则的执行与争端的解决也无须恪守僵化规则的要求，而是享有更高程度的灵活性，从而更能适应具体企业的特殊性。第四，自我规制的成本通常可以由被规制企业来承担，而政府规制则往往要由纳税人来承担成本。第五，自我规制也可以作为一种制度试验。如果产业界为实施自我规制而制定的规则被实践证明确实有效，也有可能转化为国家的正式立法。行业自我规制在美国和欧盟的历史都证明了其可以成为一个有效规制策略。

但自我规制也有其弊端。③ 第一，在于"规制者被待规制利益所俘获的风险"，因为自我规制机构往往不愿意惩罚业内人员的行为，其也可能服务于行业或职业的利益而非公共利益，例如对市场准入采取限制措施。第二，自我规制往往具有溢出效应或外部性，也即对其行业自我规制成员之外的人产生影响，此时其正当性就会令人怀疑。第三，在自我规制中结合了规则制定、解释、执行和裁决等多种职能，与分权的理念不符。第四，自我规制缺乏政府规制应遵守的程序公开（透明度）和问责机制。第五，自我规制机构作为私人机构，缺乏公共规制机构所掌握的某些有效的强制执行手段。第六，当产业规模越是庞大、所涉及企业越是众多，"集体行为的难题"就越凸显，进行有效的自我规制就越困难。

---

① Julia Black, Constitutionalising Self-Regulation, *59 The Modern Law Rev.* 27 （1996）.

② Ogus, Rethinking Self-Regulation, *15 Oxford Journal of Legal Studies* 97 （1995）；Robert Baldwin & Martin Cave, *Understanding Regulation*, Oxford University Press, 1999, pp. 126 – 129.

③ Ogus, Rethinking Self-Regulation, *15 Oxford Journal of Legal Studies* 99 （1995）.

经验表明，自我规制组织要有效发挥作用，需具备一些前提条件。第一，私人部门具有进行自我规制的动力。或者是经济上的动力，这来自对本行业繁荣发展的关切。或者是如果不进行自我规制，政府将会直接介入。从业界的角度来讲，一般不希望受政府的直接规制而丧失自由，它们自然更倾向于由"自己人"来规制。第二，要有一个较为权威、具有代表性的行业组织。第三，自我规制的程序比较公平，为利害关系人提供有效的参与途径。例如在制定规则时，要事先公布，邀请利害关系人评论，认真对待重要的、有价值的评论并加以回应。第四，提供外部参与的机会。自我规制的利害关系人不仅包含从业者，也包含公众（公共利益）和使用者，自我规制的组织和程序设计应吸收更多的外部参与，以保证其决策的正当性。第五，政府要有权力和能力对自我规制进行监督。成功的自我规制，大多有政府监督隐藏于后。一个好的规制体制是能够充分发挥二者的优势并同时控制其滥用的体制。这也是西方国家自我规制模式发展的一个趋势，即与不断增强的监督机制相结合的自我规制，这种趋势赞同使自我规制服从于更为紧密的控制或监督，即所谓政府监督下的自我规制（audited self-regulation）或共同规制（co-regulation）。①

（二）国外互联网领域的自我规制

互联网的特点使得政府规制的一些缺陷变得非常明显。例如政府规制一般要受边界和地域管辖的限制，但互联网在一定意义上恰恰是没有边界的场域，而是开放的世界性网络。网络社会的信息传播打破了原有的线性传播方式，成为网状的全球性传播。世界上任何一地的网民都可以足不出户，轻松访问全球网站，而在全球任何一个网站上登载的内容都有可能为全球网民所访问。在开放的互联网中，信息可以进行跨国、跨地区的超大规模传播。在这种情形下，相对而言不受地域管辖限制的自我规制团体就显示出其优势。另外，互联网是新生事物，政府对行业发展的情况往往缺乏足够的知识和信息从而难于就行业的规制做出决策，但行业发展中又必然会产生诸多的问题，包括消费者利益的保护以及同行之间的竞争秩序等等，在这种情形下，行业性的自我规制就成为很好的替代。因此，各国在互联网领域普遍都极为重视行业自我规制的作用。在美国，除了传统的行业协会以外，专门针对互联网活动的协会即有互联网地方广告和商业协会

---

① Douglas C. Michael, Federal Agency Use of Audited Self-Regulation As a Regulatory Technique, *47 Admin. L. Rev.* 171（1995）.

（Internet Local Advertising and Commerce Association，ILAC）、互联网服务协会（Internet Services Association）、更佳商务局（Better Business Bureau，BBB 或 BBBOnline）、消费者银行协会（Consumer Bankers Association，CBA）、直销联合会（Direct Marketing Association）以及互联网隐私工作组（Internet Privacy Working Group，IPWG）① 等。法国则先后成立了"法国域名注册协会"、"互联网监护会"和"互联网用户协会"等网络自我规制机构。从自我规制组织所涉及的议题来看，则有网络广告、电子商务、网络色情、网络隐私权保护、电子游戏、过滤软件的准确性或其应用等等。由于这些领域往往涉及众多的利益攸关方，行业协会的设立存在很大的集体行动困境，政府应采取措施促进行业协会的设立与发展，例如政府可以向产业界释放出这样的信号，即"如果你们不采取有效的措施那么我将介入"，这对自我规制组织的设立将发挥重要的激励作用。

　　互联网由于其所涉及范围的广泛性、复杂性和动态性，单纯由政府来进行规制是不切实际的，而纯粹的自我规制又有其缺陷，因此共同（合作）规制和协作式治理（collaborative governance）也成为很多国家的选择。② 例如法国政府在 1999 年初提出并开始执行对互联网的"共同调控"（共同规制）政策，并在这种思想指导下拟定了《信息社会法案》。这宗"共同调控"是建立在以政府、网络技术开发商与服务商、用户三方经常不断的协商对话基础上的。为了使"共同调控"切实地发挥作用，法国还成立了一个由个人和政府机构人员组成的常设机构——互联网国家顾问委员会。③ 英国在互联网的内容规制上一贯倡导自我规制，但这并不意味着政府无为而治。1996 年成立的互联网观察基金会（Internet Watch Foundation，IWF）是对互联网进行内容规制的自我规制机构，基金会的资金主要由网络服务提供商、移动开发制造商、信息内容提供商以及通信软件公司等私人公司提供。董事会由 12 人组成，其中 4 人是网络业主，8 人是非网络人士。但互联观察基金会实际上是在英国政府支持下设立起来的，英国贸工部在其中

---

① 这是一个由公益组织和私人企业组成的致力于互联网上贸易和交流的非正式组织，其成员包括美国在线（America Online）、迪斯尼、微软、媒体教育中心（Center for Media Education）、国际商业机器公司（IBM）、美国电话电报公司（AT & T）、全国消费者联盟（National Consumers League）、万维网联盟（W3C）和直销联合会等。

② 参见 Philip J. Weiser, The Future of Internet Regulation, *43 U. C. Davis L. Rev.* 529（2009）。

③ 《法国互联网发展政策与管理体制特点》，法国中文网，http://www.cnfrance.com/info/pinglun/20110425/4748.html，2013 年 11 月 19 日最后访问。

发挥了关键作用。①

（三）中国互联网领域自我规制的问题与改进

中国作为网民人数全球第一的互联网大国，近年来在互联网领域的行业自我规制方面已经取得了一定的进展，但其作用发挥得仍不足，存在很大的改进空间。

1. 关于互联网自我规制组织的数量

从国外来看，在与互联网相关的诸多领域都有设立自我规制组织、进行行业性自我规制的需求。但在我国，由于《社团登记管理条例》等对设立社团条件的严格限制，行业协会的发展存在诸多障碍，已经设立的社团在代表性、民主性等方面也存在严重的缺陷，自我规制功能不彰，互联网领域的自律组织更是寥寥无几，作用有限。目前中国互联网领域的行业协会在全国层面比较有影响力的主要是中国互联网协会和中国电子商务协会等，在地方层面上，除了各省份的互联网协会、电子商务协会外，为数寥寥。基于行业协会在维护公平竞争、促进市场经济健康发展中所可能发挥的积极作用，应修改相关法规，为行业协会，包括与网络相关的行业协会的发展"松绑"，大力促进行业协会发展。

2. 关于互联网自我规制组织的代表性

因为自我规制活动的溢出效应，产业自我规制组织的成员，一般不应限于一个产业的企业或从业人员，而应具有高度的开放性，这有利于提高自我规制组织决策的公益性。而在互联网自我规制中，其溢出效应尤其明显，几乎所有的自我规制活动都不仅仅影响产业界的利益，也同时与普通网民利害攸关。在我国目前的互联网协会会员中，除一些大学等少数事业单位以外，没有具有较高信用度的非企业会员，如具有较高知名度的网民或者公益性组织，这严重影响了其代表的包容性和决策的正当性。我国未来互联网自我规制组织，在组成上应增强开放性和代表性，让更多的普通网民、非政府组织或者公民行动团体及其代表参加进去。

3. 关于互联网自我规制组织的民主性

我国目前的互联网协会在内部治理民主化方面有很大欠缺，其运作带有严重的官僚化色彩，这导致成员的利益和关切不能得到及时、充分和有

---

① Cyber-Rights & Cyber-Liberties (UK) Report, Who Watches the Watchmen Part Ⅱ: Accountability & Effective Self-Regulation in the Information Age, September 1998, http://www.cyber-rights.org/watchmen-ii.htm, 2013 年 11 月 19 日最后访问。

效的反映，成员活动的积极性和主动性不足。未来的互联网自我规制组织在内部治理结构上应体现民主性的要求，赋予普通会员及其代表在重大事项上更多的决策权，并通过程序设计使会员对协会决策的参与渠道更加畅通。

4. 关于互联网自我规制组织功能的发挥

目前，互联网自我规制组织的功能尚未得到充分发挥。一方面，我国政府对行业协会仍抱有一种怀疑的态度，对于互联网中很多具有高度争议性的议题，政府仍事必躬亲，不敢放手让行业协会进行自我规制。未来互联网行业协会自我规制的发展，需要政府更多地赋权。当然，如前所述，自我规制组织要发挥作用，政府监督仍然是必要的，但这种监督应当主要是对设立过程的督导和事后的监督，而不是对行业协会组织与活动过程本身的直接介入。另一方面，政府在出台互联网规制政策或做出其他重大决策前，也没有听取相关协会意见的正式程序。行业自我规制不能取代政府规制，但即使是在政府规制的范围内，规制机构在做出决策前也应当广泛听取、认真对待行业协会的意见，以保证决策的科学性和可接受性。

5. 关于互联网自我规制组织的国际化

互联网规制具有非常强的国际性，目前许多互联网发展方面的重要决策，实际上是由国际性的非政府组织做出的，如互联网协会（Internet Society）和互联网工程工作组。这些组织所制定的标准或者做出的决定对于互联网的发展具有重要的影响，中国人必须发出自己的声音。但基于这些组织的非政府性质，由政府出面并不合适，此时如果由我国的互联网自我规制组织以自己的名义，或者组织相关人员参加，将会产生很好的效果。

五　结语

网络空间并非世外桃源或者理想国，其中的问题甚至罪恶并不少于现实物理世界，单纯依赖个人的自律并不能保证互联网的良好秩序，这就使得集体性的规制成为必需。但互联网的高度技术性、快速变化性、开放性和全球性等特点，要求我们不能将适用于传统社会的规制模式简单照搬到对网络空间的规制中，以免阻碍互联网在技术发展和商业模式等方面的创新、扼杀其发展潜力，并保证规制成效。一个成功的互联网规制体制，应当能够在自我规制和政府规制之间获致恰当的平衡，以充分发挥二者的比较优势。当然，由于各国互联网发展阶段、文化传统、经济社会条件和政治背景等方面的差异，这种平衡点的选择应有所不同，但总的目标都应是维护互联网的自由创新精神，增进公共秩序、公共安全和公共利益，促进互联网的良性健康发展。我国未来互联网规制体制的健全和完善，一方面应当加强政府规制的法治化、规范化和公开化水平，提高政府规制的效能和正当性；另一方面应根据社会优先的理念，更多地放权于社会，让行业团体在更大范围内和更高程度上发挥自我规制作用。此外，在政府规制过程中也应注意促进行业团体对规制决策的参与，而在自我规制过程中政府也应发挥激励与监督作用。迈向政府规制与自我规制互相补充、互为支持的合作式规制体制，应当成为我国互联网规制的发展方向。

On the Regulatory Regime of the Cyberspace in China: between Government Regulation and Self-regulation

*Li Honglei**

【Abstract】With the rapid development of the Internet, it has become more and more evident that regulation is indispensable for maintaining the order in the cyberspace and protecting stakeholders' interests therein. Nevertheless, it does not mean government is the only regulator of the Internet. Actually, self-regulation organizations should play a more important role in the cyberspace than in the real world. One of the key questions for Internet regulation is how to establish a regulatory regime which combines government regulation and industrial self-regulation effectively. Based on a comparative law study of Internet regulation, this essay describes the regulatory regime of the Internet in contemporary China, analyses its defects, and suggests its reform. On one hand, China should improve the effectiveness and legitimacy of governmental Internet regulation by strengthening the rule of law and increasing the standardization and transparency level of administrative actions. On the other hand, in accordance with the idea of the priority of society, China should empower self-regulation organizations (SROs) so that they could play a much more important role in Internet

---

* Associate Professor, Institute of Law, Chinese Academy of Social Sciences.

regulation. SROs should be allowed to participate in government's decision-making, while the government should be involved in self-regulation process by way of stimulatingor supervising. The direction for the reform of China's Internet regulation should be a collaborative system, in which government regulation and self-regulation complements and supports each other.

【 **Keywords** 】 Cyberspace; Regulatory Regime; Goverment Regulation; Self-regulation

Rule of Law and
Administrative Justice

Pekka Hallberg[*]

【Abstract】 Although we are familiar with the principle of rule of law, it is not easy to analyse the legal development. An approach is needed, which takes into account the different stages of development of the rule of law.

Three stages may be distinguished: 1) classical rule of law, referring to the emergence of the principles, 2) democratic rule of law, underlining the role of participation and common laws, and 3) rule of law in social context, paying attention to the social functioning of law.

A symbolic functional model of the rule of law development is "a house built on solid ground". The four-corner examination-legality, separation of powers, rights and obligations of citizens and functionality of the house-lays a firm and sound foundation for observing legal development.

Ensuring the legality of administration is also connected to the right to question the actions of public power. From the citizens' point of view, this implies having sufficient means to render the legality of the decision made by the administrative authority to be examined by an independent court.

---

* LL. D. and D. Soc. Sc. Pekka Hallberg is President Emeritus of the Supreme Administrative Court of Finland (1993-2012). Prior to this function, he has performed law-drafting duties at the Ministry of Justice, worked as a researcher and judge as well as a university professor in administrative law. He has directed the preparation of several constitutional reforms and other extensive legislative projects.

Although we are familiar with the principle of rule of law, it is not easy to analyse the concept. Rule of law should not be defined too narrowly, only by referring to different sectors of the use of public power, legislative, administrative and judicial branches. A more balanced approach to the concept is needed, which takes into account the different stages of development of the rule of law.

My presentation consists of some relevant questions: What is Rule of Law? How to monitor the legal development? How to guarantee good administration and administrative justice? I will not introduce any new concept, instead of that to examine rule of law development in a social context, with a view to understanding the importance of the legal principles in social development.

Research studies of the World Bank (Where is the Wealth of Nations? Measuring Capital for the 21st Century, 2005) indicate that human capital and the value of institutions (as measured by rule of law) constitute the largest share of wealth in virtually all countries. However, the World Bank's own rule of law indicators are based on quite restricted legal principles. Consequently, there is a growing need to elaborate a new rule of law − indicator from wider foundation, i. e. an indicator that would rest on a functioning society and also on some economic barometers.

Vision of Rule of Law. A symbolic functional model of the rule of law is like "a house built on solid ground". The rule of law principles can be analysed on the basis of four variables − the four corners of the house: 1) the principle of legality, 2) the balanced separation of powers, 3) the implementation of fundamental and human rights, and 4) the functionality of the house from the point of view of its "residents".

It is not enough to talk about rule of law, but, in addition, the requirements of definite laws, good administration, and access to justice − especially administrative justice − must be reality. In decision-making, it is essential to have the perspective of the people, and not that of the institutions. Practically it also means right to be heard and to appeal. Modern constitutional law and political science, indeed, already highlight the significance of human rights and fundamental rights, as well as the rights and obligations.

The State, power structures and institutions are relevant tools for the purpose of constructing a balanced and functional legal system. Based on my experiences of international cooperation, I would say that the symbolic reference to a house − with the four corners − provides a good basis for the analysis of the legal development of society, and a lasting foundation for different kinds of development programmes.

Development of Rule of Law

The rule of law development is tied to its national, historical, and cultural background, and there are significant differences in legal thinking between different regions of the world. The influence of religious and social circumstances is of great importance. We can also see differences between the Nordic pragmatic, American federal liberal, British parliament-oriented, Continental European normative constitutional, Eastern European post-socialist formal, Russian "democratic federal-governed", Chinese hierarchical, and African poverty and instability-related systems.

These rough descriptions also reflect differences in the attitudes towards the concept of rule of law. One worldwide change can be seen in the attitudes towards terrorism. In some countries, the recent legal reforms, aiming at supporting the fight against terrorism and security arrangements, have switched the focus of legal thinking from the traditional ideology of liberty and citizens' rights towards a security-oriented approach.

So in order to understand the legal differences, it is important to examine cultural and social conditions, i. e. place the development of the rule of law in a social context. In certain studies, for example, an interesting conclusion has been drawn concerning many African countries where there are countries with both statutory law and common law traditions. In the combat against corruption and maladministration, education and access to information have more relevance than the basic differences of legal systems. I believe, however, that it is easier to export elements of statutory law systems than common law systems to developing countries, for example, as common law systems are based on long traditions of case law.

Differences in Legal Culture

Finland is a small country and cannot take on a role of a teacher in legal issues.

Internationally, Finland has attracted attention because of its low level of corruption and efficient administration. Consequently, Finland has been placed among the leaders in the competitiveness reports of the World Economic Forum (WEF) and of the Institute for Management Development (IMD). On the other hand, in Finland, the labour market is having structural problems, wage taxes are high, and some branches are fairly closed.

A general reason is that Finland has a historical uninterrupted tradition of conformity to law and of respect of fundamental rights. Finland also adheres to a pragmatism shaped by its position between the East and West. Finland could perhaps be regarded as a laboratory in which it is possible to conduct legislative and administrative experiments.

An analysis of the rule of law runs into serious difficulties in the European Union (EU), too. Although the EU itself is an entity governed by law, its Member States have different traditions. In the largest Member State, Germany, the development is characterised by constitutionalism, an emphasis on the constitution, and by the federal structure, whereas England has no written constitution at all. There, the position of Parliament and civil liberties come to the fore, and the entire legal system is dominated by the common law tradition, which however is gradually gaining statutory law features due to the influence of the EU.

In the USA, legal development has been influenced by Liberalism as a counterbalance to the old European aristocracy and by the strong state system. It is not easy for an outsider to fully grasp the complexities of the checks-and-balances system of Capitol Hill. In recent years the fight against terrorism has shifted the focus from the ideals of civil liberties to legal thinking stressing security.

In Russia, the development has progressed from the collapse of socialism towards a State ruled by law. The Constitution of 1993 defines the system as a "democratic federally-governed state". The structure of the Russian Constitution resembles Western ones, but of course there are still needs as regards to the observance of the law, the legal validity of contracts, and the establishment of traditions.

In China, the development has interestingly and consistently progressed towards openness since 1978. This is clearly demonstrated by amendments to the Chinese Constitution of 1982. Furthermore, it became possible to supplement the public economy with private economy in 1988, the concept of socialist market economy was introduced in 1993, the goal of constructing a State ruled by law was set in 1999, and the protection of private ownership and respect of human rights were added to the Constitution in 2004.

In China tradition has also played a significantrole in guaranteeing justice. The status of hierarchy, community and family values can be found on the background nowadays as well. The possibility to appeal administrative authority's decisions in court was affirmed by law in 1989, after which the administrative official's liability for costs was legislated in 1994; in 1996 a system of administrative sanctions was introduced. When a provision to the Constitution of 2004 stated as a principle, that the state respects and protects human rights, the foundation of the development of legality grew more solid, but still there is a long way to go.

On the African continent the development of the rule of law is — as I mentioned — hindered by unstable conditions and poverty. An interesting observation is that legal development is not greatly influenced by the traditions of the colonial period, *i. e.* whether a country has a common law or civil law system. Much more important issues are education and functioning of the institutions.

Thus, already a short trip on different continents shows that it is difficult to identify a single rule-of-law concept. Although we are familiar with the principle of the rule of law, as noted above, the concept is not easy to define. The rule of law should, however, not be defined too narrowly by only referring to specific sectors such as the police, legislation, courts, administration or market and competition. A more balanced approach to the concept is needed, and the different stages of rule-of-law development have to be taken into account.

Theory of Rule of Law

In respect of the development of the theory of rule of law, it is sufficient to note that three stages may be distinguished: 1) classical rule of law, referring to the emergence of the principles, 2) democratic rule of law, underlining the role of participation and common laws, and 3) rule of law in social context, paying attention to the social functioning of law. We do not, however, need theories but an efficient legal system. In the following I will try to present this vision in concrete terms.

The concept of the rule of law has also been used in several international

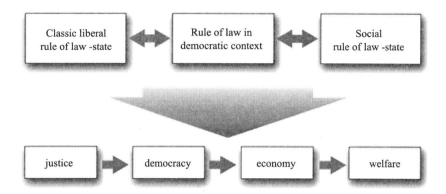

contexts, as a criterion for accession to human rights conventions, and for the membership of certain international organisations, such as the EU, as well as a precondition for several development cooperation programmes. One observation relates to the fact that after a state has already accessed EU, there is no systematic way of monitoring its rule of law development. Although it is natural that there is no system of monitoring full members, systematic research would be useful in order to ensure the implementation of the rule of law and the final objective, Europe of Europeans.

Possibly, the rule of law is now addressed in more practical terms even in Europe, the place of birth of the rule of law principles. However, some scholars have raised the question of possible double standards in Europe: new member states of the EU are subject to strict scrutiny, whereas there are even greater deficiencies, for example, in the treatment of minorities in some of the old member states.

Rule of Law – Principle of Legality

The principle of legality has been considered a distinctive mark of the rule of law. According to that principle, all public authority has to be based on law. The development of judicial systems and internationalisation can be viewed as a certain kind of a reciprocal action, where the national and international levels constantly interact.

The principle of legality is usually considered a distinctive mark of the rule of law. In fact, this is a usual interpretation of the whole concept. However, as discussed above, if we understand the rule of law merely as a principle of legality, we forget the requirement of equity, which is part of the interpretation of the rule of law in British legal culture. The requirement of equity is also clearly present in the roots of Finnish-Swedish legal culture.

When emphasising the social and democratic nature of the principle of legality, the protection of citizens by law deserves attention. Demands for the protection of individuals and their property vis-à-vis public authorities, and for access to justice, to ensure the lawfulness of official acts, were part of the historical development of rule of law thinking. Formally, the state was bound by law produced by the state itself.

Historical discussion points to the significance of a broad understanding of the requirement of lawfulness of the measures of authorities as a principle of protecting citizens. Thus, the principle of legality should always be studied from the perspective of citizens, as a guarantee for legality and justice.

Separation of Powers – Balance Between Institutions

The separation of powers is the second cornerstone of the rule of law. The doctrine of separation of powers is a result of historical development. Generally, historical doctrines do not have exact equivalents at present. Therefore, the origins of the doctrine of separation of powers easily lead to a dogmatic approach to the analysis of the duties and functions of state organs. Despite that, a brief account of the roots of the separation of powers is presented in the following.

The doctrine of separation of powers is usually associated with the French Enlightenment philosophy of the 18th century and *Montesquieu's* (1689 – 1755) writings. *Montesquieu's* basic work "De l'Esprit des Lois" (Spirit of the laws) was published in 1748. However, there were practical applications of the separation of powers already in earlier days.

The principles were first applied during the period of the Roman reign. However, it was not before the 17th century, before the first presentation of functionally separated powers was published in Oceana 1656 by *Harrington* in England. The English philosopher *John Locke* (1632 – 1704) presented, before *Montesquieu*, practical suggestions concerning the restriction of executive and legislative powers.

In practice, *Montesquieu's* doctrines were first manifested in the United States. In contrast, the development in England did not strictly follow the doctrine, but

Parliament possessed the supreme powers. A parliamentary system was developed between legislative powers and administrative authorities. However, the traditional independent status of judicial powers was preserved. In France, the republican constitutions have been shaped by doctrines of separation of powers and sovereignty in turns.

In Finland, the state system and the organisation of power have since early times been based on principles which are in a way independent from the historical development of the doctrine of separation of powers. The legislative powers were separated from the other functions of the state in Sweden-Finland already in the 17th century. Even before that, the application of law was distinct from administration. Since the first constitutions, the Parliament Act of 1617 and the Constitution Act of 1634, the administrative judicial procedure, too, has been separate from other administration of justice.

Models of the separation of powers. The various models of the separation of powers doctrine are culture-bound and they have developed differently in different countries. The French state system can be characterised as being hierarchical and underlining the powers of officials. In fact, the French tradition has been influential in the development of the administrative culture of the EU.

In Great Britain, the state is conceived in a more informal manner. State traditions, customary law, the liberties of the individual, and the sovereignty of Parliament have greater weight. This has created a kind of a liberal-democratic administrative organisation. The thoughts of *Locke* are visible: the powers of subsequent parliaments cannot be restricted. Other characteristics of the British system are that there is no written constitution and, which is typical of common law countries, the great importance of precedents in the administration of justice.

The separation of powers doctrine is viewed from a different perspective in federalist thinking, according to which society constructs itself rather on co-ordination between entities than on hierarchy. Thus, neither the constituent state nor the federal state is subordinate to the other, but the objective is to balance unity and diversity in state development. Nevertheless, in most federations, the constituent states are weaker than the federal state, both politically and economically, and there are several other tensions present in federations.

The principle of subsidiarity is among the central principles of a federalist organisation of state functions. Subsidiarity was also one of the central themes in EU. According to the principle of subsidiarity, the competence of the federal state should be restricted to those issues which the constituent states, by common decision, have considered requiring federal legislation or which cannot be handled at the member state or constituent state level. Typical federal or union level functions include foreign and security policy, and monetary and economic policy.

Pursuant to the principles written in the Constitution of Finland, the Grand Committee of Parliament shall be informed of the preparation of such EU matters as fall within the field of legislation. It is remarkable that the national system of separation of powers has been preserved and developed in new circumstances. Essentially, this is an example of the state as a learning organisation as defined in literature concerning globalisation (See *World Public Sector Report* 2001 : *Globalization and the State*).

Fundamental and Human Rights

Fundamental rights are an important standard of the rule of law. The functionality of rule of law must be evaluated before all from the citizens' viewpoint, observing the development from the third corner of the before presented structure.

The rights and duties of citizens open up a perspective for the understanding of the whole legal order. Also, they underline a view according to which the substance of the law must be examined from the perspective of the people. We will observe how the so-called Western legal culture emphasises individuality, whereas the Asian, especially Chinese, legal culture is more sensitive to communality.

The *Magna Charta* of England of 1215, the *Bill of Rights* in the constitutions of North-American colonies of the late 18th century, and the declaration of human rights originating from the *French Revolution* in 1789, as well as the references to it in subsequent French constitutions, are usually considered as the most significant international landmarks of the development of the fundamental rights institution.

Despite differences in social systems, there are many common features in the protection of fundamental rights in different countries. These kinds of universal rights have achieved a special guaranteed status in the legal order. The fundamental rights institution is generally secured in the constitution of each country. Human rights can be viewed as common, international minimum criteria for the national protection of fundamental rights.

Comparison between different fundamental rights traditions. Most constitutions include some fundamental rights provisions. The most important exception is the United Kingdom, which has no written constitution and therefore no list of individual rights in the constitution either. The constitutions of European countries have traditionally guaranteed particularly civil liberties (e. g. freedom of speech, freedom of religion and right of ownership) and equality, following the model of the French Revolution.

The inclusion of economic, social, and cultural rights is characteristic of post-World War II constitutions. In the past few decades, Sweden (1974, 1976, 1979), Canada (1982) and the Netherlands (1983) have created fundamental rights institutions comparable to that of Finland. In addition, reforms have been long under way in Switzerland and in Austria.

Fundamental rights provisions are usually placed at the beginning of the text of the constitution. The scope of application of the constitution varies from country to country, and this is dependent on the age of the constitution as well. Older constitutions lack specific fundamental rights provisions, and the fundamental rights mainly concern traditional civil liberties.

For example, fundamental rights provisions are virtually absent in the **French** constitutions, and the fundamental rights are mainly based on the human rights declaration of 1789. In Austria, the inadequate provisions of the constitution have been supplemented by giving the European Convention on Human Rights a constitutional status. In contrast, there are considerably extensive sets of fundamental rights norms in several South-European countries.

In legal comparisons, we must not restrict ourselves to the comparison of Western constitutions, however, as most fundamental rights were guaranteed by e. g. the 1977 Constitution of the **Soviet Union**, at least formally. Also, the development of increasingly detailed legislation on fundamental rights, and a shift towards the principles of socialist market economy and better comparability with **Western constitutions** can be seen in the Chinese constitutional reform since 1982. Generally, it may be observed that the focus of constitutions is gradually shifting towards fundamental rights legislation.

Yet there are clear differences in the emphases, and in the precision of legislation, between civil liberties on one hand, and economic, social and cultural rights, on the other. More recent constitutions often also include third-generation collective fundamental rights in order to ensure protection under the law for minorities, and to create constitutional basis for citizen's protection under the law, the right of access to justice. The question is, of course, also about the existence of economic resources for the implementation of different fundamental rights.

Increasingly specified determination of rights and duties of the individual and the protection of the individual's status in relation to public authorities, in particular, has been an overarching trend. With regard to the history of ideas, it seems that in the Anglo-American world the inspiration of *Locke* is more prevalent: human rights are essentially viewed as meaning freedom from the state. *Rousseau* as a source of inspiration is more common on the European continent: human rights are more than a mere freedom from the state. Thus, the latter tradition has a more positive attitude towards the state as an instrument of common welfare.

The rule of law is not merely a formal principle. It takes a dynamic, societal character as the number of laws increases and they gain material substance. In this sense, justice and democracy have to be viewed dynamically and in relation to each other.

Therefore, it is essential to examine the rule of law in a broad sense, as referring to the process of interaction between public institutions, public authority and civil society. Therefore, the emphasis is laid on the citizens'perspective, the significance of fundamental and human rights, the requirements set for the functioning of the system, and the expectations concerning judicial development.

Monitoring the Rule of Law

Dimensions and Indicators

Respect for the Rule of Law and justice are fundamental principles of a functioning society. However these basic values have not been formulated in a manner, which would facilitate monitoring and evaluation. Moreover, the lack of conceptual clarity has been exacerbated by the introduction of related values and principles into legal and political framework-freedom, equality, and respect for fundamental rights, efficient justice systems, and access to justice.

The question is: can we find indicators to evaluate rule of law development? What are the rule of law dimensions? There have been listed some relevant issues:

1) **Accountability to the law** refers to the processes, norms, and structures that hold the population, organizations and public officials legally responsible for their actions and imposes sanctions if they violate the law.

2) **Access to information** refers to the ability of citizens and organizations to request, receive and process public information.

3) **Independent judiciary.** Judges and other dispute resolution professional are not subject to external pressure notably from the executive and legislative branches of government and resolve disputes according to the law.

4) **Effective judicial system (criminal, civil and administrative)** provides mechanisms for recognising, protecting and enforcing rights and legitimate interests. The emphasis of this dimension is on the effectiveness of the legal system, which means that the disputes are resolved in a predictable, timely and cost-effective manner.

5) **Respect for the fundamental rights** means that there are accessible and reliable mechanisms for remedying violations of fundamental rights and the citizens have equal opportunities to use these mechanisms to seek redress.

6) **Effective implementation of laws** refers to the extent to which laws, regulations and case law are implemented in an equal and fair manner.

7) **Access to justice** refers to the equal availability to dispute resolution mechanisms which lead to fair outcomes in all areas of law-civil, family, criminal, administrative etc. Access to fair dispute resolution mechanisms and outcomes should not be contingent on wealth, social or political power, ethnicity, gender, religion or any other characteristic of the person. Geographical location, access to technologies and legal awareness should also not be factors that impede access to justice.

8) **Absence of corruption.** Corruption is the abuse of public powers for private gains. Public and private officials who are entrusted with powers have to use this power for achieving legitimate outcomes. Use of entrusted power for attainment of illegitimate private gains is corruption.

There is also a need to **operationalise justice**. Otherwise justice is only an overused term. Some starting points are very important: 1) Justice as fairness refers to having equal rights to basic liberties and ensuring that inequalities benefit the least advantaged members of society. 2) Empirical justice research has to be identified with many specific factors that make a procedure or an outcome fair as experienced by the people involved. 3) Dimensions of bottom up justice consist of accessibility of dispute resolution (low costs of access to justice), fair dispute resolution processes (procedural, interpersonal and informational justice) and fair outcomes (distributive justice, functionality, transparency etc.)

Rule of Law Indicators

Moreover, research organizations and international institutions are presently creating indicators for the evaluation of justice, economy, as well as human rights. Many of the analyses are very limited in scope, and a broader dialogue for rule of law monitoring in Europe is necessary. I have found over 20 global rule of law datasets. There are several references to the materials online.

These databases comprise an enormous amount of information that can be combined in different ways in order to monitor judicial, economic and social development. Even though most of the indicators are based on interviews, and therefore opinions, their significance as guideposts of development is evident. This may, however, narrow down the perspective of analyses to mere evaluation of first-hand experiences. Consequently, the more general issues, related to power structures and the functioning of legislative policy and public authority, would be left in the background.

An interesting question is whether or not the emphasis of the monitoring system should be shifted from input and process to output and outcome. The results and the approach angle we take on them will indeed be the key factors. On the other hand, rule of law development is a continuous process, which means we must also examine the factors that affect the process indirectly.

In the following I will contemplate on rule of law development and the elements that affect it from a broader perspective. Even a singular indicator may illustratively point out defects in the functioning of a rule of law system. However, we also need a strategy, based on combining experiences, for how to generate more coherent legislation, increase the legitimacy of the exercise of power and balance of separation of powers and improve the functionality of the justice system from the citizens' standpoint. It is not enough to speak highly of the rule of law — clear laws, good administration, and access to justice also have to be a reality.

Clear legislation and legislative policy. Legislation plays a key role in the development of the rule of law. As legislation develops, the rule of law gains substance. In this regard, the rule of law is a dynamic principle. Therefore, law should be seen as a means, not as an outcome.

However, the law of today is not an unambiguous building material. Legislation has become more fragmented and somewhat more indirect. Instead of rights and duties, more and more regulatory instruments are related to the interests of limited groups of persons and to the duties of authorities. This is not a problem of civil law systems only. The same is true of common law systems.

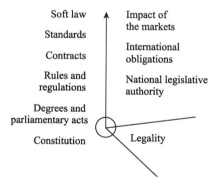

Regulatory system quality and policy

Generally speaking, the problems of legislation lie in its distance to reality. Laws that feel real are also easy to understand. One of the greatest problems in legal policy today seems to be that laws are too often prepared short-sightedly and by individual administrative sectors. Is legislation thus turning into " defective legislation" that merely addresses current, acute problems instead of constructively guiding long-term development?

There have been different projects to decrease the amount of legislation and to improve its quality. The OECD Recommendation of the Council on Improving the Quality of Government Regulation of 1995 includes a ten-item OECD Reference Checklist for Regulatory Decision-Making.

Earlier the role of the public sector was mainly to protect the economy from risks, but recently it has also been charged with the task of identifying methods for protecting economic agents in situations where economic risks have occurred. Legislation thus also has a global dimension.

The newest tiers of the legislative pillar house several soft law norms (See the picture above). One of the best known soft law systems is Lex Mercatoria, which is based on gradually shaped commercial practices and rules. These rules of commerce were originally used in places of international trade, and have prevailed as significant common rules of the game in global markets. Some have been included in national legislation and harmonised, but the entity of the rules is still based on tradition. Different standards have also been growing in importance. Their main goal is to guarantee uniformity and define best practices. Norms are more easily accepted internationally if they are not legally binding.

Development of the separation of powers. The separation of powers is the second cornerstone of the rule of law development. The doctrine of the separation of powers is a result of historical development. Because generally historical doctrines do not have exact equivalents at present, the origins of the doctrine can easily lead to a dogmatic approach towards the state organs.

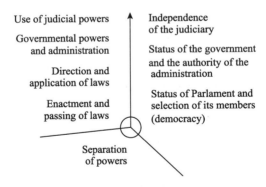

Origins of the state-separation of powers

Although the independence of the courts is essential to the development of the rule of law, as a judge I would like to emphasise that independence does not mean isolation, but rather dependence on general social development. There are two crucial points: First, the power of decision on the interpretation of laws, including the constitution, belongs to the courts and not to parliamentary bodies. Parliament may always change the law, but it may not issue recommendations on its interpretation to the courts. The second principle is that a judge shall not be suspended from office, except by a judgment of a court of law.

The importance of human rights obligations. Rights and obligations should be viewed as a single entity, and–in accordance with modern fundamental rights law — as a pursuit of balance between conflicting rights. When it comes to news media it is, for instance, difficult to strike a balance between the freedom of expression on the one hand and the protection of privacy on the other. As a political right, freedom of expression naturally constitutes a social cornerstone and therefore should not be infringed upon unless there are extremely well-founded reasons for it.

Status of the people

Functionality of the rule-of-law house. As mentioned earlier, the fourth corner of the house is the functionality of the system: acts should be comprehensible, bureaucracy decreased, decisions taken promptly and access to

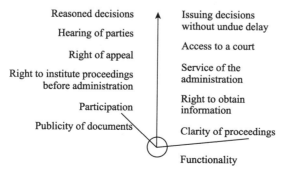

Functioning of the rule of law

justice simple. In other words, public authority is the servant and the citizens are the masters.

Many people find my house metaphor too simple. How does it for instance enable us to consider corruption? What connection is there between anti-corruption and good governance and the principles of the rule of law? My claim is that the fundamental principles of the legal system – including participation in administration, proper management of public affairs and public property, integrity, transparency and accountability – play a key role in preventing corruption.

Durability of the rule of law. In my opinion, this four-corner examination lays a firm and sound foundation for observing legal development. It creates a kind of rule-of-law indicator. To continue with this imagery, we notice the need to support the different corners of the house with interlocking support structures in order to sustain the rule of law. This in turn highlights the importance of social capital – a concept studied by political science and sociology – as a factor providing for the durability of the rule of law.

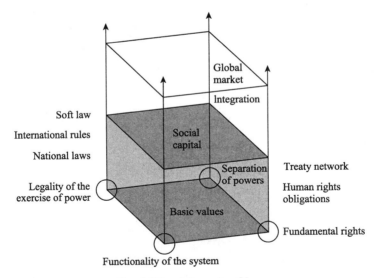

Durability of the rule of law

The foundation of the house requires strong values. Correspondingly, by measuring the height of the building one can estimate the level of economic development present in the country.

The construction of skyscrapers-competitive economies – also requires solid support structures, confidence in the durability of the system. The importance of human resources and their interaction, i. e. of social capital, should be discussed not only with regard to economic growth, but also in view of more general social welfare.

Social capital is considered both an important condition for economic growth as well as a stabiliser of liberal democracy. The importance of social capital and its increase have been discussed as a second generation model of economic reform. A question thus arises: How can we increase the stock of social capital? As social capital is essentially a resource of civil society, there are limits to what extent state actions can contribute to it.

What is the core substance of this key concept, social capital? Essentially, it is certain kind of communality that is not bound to explicit norms but based on the feeling of solidarity and trust between people. *Fukuyama* suggests a short practical definition: "social capital is an instantiated informal norm that promotes co-operation between two or more individuals". *Putnam* argues that one special feature of social capital, trust, norms, and networks, is that it is ordinarily a public good. Social capital, unlike other forms of capital, must often be produced as a by-product of other social activities.

From a historical perspective it is interesting to see that in the field of political research social capital is often associated explicitly with the democratic concepts of *Alexis de Tocqueville*, that is, communality as experienced by the people. The Finnish emeritus professor *Aulis Aarnio* has examined non-material questions such as the relationships between social capital, happiness and trust on the one hand and income and wealth inequalities on the other, in addition to his work on the variables linked to physical well-being. In the field of business research, there are even studies whose scores show that this kind of team spirit considerably promotes economic efficiency.

More generally, drawing from the Italian experience, *Putnam* argues that social capital supports the functioning of both the market and the state: "Social capital, as embodied in horizontal networks of civic engagement, bolsters the performance of the polity and the economy, rather than reverse: Strong society, strong economy; strong society, strong state." Moreover, "for political stability, for government effectiveness, and even for economic progress social capital may be even more important than physical or human capital. "

It is important to analyse the essence of social capital and its promotion from the perspective of civil society, the people. Therefore, in the context of the legal system the focus of reforms should be on the practical development of fundamental rights and freedoms, and not on the definition of institutional competences. Furthermore, the connections between the legal system and the broader social system should be considered in order to reach the next, even more important, step of the analysis.

How to Guarantee Good Administration and Administrative Justice

Good Governance and Accountability

The functionality of the administration is in a key position with regard to the rule of law development. Especially in Nordic welfare society the public administration has extended to all fields. As the competitive aspects of the state become more pronounced, the role of public administration and the courses of action should be considered more critically.

Furthermore, the Code of Good Administrative Behaviour prepared by the European Ombudsman and approved by the European Parliament in September 2001 is worth noting. In addition, the good official administration has been emphasised in the White Paper on European Governance submitted by the Commission on 25 July 2001.

In international contexts, there are two competing approaches to good governance. First, we may talk about a tradition of democratic governance, according to which good governance is mainly defined as being a method of governance that serves democracy and equality. The other approach has been to characterise good governance as meaning efficient governance, in which the governance is viewed more narrowly on the basis of neo-liberal economic policy, as principles underlining the productivity and efficiency of public administration. The tradition of democratic governance attempts at giving politics a central role. The question is about participatory governance, to which it is easier for the people to commit themselves.

An important recommendation is related to improving administrative structures and the course of action taken in the process. Before all else, it is necessary to have a clear public law on how matters are conducted with authorities, how to take legal action, how to organize the hearing of concerned parties and give a reasoned decision, and how to proceed if the decision is not satisfactory.

Behind these laws on general administrative procedure are often the general principles of administrative justice, such as:

1) the principle of equality, hence the authority has the duty to treat every customer of the administration in an equal manner,

2) the principle of purposefulness, hence the duty to exercise the power of the authority solely for the justified purposes,

3) the principle of objectivity, according to which the actions of the authorities must be impartial,

4) the principle of relativity, according to which the actions of the authority must be in correct proportion to the identified goal, and

5) the principle of the protection of trust, according to which the actions of the authority must protect expectations based on the legal order. This refers to the legitimacy of action.

Achieving a general administrative law and at the same time emphasizing the service principle and the administrative authorities' duty of guidance is an important goal.

An important issue in this context is combating corruption. There is hardly a country that is absolutely free from corruption. But the consistently high rating for relative freedom from corruption that Finland receives in international surveys nevertheless indicates certain strengths that Finnish society has gained in following its historical path to development.

The prevention of corruption requires a comprehensive system of legislation, a well-functioning judiciary, efficient law enforcement and proactive monitoring of abuses, as well as up-to-date and transparent financial management (see publications Combating Corruption, The Finnish Experience published by the Ministry for Foreign Affairs of Finland, 2005 and Corruption and the Prevention of Corruption in Finland, Ministry of Justice, 2009.)

Finland's constitution stipulates that good governance must be guaranteed by law. Finnish laws proscribe a wide range of special abuses and treat them as criminal offences. The main laws that safeguard against corruption include the Constitution of Finland, the Administrative Procedure Act and the Act on the Openness of Government activities.

The Right of the Citizens to Make Appeals

Ensuring the legality of administration is also connected to the right to question the actions of public power. From the citizens' point of view, this implies having sufficient means to render the legality of the decision made by the administrative authority to be examined by an independent court. These systems of appeal proceedings can be categorised in many ways: Firstly, we have countries where administrative legal disputes belong to general courts, where separate divisions have been founded, if needed, to deal with administrative matters. The second main group is formed by countries, and this includes most European countries, where there are separate administrative courts designated for administrative disputes.

Thus, on an organisational basis, the countries where settlement of administrative disputes has been assigned to general courts, without making a distinct separation to civil and criminal cases, can be grouped together. The other alternative is the establishment of separate administrative courts. The latter is commonly the alternative chosen in the EU Member Countries. A functional administrative court system and also procedural guarantees for justice are integral elements of the modern understanding of the rule of law principle in Europe.

Also a development trend has occurred in the common law countries, as we may note further, where rectifying errors of the administration in a rational way is aspired to, as opposed to the civil court system, where taking actions against the administration is slow and expensive. The procedure is considerably less expensive in administrative courts than in courts abiding by the civil procedure. That is why many of the so-called common law countries have also developed alternative systems, the so-called tribunal-type bodies of appeal.

In principle, it is important to emphasise that the citizen's right to appeal a decision made by an administrative authority should not be observed as a function of administrative oversight, as was mainly the case in the socialist system, but rather from the viewpoint of the rationale underlying the exercise of justice, i. e. as a guarantee for realising the rule-of-law principle in an individual case and as a negation of despotism.

The Purpose of Administrative Justice

When organising the structure of administrative courts, independence of the judges plays a specifically important role because when there is a dispute, it usually occurs between a private person and an administrative authority, an instrument of public power. The independence of the use of judicial power is a part of the balance of the separation of powers. Indeed, the independence of courts is mainly about guaranteeing conformity to law and this way indirectly securing the status of the legislator, or basically the parliament.

I will only state here that the significance of independent courts, and of specialising in these legal matters that are important in the daily lives of the citizens, have formed a solid guarantee of justice.

Countries like Finland, who have adopted the separate system of administrative courts, benefit from the fact that an appeal can be made directly on the decision of the administrative authority. Similarly, leadership over the process is more active in the administrative court because also the court has the duty to acquire further information.

Moreover, the procedure is considerably less expensive in administrative courts than in courts abiding by the civil procedure. That is also why many of the so-called common law countries have developed alternative systems, the so-called tribunal-like bodies of appeal.

I will here bypass thinking about the function of the right to appeal more broadly. The activity of administrative courts is not about having "an overcoat of administration and supervision", but of securing legal protection and justice in individual matters.

Bibliography

Bauer, Horst (1973): *Gerichtsschutz als Verfassungsgarantie*, *Zur Auslegung des Art. 19 Abs. 4 GG*. Berlin.

Becker, Franz-König, Kalus (1967): Allgemeide Einleitung. Verwaltungsverfahrens gesetze des Auslandes. pp. 3 − 84. Schriftenreihe der Hochschule Speyer. Band

31/I －II. Berlin.

Bradley, A. W. （1971）: Judicial protection of the individual against the Executive in Great Britain. Gerichtschutz I pp. 327 －372. Köln.

Buhler, Ottmar （1914）: *Die subjektiven öffentlichen Rechte und ihr Schutz in der deutschen Verwaltungsrechtssprechung.*

Dicey, A. V. （1885）: *Introduction to the Study of The Law of the Constitution.*

Eichenberger, Kurt （1960）: *Die Richterliche Unabhängigkeit als staatrechtlilihes Problem.* Bern

Fukuyama （1995）, *The Primacy of Culture*, Journal of Democracy, pp. 7 －14.

Gardner, Warner W （1959）: *The Administrative Process. Legal institutions today and tomorrow. The central inference volume of the Columbia law school*, pp. 108 －148. New York.

Garner. J. F: *Administrative Law.* London 1967.

Hallberg, Pekka （2009）: *Constructing Rule of Law* （published in Chinese）, Edita Publishing Oy.

Harrington, James （1656）: *The Commonwealth of Oceana.* London.

Hsu, C. Stephen （editor）, （2003）: *Understanding China's Legal System*, Essays in Honor of Jerome A. Cohen, New York.

Ministry for Foreign Affairs of Finland （2005）: *Combating Corruption, The Finnish Experience.*

Ministry for Foreign Affairs of Finland （1998）: *Fundamental Rights in the Constitution of Finland.*

Ministry of Justice （2009）: *Corruption and the Prevention of Corruption in Finland.*

Montesquieu （1748）: "*De l'Esprit des Lois*" （Spirit of the laws） available at http://www. constitution. org/cm/sol. htm （Last accessed 19. 9. 2012. ）.

Supreme Administrative Court 90th anniversary book （2008）: Allan Rosas, Free movement of persons and social benefits, p. 644 and Vassilis Skouris, Aspects de la sécurité legal dans.

World Bank （2006）: Where is the Wealth of Nations? Measuring Capital for the 21st Century, the International Bank for Reconstruction and Development/ The World Bank, Washington, D. C. .

World Public Sector Report 2001: Globalization and the State.

法治与行政司法

佩卡·哈尔贝格[*]

【摘要】 虽然我们都熟悉法治的原则，但是分析法治的发展并非易事：我们需要找到一种能够考虑到法治发展各个不同阶段的方法。法治的发展可以分为三个阶段：（1）法治原则产生的传统法治阶段；（2）强调参与和普通法的作用的民主法治阶段；（3）注重法律的社会功能的社会语境中的法治阶段。法治发展的一个象征性的功能模式就是"建立在坚实基础之上的房子"。对法治这座房子的四个角落——合法性、分权、公民的权利和义务以及功能性——的审查为考察法治的发展提供了坚实的基础。确保行政的合法性也是与质疑公权力行为的权利相联系的。从公民的角度来看，这意味着他们应该有充分的手段将行政机构所做决定的合法性问题提交独立的法院审查。

---

* 芬兰最高行政法院前荣誉院长。

政府信息主动公开制度实施现状与问题[*]

吕艳滨[**]

【摘要】 本文对连续 5 年来国务院部门、省及较大的市实施政府信息公开制度的情况进行了观察、验证、统计、分析，据此研究了当前政府主动公开信息中存在的问题，总结了原因，并从提升立法位阶、加强机构建设、细化公开标准等方面提出了完善建议。

【关键词】 政府信息公开　主动公开　知情权　实施

一　引言：政府信息公开制度实施面临的形势

2007 年颁布的《政府信息公开条例》（以下简称《条例》）首次以行政法规的形式规定了行政机关等的信息公开义务，认可并保障公众申请公开政府信息，以及对政府信息公开的决定申请行政复议或者提起行政诉讼的权利。《条例》一出，以公开为原则、不公开为例外的观念渐入人心，政府信息公开申请量不断增加，行政机关的公开程度日益提升，及时、全面、准确、有效地公开信息也已成为政府管理经济社会事务、维护自身公信力所不可或缺的手段。

为了推动和规范政府信息公开工作，近年来，国务院及各地方政府发布了大量涉及政府信息公开工作的文件。诸如《国务院办公厅关于做好施行〈中华人民共和国政府信息公开条例〉准备工作的通知》（国办发〔2007〕54 号）、《国务院办公厅关于施行〈中华人民共和国政府信息公开

---

　　* 本文为中国社会科学院法学研究所法治指数创新工程项目阶段性成果。
　　** 吕艳滨，中国社会科学院法学研究所副研究员。

条例〉若干问题的意见》（国办发〔2008〕36号）、《国务院办公厅关于做好政府信息依申请公开工作的意见》（国办发〔2010〕5号）、《国务院办公厅关于进一步加强政府网站管理工作的通知》（国办函〔2011〕40号）、《国务院办公厅转发全国政务公开领导小组关于开展依托电子政务平台加强县级政府政务公开和政务服务试点工作意见的通知》（国办函〔2011〕99号）、中共中央办公厅与国务院办公厅《关于深化政务公开加强政务服务的意见》（中办发〔2011〕22号）、《国务院办公厅关于印发当前政府信息公开重点工作安排的通知》（国办发〔2013〕73号）、《国务院办公厅关于进一步加强政府信息公开回应社会关切提升政府公信力的意见》（国办发〔2013〕100号）等，可谓不胜枚举。各级各类行政机关也纷纷强化对政府信息公开工作的重视程度，政府网站等公开载体建设水平不断提升，主动公开信息的数量不断增加。

但从公开渠道反馈的情况看，公众获取政府信息的难度依然很大。应主动公开的信息不公开，或者公开效果不理想导致公众不能有效获取。尤其是，政府信息公开的滞后逐步侵蚀着政府公信力。从2008年的瓮安事件、广元柑橘事件,① 到2009年的杭州三菱跑车事件,② 再到2012年的什邡钼铜事件以及发生在厦门、大连、宁波、昆明等地的PX事件，无不在一定程度上肇因于信息公开的不及时、不准确。分析2012年什邡钼铜事件和近年来频发的PX事件的诱因及过程，可见相关地方政府引入此类项目无疑都基于发展本地经济的良好初衷，且都履行了各种审批手续，甚至有些地方还建有完善的决策参与机制和风险评估机制，但由于决策过程中未能妥善处理决策与民众的关系，没有认真听取和反映民意的意见，没有及时公开有关信息，从而引发公众的怀疑、不满，形成了政府、公众、项目运营投资方多方皆输的局面。

本文基于笔者所在研究团队2009年至2013年连续5年对国务院部门、③

---

① 2008年10月因有关部门面对"柑橘长蛆"的信息广泛传播，事前宣传不够，事后回应滞后，导致公众产生恐慌心理，导致当年大量柑橘滞销，柑橘产业遭受巨大损失。

② 2009年5月，在处理一起三菱跑车肇事致人死亡事件时，警方面对媒体和公众提供的信息闪烁其词、不严谨，引发公众对交警部门的强烈指责和对交警部门是否能公正办案的质疑，甚至一度质疑之后出庭受审的嫌疑人是否被人"顶包"。

③ 国务院部门限于国务院组成部门、国务院直属特设机构、国务院直属机构、国务院直属事业单位、部委管理的国家局中，对外行使行政管理职权、与公众生产生活具有密切关系的部门。

省级政府和较大的市①政府开展的政府透明度测评与调研活动获取的一手数据，着重分析当前政府信息公开制度实施中存在的问题，研讨完善制度、加强实施的对策。

二　主动公开落实不到位

《条例》第二章明确了行政机关的主动公开义务，此外，行政审批、食品安全监管、环境保护等众多领域的法律法规也规定了行政机关应当主动公开的信息。但通过5年的连续跟踪测评调研可以发现，虽然相关领域的主动公开工作进步明显，但应公开信息未公开、公开不全面、公开不及时等问题仍然十分突出。

（一）应公开的未公开

相关法律法规及《条例》已经明确了主动公开义务及其范围，但实践中应公开的信息未依法公开的情况还比较普遍。

以拆迁信息为例，根据2009年和2010年连续两年对43个较大的市公开拆迁信息的情况进行的调研，结果显示，提供有效的拆迁公告信息的，2009年为25个（占58.1%），2010年为26个（占60.5%）。2010年，在其各类网站中提供拆迁补偿指导性标准的城市为20个（占46.5%），略低于2009年的23个（占53.5%）。除此之外，2010年，能够有效提供拆迁公司资质信息的有14个（占32.6%），2009年为13个（占30.2%）；提供拆迁评估公司信息的有13个（占30.2%），与2009年持平。安置房方面，2010年，仅有4个城市能够在网站提供其位置信息（占9.3%），2009年为9个（占20.9%），有4个可以提供其价格信息（占9.3%），2009年为3个（占7%）。而上述信息都是原《城市房屋拆迁管理条例》明确要求公开的。

再以食品安全信息公开为例，《食品安全法》等法律、法规、规章中对公开哪些涉及食品安全监管的信息有明确规定，但众多信息并没有得到很好的公开。调研组以较大的市为对象，2010年对工商、质检、食品药品监督管理等部门公开食品安全信息、2011年对餐饮服务监督管理信息（主要涉及食品药品监督管理部门）、2012对食品生产监督管理信息（主要涉及质

---

① 根据《立法法》第63条第4款，较大的市是指省、自治区的人民政府所在地的市，经济特区所在地的市和经国务院批准的较大的市。这些城市都有地方立法权，相对于省级政府与公众生产生活联系更为紧密，相对于地级市和区县具有更大的决策空间。

检部门）的公开情况，进行了测评调研。

2010 年的调查结果显示，仅有 22 个较大的市的质量监督管理部门网站公布了所做出的食品生产许可的信息（占 51.2%），仅有 5 个城市的工商行政管理部门网站公布了所做出的食品流通许可信息（占 11.6%），仅有 10 个城市的食品药品监督管理部门网站公开了所做出的餐饮服务许可信息（占 23.3%）。2011 年调研显示，一些法定应当公开的信息未在其政府网站公开。仅 28 个城市公布了餐饮服务许可办理流程（占 65.1%），24 个城市介绍了此类许可的办理指南（占 55.8%），29 个城市公开了办理此类许可需要提供的申请材料（占 67.4%），19 个城市向社会公布了许可的办理结果（占 44.2%）。监督检查方面，仅有 10 个城市公布了对违法行为的查处情况（占 23.3%），3 个城市设立了"餐饮服务提供者食品安全信用档案"栏目（占 7%），17 个城市公开了食品安全的预警、警示信息（占 39.5%）。

2012 年调研显示，食品生产监督管理信息公开很不理想。43 个较大的市中，仅有 26 个城市的质量技术监督部门在网站上公开了本地食品安全监管方面的规范性文件，仅占 60.5%。有 5 个城市的质量技术监督局没有公开食品生产许可办理指南（占 11.6%），而公开信息全面（包括核发新证、补领、变更、更正、注销等各类业务流程）的仅有 5 个（占 11.6%）。公开食品生产企业委托加工备案办理指南的仅有 21 个（占 48.8%）。行政审批的办理结果对于公众获知食品生产企业的资质至关重要，但这些信息的公开程度并不高，仅有 24 个公开了食品生产许可证发证结果信息（占 55.8%），仅有 5 个公开了食品生产企业委托加工备案结果信息（占 11.6%）。仅有 30 个城市的质量技术监督部门公开了食品生产监督抽查信息（占 69.8%），公开一个月内此类信息的仅有 10 个（占 23.3%）。仅有 16 个城市的质量技术监督部门公开了食品企业安全信用档案（占 37.2%），而能够在其中详细公开企业各类基本信息的则更少。比如，公开全面的食品生产企业基本信息的仅有 3 个城市（占 7%），公开企业守法或者违法记录的仅有 4 个城市（占 9.3%）。

再以环境信息公开为例，调研组连续对 26 个省级政府和 43 个较大的市的政府在空气质量信息、水质量信息、固体废弃物监管信息、辐射安全信息、建设项目环境影响评价信息和环境行政处罚结果方面的公开情况进行了测评调研。2012 年的调研显示，省级政府环境保护部门中，公开下辖区域空气质量预报信息的仅有 9 个（占 34.6%）；公开下辖区域饮用水质量月报信息的仅有 10 个（占 38.5%）；公开危险废物跨省转移申请审批情况信息的仅有 11 个（占 42.3%）；全面公开建设项目环境影响评价受理公告、审批前公示、审批后公告三类信息的仅有 12 个（占 46.2%）；公开建设项目竣工环境保护验收受理公告的仅有 9 个（占 34.6%）；全面公开建设项目竣工环境保护验收受理公告、审批前公示和审批后公告三类信息的仅有 6 个（占 23.1%）。较大的市环境保护部门在这方面的问题更为突出，其与省级政府上述指标相对应的数据分别是 11 个（占 25.6%）、20 个（占 46.5%）、13 个（占 30.2%）、15 个（占 34.9%）、6 个（占 14%）和 4 个（占 9.3%）。

（二）公开不全面

课题组对较大的市的房屋拆迁信息公开情况进行测评和调研时，主要集中于拆迁法规、政策、拆迁公告、拆迁补偿指导性标准、拆迁工作流程等信息的公开情况。2009、2010 年拆迁信息公开的调研显示，拆迁公告中能够提供拆迁地段示意图的仅有 3 个，2009 年为 2 个。

2012 年调研组在对较大的市质量技术监督部门公开食品安全政策法规、食品生产许可（含办理流程、指南及发证信息）、食品生产企业委托加工备案（含办理流程、指南及备案信息）、食品安全监督检查信息、食品企业质量信用信息、食品安全常识等的情况进行测评和调研时发现，食品生产企业委托加工备案办理指南中公开全面的食品生产企业委托加工备案办理指南（包括办理依据、办理部门、办理地址、联系方式、需提交的材料、办理程序、办理期限）的仅有 9 个（占 20.9%）。

环境信息公开的目的是让公众获取相关信息，并推动公众参与环境保护，如果公开的信息过于简单就无法达到此目的。不少环境保护部门在建设项目环境影响评价的受理公告信息和审批前公示信息中不提供便于公众理解的环境影响评价报告书的简本。有的环境保护部门只是以简单列表的形式提供一个月或是几个月的建设项目环境影响评价的审批情况，有的在列表中只提供批准时间、批准文号和文件题名等一些简单的信息，不提供项目及环境影响评价的详细内容。由于缺失关键内容，公众难以了解项目对环境影响的真实情况，这也是一些项目上马后招致公众质疑的原因之一。

在行政审批信息的公开方面，大部分网站公开的行政审批相关信息不够全面，2012 年调研发现主要存在如下问题。其一，机构联络信息不全面。为了推动行政审批制度改革，实现行政审批的集中管理、便民高效，不少地方建设了政务服务中心。这就需要详尽地公开政务服务中心的基本信息，如中心地址、联系电话、电子邮箱、中心交通路线（如自驾车信息或者交通换乘信息）或者地理位置示意图、中心工作时间（应当精确到工作日、上下班时间）等。但在43个较大的市中，只有2个城市公开了上述全部信息；所有省级政府均未能全部公开上述信息。其二，审批事项信息不全面。公开审批依据、审批条件、审批申请材料、审批程序、审批期限、审批办理地点、审批部门联系电话等办事信息，是实现行政审批透明、便民的前提。但经对调研的省市随机抽查10条审批信息发现，只有5个城市和5个省级政府在办事指南中提供了所有事项信息。其三，审批办件动态信息不全面。为方便公众及时了解审批的办件动态，应该及时进行办件状态公示，提供受理审批的主办部门信息、受理事项信息、申报时间、办理状态信息（如在办理中、已办结等）。公开办件公示栏目的较大的市有35个，其中有4个城市提供了上述所有动态信息；公开办件公示栏目的省有13个，只有2个省提供了上述所有动态信息。行政审批信息的缺失说明各级政府在构建服务型政府方面仍然需要做出较大的努力。

（三）公开不及时

政府信息公开应当确保所公开的信息是最新且准确的，否则，非但信息无用，还可能误导公众，影响政府公信力。但目前，公开不及时、信息不更新的问题比较普遍。

食品安全信息方面，2010年调研时，43个较大的市的市政府官方网站、食品安全信息网以及卫生行政管理部门、质量技术监督部门、工商行政管理部门、食品药品监督管理部门的所有网站中，提供的食品安全宣传普及知识包含2010年信息的仅有23个（占53.5%）。而2011年调研发现，有35个城市公布了调研之前3个月内对餐饮服务提供者的监督检查信息（占81.4%），公开之前3个月内对违法行为查处情况的有8个城市（占18.6%），公开3个月内的食品安全预警、警示信息的有7个城市（占16.3）。2012年调研发现，各地质量技术监督部门中，仅有12个城市发布了6个月内的食品生产许可结果（占27.9%）；仅有4个城市发布了6个月内食品生产企业委托加工备案信息（占9.3%）；仅有10个城市提供了近1个月内食品监督抽查情况（占23.3%）；没有1个城市提供1个月内的"食品安全信息档案"信息；仅有13个城市提供了6个月内的食品安全常识信息（占30.2%）。

环境信息方面，2012年调研发现，在43个较大的市环境保护部门中，提供调研日前6个月内的危险废物经营许可证发证信息、废弃电子产品处理资格审批情况信息、辐射安全许可证发证审批信息的分别仅有 19 个（占 44.2%）、5 个（占 11.6%）和 9 个（占 20.9%）。省级政府公开调研日前 6 个月内的危险废物经营许可证发证信息、危险废物跨省转移申请审批信息、辐射安全许可证发证审批信息的，分别是 21 个（占 80.8%）、7 个（占 26.9%）和 21 个（占 80.8%），仍有一部分网站存在信息更新滞后的问题。

（四）公开信息不一致

随着信息化的推进，政府机关公开信息的平台越来越多，不仅《条例》规定的政府公报、政府网站、新闻媒体等平台，就连政府网站也越来越多元化，相同信息可能会发布在不同网站或同一网站的不同栏目中。这些网站如当地政府门户网站、业务部门网站，甚至一些专业性的政府网站（如食品安全信息网）。这一方面增加了公众获取信息的渠道，但随之而来的问题则是，信息公开的随意性大，相关信息在不同平台发布的时候存在内容不一致的现象。

以行政审批的信息公开为例，各省、较大的市政府的门户网站以及所属部门的网站基本都设立了在线办事栏目，其中大部分内容都是行政审批事项，同时，当地的政务服务中心（或行政服务中心）也建有网站，公开相关行政审批信息，各业务部门也往往在自家网站公开本部门的行政审批信息。换言之，每个地方仅网站公开渠道就至少同时存在两到三个针对同一行政审批事项的信息。根据 2012 年调研情况，调研组在对政务服务中心（或行政服务中心）与政府门户网站或者所属部门网站上的行政审批事项信息、特定审批事项的办事指南等信息进行对比验证后发现，各网站所公开的行政审批事项信息不一致的情况并不鲜见。课题组对同一地方上述网站公开的审批事项列表、特定审批事项的办事指南等信息进行了抽查比对，按理说，同一地方的同一审批事项在各不同网站上公开的内容应当一致，但结果显示各网站均一致的只有 4 个省和 8 个较大的市。如宁波市政府门户网站"网上办事"栏目公开的"转外地就医核准"审批事项中注明审批时限为 2 个工作日，申报材料的第一项为"1. 由市级定点医疗机构或鄞州人民医院、113 医院、镇海龙赛医院、北仑宗瑞医院及开发区中心医院等医疗机构的副主任以上职称医师开具的《宁波市城镇职工基本医疗保险转院证明》（医疗机构盖章）"（见图 1，链接为 http://gtog. ningbo. gov. cn/col/col10265/index. html? type = 9999）；但其行政服务中心网站显示的则是"法定时限 20 个工作日；承诺时限 0 个工作日"，申报材料第一项为"1. 由指定的定点医疗机构（即有出具转外就医证明资格的医院）副主任以上职称医师开具的《宁波市医疗保险转院证明》（加盖医疗机构章）；出具精神病转院证明限在宁波市康宁医院"（见图2，链接为 http：//www. nbxzfw. gov. cn/txweb/service/item_ detail. jsp？ uuid = v8qyun1xk9r3m7e3dzpj）。

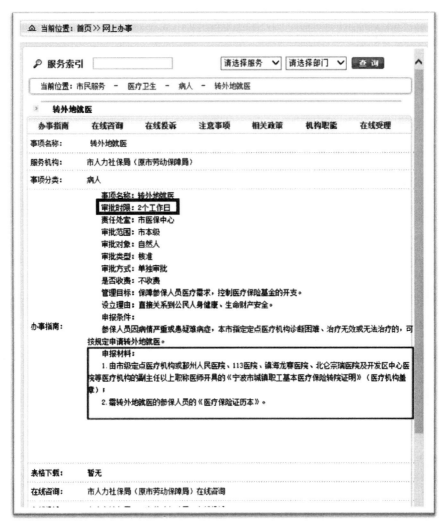

图 1　宁波市政府门户网站"网上办事"栏目中
"转外地就医"审核事项信息

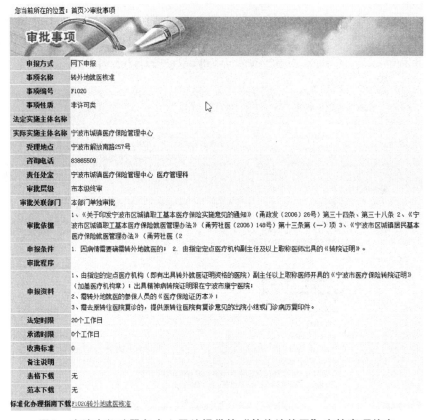

图 2 宁波市行政服务中心网站提供的"转外地就医"审核事项信息

三 存在问题的原因

政府信息公开制度实施中存在诸多问题，其原因值得关注。首先，《条例》的位阶低，受制于其他法律，影响实施效果。以行政法规而不是法律的形式出台政府信息公开制度，有其特定的时代原因，[①] 从尽快构建政府信息公开制度，推动政府信息公开工作角度看，其积极意义不可否定。但受上位法制约的问题自《条例》颁行伊始就一直存在并且无法得到根本解决。《保密法》《档案法》等成为掣肘的问题早有著述讨论，本文不赘述。虽然《条例》可以视为政府信息公开的专门法，但特别法优于一般法、新法优于

---

① 参见周汉华主编《政府信息公开条例专家建议稿——草案·说明·理由·立法例》，中国法制出版社，2003，第 16－19 页。

旧法的原则只能适用于行政法规一级，遇到法律就只能适用上位法优于下位法的原则，许多领域公开的推动，与其说是依靠法的手段，不如说依靠的是行政命令，预决算公开及三公经费公开可谓较为典型的一例。

其次，《条例》自身规定存在缺陷。《条例》自身规定的不完善之处也导致政府信息公开制度的实施面临重重困难。第 8 条将不危害"社会稳定"作为公开的前提，为不公开提供了无形且巨大的口袋。第 13 条"除……主动公开的政府信息外，……还可以根据自身生产、生活、科研等特殊需要"申请公开信息的表述，为审查申请人的目的用途提供了解释的空间甚至直接的依据，这种做法在全世界实行政府信息公开制度的国家和地区中都是较为罕见的。第 14 条将国家秘密、商业秘密、个人隐私作为公开的例外，看似规定了有限且较小的不公开信息的范围，但既不明确也不具有操作性，令执行者依旧保有较大裁量权，且易使其无所适从，更漏掉了"过程信息""执法信息"等其他国家地区普遍允许作为例外的内容。此外，《条例》中存在大量的适用例外，涉及信息发布的审批（第 7 条第 2 款）、主动公开事项的确定（第 9 条第 4 项）、信息公开之前的保密审查（第 14 条第 2 款、第 3 款）、信息的公开权限（第 17 条）、信息的主动公开期限（第 18 条）等内容，使《条例》可以轻易被位阶不高的"红头文件"架空。如其第 7条第 2 款、第 9 条第 4 项、第 14 条第 2 款和第 3 款中的"国家有关规定"都足以使一些"红头文件"成为不适用《条例》的特别规定。可以说，上述制度设计上的不严谨几乎为不公开提供了充分的依据。

再次，政府信息公开工作机构和人员配置不到位。政府信息公开机构设置不理想的情况在很多行政机关都普遍存在。早在 2009 年和 2010 年的测评调研中，调研组对被调研对象《政府信息公开指南》提供的政府信息公开工作机构的电话进行验证，其中，2009 年在 29 个提供了联系电话的较大的市中，有 3 个一直无人接听，5 个系两周内多次拨打才打通的。2010 年，在提供电话号码的 46 个国务院部门中，有 6 个是一周内经过多次拨打才打通并解答咨询的，有 7 个未能在一周内打通；在提供电话号码的 36 个较大的市中，有 4 个是一周内经过多次拨打才打通，有 2 个则完全未能在一周内打通。即便到了 2012 年调研时，仍有个别行政机关尚未设置专门的政府信息公开机构，在收到申请时临时安排工作人员处理相关申请，而这些工作人员对政府信息公开工作缺乏相关的业务知识，在处理相关申请时业务不熟练、解决问题能力差。

另外，各级政府机关对自身家底没有摸清。从主动公开的情况看，应公开而未公开的情况较为普遍，主要是因为各政府机关对本机关职责范围内的法律法规等所规定的应主动公开的信息究竟包括什么、应该如何公开，并不是十分清楚，这就导致许多本该公开的信息，由于政府机关自身工作的原因，而没有意识到应当公开。

最后，公开文化的培育需要时间。构建透明政府离不开培育成熟的公开文化，但现实的情况是无论公众，还是政府机关工作人员，公开意识都还在培育过程中。2011 年，调研组为了解公众对政府信息公开的认知程度，在北京、四川、山东、河北、天津、吉林、甘肃、安徽、辽宁、浙江、江西开展了随机的问卷调查。[①] 结果显示，公众对于政府信息公开制度的认知程度还不够高。比如，仅有 6.4% 的人会选择向政府机关了解自己需要的信息，仅有 58.4% 的人知道《条例》，有 31.7% 的人不知道自己有权申请政府机关公开自己需要的信息。而政府机关工作人员的公开意识低的问题更不容忽视。我们通过调研访谈发现，有的政府机关工作人员甚至不知道还有政府信息公开制度，不少政府机关的工作人员仍将政府信息公开工作视为负担，反感甚至抵触公开，甚至将这种情绪带到了与政府信息公开申请人的接触之中，有的工作人员只考虑自己如何完成工作，完全不考虑如何方便公众获取信息。特别是，不少政府机关在与调研组的接触中反馈最多的竟然是不知道如何公开、如何界定应否公开，并表示专门的政府信息公开培训少之又少，少有的培训也往往只能涉及政府信息公开的一点"皮毛"。

四　完善政府信息公开制度的建议

透明是法治的基石，没有透明的权力运行机制，法治政府、诚信政府建设则无从谈起。同时，透明不是无限的、绝对的，否则，政府管理、社会秩序同样会遭受不利影响。为此，在实践的基础上，逐步完善政府信息公开制度是法治政府建设的重要任务。

第一，加快政府信息公开制度上升为法律的进程，完善政府信息公开的相关制度。经过 6 年的实施，政府信息公开制度已深入人心，成为政府管理和公众办事的重要手段，《条例》相关制度也经历了实践的检验，各种不足也基本暴露了出来。为了进一步推进政府信息公开工作，应尽快启动政

[①]　此次问卷调查共计发放 850 份问卷，回收有效问卷 793 份。其中，男性 457 人，女性 323 人，13 人拒答性别；初中及以下 32 人，高中 94 人，大学专科 229 人，大学本科 364 人，研究生以上 72 人，2 人拒答学历。

府信息公开法的立法程序。立法中应将重点放在依申请公开制度和不公开信息的界定上，取消对政府信息公开申请人资格、申请用途的审查，明确界定不公开信息的范围，如舍弃个人隐私的表述，改为"与个人有关，公开后可能对其合法权益造成损害的信息"，增加过程信息、执法信息等内容。此外，还应配合立法，彻底清理和修订包括《保密法》《档案法》等在内的法律法规，使其适应信息化发展和推动政府信息公开的需要。特别是确立信息公开优先的原则，防止使行政机关及其工作人员陷入有的法律法规要求其保密，有的则要求其公开的两难境地。①

第二，加强政府信息公开工作机构建设。政府信息公开工作具有较强的专业性、时效性，需要各机关为此做好统筹安排，有序推动。为此，各级各类政府机关应当配备必要的机构和人员专门负责政府信息公开工作，维持工作人员的稳定性，并确保其具备管理、法律、信息技术等方面的专业知识。为确保工作人员具备相应的工作能力，还必须注重提升其公开意识，使其真正认识到公开是政府管理的基本要求，也是创新政府管理的重要手段。应彻底摆脱开大会、念文件式的培训模式，系统化、有针对性地对各类机关中的不同群体工作人员开展深入持久的培训，使其将公开文化内化为自己的工作态度和工作方式。

第三，明确政府信息公开的标准。无论是在推动《条例》上升为法律的过程中，还是贯彻落实《条例》的过程中，都必须明确政府信息公开工作的标准，包括应主动公开什么、如何公开、何时公开，如何在处理依申请公开时准确界定不公开信息、如何处理政府信息公开与相关法律法规的关系等。为此需要有关上级部门及时根据政府信息公开工作的要求、面临的形势等制定相应的指南性的文件，指导下级机关的活动。

第四，清理主动公开信息。主动公开在政府信息公开工作中至关重要，因为如果大部分信息通过依申请来公开会给政府机关带来被动。准确、全面、及时、有效地公开政府信息，既可以减少因处理依申请公开而使政府自身和公众需要付出的成本，又可以提升政府公信力，更可以使公众从中获益。各政府机关应当对本部门职责范围内的法律法规等进行全面清理，理清究竟涉及哪些主动公开信息，明确其公开范围和公开方式。此外，应确保依法应主动公开的信息可以令公众方便地获取，提高其公开质量，避

---

① 参见托比·曼德尔《信息自由：多国法律比较》，龚文庠等译，社会科学文献出版社，2011，第53－54页。

免出现公开不全面、不准确、不及时、不统一等问题。对于申请量大、涉及面广的信息，则应做好评估，适时转为主动公开，减少公众获取信息的成本和各部门处理申请的压力。

Implementation of the System of
Active Disclosure of Government Information:
Current Situation and Existing Problems

Lyu Yanbin *

【Abstract】 This article conducts observation, verification, and statistical analysis of the situations of implementation of the system of active disclosure of government information by various ministries and commissions under the State Council and the governments of various provinces and relatively large cities during the past five consecutive years and, on the basis of such analysis, examines the existing problems in the current system of active disclosure of government information, summarizes the causes of these problems and puts forward suggestions on improving the system, including adopting higher-level laws, strengthening institutional construction, and elaborating on the relevant standards.

【Keywords】 Disclosure of Government Information; Active Disclosure of; The Right to Know; Implementation

* Associate Professor, Institute of Law, Chinese Academy of Social Sciences.

Regulation of Regional Policy

Matti Niemivuo *

【**Abstract**】 The aim of this article is to give an overview on the regulation of regional policy and how it has been implemented in Finland. The article is based on the author's two books from 1979 and 2013. [1]

A conscious regional policy started in Finland at the end of 1950. A main idea in the Finnish politics was that the State must take care of the whole country and, especially, support undeveloped regions. For this reason, many legislative and other measures were initiated in the public and private sector in order to build the Finnish society as a welfare state. In the first half of the 1990's, when there was a serious financial crisis in Finland, many cutbacks were made to the Finnish welfare state. The economy became the most important factor in all political decision-making.

After Finland became a member of the European Union (1995), there was less and less room for national decision-making in regional policy. Indeed, the State gave up its leading position to the EU, to regional authorities and to private sector partners in regional policy. The results of this new regional policy have not been very good. During last twenty years the disparities have increased between rich and poor regions in Finland. Also the OECD has criticized the Finnish regional policy in 2010.

---

* Professor emeritus, University of Lapland (Finland).

[1] Matti Niemivuo, *Aluehallinto ja aluepoliittinen lainsäädäntö julkisen vallan välineinä* (Helsinki: Juridica, 1979) and Matti Niemivuo, *Aluehallinto ja aluepoliittinen lainsäädäntö* (Helsinki: Lakimiesliiton Kustannus, 2013).

A well-functional regional government is necessary in developing regions of the country. In Finland, there has never been a democratic provincial self-government like in many other European countries. As such, inter-municipal corporations have acted as democratic authorities on the regional level. The main tasks of these organs was planning and taking care of hospitals, social services and educational institutions. In 1994, the status of the Regional Councils was strengthened, especially in regional policy. From the beginning of 2010, a reform of regional state administration made the Regional Councils still more powerful compared with State authorities. This new regional state administration is quite complicated and weak because of its vast tasks and lack of personnel.

Regional development is one of the priorities of the programme put in place by Prime Minister Jyrki Katainen's Government. The objective is an economically, socially and environmentally sustainable Finland. In terms of regions, cities and municipalities, the Government promise to support "their dynamic vitality, development potential and competitiveness in the global economy". This kind of language is typical in the new regional development policy. It sounds nice, but "development" in this rhetoric means cutting back funding or not investing in poor regions like Northern and Eastern Finland. There in the article are a lot of examples of this kind of policy-making.

At the end of the article there are some conclusions with positive future perspectives to develop the Northern Finland. The main reason is that the Arctic has become an increasingly interesting region of the world from a political, economic and scientific standpoint.

I. Introduction

In 1952, Dr. Urho Kekkonen, former president of the Republic of Finland, published a book on increasing economic and social welfare in Finland.[①] In particular, the book contained several concrete measures on how to develop Northern Finland, namely Lapland. On the whole, President Kekkonen's vision was completed during his long presidency (1956 –1981). Finland changed from

---

① Urho Kekkonen, *Onko maallamme malttia vaurastua* (Helsinki: Otava, 1952).

an agrarian to an industrial society and became a modern welfare state according to the so-called Nordic model. Local government was in a key position in this model.

A common feature of the post-war development in Finland was the increase, change and diversification in the functions of municipal government. As a result of the development, the municipal government was primarily responsible for education, health care and social welfare. In addition, the sphere of activity of municipal government was expanded to include many other functions, for example housing, employment and environment issues.

There were many reasons for the increase in municipal functions. The most important was the general change in society, which was apparent, for example, in technological developments, industrialisation and urbanisation. Various pressures led to the expansion of public services so that all citizens could enjoy such services on an equal basis regardless of their place of residence. In particular, the principles of social justice and the equality of citizens lay behind the expansion of public services.

Despite economic growth and positive developments in people's standard of living in Finland, some regions, such as Northern and Eastern Finland as well as other remote and sparsely populated areas, had a number of problems, including unemployment and the long distances to public services (education, health care and social welfare). State funding was an important source of income for municipalities, which also had the right to levy taxes on their residents.

A central idea in the political decision-making process was that the State must take care of the *whole country* and, especially, *support undeveloped regions*. For this reason, a number of important measures were initiated in the public and private sector in order to build the Finnish society as a welfare state.

In the first half of the1990's, when there was a serious financial crisis in Finland, many cutbacks were made to the Finnish welfare state. The economy became the most important factor in all political decision-making. After Finland became a member of the European Union (1995) , there was less and less room for national decision-making in regional policy. Indeed, the State gave up its leading position to the EU, to regional authorities and to private sector partners in regional policy.

In order to understand and explain the Finnish regulation on regional policy, it is essential to know its history. It is important to know various developments in the regulation before it is possible to find out *how* and above all *why* the regulation has obtained the form it has now. Moreover, it is absolutely necessary to know the aims and effects of the regulation.

II. Impact of Regulation on Regional Policy

The developments that have taken place in Finnish society since the end of the Second World War have been, even in comparison to those that have taken place in other countries, rapid and intensive. As with the other Nordic countries, full employment was the main policy goal. [1] In this respect, industrialisation was a key issue for the political decision-makers and actors in the private sector. In addition, there was a general political consensus that there was a need to expand of the public sector, especially in order to promote education, healthcare and social services.

State subsidies to municipalities could be seen as a first measure of regional policy. Little by little, State subsidy policy started to take into account the different financial possibilities of the municipalities. At the end of the1960s, the new State subsidy legislation made it possible to even out the financial possibilities of different municipalities.

Conscious regional policy in Finland started at the end of the 1950s. The first step was the Act on tax relief for the industry in Northern Finland (190/1958). The main aim of this Act was to revitalise business activities in the northern part of the country. At the same time, other important regional policy measures were initiated, for instance, the University of Oulu was founded.

The first acts on undeveloped regions were regulated *for the years* 1966 − 1969 and second respective series of acts *for the years* 1970 − 1975. In this legislation, undeveloped regions were divided into two zones (I and II), industry and other business activities received different kinds of economic benefits based on these divisions. Industrialisation was a key concern during this period. However, the legislation and its measures could not stop unfavorable development, especially in sparsely populated rural municipalities. People moved to the south and south-western parts of Finland, and, in the worst cases, they immigrated to Sweden in

---

① Mary Hilson, *The Nordic Model. Scandinavia since* 1945 (London: Reaktion Books, 2011), p. 74.

particular. In 1972, a new department was created at the Prime Minister's Office to intensify and coordinate regional policy planning.

New acts on regional policy were adopted for the *years* 1976 −1979 after much heated political discussion in Parliament. According to these acts, regional policy included the whole country, not only the undeveloped regions. In 1979, Parliament prolonged the application of these acts to the end of 1981.

Many important political decisions were made during this period. For instance, public services, such as the reform of the primary school system, started in the northern part of Finland and new universities (in Kuopio, Joensuu, Lappeenranta and Rovaniemi) were founded in Eastern and Northern Finland. In addition, not only State-owned industries but also privately owned and market-oriented industries located their activities in Northern Finland. Furthermore, the State provided economic support for the industrial developments. Also, municipalities made a lot of improvements in the country's infrastructure in order to support the private sector in building factories and creating jobs for citizens. At the beginning of 1982, a new era started in regional policy. Again, new legislation on regional police was adopted for the *years* 1982 −1989. Its content was almost the same as that of the preceding legislation. The aim of the new legislation was to promote a balanced welfare state. In 1984, the coordinative role in regional policy was transferred to the Ministry of the Interior. Now *regional differentiation* between the provinces became a magic word. It was not necessary to develop regions according to the same formula, because regions had different needs and challenges.

The deepest reform was made through the acts on regional development, which were adopted for the *years* 1989 −1993 and 1994 −2002. The basic idea in these legal frameworks was programme-based regional development. In 1994, Regional Councils (joint municipal organs) began to serve as regional development authorities in the regions. After Finland joined the European Union, the Regional Councils also acted as regional development authorities for the EU's Structural Fund projects.

In 2002, a new Regional Development Act (602/2002) was adopted. According to Section 1, the purpose of this act is "to create the preconditions for economic growth, industrial and business development, and a higher employment rate". These factors will guarantee regional competitiveness and well-being on the basis of competence and sustainable development. The Act also aims "to reduce differences between regions in the level of development, improve their people's living conditions, and promote balanced development among regions". To achieve the aims of the Act, attention should be paid to the varying potential of the different regions and the need to develop their population, business and industry, and regional structure in different ways. In addition, the objectives of the European Union's regional and structural policies should be taken into account. The Structural Fund Act (1401/2006) was passed several years later for such purposes.

At the same time that regional administration was being reformed, a new Act on Regional Development (1651/2009) and an amendment to the Structural Fund Act (1653/2009) were adopted.

What are the results of this new regional policy? During last twenty years the disparities have increased between rich and poor regions in Finland. Also the OECD has criticized Finland quite recently: "Disparities have also been increasing across regions, particular in labor market outcomes. This reflects the dramatic structural change that has occurred since the early 1990s, and the lack of policy success in tackling this transition. These growing disparities in regional labour market outcomes have contributed to serious demographic imbalances building up in the regions. These are especially prevalent in the smaller municipalities and challenge the very sustainability of these entities."[1]

Northern and Eastern Finland in particular have lost jobs, public services and people. It is evident that the financial crisis of 1991 − 1995, the crisis at the beginning of the 2000s and financial crisis starting in 2008 served to exacerbate the problems. Moreover, discussions on globalisation and national and international competitiveness in business are typical of our time. The question also has to do with the fact that common values have changed in our social policy over the years. In addition, political parties have lost their positions to market-forces. However, this new regional policy, with its odd rhetoric, is seen as being modern compared with the previous, old-fashioned regional policy.[2]

---

[1] See OECD Economic Surveys, Finland, 2010, p. 105 and pp. 106 − 120.

[2] Sami Moisio, *Valtio, alue, politiikka* (State, Region, Politics) (Ph. D. diss., Tampere: Vastapaino, 2012).

III. Administrative Structure of Regional Government

The Finnish administrative machinery is divided into central, regional and local levels. Originally, the state regional administration consisted of State Provincial Offices led by Governors. Especially during the years 1970 – 1990, this authority was strong and also important in the planning of regional policy. In addition, there were other regional State authorities in different fields. Since the 1990's, Employment and Economic Development Centers, the Finnish Road Administration and Regional Environment Centers have been central authorities at the regional level.

In 1997, the number of provinces was reduced from twelve to six. The main reason for the reform was the difficult economic situation. In addition, this reform strengthened self-government in the regions.

In Finland, there has never been a democratic provincial self-government, although this has been possible according to the Finnish Constitution since 1919. As such, inter-municipal corporations (joint municipal authorities) have acted as democratic authorities on the regional level. The main tasks of these organs was planning and taking care of hospitals, social services and educational institutions. In 1994, the status of the Regional Councils was strengthened, especially in regional policy.

From the beginning of 2010, a reform of regional state administration made the Regional Councils still more powerful compared with State authorities: six regional State administrative agencies and 15 centers for Economic development, Transport and the Environment were created. This new regional state administration is quite complicated and weak because of its vast tasks and lack of personnel.

IV. Discussion and Future Perspectives

Regional development is one of the priorities of the programme put in place by Prime Minister Jyrki Katainen's Government. The objective is an economically, socially and environmentally sustainable Finland. In terms of regions, cities and municipalities, the Government promise to support "their dynamic vitality, development potential and competitiveness in the global economy". This kind of language is typical in the new regional development policy. It sounds nice, but "development" in this rhetoric means cutting back funding or not investing in poor regions like Northern and Eastern Finland.

Let's take some examples.

According to the Finnish Constitution, there are three kinds of courts of law: general courts, administrative courts and special courts. As the result of a long development process, Finland now has a *two-level system of general administrative courts*. The higher level is formed by the Supreme Administrative Court and the lower level by the regional administrative courts. In certain sectors, such as taxation, the regional administrative courts are, in effect, the final instance of appeal, as leave is required for a further appeal to the Supreme Administrative Court. The most important *special courts* in the field of administrative law are the Insurance Court and the Market Court.

Nowadays, there are eight *regional administrative courts*, which are situated in Helsinki, Turku, Hämeenlinna, Kouvola, Kuopio, Vaasa, Oulu and Rovaniemi. In addition, there is the Administrative Court of the Åland Islands, which was founded in 1994. This Court is, however, connected to the Åland District Court, i. e. to the general court of law in the first instance.

In May 2012, the Ministry of Justice decided to develop a system of regional administrative courts. Two regional administrative courts-in Rovaniemi and Kouvola-will be merged with regional administrative courts in Oulu and Kuopio. The decision was mainly based on economic reasons. In particular, transferring the court from Rovaniemi, in the centre of Lapland, to Oulu is a regional policy question, too. Why was it not possible to transfer the court from Oulu to Rovaniemi? At present, there are also other general courts of law and the Faculty of Law of the University of Lapland in Rovaniemi.

Parliament has adopted the Government proposal and the reform will enter into force in 2014.

The programme put in place by Prime Minister Jyrki Katainen's Government states that *police services* can be secured throughout the country. The reality is quite different. Especially in Northern and Eastern Finland, there are only police resources in big cities. In addition, in June 2013 Parliament adopted a reform that will reduce police resources by seven million euros. In this connection, traffic police-who have operated throughout the country-will be abolished.

The Ministry of Defence will *abolish six military bases* in different regions. The termination will result in the loss of more than 2000 jobs (both civilian and military). In particular, abolishing of the North Karelia Brigade in Kontiolahti is a difficult regional policy matter. Luckily, the Government has promised to support the Brigade in this case.

Founding new universities in Northern and Eastern Finland was a typical example of good regional policy. Today, the political decisions are otherwise. Aalto University, a public foundation university, was established on 1 January 2010. It consists of three former universities (Helsinki University of Technology, the Helsinki School of Economics and the University of Art and Design Helsinki) and it is situated in the Helsinki Metropolitan Area. The State provided it with enormous amounts of support compared with other universities. Why this university? Why not the University of Helsinki or the University of Oulu? Maybe the future will make it clear that the political decision was not incorrect, although it was not fair from the perspective of regional policy or the equality of other universities.

The Government agenda includes two important reforms: *the reform of local government* and *social and health service reform.* Both of these reforms are linked together. At present, there are 320 municipalities in Finland. The aim of the former reform is clear that there will be fewer municipalities in the future, it supports in particular those municipalities that are economically stronger. The idea is that there will be no municipalities with less than 20,000 inhabitants. The problem is that such a reform is not in line with the Finnish Constitution, which guarantees self-government for the municipalities.

The social and health service reform is linked to the reform of local government. The central idea is that only big cities can arrange social and health services. There are two problems with this thinking. First, small municipalities then will not have the right to arrange social and health services, they only have to pay the costs of those services. Second, many cities are too small to be responsible for all social and health services. For instance, special health services need to be arranged in a municipality with at least at least 200,000 inhabitants.

Finally, here are some conclusions with positive future perspectives. In January

2013, a working group set up by the Ministry of Employment and the Economy proposed many new and innovative measures for the development of Northern Finland in its report.[①] Behind the ideas is the argument that the Arctic has become an increasingly interesting region of the world from a political, economic and scientific standpoint. The main reasons for increasing interest in the region are globalisation, climate change and the need for energy. In particular, its natural resources like oil, gas and minerals have caused tension and competition in the region. Furthermore, new opportunities for traffic connections via the Arctic Ocean to the Far East are fascinating. Many governments and parliaments in different countries in this area and also international organisations like the European Union have prepared Arctic strategies or other political documents.

Hopefully, the working group report will be the same kind of document as President Urho Kekkonen's pamphlet "Onko maallamme malttia vaurastua?" It was a start for a l'avenir rose in the North. In addition, there is a need for more independent national regional policy. Unfortunately this change is not seen in the new regional policy legislation, which our Parliament adopted in December 2013.

对区域政策的规制

玛蒂·尼米弗欧[*]

【摘要】本文基于作者在 1979 年和 2013 年所出版的两本专著，其目的在于概要介绍对区域性政策的规制及其在芬兰的实施。

---

① TEM (Ministry of Employment and the Economy) reports 2/2013. Katse pohjoiseen (Looking at the North).

* 芬兰拉普兰大学荣誉教授。

八二宪法实施以来宪法观念与
理论基础的变迁

翟国强[*]

【摘要】 八二宪法颁布实施以来，中国的政治秩序逐渐趋于稳定，法律制度不断健全，逐步形成了中国特色的社会主义法律体系。三十多年来，伴随着大规模政治运动状态的终结和经济领域的改革开放，主流的宪法观念和宪法理论也发生了不同程度的变化。在宪法实施和宪法修改过程中，宪法制度变迁与其背后的价值理念在发展过程中相互影响，促成了今日的宪法理论与实践的格局。与此相关，宪法学方法论、基本范畴体系和价值理念在与宪法实践的不断互动中也不断变迁，丰富并完善了中国的宪法学说体系。

【关键词】 宪法观念　变迁　宪法实施　方法论

一　引言

1978 年 12 月召开的中共十一届三中全会被认为是开启了中国改革开放历史新时期的一个关键转折点。结束"文化大革命"中大规模的群众运动，如何使政治活动进入一种有序可控的状态，是当时摆在中国共产党面前的主要政治任务。1982 年 12 月 4 日，第五届全国人民代表大会第五次会议以无记名投票方式正式通过了《中华人民共和国宪法》，学界一般通称为八二宪法。这次宪法修改是对 1978 年宪法进行的全面修改，内容上回归 1954 年宪法设定的基本制度，在宪法的修改程序和方式、宪法结构安排、国家机构的设置、公民基本权利和义务的规定等方面体现了对 1954 年宪法的继承

---

* 翟国强，中国社会科学院法学研究所副研究员。

和发展。八二宪法制定的一个重要背景就是以法律来为政治设定规范这样一个价值目标。通过宪法的颁布实施，法律制度进一步健全，中国的政治格局逐渐趋于稳定，逐渐从非常政治返回到常态政治，执政党的重心逐渐由政治领域阶级斗争向经济建设转移。

　　受马克思主义对经济基础决定性理论的影响，执政者认为改革应当首先改变经济制度。根据八二宪法的制度设计，国家的主要任务是以经济建设为中心，政治领域的改革都是为经济体制改革服务的。与此相对应，历次宪法修改的重要内容就是对经济体制改革的成果进行确认。而回顾中国三十多年来的经济体制改革实践，其基本路径是地方进行先行先试的探索，摸着石头过河，等经验成熟后再进行利弊权衡，归纳总结，上升为正式法律制度，推广到全国范围实施。但作为社会主义宪法的一个重要特征，中国宪法对经济制度的规定比较具体，因此经济体制改革的实践不免会产生突破宪法对经济体制的具体规定的现象。① 对此，有学者称之为"良性违宪"。② 随着我国市场经济体制的不断发展和完善，宪法修改中对经济体制进行的实质性修正条款逐渐减少，其他方面的内容逐渐增加。在 1999 年的宪法修正案 13 条将法治国家确立为宪法原则之后，要实现法治国家所要求的"有法可依"，各项具体法律制度的完善就成为当务之急，因此如何完善法律制度成为宪法实施的主要任务。在此背景下，立法成为宪法实施的主要方式。三十多年来，在全国人大的主导下，中国各级立法机关积极完善各个不同领域的法律制度，形成了中国特色的社会主义法律体系。三十多年间，伴随着大规模政治运动状态的终结和经济领域的改革开放，主流的宪法观念和宪法理论也发生了不同程度的变化。在宪法实施和宪法修改过程中，宪法制度的变迁与其背后的价值理念在发展过程中相互影响，促成了今日的宪法理论与实践的格局。

---

① 对于这种过于详细的规定，张庆福曾提出不同看法，他指出："各国的宪政建设实践表明，凡是对经济问题规定得比较简明扼要的，其稳定性就比较强，权威性就比较高。而相反，规定得越详细的，宪法的稳定性就差。宪法如何规定经济关系才适度呢？我认为，宪法对经济问题的规范要比对其他问题更概括更原则，要留给法律更大的空间。具体说，重点规定公民的经济权利，特别是对公民财产权利的保护。在总则或总纲中只简要概括规定国家的基本经济政策，主要规定国家的基本经济制度。"《纪念宪法颁布 20 周年座谈会纪要》，《法学研究》2003 年第 1 期。

② 郝铁川：《论良性违宪》，《法学研究》1996 年第 4 期。

二　八二宪法实施以来主流宪法观念的发展

八二宪法颁布实施至今已经三十多年，这三十多年间，中国的经济、政治、文化等社会背景发生了大幅度的变化，与此相适应，全国人民代表大会分别于 1988 年 4 月 12 日、1993 年 3 月 29 日、1999 年 3 月 15 日和 2004 年 3 月 14 日对八二宪法进行了四次局部修改。三十多年来，随着经济体制改革的深化和对外开放程度的提高，中国的主流政治观念在不断变化，与此相关的宪法学方法论和基础理论体系也发生了一系列的变化。

（一）从根本意志到根本规范

宪法变动频繁的时期，主流宪法观念往往会强调宪法背后的人民意志，从 1954 年宪法到八二宪法，各个宪法草案报告中的人民意志出现的频率逐渐提高。1954 年宪法制定时，刘少奇《关于中华人民共和国宪法草案的报告》中出现了 6 次。在 1982 年宪法修改的时候，人民的意志在彭真的《关于中华人民共和国宪法修改草案的报告》中一共出现了 7 次。随着宪法秩序趋于稳定，主张宪法是根本法，并以此为依据来规范政治活动成为政治观念的主流。1982 年《关于中华人民共和国宪法修改草案的报告》指出："中国人民和中国共产党都已经深知，宪法的权威关系到政治的安定和国家的命运，决不容许对宪法根基的任何损害。"将宪法看作根本规范的观念必然要求重视宪法的实施，发挥宪法的规范功能。1992 年在纪念宪法颁布十周年会议上的讲话中，全国人大常委会委员长乔石再次提到了"决不允许对宪法根基的任何损害"。并进一步指出："贯彻实施宪法，还要求全国人大和全国人大常委会认真把监督宪法实施的职责承担起来。要加强对法律、法规是否违宪的审查，对任何违宪行为都要坚决纠正。地方各级人大及其常委会都要在本行政区域内保证宪法的遵守和执行。全国人大常委会要很好地运用解释宪法的职能，对宪法实施中的问题作出必要的解释和说明，使宪法的规定得到更好的落实。"根本规范的理念同时要求一切国家权力的正当性都源于宪法的授予。李鹏在 2001 年法制宣传日的讲话中曾指出："全国人大及其常委会是宪法规定的最高国家权力机关，其权力来源于宪法，也必须在宪法范围内活动，必须在宪法规定的范围内行使立法、监督等职权，不得超越宪法。"迄今，主流宪法观念仍然强调宪法是人民意志的体现，在宪法修改过程中更加重视扩大公民的有序参与，并致力于完善参与的法律程序。只是在宪法实施的语境下，更加强调宪法作为根本法律规范的功能。

（二）坚持审慎的修宪理念

基于"文化大革命"中政治秩序极度混乱的动荡，执政者试图通过宪法来追求政治秩序的稳定的期望很高，八二宪法及其修正案都体现了中国共产党追求稳定政治秩序的价值诉求。八二宪法修改时彭真在全国人大会议上所做的《关于中华人民共和国宪法修改草案的报告》，对这部宪法的功能定位是"一部有中国特色的、适应新的历史时期社会主义现代化建设需要的、长期稳定的新宪法"，并寄希望于通过确立一种约束政治活动的根本规范，来实现这种对稳定政治秩序的追求。因此在草案说明中，特别强调"宪法的权威关系到政治的安定和国家的命运，决不容许对宪法根基的任何损害"。这种追求政治秩序稳定的价值诉求直接影响了历次宪法修改。1988年，第一次修改八二宪法时，根据中共中央的建议正式名称采取的是"修改宪法个别条款"的表述。1993年3月14日，《中国共产党中央委员会关于修改宪法部分内容的补充建议》指出："必须进行修改的加以修改，……这次修改宪法不是作全面修改，可改可不改的不改。"1998年12月，李鹏在修改宪法征求专家意见会上指出："修改宪法事关重大，这次修改只对需要修改的并已经成熟的部分内容进行修改，可不改和有争议的问题不改。"1999年3月14日，《第九届全国人民代表大会第二次会议主席团关于中华人民共和国宪法修正案（草案）审议情况的说明》指出："属于可改可不改的内容，可以不作修改。"2004年3月8日，《关于〈中华人民共和国宪法修正案（草案）〉的说明》也指出："这次修改宪法不是大改，而是部分修改，对实践证明是成熟的、需要用宪法规范的、非改不可的进行修改。"回顾历次宪法修改，一个基本的态度就是坚持宪法修改的"绝对必要性原则"，最大可能地维护和实现政治和法律格局的有序稳定，这种对于宪法修改的谨慎态度已经成为指导历次宪法修改的一个主流宪法观念。

（三）从政治象征到法律规范

八二宪法的修改是以1954年宪法为基础的，该宪法继受了苏联的宪法制度，同时其原理受苏联宪法学说，特别是斯大林的宪法观念影响很大。由于接受了马克思主义经济基础决定上层建筑的原理，社会主义宪法的一个重要特征就是将宪法理解为是对某种政治事实的确认和宣示。在中国共产党的主流宪法理念中特别强调对事实问题的确认。毛泽东曾经认为"革命成功有了民主事实以后，颁布一个根本大法，去承认它，这就是宪法"。因此，在八二宪法的起草过程中，有关的政治家和领导人非常重视宪法序言中对"四件大事"等历史事实的叙述，宪法序言的内容系在邓小平直接过问下，由彭真亲自执笔起草的。①

　　毋庸讳言，从政治的视角看，在任何国家，任何政治体制下，宪法不仅是法，也是一个政治象征或者政治宣言。② 特别是通过革命取得政权后制定的宪法，往往需要对一些事实进行宣告和确认，通过以宪法规范确认事实的方式来寻求政权的历史正当性。但宪法更重要的功能在于为政治过程提供根本法律规范，因此需要以法律的方式来实施。三十多年来，随着法治化进程的不断深入，宪法的法律性逐渐被社会各界接受并强化，主流宪法观念逐渐将宪法看作法律体系的基础，因此是一种需要在法律系统内贯彻实施的规范。而这种实施主要是通过立法的方式加以实现，实施宪法的一个主要机构是全国人大。③ 随着法律体系的不断完善和健全，宪法确认的基本权利和国家组织规范在普通法律层面得以具体化并建立了相应的保障机制。在这个过程中，宪法的法律性逐渐被各级立法机关和行政机关乃至社会公众所普遍接受。

（四）从确认改革到规范改革

　　回顾中国的改革开放进程，其中一个重要的特征就是所谓的"摸着石头过河"，不断进行探索改进。因此，改革过程中的法治建设的整体思路采取的是一种经验主义的方法。国家层面的立法大多是以地方的立法经验为基础，成熟后上升到国家层面。因此，立法更多的是对改革成果的法律确认。但随着宪法实施的深入，各项规范公权力的宪法制度不断健全，主流宪法观念逐渐由被动的确认改革发展到能动的规范改革。在 1993 年宪法修改时，《中国共产党中央委员会关于修改宪法部分内容的补充建议》指出，宪法修改是根据十多年来中国社会主义现代化建设和改革开放的新经验，着重对社会主义经济制度的有关规定做了修改和补充，使其更加符合现实情况和发展的需要。这些表述和提法，体现了主流政治观念中以宪法来确认改革成果的主张。随着宪法上的程序法不断完善，在宪法和法律的轨道上进行改革逐渐成为主流的宪法观念。在立法法制定过程中，对于改革相关的授权立法和中央地方立法权分配等问题的讨论体现了这种将改革纳入

---

① 参见王汉斌《王汉斌访谈录》，中国民主法制出版社，2012，第 66 页。
② Larry R. Baas, "The Constitution as Symbol: The Interpersonal Sources of Meaning of a Secondary Symbol", *American Journal of Political Science*, Vol. 23, No. 1 (Feb., 1979), pp. 101 – 120.
③ 参见王汉斌《王汉斌访谈录》，中国民主法制出版社，2012，第 80 页。

法制轨道的宪法观念。①

（五）宪法叙事的理性化

三十多年来，主流政治观念逐渐以更加理性的态度看待宪法，在有关宪法的政论叙述中出现了理性化或者去情感化的特征。这也是自新中国成立以来主流宪法观念的一个整体发展趋势。不可否认，政治叙事必然带有情感（甚至是激情）色彩，在中国主流的政治叙事的一个重要样本就是人民日报或者新华社等主流媒体的表述。在1954年宪法制定后，《人民日报》的标题是《首都人民热烈欢呼宪法的通过》，新华社的消息题目是《北京、上海等城市广大人民欢庆中华人民共和国宪法的公布》。而在八二宪法通过后，《人民日报》社论的标题是《人人学习宪法，人人掌握宪法》《新时期治国安邦的总章程》等。1993年宪法修改后，新华社的新闻标题是《首都各界座谈宪法修正案，与会者认为意义重大影响深远》。2004年宪法修改时，新华社的新闻标题是《从宪法修改看中国特色社会主义》。此外，从历次宪法修改的草案说明中也可以看出政治修辞运用更加趋于谨慎，概念表述尽量不带感情色彩成为宪法修正案草案说明的一个重要发展趋势。导致这种变化的原因有很多，其中一个重要的原因就是主流宪法观念更多地将宪法看作一种法律规范，而不单是凝聚意志和力量的政治性文件，因此在宪法叙事中尽量回避情感色彩。这种变化也是中国政治过程中个人魅力型权威逐渐向法治权威过渡的必然要求。

三　宪法基础理论的发展

与上述主流宪法观念的变化同步，宪法实施以来宪法学理论研究也出现了繁荣发展的趋势。这种变化的原因可以追溯至中共十一届三中全会宣告了政治领域极"左"思潮的结束，执政党所提出的政治领域的思想解放要求是："在人民内部的思想政治生活中，只能实行民主方法，不能采取压制、打击手段。要重申不抓辫子、不扣帽子、不打棍子的'三不主义'。各级领导要善于集中人民群众的正确意见，对不正确的意见进行适当的解释说服。"伴随着这种思想解放的进程不断深入，理论研究逐渐走向正轨，出现了学术观点的争鸣和交锋。特别是最近十年以来，中国的宪法学研究在方法论和基本理论体系上出现了明显的变化。三十多年来，宪法学理论研

---

① 参见李鹏《立法与监督：李鹏人大日记》，新华出版社、中国民主法制出版社，2006，第316页。

究也间接地影响着主流宪法观念的变化，进而影响着宪法制度的发展。①

（一）方法论的转型

新中国成立后，宪法学的研究完全摒弃了民国时期的宪法学说，在马克思主义的指导下，创立了以阶级分析方法为根本方法的宪法学。以阶级分析方法为根本方法的宪法学强调宪法在内容上是统治阶级意志和利益的集中体现，认为宪法是阶级力量对比关系的表现。党的十一届三中全会以后，法学理念的革新之一就是对阶级斗争思维方式进行了一定程度的反思。② 随着时代发展和学术界思想的进一步解放，将"政治力量对比关系"作为宪法的本质特征逐渐成为代替阶级理论的新学说。这种宪法理论研究可以称为"政治教义宪法学"。③ 这些理论在方法论上，坚持马克思主义的立场，对宪法规范采取政治化的解说性研究。在宪法制定或者修改时，这种政治化的方法有其存在的历史合理性。即政治势力和政治理念主导着宪法规范的生成，宪法学理论的研究也不免受当时的政治和社会环境的影响。再加上中国自 1954 年宪法制定以来一贯采取的是政治动员式的制宪和修宪模式，政治理念对宪法学影响深刻也在情理之中。而且，当时一些主流宪法学家兼具学者与政治家的双重身份，比如张友渔、王叔文等，加上高度政治化的学术环境，也导致了宪法学方法的政治化特征。因此，宪法学者在宪法起草、全民讨论和宣传过程中的功能不是研究问题，而是普及宪法知识，宣传解释宪法背后的政治原理。④

进入 21 世纪以来，关于宪法学的方法，大多数宪法学者认为，宪法学应当具有独立于其他邻近学科，尤其是政治学的方法。⑤ 宪法学研究在整体上经历了一次由宏大叙事到精细化研究的法学方法的转型。这种方法论转型的一个重要思路就是将宪法看作一种具有法律约束力的规范，并突出其实践导向性。因此主张采取法解释学的方法对宪法文本进行一种规范性解

① 比如，1998 年 12 月 22 日，在李鹏主持的修改宪法征求意见座谈会上，张庆福、曾宪义提出宪法修改增加"保护公民私有财产权"；黄子毅、王家福、陈光中提出宪法修改增加"国家尊重和保护人权"。虽然在 1999 年宪法修改时这些观点没有被采纳，但是在 2004 年宪法修改时被采纳。

② 参见周凤举《法单纯是阶级斗争工具吗？——兼论法的社会性》，《法学研究》1980 年第 1 期；苏谦《也谈法律的继承性》，《法学研究》1980 年第 1 期。

③ 林来梵：《中国宪法学的现状与展望》，《法学研究》2011 年第 6 期。

④ 参见张友渔主编《中国法学四十年》，上海人民出版社，1989，第 154 页。

⑤ 郑贤君：《宪法学为何需要方法论的自觉？——兼议宪法学方法论是什么》，《浙江学刊》2005 年第 2 期。

释，进而形成一个解释理论体系。晚近中国法学界兴起的宪法解释学或者规范宪法学正是以此作为学术努力的方向，试图建构中国的宪法学体系的。这种现实问题导向的研究方法和思路正在被越来越多的学者所肯定，成为学界的主流学说。这种方法论转型的原因是宪法法律实施的必然要求。此外，法律实践中不断出现大量的宪法问题也需要从理论上给予解答，由此产生了对抽象宪法条文进行法律解释的需求。

八二宪法实施以来，在官方主流的政治理念中采取的是一种谨慎的宪法变迁观念。在此背景下，宪法解释的方法最初是为了回应现实变迁的需要对宪法条文的含义进行新的理解，其功能定位是作为宪法修改的一种替代手段。1993 年 3 月 14 日，中国共产党中央委员会《关于修改宪法部分内容的补充建议》指出，"有些问题今后可以采取宪法解释的方式予以解决"，"宪法第六条规定社会主义公有制实行按劳分配的原则，并不排除按劳分配以外的其它分配方式。必要时可作宪法解释"。在 1999 年 3 月 14 日，《第九届全国人民代表大会第二次会议主席团关于中华人民共和国宪法修正案（草案）审议情况的说明》指出，有些修改意见和建议可以通过宪法解释予以解决。2004 年 3 月 8 日，王兆国在《关于〈中华人民共和国宪法修正案（草案）〉的说明》中指出："这次修改宪法不是大改，而是部分修改，对实践证明是成熟的、需要用宪法规范的、非改不可的进行修改，可改可不改的、可以通过宪法解释予以明确的不改。"2004 年 3 月 12 日，第十届全国人民代表大会第二次会议主席团关于《中华人民共和国宪法修正案（草案）》审议情况的报告进一步重申了有的（修改建议）可以通过宪法解释予以明确。这种在宪法修改实践中贯彻的主流宪法观念刺激了宪法学研究对于宪法解释的关注，宪法学理论界与宪法决策者就宪法解释问题在宪法修改过程中也进行了一定程度的互动。① 早期的理论更多的是将宪法解释作为回应社会现实的一种方式，与宪法修改相对应进行思考。因此，主要关注的是宪法解释的一般方法、宪法解释的界限等问题。② 与理论界对宪法解释

---

① 根据李鹏日记记载，在征求意见会上一些学者提出的运用宪法解释来应对社会发展的思路被肯定："修改宪法事关重大，这次修改只对需要修改的并已成熟的部分内容进行修改，可不改和有争议的问题不改。宪法赋予全国人大常委会解释宪法的职权，因此有些问题将来可以通过全国人大常委会关于宪法的解释来解决。"参见李鹏《立法与监督：李鹏人大日记》，新华出版社、中国民主法制出版社，2006，第 260 页。

② 韩大元、张翔：《试论宪法解释的客观性与主观性》，《法律科学》1999 年第 6 期；韩大元、张翔：《试论宪法解释的界限》，《法学评论》2001 年第 1 期；韩大元：《"十六大"后须强化宪法解释制度的功能》，《法学》2003 年第 1 期。

热切关注形成鲜明对比的是，宪法解释的法定机关全国人大常委会却并未做出任何具有法律效力的宪法解释。鉴于这种现状，理论界开始反思仅仅在抽象层面研究宪法解释的一般方法和原理的现实意义，并逐渐认识到仅仅关注宪法条文的宪法解释学无法有效回应现实的需求，也无法促成现实中宪法制度的发展，因此理论界对于宪法解释的研究开始出现了两种发展趋势。一是以现实问题为切入点，进行一种问题导向的宪法解释学研究。最近十年以来出现的大量宪法案例或事件的研究体现了这种思路。二是将宪法解释与普通法律论证相结合寻求宪法在一般法律中的贯彻落实。宪法理论界对合宪解释方法、宪法权利的辐射效力等问题的关注体现了这种思路。

三十多年来，宪法学理论在方法论上更加多元化。除了从法解释学角度进行宪法学理论研究之外，学界也不乏基于外部视角对宪法现象进行社会学、政治学方法的研究，即作为"社会科学的宪法学"研究。而且，在宪法解释学或规范宪法学的思考过程中，并没有排斥政治学和社会学的研究方法。持论平稳的学者更趋向于以实践问题为导向，以法学方法为根本方法，同时引入其他学科的研究方法，围绕宪法规范来寻求对中国宪法现实具有解释力度的宪法学说。三十多年来，中国的法治建设取得了一些成就，法律制度获得了一定程度的自主性。但是政治对法律而言仍处于绝对优势地位，因此从政治的外部视角来思考中国宪法问题的研究方法仍颇有市场。这些政治学的方法体现为透过宪法来探求其背后的利益关系或政治理念。有些研究直接根据政治逻辑对政治话语中的宪法概念进行解读，甚至进行理论续造，再有就是基于研究者的价值立场对其进行学术化解读。但是就整体而言，这种作为"社会科学的宪法学"仍缺乏从中国历史、中国社会角度进行认真严肃的学术研究，有的只是一种政治哲学的解读，有的只是一种有关宪法的叙事或修辞。目前中国的主流政治观念并不排斥国外的制度经验，明确提出"要借鉴人类政治文明有益成果"。宪法学研究中参考借鉴国外的宪法理论和制度实践成为近年来宪法学研究的一个重要特征。毋庸讳言，无论从立宪主义思想上还是宪法制度的演进上，西方理论和制度对中国的影响都是无法回避的现实。但是就目前研究现状而言，如何对域外理论进行本土化也是一个重要的挑战。目前，应对这种本土化的挑战需要重视中国宪法（思想）史的研究和宪法社会学的研究。

（二）基本范畴与理念的变迁

宪法学方法的变迁论决定了宪法学范畴体系的发展。中国宪法学的方法曾长期受到苏联宪法的影响，早期的宪法学体系"明显地是历史唯物主义原理这一学科的机械性延伸，如阶级分析的方法和国体、政体、阶级、革命、经济基础、上层建筑、生产力、生产关系等用语"。① 在具体于特定问题的分析时，一般惯于引用政治性的概念解释宪法条文，甚至反其道而行，直接将宪法条文作为论证政治决断正当性的依据。受到这种思路的影响，中国的宪法学理论曾将国体、政体等政治学的基本范畴作为宪法学的基本范畴。随着法学研究整体水平的提高，法学逐渐成为一门具有独特方法的学科，此外独立的范畴体系也是形成独立学科品格的重要标志。中国宪法学应当逐渐抛弃那些陈旧的范畴，建立中国宪法学自己的话语系统，成为学界的共识。② 在这种理念指导下，许多政治学的概念逐渐被宪法学所边缘化，宪法学的范畴体系开始逐渐独立于政治学。国体、政体、阶级、革命、经济基础、上层建筑、生产力、生产关系等政治学的范畴逐渐成为宪法学理论体系的边缘。自 2005 年以来，宪法学界针对宪法学基本范畴问题已经召开了数次专题的研讨会，但是对于基本范畴究竟包含哪些仍然没有达成共识。③ 对于中国宪法学基本范畴的发展，韩大元指出，"中国宪法学"与"中国的宪法学"是不同的，在构建"中国宪法学"过程中，必然经历"中国的宪法学"阶段，可能沿用政治现象与宪法现象之间灰色地带中的术语，但随着学术的进一步发展，中国宪法学能够成立和成熟的时候，应当逐渐抛弃这些陈旧的范畴。④

八二宪法颁布实施以来，基本权利作为宪法核心价值的观念成为理论研究的共识，有关基本权利的研究逐步升温，特别是法理学界对于权利义务基本范畴的研究，更促使宪法学界对于基本权利的关注。基本权利成为

---

① 童之伟：《宪法学研究方法之改造》，《法学》1994 年第 9 期。
② 韩大元：《对 20 世纪 50 年代中国宪法学基本范畴的分析与反思》，《当代法学》2005 年第 5 期。
③ 如，李龙和周叶中认为，宪法学的基本范畴包括：宪法与宪政、主权与人权、国体与政体、基本权利与基本义务、国家权力与国家机构共五对基本范畴。韩大元认为，宪法学基本范畴主要包括：国家－社会；宪法－法律；立宪主义－民主主义；人权－基本权利；主权－国际社会。李龙、周叶中：《宪法学基本范畴简论》，《中国法学》1996 年第 6 期；韩大元：《对 20 世纪 50 年代中国宪法学基本范畴的分析与反思》，《当代法学》2005 年第 5 期。
④ 林来梵、郑磊、翟国强：《对话与约定的狂想——一场中国宪法学圆桌学术会议的述评》，《浙江社会科学》2005 年第 3 期。

宪法学的一个重要的核心范畴，甚至被认为是最为核心的基本范畴。目前，中国的宪法学理论体系大致可以分为国家机构和基本权利两大部分，其中基本权利体系的比重在逐渐增加。迄今，我国宪法学界对于基本权利在宪法规范体系中的核心地位达成了学说上的基本共识，中国的宪法学研究已经逐步转向以基本权利为核心的研究。① 而且，近年来的基本权利理论研究已经开始将基本权利的保障理念渗透至国家机构和各种公法制度中进行研究，进而试图构建以基本权利为轴心的宪法学。加上宪法学方法论转型的影响，对于基本权利法解释学的构建成为近十年来中青年宪法学者的努力目标。目前，有关基本权利法解释学的研究成果已经颇具规模。

八二宪法实施以来，在国家公权力研究领域也产生了一些价值立场的变化。其中一个重大的理念变化，就是对所谓"议行合一"原则的反思。所谓"议行合一"是指立法机关和行政机关合二为一，制定法律的机关同时负责执行法律。② 中国宪法学界曾经一度把"议行合一"看成社会主义国家政权组织的普遍原则，并将之作为与资本主义之"三权分立"相对立、体现社会主义制度优越性的体制或原则，并将此作为姓"资"还是姓"社"的区分标准。1989年王玉明旗帜鲜明地提出"议行合一不是我国国家机构的组织原则"。③ 此后，吴家麟对"议行合一"学说进行了深刻反思，并从巴黎公社是怎样实行议行合一的、为什么巴黎公社要实行议行合一、马克思和列宁是怎样肯定议行合一的、议行合一的利弊何在、我国政权组织原则是民主集中制还是议行合一、议行合一与议行统一是否相同等六个方面论证了议行不宜合一。④ 时任全国人大常委会办公厅研究室主任的刘政也撰文指出议行合一不是我国人大制度的特点。⑤ 大多数学者认为强调"议行合一"容易忽视政权之间的合理分工和相互制约，不利于保障各国家机关依法行使职权，而且由于其实际上主张人大代表和人大常委会委员兼职，不

---

① 对此张千帆指出，宪法学过去将眼光放在"人民""国家""主权"等宏观概念上，现在的焦点则转移到个人的基本权利方面。张千帆：《从"人民主权"到"人权"——中国宪法学研究模式的变迁》，《政法论坛》2005年第2期。

② 蔡定剑：《中国人民代表大会制度》（第4版），法律出版社，2003，第92-93页。

③ 王玉明：《议行合一不是我国国家机构的组织原则》，《政法论坛》1989年第4期。

④ 吴家麟：《"议行"不宜"合一"》，《中国法学》1992年第5期。

⑤ 刘政、程湘清：《人民代表大会制度的理论与实践》，中国民主法制出版社，2003，第108-115页。

利于加强人大监督权的发挥。① 经过一番激烈的争论之后，"议行合一"说在中国的理论研究和实践中的影响逐渐式微。这种理念变化是承认国家机关之间权力分工和相互制约的一个重要标志，也为通过国家机构组织法和监督法等法律来实施宪法提供了理论基础。

　　上述价值观念转变的另一个体现就是承认人民代表大会之外的司法机关具有相对的独立性，人大不宜对司法过程进行个案监督，司法机关是适用法律的机关，在宪法上具有独立地位。在这种司法优位的理念下，宪法学理论曾一度主张法院在具体案件中有选择适用法律的权力，甚至有拒绝适用违反宪法的法律的义务。但是这种主张并未被主流政治观念所接受，特别是由司法机关来决定代议机关制定的法律的正当性，与中国宪法制度设计的初衷不符合。为此，主流政治观念旗帜鲜明地"坚决不搞三权分立"，其中包含着反对由司法机关来审查法律合宪性的观点。自八二宪法颁布实施以来，在保持现有的政治观念和政治格局不变的前提下，由全国人大常委会（或者人大内部特设机构）来监督宪法实施的思路为大多数学者所肯认。但自宪法实施以来全国人大常委会尚未做出过具有法律效力的宪法解释或宪法判断。这是目前中国宪法学理论，特别是宪法解释学所面临的最大实践困境。因此，近年来宪法学研究的一个重要课题就是宪法如何在一般部门法领域发生规范效力，并结合具体的案件或者事例在一般法律问题中寻求宪法实施的迂回路径。

四　结语：评析与展望

　　与之前的几部宪法相比较，八二宪法在四个方面扩大了人大常委会的职权：立法权；监督宪法实施，解释宪法的权力；审查和批准计划预算在执行过程中所必须做的部分调整；根据总理提名，决定部长、委员会主任和审计长、秘书长的人选。② 在上述四个职权行使方面，立法权行使最为充分，法律依据也比较明确。在1954年宪法中，全国人大常委会并没有立法的权力，到1982年通过了现行宪法，才赋予了全国人大常委会以立法的权

---

① 蔡定剑：《中国人民代表大会制度》（第4版），法律出版社，2003，第88-91页；童之伟、伍瑾、朱梅全：《法学界对"议行合一"的反思与再评价》，《江海学刊》2003年第5期。

② 参见王汉斌《王汉斌访谈录》，中国民主法制出版社，2012，第79-80页。

力。① 以这部宪法为根本法律依据，包括人民代表大会在内的国家组织机构逐渐完善，各级立法机关也制定了大量的法律，政治、经济、文化、社会等各个领域的法律制度逐步得到完善。根据八二宪法的授权，全国人大常委会加快立法进度，迄今大约80%的法律都是全国人大通过的。② 第三项和第四项主要是程序性的权力，全国人大据此也制定了相应的法律来进行具体化实施。但第二项职权，即监督宪法实施和解释宪法的权力，至今还没有法律层面上的规范依据。

回顾八二宪法颁布实施以来三十多年的法律实践，人大常委会在监督宪法实施方面作为不大，在解释宪法方面基本没有做出过具有法律效力的宪法解释或宪法判断。在中国特色社会主义法律体系形成后，人大立法的主要职能是根据社会发展对法律体系进行修补和完善，大规模立法的时代即将结束。此后如何避免法律体系的碎片化，维持法律制度的统一性将成为法治建设的一个重要任务。整体来看，现有的法律制度仍缺乏一种从宪法层面对法律体系的合宪性和正当性进行统合的优化机制，因此，如何对法律体系进行宪法性控制是全国人大发挥宪法监督职能的一个紧迫课题。由于主流政治观念无法接受司法机关做出合宪性判断的制度模式，宪法学界对于宪法实施监督的理论主张主要还是寄希望全国人大能够选择合适的切入点推进宪法监督的实践。

八二宪法实施三十多年来，随着依法治国方略的实施，特别是中国特色社会主义法律体系的形成和完善，法律系统相对于政治系统的独立性已经逐渐显现。在中共中央的正式文件中，逐渐开始将中国特色社会主义法律体系与政治制度加以并列表述，法治话语逐渐获得了相对独立的地位。这种政治话语的逐渐发展，在为宪法的法律化实施提供政治理论支持的同时，也将为宪法基础理论的研究提供一种较为明确的政治坐标。为此，如何结合中国的政治实践并基于法学的立场研究宪法实施以及宪法监督问题将是宪法学研究的一个重要课题。与此同时，实践问题导向的宪法理论研究将成为主流。当然，受制于中国的政治和法治现实，单纯的逻辑分析和宪法条文释义固然不足以解释和解决现实中出现的宪法问题。引入其他学科的知识特别是政治学、社会学的研究来强化宪法论证也是必需的。但是

---

① 参见李鹏《立法与监督：李鹏人大日记》，新华出版社、中国民主法制出版社，2006，第8页。

② 参见王汉斌《王汉斌访谈录》，中国民主法制出版社，2012，第80页

也要警惕其他方法运用过度而导致喧宾夺主的局面。完全专注于宪法背后的社会和政治背景，可能会使宪法学研究在方法论上重新返回过去的宏大叙事而脱离其实践品格，或者过于关注宪法背后的意识形态从而被政治内卷化（involution）。

（原载《华东政法大学学报》2012 年第 6 期，收入本书时略有修改）

The Evolution of the Concept and Theoretical Basis of Constitution since 1982

Zhai Guoqiang [*]

【Abstract】Since the promulgation and implementation of the 1982 Constitution, the political order has been gradually stabilized, the system of law continuously improved, and a social legal system with Chinese characteristics gradually taken form in China. During the past thirty plus years, with the end of large-scale political movements and the reform and opening up in the economic field, the mainstream constitutional concept and theory have been undergoing a process of evolution. In the process of implementation and revision of the Constitution, the evolution of the constitutional system and the development of the values behind it have interacted with each other, resulting in the current structure of constitutional theory and practice in China. Related to the above process are the continuous evolution of the methodology, the basic category system and the value system of constitution and their interaction with constitutional practice, which have enriched and improved the system of constitutional theory in China.

【Keywords】Constitutional Ideas; Evolution; Enforcement of the Constitution; Methodology

---

* Associate Professor, Institute of Law, Chinese Academy of Social Sciences.

论中国司法管理体制改革的切入点

莫纪宏*

【摘要】本文通过分析司法活动的性质和特点，对一个国家的司法体制做了两个角度的划分，指出一个国家的司法体制是由司法组织管理体制和司法运行体制构成的。司法管理体制主要解决的是司法机关如何设置以及如何配置司法权力；司法运行体制主要涉及司法机关运用司法权力解决具体案件的法律程序和法律机制。司法管理体制是国家司法权力配置、组织和运行的机制和制度，其中司法机关的法律性质和法律地位如何确定、上下级司法机关之间的相互关系、司法人员如何产生和履行职务、司法职权如何设定和配置、司法功能如何得到充分和有效发挥等，是司法管理体制的重要制度内涵。司法管理体制在一个国家的司法体制中具有基础性的建构作用，有什么样的司法管理体制，就有什么样的司法运行体制；司法运行体制运转不畅，主要来源于司法管理体制的设计缺陷。本文通过分析我国司法政策的演变，认为司法管理体制改革在我国当下的合法性依据来源于司法政策，特别是党的十八届三中全会通过的《中共中央关于全面深化改革若干重大问题的决定》（以下简称《决定》），对司法体制改革，特别是司法管理体制改革提出了明确的要求。笔者认为，要正确地贯彻落实《决定》的要求，应当将司法活动通过宪法修改纳入国家基本制度范畴，依托人民代表大会制度的基本制度框架，建构由全国人大常委会作为最高司法机关的"大司法"管理体制，同时还要正确处理党委政法委与法院、检察院和公安机关之间的关系，协调公、检、法、司在刑事案件审理中的相互监督和制约关系，健全司法队伍，推进法官、检察官和警官的职业化，并尝试建立与行政管辖区适当分离的审判制度，进一步保证司法机关依法独

---

* 莫纪宏，中国社会科学院法学研究所副所长、研究员。

立行使司法职权，维护司法正义。

　　【关键词】司法管理体制　司法运行体制　司法体制　司法改革　司法政策

一　我国司法管理体制的现状及特点

　　司法是国家专门机关将宪法和法律适用于具体的案件解决法律矛盾和纠纷的体现国家意志的国家权力活动。司法最重要的制度功能就是适用法律，运用法律来解决具体的法律矛盾和纠纷。司法在最狭义上被仅仅理解为法官的适用法律的活动。[①] 司法在国家权力活动体系中具有非常重要的地位，与立法、执法、法律监督、法律遵守、法律教育等共同构成了现代法治社会国家权力依法运行的制度基础。由于司法处于一个国家法治运行的最终环节，因此，司法通常被称为守卫法治原则、保障人权的最后一道制度防线。司法的最大制度特征是司法活动解决的是一个个具体问题，司法在法制建设中的主要功能是保障"具体法治"的实现。

　　一个国家的司法体制是由司法组织管理体制和司法运行体制构成的。司法管理体制主要解决的是司法机关如何设置以及如何配置司法权力；司法运行体制主要涉及司法机关运用司法权力解决具体案件的法律程序和法律机制。司法管理体制是国家司法权力配置、组织和运行的机制和制度，其中司法机关的法律性质和法律地位如何确定、上下级司法机关之间的相互关系、司法人员如何产生和履行职务、司法职权如何设定和配置、司法功能如何得到充分和有效发挥等，是司法管理体制的重要制度内涵。司法管理体制在一个国家的司法体制中具有基础性的建构作用，有什么样的司法管理体制，就有什么样的司法运行体制；司法运行体制运转不畅，主要来源于司法管理体制的设计缺陷。所以，只有不断地改革和完善司法管理体制，才能保证司法机关有效地行使司法权力，并通过司法活动来正确地

---

　　① 《牛津法律大辞典》虽然没有"司法"词条，却有描述"司法"性质的派生性词条"司法的"。该辞典对"司法的"（judicial）解释为：关于法官的术语，在很多情况下区别于"立法的""行政的"，在另外一些情况下，区别于"司法以外的"，后者指不经法院处理以及没有法官干预的处理。很显然，《牛津法律大辞典》是以法官的职务活动为核心来定义"司法"的，也就是说，凡不是法官履行职务的活动都不属于"司法"概念的范围。这是对"司法"的实质性内涵做的"狭义"解释。参见〔英〕戴维·M. 沃克：《牛津法律大辞典》，北京社会与科技发展研究所组织翻译，光明日报出版社，1988。

适用法律，保障公民的权利。

　　我国现行的司法管理体制是在长期的司法实践活动中不断总结经验产生的，许多司法管理制度带有非常明确的时代特征和探索及改革的性质。目前存在的主要问题是司法管理体制的"法律依据"不足，主要是依靠执政党的司法政策来指导，在国家基本宪法和法律制度与司法管理体制之间还需要一定的制度关联。司法管理体制的法律性质和法律地位也需要通过法律文本的形式加以明确。总体上来看，司法管理体制存在着政策主导、检审为主体、以人民代表大会制度为依托的实用主义特色，许多与司法管理体制相关的基本法律关系需要进一步加以澄清。

　　尽管宪法文本中没有涉及"司法"，但这并不意味着"司法"一词就不可以研究或者在实际中禁止加以使用。事实上，改革开放之后，从党的十一届三中全会到党的十八大，都对"司法"保持了高度的关注。以党的十二大以来的历次党代会的重要文件为例，党的十二大工作报告没有出现"司法"一词，党的十三大报告正式提出了"司法机关"的概念和加强"司法"的理念。赵紫阳在《沿着有中国特色的社会主义道路前进》工作报告中指出："我们必须一手抓建设和改革，一手抓法制。法制建设必须贯串于改革的全过程。一方面，应当加强立法工作，改善执法活动，保障司法机关依法独立行使职权，提高公民的法律意识。"这里已经提及"保障司法机关依法独立行使职权"。上述规定实际上是对执政党的各级党组织提出的要求。党的十四大报告没有提及"司法"概念。党的十五大报告对"司法"概念有了进一步深化，提出了"司法工作"、"司法改革"、"司法机关"和"司法队伍"的概念，执政党关于"司法问题"的认识逐渐系统化。党的十六大报告完整提出了"司法体制"的概念，并且专项阐述了"司法体制改革"问题。江泽民在《全面建设小康社会，开创中国特色社会主义事业新局面》工作报告中指出："推进司法体制改革。社会主义司法制度必须保障在全社会实现公平和正义。按照公正司法和严格执法的要求，完善司法机关的机构设置、职权划分和管理制度，进一步健全权责明确、相互配合、相互制约、高效运行的司法体制。从制度上保证审判机关和检察机关依法独立公正地行使审判权和检察权。完善诉讼程序，保障公民和法人的合法权益。切实解决执行难问题。改革司法机关的工作机制和人财物管理体制，逐步实现司法审判和检察同司法行政事务相分离。加强对司法工作的监督，惩治司法领域中的腐败。建设一支政治坚定、业务精通、作风优良、执法公正的司法队伍。"党的十七大工作报告则进一步深化了党的十六大工作报告关于加强司法体制改革的司法工作精神，提出了完善司法制度、优化司法职权和规范司法行为的要求，从而在更加科学和规范的意义上确立了"司法工作"的政策依据。胡锦涛在党的十七大报告中强调指出："深化司法体制改革，优化司法职权配置，规范司法行为，建设公正高效权威的社会主义司法制度，保证审判机关、检察机关依法独立公正地行使审判权、检察权。"党的十八大报告中直接提到"司法"一词的地方共有五处：进一步深化司法体制改革，坚持和完善中国特色社会主义司法制度，确保审判机关、检察机关依法独立公正行使审判权、检察权"；"推进权力运行公开化、规范化，完善党务公开、政务公开、司法公开和各领域办事公开制度"；"加强政务诚信、商务诚信、社会诚信和司法公信建设"；"完善立体化社会治安防控体系，强化司法基本保障，依法防范和惩治违法犯罪活动，保障人民生命财产安全"；"民主制度更加完善，民主形式更加丰富，人民积极性、主动性、创造性进一步发挥。依法治国基本方略全面落实，法治政府基本建成，司法公信力不断提高，人权得到切实尊重和保障"。

可以说，改革开放以来，如果说党的十三大报告首先肯定了"司法工作"的合理性和重要性的话，党的十六大、十七大和十八大报告则比较科学、系统和完整地描述了我国司法制度的构成、司法工作的基本政策要求以及司法体制改革的目标，自此，执政党指导下的司法工作得到了全面的政策保障。从党的历次代表大会关于"司法"的政策和指示精神来看，目前在政策层面中使用的"司法"一词主要涉及审判机关和检察机关，司法行政机关的司法行政事务属于"行政"的范畴，通常不在"司法"意义上来理解。因此，尽管缺少对"司法"内涵的权威性和确定性的解释，但在我国现行的法律制度下，司法作为国家权力活动的一种重要形式，主要是指国家审判机关和国家检察机关依据宪法和法律规定行使审判权和检察权的行为。

二　我国司法管理体制改革的方向和主要目标

如果在司法政策的层面将"司法"一词仅仅限制在审判机关行使审判权和检察机关行使检察权的行为上来理解，近十年来，围绕着不断完善我国的审判组织体制和检察组织体制，中央政法委、最高人民法院、最高人民检察院都先后发布了司法体制改革的规范性文件，对于司法管理体制的改革方向进行了适时指导，取得了一定的改革成效。

（一）审判组织管理体制改革的历史演变及特点

我国现行的审判组织管理体制是由现行《宪法》、《人民法院组织法》

和《法官法》等法律确定的。现行《宪法》第 124 条第 1 款规定：中华人民共和国设立最高人民法院、地方各级人民法院和军事法院等专门人民法院。第 127 条规定：最高人民法院是最高审判机关。最高人民法院监督地方各级人民法院和专门人民法院的审判工作，上级人民法院监督下级人民法院的审判工作。第 128 条又规定：最高人民法院对全国人民代表大会和全国人民代表大会常务委员会负责。地方各级人民法院对产生它的国家权力机关负责。第 126 条又确定了人民法院依法独立行使审判权的原则，即"人民法院依照法律规定独立行使审判权，不受行政机关、社会团体和个人的干涉"。1979 年 7 月 1 日第五届全国人民代表大会第二次会议通过 1979 年 7 月 5 日全国人民代表大会常务委员会委员长令第三号公布，自 1980 年 1 月 1 日起施行，根据 1983 年 9 月 2 日第六届全国人民代表大会常务委员会第二次会议《关于修改〈中华人民共和国人民法院组织法〉的决定》、1986 年 12 月 2 日第六届全国人民代表大会常务委员会第十八次会议《关于修改〈中华人民共和国地方各级人民代表大会和地方各级人民政府组织法〉的决定》和 2006 年 10 月 31 日第十届全国人民代表大会常务委员会第二十四次会议《关于修改〈中华人民共和国人民法院组织法〉的决定》修正的《中华人民共和国人民法院组织法》详细规定了人民法院的审判组织体制。根据《人民法院组织法》的相关规定，中华人民共和国的审判权由下列人民法院行使：（1）地方各级人民法院；（2）军事法院等专门人民法院；（3）最高人民法院。地方各级人民法院分为：基层人民法院、中级人民法院、高级人民法院。人民法院审判案件，实行两审终审制。

根据我国现行《宪法》第 3 条第 3 款确立的国家机构组织设置原则，国家行政机关、审判机关、检察机关都由人民代表大会产生，对它负责，受它监督。因此，从总体上来说，我国现行的法院审判组织体制是与人民代表大会的组织体制相适应的。分为中央层面的最高国家审判机关，即最高人民法院；地方层面的人民法院分为三级，包括县级、地市级和省级人民法院。全国的法院组织系统分为四个层次，每一个层次的人民法院都由相应的人民代表大会选举产生，在权力隶属关系上，由同级人民代表大会产生，对同级人民代表大会负责，受同级人民代表大会监督。司法审判实行两审终审制，最高人民法院是享有终审权的最高审判机关。各级人民法院的院长、副院长和审判委员会委员由同级人民代表大会选举产生，根据《人民法院组织法》的规定，在省、自治区内按地区设立的和在直辖市内设立的中级人民法院院长、副院长、庭长、副庭长和审判员，由省、自治区、直辖市的人民代表大会常务委员会任免。《法官法》规定：初任法官采用严格考核的办法，按照德才兼备的标准，从通过国家统一司法考试取得资格，并且具备法官条件的人员中择优提出人选。人民法院的院长、副院长应当从法官或者其他具备法官条件的人员中择优提出人选。关于审判体制，《人民法院组织法》第10条第1款规定：各级人民法院设立审判委员会，实行民主集中制。审判委员会的任务是总结审判经验，讨论重大的或者疑难的案件和其他有关审判工作的问题。此外，《人民法院组织法》还规定：各级人民法院按照需要可以设助理审判员，由本级人民法院任免。助理审判员协助审判员进行工作。助理审判员，由本院院长提出，经审判委员会通过，可以临时代行审判员职务。有选举权和被选举权的年满二十三岁的公民，可以被选举为人民陪审员，但是被剥夺过政治权利的人除外。人民陪审员在人民法院执行职务期间，是他所参加的审判庭的组成人员，同审判员有同等权利。据此可知，我国的审判机关的审判人员队伍是由法官、助理审判员和人民陪审员共同组成的，院长、副院长和审判委员会委员应当从法官中推荐人选。

对于《宪法》、《人民法院组织法》和《法官法》等法律确立的我国审判组织体制，应当说，基本上适应了我国人民代表大会制度政权建设的特点，既考虑到法官职业的专门性，又关注到司法审判业务的民主性。但是，上述依法设置的法院审判组织体制在实际运行过程中也存在着一些问题无法得到有效解决，主要涉及司法地方保护主义、司法审判机关缺少公信力、审判与裁决相分离、法官素质差、人民陪审员制度低效等。有鉴于此，最高人民法院从1999年10月开始就着手法院审判组织体制的改革，先后发布了三个"五年改革纲要"。《人民法院第一个五年改革纲要（1999－2003）》①对改革的总目标设定为：从1999年起至2003年，人民法院改革的基本任务和必须实现的具体目标是：以落实公开审判原则为主要内容，进一步深化审判方式改革；以强化合议庭和法官职责为重点，建立符合审判工作特点和规律的审判管理机制；以加强审判工作为中心，改革法院内设机构，使审判人员和司法行政人员的力量得到合理配备；坚持党管干部的原则，进一步深化法院人事管理制度的改革，建立一支政治强、业务精、作风好的法官队伍；加强法院办公现代化建设，提高审判工作效率和管理水平；健全各项监督机制，保障司法人员的公正、廉洁；对法院的组织体

---

① 1999年10月20日，法发〔1999〕28号。

系、法院干部管理体制、法院经费管理体制等改革进行积极探索，为实现人民法院改革总体目标奠定基础。由上可见，《人民法院第一个五年改革纲要》将改革的重点还是放在了法院审判组织体制上，重点解决的问题是法官素质以及法院内设机构、法院干部管理体制。从 1999 年至 2003 年，在《人民法院第一个五年改革纲要》实施期间，全国各级人民法院以公正与效率为主题，以改革为动力，认真贯彻落实《人民法院第一个五年改革纲要》，基本完成了各项改革任务，初步建立了适合我国国情的审判方式，为司法公正提供了一定制度保障；基本理顺了我国的审判机构，完善了刑事、民事、行政三大审判体系，使法院组织制度更加合理化；扩大了合议庭和独任法官的审判权限，为实现审与判的有机统一打下了基础；实施了法院执行工作新机制，在一定程度上缓解了执行难问题，并为深化体制改革进行了有益的探索；确立了法官职业化建设的目标，合理配置司法人力资源，使人民法院的整体司法能力明显提高；加速了司法装备现代化建设，全国大部分法院的基本建设和物质保障有了较大改善。

2004 年，最高人民法院又推出了《人民法院第二个五年改革纲要（2004－2008）》①，该纲要在总结第一个五年改革纲要实施经验基础上，适当调整了审判组织体制改革的重点，将 2004 年至 2008 年人民法院司法改革的基本任务和目标确定为：改革和完善诉讼程序制度，实现司法公正，提高司法效率，维护司法权威；改革和完善执行体制和工作机制，健全执行机构，完善执行程序，优化执行环境，进一步解决"执行难"；改革和完善审判组织和审判机构，实现审与判的有机统一；改革和完善司法审判管理和司法政务管理制度，为人民法院履行审判职责提供充分支持和服务；改革和完善司法人事管理制度，加强法官职业保障，推进法官职业化建设进程；改革和加强人民法院内部监督和接受外部监督的各项制度，完善对审判权、执行权、管理权运行的监督机制，保持司法廉洁；不断推进人民法院体制和工作机制改革，建立符合社会主义法治国家要求的现代司法制度。很显然，《人民法院第二个五年改革纲要》的实施重点在于"审"与"判"的有机结合，同时还要着手保证法官职业化，有效分离司法审判管理与司法政务管理，建立更加有效的人民法院体制和工作机制。

为贯彻党的十七大精神，落实中央关于深化司法体制和工作机制改革的总体要求，维护社会公平正义，满足人民群众对司法工作的新要求、新

① 最高人民法院，法发〔2005〕18 号。

期待，实现人民法院审判组织体制的科学发展，最高人民法院于 2008 年又制定《人民法院第三个五年改革纲要（2009－2013）》[①]。《人民法院第三个五年改革纲要》将深化人民法院司法体制和工作机制改革的目标定位为：进一步优化人民法院职权配置，落实宽严相济刑事政策，加强队伍建设，改革经费保障体制，健全司法为民工作机制，着力解决人民群众日益增长的司法需求与人民法院司法能力相对不足的矛盾，推进中国特色社会主义审判制度的自我完善和发展，建设公正高效权威的社会主义司法制度。《人民法院第三个五年改革纲要》实施效果比较显著，据最高人民法院新闻发言人孙军工 2012 年 3 月 20 日在最高人民法院新闻发布会上透露，《人民法院第三个五年改革纲要》共提出 30 项改革内容，涉及 132 项具体改革任务，截至目前，已完成 103 项，25 项取得实质性进展，其他 4 项也在有序推进之中。[②]

　　为了进一步巩固和扩大人民法院审判组织体制改革的成果，2014 年 1 月 8 日，最高人民法院周强院长在全国法院院长会议上明确指出：随着党的十八届三中全会关于全面深化改革各项工作的推开，新一轮司法体制改革已经拉开序幕。各级人民法院要着眼于加快建设公正高效权威的社会主义司法制度，始终坚持司法体制改革的正确方向，准确把握司法体制改革的目标任务，坚持依法有序推进改革，确保圆满完成改革任务。要大力加强思想政治建设，积极推进正规化、专业化、职业化建设，进一步加强和改进司法作风，坚决查处违纪违法行为，不断加强人民法院队伍建设，为坚持司法为民、公正司法提供有力组织保障。[③] 可见，新一轮司法体制改革是从更宏观的层次出发，对我国司法审判组织体制和运行体制提出了带有方向性的改革要求，其改革的着力点集中在"加快建设公正高效权威的社会主义司法制度"上。其中，法院组织管理体制的改革也是法院改革工作的重中之重。

（二）检察组织管理体制改革的历史演变及特点

　　与人民法院的审判组织管理体制相似的是，我国现行的检察组织管理体制也是由现行《宪法》、《人民检察院组织法》和《检察官法》等法律具

---

①　最高人民法院，法发〔2009〕14 号。

②　中央人民政府网站，参见 http://www.gov.cn/jrzg/2012－03/20/content_2095954.htm，2014 年 2 月 25 日最后访问。

③　中央人民政府网站，参见 http://www.gov.cn/jrzg/2014－01/14/content_2565946.htm，2014 年 2 月 25 日最后访问。

体加以规定的。现行《宪法》从第 129 条到第 133 条详细规定了人民检察院的法律性质以及人民检察院的组织管理体制，主要内容包括：中华人民共和国人民检察院是国家的法律监督机关（第 129 条）。中华人民共和国设立最高人民检察院、地方各级人民检察院和军事检察院等专门人民检察院（第 130 条）。人民检察院依照法律规定独立行使检察权，不受行政机关、社会团体和个人的干涉（第 131 条）。最高人民检察院是最高检察机关。最高人民检察院领导地方各级人民检察院和专门人民检察院的工作，上级人民检察院领导下级人民检察院的工作（第 132 条）。最高人民检察院对全国人民代表大会和全国人民代表大会常务委员会负责。地方各级人民检察院对产生它的国家权力机关和上级人民检察院负责（第 133 条）。与人民法院的组织管理体制相同的是，我国的各级人民检察院也是由同级人民代表大会选举产生的，对同级人民代表大会负责，受同级人民代表大会的监督。与人民法院的组织管理体制略有不同的是，人民检察院由于其法律性质是国家的法律监督机关，因此，在行使国家检察权的上下级关系上，地方各级人民检察院对产生它的国家权力机关和上级人民检察院负责。而地方各级人民法院只需要按照两审终审原则接受上级人民法院的依法监督。此外，根据《人民检察院组织法》①的规定，省、自治区、直辖市人民检察院检察长的任免，须报最高人民检察院检察长提请全国人民代表大会常务委员会批准；自治州、省辖市、县、市、市辖区人民检察院检察长的任免，须报上一级人民检察院检察长提请该级人民代表大会常务委员会批准。下级人民检察院检察长由上级人大常委会批准，这一制度设计也充分体现了上下级检察机关之间的领导与被领导关系。根据《检察官法》的规定，检察官职务的任免，依照宪法和法律规定的任免权限和程序办理。人民检察院的助理检察员由本院检察长任免。初任检察官采用严格考核的办法，按照德才兼备的标准，从通过国家统一司法考试取得资格，并且具备检察官条件的人员中择优提出人选。人民检察院的检察长、副检察长应当从检察官或者其他具备检察官条件的人员中择优提出人选。

　　针对人民法院不断改革司法体制的具体举措，最高人民检察院也先后就检察组织管理体制改革发布了若干重要的规范性指导文件。2000 年 2 月

---

① 1979 年 7 月 1 日第五届全国人民代表大会第二次会议通过，根据 1983 年 9 月 2 日第六届全国人民代表大会常务委员会第二次会议通过的《关于修改〈中华人民共和国人民检察院组织法〉的决定》修订。

15 日，最高人民检察院发布了首个《检察改革三年实施意见》①，该意见指出，改革检察官办案机制，全面建立主诉、主办检察官责任制。用人制度的管理也被列入改革范围。各级检察机关录用主任科员以下职务的工作人员，一律实行考试录用制度；逐步实行最高人民检察院、省级人民检察院业务部门的检察官从下级检察院优秀、资深检察官中选任的制度，有计划地选调高层次法律人才到检察机关担任领导职务和检察官。2005 年最高人民检察院颁发的《关于进一步深化检察改革的三年实施意见》② 对检察组织管理体制改革提出了若干改革要点，其中有两个大的改革事项直接关系到检察组织管理体制的改革。一是完善检察机关组织体系，改革有关部门、企业管理检察院的体制。其中改革措施包括：逐步改革铁路、林业等部门、企业管理检察院的体制，将部门、企业管理的检察院纳入国家司法管理体系，明确有关检察院的经费来源、人员编制、选拔任用以及案件管辖权等。规范人民检察院派出机构的设置。研究制定人民检察院派出机构管理办法，明确派出机构的设置条件和审批程序，规范派出机构的法律地位和职权范围。改革检察机关司法鉴定机构。按照全国人大常委会关于司法鉴定管理问题的决定的要求，最高人民检察院制定相关规定，完善检察机关司法鉴定机构和人员的管理机制，明确检察机关内设鉴定机构的职责和工作程序。二是改革和完善检察干部管理体制，建设高素质、专业化检察队伍。具体内容涉及：落实宪法和法律规定的上下级人民检察院的领导体制，采取措施加大上级人民检察院对下级人民检察院领导班子的协管力度，探索实行上级人民检察院对下级人民检察院检察长人选的提名制度。落实地方各级人民检察院通过考试录用工作人员的制度，实行面向社会、从通过国家统一司法考试取得任职资格的人员中公开选拔初任检察官的制度。逐步建立上级人民检察院检察官从下级人民检察院检察官中择优选拔的工作机制。省级人民检察院每年要有计划地从高等院校法律专业应届毕业生中选调优秀学生充实基层人民检察院。完善检察官教育培训制度，建立与国家司法考试、检察官遴选制度相配套的任职培训制度。推行检察人员分类改革，对检察人员实行分类管理。在总结试点经验的基础上，完善检察人员分类改革的方案。会同有关部门制定检察官单独职务序列，确定检察官职务与

---

① 高检发〔2000〕3 号，2000 年 1 月 10 日最高人民检察院第九届检察委员会第五十二次会议通过。

② 2005 年 9 月 12 日最高人民检察院文件高检发〔2005〕17 号公布，自公布之日起施行。

级别的对应关系。完善检察官晋升、奖惩、工资、福利、退休、抚恤、医疗等保障制度，协调落实检察津贴。最高人民检察院会同有关部门研究制定相关规定。研究制定贫困地区检察官选任录用的特殊政策，采取措施吸引人才到贫困地区、少数民族地区检察机关工作。通过实行干部交流、挂职、特殊津贴等措施，保障贫困地区检察机关的队伍稳定和检察工作的协调发展。

2008 年 3 月 10 日最高人民检察院检察长贾春旺在第十一届全国人民代表大会第一次会议上所做的《最高人民检察院工作报告》中又对检察组织体制改革提出了若干明确意见。贾春旺检察长指出：改革和完善检察机关内部制约机制。加强办理职务犯罪案件的内部制约，规定案件受理、立案侦查、审查逮捕、审查起诉必须由不同内设机构承办，由不同院领导分管。建立并推行讯问职务犯罪嫌疑人全程同步录音录像制度，促进侦查讯问活动规范化，加强了人权保障。建立查办职务犯罪工作备案、审批制度，规定职务犯罪案件立案、逮捕必须报上一级检察院备案审查，撤案、不起诉必须报上一级检察院批准。制定执法过错责任追究条例，完善执法责任制和责任追究机制。最高人民检察院和一些地方检察院建立检务督察制度，重点对检察人员执法办案中履行职责、遵守纪律等情况进行监督。改革和完善检察机关接受监督的机制。为加强对查办职务犯罪工作的外部监督，最高人民检察院经中央同意并报告全国人大常委会，从 2003 年 9 月起开展了人民监督员制度试点工作。规定职务犯罪案件中拟作撤案、不起诉处理和犯罪嫌疑人不服逮捕决定的"三类案件"，全部纳入人民监督员监督程序。截至 2007 年底，全国已有 86% 的检察院开展试点。人民监督员共对21270 件"三类案件"进行了监督，其中不同意办案部门意见的 930 件，检察机关采纳 543 件。深化检务公开，对检察机关工作制度、办案规程等规定，依法能够公开的全部向社会公开。完善诉讼参与人权利义务告知、检察人员违纪违法行为投诉制度，推行不起诉案件公开审查、多次上访案件听证制度，健全特约检察员、专家咨询委员会制度，建立保障律师在刑事诉讼中依法执业的工作机制，增强了执法透明度，促进了司法公正。①最高人民检察院在有序推进检察组织管理体制改革的过程中，始终把握住改革的正确方向，采取比较可靠的改革措施，取得了明显的效果。最高人民检

---

① 《最高人民检察院工作报告》，新华网，http://www.ce.cn/xwzx/gnsz/gdxw/200803/22/t20080322_14923523.shtml，2014 年 2 月 25 日最后访问。

察院常务副检察长胡泽君曾经对此有比较好的总结。在 2012 年 2 月 9 日于福州召开的全国检察改革推进会暨经验交流会上，胡泽君指出，根据中央的司法体制改革精神，高检院分别于 2000 年和 2005 年制定了两个检察改革的三年实施意见。2008 年底，《中共中央转发〈中央政法委员会关于深化司法体制和工作机制改革若干问题的意见〉的通知》（中发〔2008〕19 号）下发，2009 年 2 月，高检院制定下发了《关于贯彻落实〈中央政法委员会关于深化司法体制和工作机制改革若干问题的意见〉的实施意见——关于深化检察改革 2009 - 2012 年工作规划》及工作方案。经过各级检察机关的共同努力，检察体制和工作机制改革呈现重点突破、整体推进、扎实有序、成效明显的良好局面，强化法律监督职能的改革取得重大进展，对自身执法活动的监督制约机制逐步完善，贯彻落实宽严相济刑事政策的工作机制更加健全，检察机关组织体系和干部管理制度改革正在深入推进，检察经费保障体制改革取得重大突破。截至目前，中央确定的司法改革任务中，由高检院牵头的 7 项改革任务已基本完成，高检院协办的改革任务和《检察改革规划》确定的各项改革任务大部分已完成。① 2009 年 2 月，最高人民检察院出台了《2009 - 2012 年基层人民检察院建设规划》，积极推进基层检察院执法规范化、队伍专业化、管理科学化和保障现代化建设。最高人民检察院党组书记、检察长曹建明在 2013 年 11 月 14 日举行的最高人民检察院机关开展学习贯彻党的十八届三中全会精神大会上进一步明确提出：最高检要按照中央的统一部署，加强对检察改革的总体设计、统筹协调，抓紧修改完善新一轮检察改革方案，进一步明确检察改革整体的路线图和时间表。坚持统筹协调，既要保证检察机关内部的各项改革措施协调配套，又要与中央司法体制改革和其他政法机关的改革协调推进。②

（三）党委政法委改革政法工作的指导思想及特点

党委政法委对政法工作进行的监督，是基于作为执政党的共产党具有对国家生活和社会生活进行全面的政治领导作用的具体政治国情产生的，它与依据宪法和法律规定，由人民代表大会及其常委会对司法进行的监督以及检察机关对司法审判活动进行的法律监督，是相辅相成、相互分工和相互配合的关系，它们共同构成了具有中国特色的统一和完整的执法监督

---

① 龙平川、张仁平：《深化检察改革六项主要任务确定》，《检察日报》2012 年 2 月 10 日。

② 《最高检：进一步明确检察改革整体路线图和时间表》，《法制日报》2013 年 11 月 15 日，参见 http://news.xinhuanet.com/legal/2013 - 11/15/c_125706848.htm，2014 年 2 月 25 日最后访问。

机制。虽然党委政法委在领导政法工作的实践中发挥了非常重要的作用，不过，由于长期以来，对于党委政法委进行的包括司法监督在内的政法工作的性质、依据、方式、效力等问题缺少系统化的理论研究，在实践中许多重要的行之有效的司法监督形式也没有完全规范化和制度化，所以，不论是在理论上，还是在实践中，党委政法委司法监督规范化和制度化的问题都没有完全得到解决。因此，对此问题需要从理论上予以进一步澄清，在实践中应当摸索出一套行之有效的做法。由于缺少宪法和法律上的明确规定，所以，党委政法委进行执法监督时的被监督主体以及监督对象的范围就很难加以确定，导致了在实践中各地做法不太统一。例如，北京市政法委司法监督的对象涉及法院、检察院、公安局、司法局、民政局、监狱局、劳教局、公安交通管理局等部门；而中共威海市委政法委执法监督的对象仅涉及法院、检察院、公安局、司法局和市交巡分局等。很显然，在实际工作中，各地党委政法委分工负责的下属部门和机构的数量和性质并不统一，这就在理论上产生了党委政法委进行司法监督的范围究竟应当有多大的问题。在党委政法委对政法工作领导过程中，最突出的问题是政法委是否有权介入审判机关所审理的具体案件。但无论如何，党委政法委通过对政法工作行使领导权从而实现对审判机关和检察机关行使审判权和检察权的监督，在实践中证明是符合中国当下具体的法治国情的，事实上，在"司法"本身尚未通过宪法规定加以制度化的前提下，司法机关的组织管理体制以及司法活动都是在党的司法政策指引下进行的，因此，司法管理体制改革不可能回避党委政法委如何改进对政法工作的领导和管理方式问题。在实践中，党中央以及中央政法委对全国范围内的司法工作经常性地发布指导性意见，是司法体制改革的主要政策性文件和合法性依据。

例如，2004年12月，中共中央转发的《中央司法体制改革领导小组关于司法体制和工作机制改革的初步意见》，把改革和完善律师收费制度作为专门问题加以规定，明确指出要完善律师收费制度，制定律师诉讼代理收费指导性标准，建立健全律师收费争议解决制度，完善对律师违法违纪收费行为的处罚办法。

2008年11月28日，中共中央政治局通过了《中央政法委员会关于深化司法体制和工作机制改革若干问题的意见》，从发展社会主义民主政治、加快建设法治国家的战略高度，对司法体制改革做出了战略部署。该意见明确规定：本次司法体制改革将建立政法系统财政保障机制，以后法院、检察院的经费将由中央财政专项确定，建立分类保障政策和公用经费正常增长机制，解决基层法院的经费保障问题，从而开始打破司法经费由地方保障的格局，逐步化解司法的地方化难题。具体有可能会采取分地区，分级别，结合案件数量和诉讼费收入情况，采用因素计算法确定各法院的财政拨款数。与此同时，该意见还对司法管理体制改革提出了几项具体改革任务，包括：（1）检察院刑侦职能划归公安局管辖，检察院专司法律监督。检察院作为法律监督机关，原有的《刑事诉讼法》规定，检察院享有对经济犯罪和职务犯罪等部分刑事案件的侦查权（自侦权）。对于公安机关侦查的案件，可以由检察院进行法律监督，但是对于检察院的自侦案件，则长期缺乏必要的制度性限制，只在检察院内部进行监督。根据"有权利就有监督"的原则，本次司法体制改革将检察院对经济犯罪和职务犯罪的刑侦职能从检察院剥离开，划归公安局管辖，检察院主要专心做法律监督建设，以实现加强权力监督制约的目标，其中包括对法院的监督和对司法系统其他部门的监督。（2）法院执行职能划归司法局管辖，法院其他有关行政职能划归司法行政机关管辖，法院专司审判。在我国，法院判决后案件"执行难"很突出，影响到法院判决的权威性和严肃性。本次司法体制改革将包括法院执行在内的有关行政职能划归司法行政机关管辖，法院专司审判。（3）看守所划归司法局管辖。长期以来，看守所作为主要的羁押场所，由同级公安机关管理。在侦查、羁押、改造主体一体化的管理模式下，看守所对侦查机关的讯问活动缺乏有效的监督，容易出现刑讯逼供现象。近年来曝光的佘祥林案、聂树斌案中，都存在刑讯逼供，这些案件主要发生在看守所。许多学者提出，为了体现程序公正和控辩平衡，必须做到侦查权和羁押权的分权与制约。本次司法体制改革将看守所的管理移交到司法部（局）体系之下。（4）加强政法队伍建设。司法体制改革本着"从严治警"与"从优待警"相结合的原则，提出完善政法干警招录和培训机制，完善政法干警行为规范和职业保障制度，加强政法机关廉政建设，严肃查处政法干警违法违纪行为，改革完善司法考试制度和律师制度等。

由此可见，从制度层面谈论司法管理体制改革不可能抛开党对政法工作的领导，由于目前我国的司法管理体制都是在党的司法政策指导下建立和运行的，所以，司法体制改革，特别是司法管理体制改革，不论是价值目标，还是具体任务，都必须认真考虑执政党对政法工作的基本立场和改革司法体制的政策走向。

（四）党的十八届三中全会通过的《中共中央关于全面深化改革若干重大问题的决定》（以下简称《决定》）提出的司法管理体制改革的主要目标

党的十八届三中全会通过的《决定》围绕着"推进法治中国建设"这个时代主题，从两个不同的角度，对我国司法管理体制改革的方向和主要目标做出了整体部署，成为我国司法管理体制改革的指导思想。

1. 司法管理体制改革的方向在于确保依法独立公正行使审判权、检察权

《决定》强调指出：确保依法独立公正行使审判权、检察权。改革司法管理体制，推动省以下地方法院、检察院人财物统一管理，探索建立与行政区划适当分离的司法管辖制度，保证国家法律统一正确实施。建立符合职业特点的司法人员管理制度，健全法官、检察官、人民警察统一招录、有序交流、逐级遴选机制，完善司法人员分类管理制度，健全法官、检察官、人民警察职业保障制度。

2. 司法管理体制改革的目标是健全司法权力运行机制

《决定》还明确提出，健全司法权力运行机制。优化司法职权配置，健全司法权力分工负责、互相配合、互相制约机制，加强和规范对司法活动的法律监督和社会监督。改革审判委员会制度，完善主审法官、合议庭办案责任制，让审理者裁判、由裁判者负责。明确各级法院职能定位，规范上下级法院审级监督关系。推进审判公开、检务公开，录制并保留全程庭审资料。增强法律文书说理性，推动公开法院生效裁判文书。严格规范减刑、假释、保外就医程序，强化监督制度。广泛实行人民陪审员、人民监督员制度，拓宽人民群众有序参与司法渠道。

总结《决定》关于司法管理体制改革的要求，可以发现它具有以下几个特点：一是《决定》所涉及的司法管理体制包括了公、检、法三机关的组织管理体制，其内涵要比通常理解的检审为主体的司法管理体制范围要宽一点，说明司法管理体制本身就存在很多不确定的因素，需要通过改革来形成比较稳定和成熟的制度；二是司法管理体制改革的突破点放在司法组织管理的集中性上，今后的趋势是司法职权逐渐集中行使，并向中央司法机关集中；三是司法管理体制改革关键还在于优化司法职权配置，其中保证审判机关和检察机关依法独立公正行使审判权和检察权是司法组织管理体制改革的重要目标；四是司法队伍职业化和分类管理是司法人员队伍建设的改革方向，目的旨在加强司法的专业化和职业化特征，提高司法人员素质；五是实行审与裁的统一，进一步强化司法人员的职业责任心。可

以预见，《决定》为司法管理体制改革指出的发展方向是非常宽广的，也是全方位的，需要在理论上做充分的准备，在实践中，要通过不断完善一系列具体的司法制度才能最终实现司法管理体制改革的价值追求。

三　在法治中国建设中司法管理体制改革的切入点

《决定》在"推进法治中国建设"的原则性要求方面突出强调了司法体制改革的重要性，而司法体制改革关键在于司法管理体制改革，司法管理体制改革到位，司法运行体制也就能够充分发挥自身的最大限度的制度效能。因此，当下深化司法体制改革的最重要的任务就是应当在法治中国建设的大背景下，通过完善和健全司法组织管理体系，建立起独立公正高效权威的司法制度，维护当事人权益，让当事人在每一个司法案件中都感受到公平正义，让全社会都树立起信赖司法制度、尊重司法制度，依靠司法制度解决纠纷、依靠司法制度维护自身权益的意识，这是法治中国建设的关键环节。

（一）要正确处理坚持党的领导和确保司法机关依法独立公正行使职权的关系

党的各级组织对司法工作的领导是通过党委政法委对政法工作的领导体现出来的，司法工作作为政法工作的重要组成部分，也必须加强党的领导，具体体现为两个方面：一是依照党管干部的原则，考察、推荐、配备优秀的司法人员和司法干部，抓好司法机关的组织建设和党的建设；二是监督司法机关遵守宪法法律情况，依法对违法乱纪司法人员提出追究处理意见与建议。在加强党对政法工作领导的同时，要彻底转变党对司法工作的领导方式，党的各级组织和各部门领导干部一律不得批示案件，不得就个案发表意见。今后凡是出现批示和意见，除涉及国家安全、军事机密等法定因素外，应当在互联网公布裁判文书时一并公开。党委政法委是党领导司法工作的专门机关，要善于运用法治思维和法治方式领导司法工作，在推进公平正义司法制度建设中发挥重要作用。在试点法检人财物省级统一管理的试点省份，上述职责由省级政法委承担。

（二）要正确处理人民代表大会制度与司法制度的关系

要通过修改宪法的方式，尽量将司法制度和司法机关纳入国家基本法律制度和国家机构的序列，尽快解决司法管理体制过于政策化的问题。同时，对于现行宪法所规定的审判机关和检察机关，要通过改革措施，不断强化审判机关和检察机关依法独立公正行使审判权和检察权的能力。进一步完善法院和检察院由人大产生、对人大负责、受人大监督制度，要使之日常化、制度化、规范化。要进一步完善法院和检察院向同级人大报告工作的制度，多增加专项报告，减低人代会会议对两院报告的投票表决影响力，防范法院和检察院片面追求高通过率而做表面文章，增强人大监督法院和检察院依法行使职权的公开性和透明度。

（三）要建立"大司法"概念，充分发挥司法的法律功能，建立更加科学和严谨的司法管理体制

在我国现行宪法所设计的国家权力体系框架中，有国家权力机关、国家行政机关、国家审判机关和国家检察机关，国家权力的分配是依托国家机关的性质而定的，没有按照"依权设机构"的"权力分立模式"分配国家权力，因此，各级人大作为各级国家权力机关在宪法上行使的是一种"集合性国家权力"，这种权力的事务功能在法理上覆盖了立法、行政和司法所有的领域，并且具有"最终性"和"最高性"。国家权力机关掌握的国家权力是独立的，不受其他国家机关掌握的国家权力的制约。国家行政机关依据宪法规定行使行政职权，而检察机关、审判机关依据宪法规定行使检察权、审判权，至于说"检察权""审判权"是否等同于"司法权"，或者说能否在法理上将检察机关行使的检察权和审判机关行使的审判权确认为宪法学理论上所认同的"司法权"，这个问题在我国现行宪法的框架内并没有得到很好的解决。但是，从宪法赋予全国人大及常委会监督宪法和法律实施的职权来看，全国人大及常委会也有权依据宪法和法律来处理一些具体的法律争议和纠纷，特别是 2000 年出台的《立法法》第 91 条赋予了全国人大常委会一定的"违宪违法"审查权[①]，因此，从法理上和现有的宪法制度来看，要将司法权的内涵仅仅限制在"检察权""审判权"的范围，

---

① 2000 年《中华人民共和国立法法》第 90 条明文规定：国务院、中央军事委员会、最高人民法院、最高人民检察院和各省、自治区、直辖市的人民代表大会常务委员会认为行政法规、地方性法规、自治条例和单行条例同宪法或者法律相抵触的，可以向全国人民代表大会常务委员会书面提出进行审查的要求，由常务委员会工作机构分送有关的专门委员会进行审查、提出意见。前款规定以外的其他国家机关和社会团体、企业事业组织以及公民认为行政法规、地方性法规、自治条例和单行条例同宪法或者法律相抵触的，可以向全国人民代表大会常务委员会书面提出进行审查的建议，由常务委员会工作机构进行研究，必要时，送有关的专门委员会进行审查、提出意见。根据《立法法》第 90 条的上述规定，全国人大常委会要依据《立法法》的规定行使违宪或违法审查权，对可能存在违宪或违法问题的行政法规、地方性法规、自治条例和单行条例进行审查，必然是面临着"法律争议"，因为没有"法律争议"，违宪或违法的案件就不可能提交给全国人大常委会解决。

很显然，与我国现行宪法所确立的基本国家权力制度不相符合，全国人大及常委会依据宪法和法律也承担了一定的司法职能，而且由于全国人大及其常委会拥有的"最高国家权力机关"的身份和地位，实际上，如果在宪法文本中引进了司法的概念，该机关在法律制度上相当于"最高司法机关"。为此，如果"司法入宪"，"司法"的性质就必须是"广义"上的，而不能采用"三权分立"体制下的与"立法""行政"相对立的"司法"。在这一点上，我国现行宪法所能接纳的司法原则应当是"议会主权"意义上的，近似 2009 年之前英国采取的上议院司法制度。狭义上的"司法"概念与我国现行宪法所确立的人民代表大会制度的根本原则是相互冲突的，因此，在可预见的将来，只要我们坚持人民代表大会制度的基本原则不变，那么，宪法中的"司法"概念就只能是"议会主权"意义上的"大司法"，将"司法"仅仅限定在"检察权""审判权"的范围，或者是限制在"审判权"的框架内，这种制度设想缺少基本的政治基础，不可能在现行宪法的制度框架内存在，因此，所谓的"司法入宪"必然是"司法"进入人民代表大会制度下的国家权力框架内，而不可能出现"司法"作为独立的国家权力进入现有的宪法制度之中，这是"司法入宪"的基本政治判断。

（四）要正确处理政府与法院和检察院的关系

各级人民政府与各级人民法院、人民检察院应当依照宪法和相关法律法规，各司其职，各负其责，互不隶属，互不领导。

各级政府召集会议、组织活动，均不得将法院、检察院列为参加单位，更不能将法院和检察院作为政府的一个职能部门看待，探索设立行政法院，强化法院对行政行为的司法审查，以补强司法力量，实现司法权力与行政权力真正各负其责、互相制约的宪治状态。

（五）完善法院审级独立制度，探索建立与行政区划适当分离的司法管辖制度

目前依照现行宪法和相关法律设立的四级法院在不同审级中职能定位不同，分别依照宪法和法律独立行使相应的审判权，不受上级法院干涉。最高人民法院保证法律统一正确实施的最主要途径是审级监督，发布司法解释，应地方法院要求对法律适用问题做出批复，不对下级法院的在审案件出具裁判性意见。要选取数个经济社会文化发展相对均衡的省份，试点跨区县法院的设置，探索建立与行政区划适当分离的司法管辖制度。从制度上掐断行政机关、社会组织和公民个人对基层法院审判活动可能施加的不良影响。选取数个经济较为活跃的地区，试点最高人民法院商事民事派

出法庭、巡回法庭制度，探索降低当事人诉讼成本、便民利民的可能途径。将最高人民法院的二审和审判监督职能直接授予最高人民法院按照大区设立的地区法院，强化最高人民法院与省级人民法院之间的业务联系，提高最高人民法院审理二审和再审案件的效率。试点设立知识产权法院，可将知识产权法院的试点设立与跨行政区划法院设立试点相结合。

（六）探索法官、检察官、警察职业化路径，初步建立符合司法职业特点的司法人事管理制度

完善司法人员分类管理制度。在司法组织系统内从事一般行政支持、后勤保障服务的人员作为司法政务人员与法官、检察官严格区分。前者依照一般公务员制度管理，后者依照法官法、检察官法管理。可选择适当时机，将司法政务人员直接划归司法行政部门管理。建立法官检察官员额制度。在司法人员分类管理实施后，由中编办根据各地经济社会发展状况和司法实际，统筹确定法官、检察官员额配备方案，由全国人大常委会批准，具有法律效力，作为经费待遇配备依据。法官、检察官员额配置制度要注意地区特点和经济文化发展状况，要鼓励年轻司法人员到中西部司法机关任职，不断积累司法工作经验。完善法官选任制度。根据司法职业特点，探索完善法官、检察官统一招录、遴选制度。根据近些年法官、检察官家庭所在地、就读大学与就业区域日趋重合的趋势，考虑到法官、检察官职业的特点，招录、遴选法官、检察官试行全国（或省级）统筹，从法官、检察官就业起始，实现必要的地籍、学籍回避。对于法官、检察官在一地司法机关工作达到一定年限的，要集中组织轮岗或异地交流，要实行全国范围内的法官、检察官人员的可自由流动制度。对于未取得"中华人民共和国法律职业证书"者，均不得遴选为法官、检察官，均不得从事法官、检察官工作。建立完善法官检察官的等级、评定与晋升制度，其核心是凸显法官、检察官的职级意识，实现工资待遇与职级的衔接，在官方文件中以职衔称谓取代院长、庭长等行政性称谓。院长、检察长由适格的法官、检察官兼任，并由本级法院法官和检察院检察官选举产生，实行任期较短的轮流任职制，充分发挥每一名法官、检察官的组织管理才能，减低院长、检察长的官员身份色彩，提升院长、检察长的专家业务能力和水平。选取数个财政状况良好、司法工作基础较好的省区市进行省以下地方法院、检察院人财物统管工作的试点。同时，要求法院和检察院所在地党委和人民政府采取积极有效的措施予以配合，确保法官和检察官的办公条件。建立法官、检察官职业保障制度。在省以下试点法官、检察官统管的地方，在

法官、检察官员额确定基础上，探索法官、检察官招录、遴选、晋升、薪酬特别保障制度，大幅提升工资福利待遇，健全法官职务豁免制度，凸显法官、检察官职业的独立性。根据国家司法改革的总体要求，修改《人民法院组织法》《人民检察院组织法》《法官法》《检察官法》等相关法律法规，将司法改革成果纳入法律，并依法推进司法体制改革。根据法院和检察官职业化管理的要求，进一步提升人民警察的法律地位，将人民警察逐渐纳入司法人员队伍序列，由司法行政部门统一管理，主要用于配合审判机关和检察机关的实施宪法和法律的活动。

The Entry Point of the Reform of Judicial Administration System

Mo Jihong [*]

【Abstract】Based on the analysis of the nature and characteristics of judicial activities, this article divides the judicial system of a state into two parts: judicial organization and administration system and judicial operation system. The former is mainly responsible for the organizational structure of judicial organs and the allocation of judicial power whereas the latter mainly consists of legal procedures and mechanisms by which judicial organs exercise their judicial power to deal with concrete cases. Judicial administration system consists of mechanisms and institutions for the allocation, organization and operation of state judicial power. Its main institutional contents include the nature and legal status of judicial organs, the relationship between judicial organs at different levels, the appointment of and performance of functions by judicial personnel, the allocation of judicial functions and powers, and mechanisms aimed at bringing judicial functions into full and effective play. Judicial administration system plays a fundamental role in the construction of judicial system in a country: judicial operation system is determined by judicial administration system. Defections in the design of judicial administration

---

[*] Professor and Deputy Director, Institute of Law, Chinese Academy of Social Sciences.

system are the main causes of the malfunction of the judicial operation system. This article analyzes the development of judicial policy in China and maintains that currently the legitimacy of the reform of judicial administration system in China comes from judicial policy, especially the Decision on Several Issues Relating to Comprehensively Deepening the Reform (the Decision), adopted at the Third Plenary Session of the CPC Central Committee. The Decision raises specific demands on the reform of the judicial system, especially the judicial administration system. The author of this article is of the opinion that, in order to correctly implement the Decision, the government should amend the Constitution so as to incorporate judicial activities into the scope of basic state system and, on the basis of the basic institutional framework of the system of people's congresses, construct a judicial administration system with the Standing Committee of the National People's Congress as the highest judicial organ, correctly deal with the relationships between political and legal affairs commissions, courts, procuratorates and public security organs, coordinate the relationship of check and balance between public security organs, procuratorates, courts and judicial administration organs in the handing of criminal cases, improve the quality of judicial personnel, promote the professionalism of judges, prosecutors and police officers, establish a trial system separated from the system of administrative precincts, and further ensure the independent exercise of judicial functions and powers by judicial organs, so as to uphold judicial justice.

【Keywords】Judicial Administration System; Judicial Operation System; Judicial System; Judicial Reform; Judicial Policy

深化司法体制改革的宏观思路与具体方案

熊秋红 *

【摘要】 中国的司法改革经历了渐进式发展的过程，深化司法体制改革意味着司法改革将进入"深水区"——重点在于改革与司法机关依法独立公正行使职权不相适应的司法体制。在深化司法体制改革中，应当辩证地看待坚持遵循司法规律与坚持依法有序改革的关系，正确处理适时修改法律与维护法律的稳定性之间的关系。从尊重司法规律的角度看，强化司法的本我定位、保障司法的独立性、提高司法保障人权的程度、促进司法品质的提升以及赢得民众对司法的信赖等，应当成为深化司法体制改革所追求的理想目标；从坚持问题导向的角度看，深化司法体制改革应当着重于解决法官的非职业化、司法的行政化和司法的地方化等问题。中央新一轮的司法改革方案列举了改革司法管理体制，建立符合职业特点的司法人员管理制度，健全司法权力运行机制，深化司法公开，改革人民陪审员制度，健全人民监督员制度，严格规范减刑、假释和保外就医程序，改革涉法涉诉信访制度等改革重点，这些改革重点有待予以具体设计。为了拓宽深化司法体制改革的研究视野，有必要将与劳动教养相类似的制度的改革、腐败犯罪案件办理机制、政法委的职能定位、看守所的归属以及法院的判决执行权改革等议题纳入讨论的范围。

【关键词】 深化司法体制改革　宏观思路　具体方案

近些年来，中国的决策层明确提出了"深化司法体制改革，确保审判机关、检察机关依法独立公正行使审判权、检察权"的改革方向。2013年1月7日全国政法工作电视电话会议将劳动教养制度改革、涉法涉诉信访工作

---

* 熊秋红，中国社会科学院法学研究所研究员。

改革、司法权力运行机制改革、户籍制度改革等"四项改革"确定为2013年政法工作的重点。2013年11月12日，中共十八届三中全会通过的《中共中央关于全面深化改革若干重大问题的决定》确立了"让人民群众在每一个司法案件中都感受到公平正义"的司法改革理念，并且对于深化司法体制改革做出了全面部署。

2014年1月的政法工作会议在名称上由"全国政法工作会议"更名为"中央政法工作会议"，国家主席习近平出席会议并发表讲话，传递出中央决策层重视司法工作，拟加强司法工作的强烈信号。习近平主席在讲话中主要强调了四个方面的内容：第一，正确处理执政党的政策和国家法律的关系，正确处理坚持执政党的领导和确保司法机关依法独立公正行使职权的关系；第二，正确处理维稳和维权的关系；第三，健全严格执法、公正司法的保障机制；第四，深化司法体制改革，推进国家治理体系和治理能力现代化。

当前所进行的新一轮司法改革是对过去十多年来所进行的司法改革的延续。中国的司法改革经历了逐步发展、逐步深化的过程，学术界用司法改革"第一阶段"（20世纪80年代末至90年代中期以审判方式改革为主导的司法改革）、"第二阶段"（从1997年至2008年因为确立依法治国方略所带来的全方位的司法改革）、"第三阶段"（从2008年至今更多地涉及体制性问题的司法改革）来描述司法改革的大致历程。[①] 司法改革的阶段性成果通过相关法律法规的修改予以了固定，例如1996年、2012年对《刑事诉讼法》的两次修改，2007年、2012年对《民事诉讼法》的两次修改。2012年10月，国务院新闻办发布《中国的司法改革》白皮书，对司法改革所取得的主要成就做了较为详细的说明。

《中国的司法改革》白皮书将改革开放以来的司法改革成就总结为以下四个方面：其一，通过优化司法职权配置、规范司法行为、扩大司法公开、加强司法民主、加强检察机关的法律监督，有力地维护了社会的公平正义；其二，加强了对人权的司法保障，具体表现为防范和遏制刑讯逼供，保障

[①] 参见公丕祥《当代中国司法改革的时代进程》，《法制资讯》2009年第2期。另外，季卫东教授将新中国成立初期的司法改革称为第一波，改革开放后的司法改革称为第二波，现阶段的司法改革称为第三波。他认为，第三波司法改革的基本目标应该设定为以适当的、有效的方式限制法官行使裁量权的任意性，其核心是在司法体系内部，通过制度性的、技术性的安排妥善地解决这个问题。参见马国川《季卫东：司法改革第三波》，《经济观察报》2009年11月13日。

犯罪嫌疑人、被告人的辩护权，保障律师执业权利，限制适用羁押措施、保障被羁押人的合法权益，加强未成年犯罪嫌疑人、被告人的权益保障，严格控制和慎重适用死刑，完善服刑人员社区矫正和刑满释放人员帮扶制度，完善国家赔偿制度，建立刑事被害人救助制度等诸多方面；其三，通过实行统一的国家司法考试制度、建立警察执法资格等级考试制度、加强司法人员职业教育培训、加强司法人员职业道德建设、加强律师职业道德建设、拓展律师发挥作用的空间、改革完善司法经费保障体制，使司法能力得到了较大程度的提高；其四，践行司法为民，采取了加强基层司法机构建设、简化办案程序、建立多元纠纷解决机制、降低当事人诉讼成本、开展法律援助、畅通司法机关与社会公众沟通渠道等多种举措。

深化司法体制改革，意味着司法改革将在现有基础上持续推进。在以往推进司法改革的过程中，由于新旧司法理念、体制机制、具体制度在理论上的对立以及司法改革的内容、程序本身的复杂性，导致已有的司法改革主要集中于工作机制、工作方法、司法程序等层面，真正触及体制性问题的改革较为有限。深化司法体制改革，意味着未来的司法改革将进入"深水区"——重点在于改革与司法机关依法独立公正行使职权不相适应的司法体制，而以体制性问题为着力点的司法改革本质上属于政治体制改革的组成部分，因此比技术性的司法改革难度明显加大。中国的司法改革一直面临着"合法改革"与"违法改革"之争，在深化司法体制改革的进程中如何看待这一问题，如何为深化司法体制改革设计整体蓝图，如何评价深化司法体制改革的若干具体方案，这些问题是深化司法体制改革中的关键性问题，本文拟对此进行探讨。

一　深化司法体制改革中的"依法改革"问题

改革开放以来，中国的法治建设围绕着"有法可依、有法必依、执法必严、违法必究"的十六字方针进行；在新的历史时期，国家决策层又提出了"科学立法、严格执法、公正司法、全民守法"的新十六字方针。2011年3月，全国人大常委会委员长吴邦国在十一届全国人大四次会议上做全国人大常委会工作报告，他宣布：一个立足中国国情和实际、适应改革开放和社会主义现代化建设需要、集中体现党和人民意志的，以宪法为统帅，以宪法相关法、民法商法等多个法律部门的法律为主干，由法律、行政法规、地方性法规等多个层次的法律规范构成的中国特色社会主义法律体系已经形成。在此背景下进行司法体制改革，改革的合法性问题成为人们关注的焦点之一，因为"作为一项法律活动，司法改革应当遵循合法性原则，但是改革的性质也决定了司法改革必须突破实在法的规定"。① 而对于实在法的突破很容易招致僭越立法权、挑战法律权威与破坏法治秩序的批评。

中央政法委书记孟建柱撰文指出：深化司法体制改革，必须"坚持遵循司法规律、坚持依法有序"。② 坚持遵循司法规律，指出了司法体制改革的基本方向，即要改变不符合司法规律的旧有体制，这必然涉及法律的修改或创设问题；坚持依法有序，指出了在深化司法体制中应当重视改革的合法性问题，防止出现随意突破现有法律进行改革的乱象。在深化司法体制改革中，应当辩证地看待坚持遵循司法规律与坚持依法有序改革的关系，正确处理适时修改法律与维护法律的稳定性之间的关系。

探讨如何深化司法体制改革问题，不能不顾及新颁行的法律对于司法体制改革的制约，避免法律"朝令夕改"所带来的弊害。深化司法体制改革的意见和建议很大程度上需在现行宪法和法律的框架内予以考虑，与此同时，应当遵循司法规律，促进司法体制朝着科学化、民主化、公正化方向发展。

过去十多年来的司法改革总体上逐步向前推进，但其间也有曲折。处于转型期的中国法治建设体现出阶段性和妥协性的特点，司法改革进程也不例外。2012 年中国相继对《刑事诉讼法》《民事诉讼法》进行了修改，两大诉讼法的修改可以视为司法改革的重要组成部分。

《刑事诉讼法》的修改将"尊重和保障人权"作为刑事诉讼的任务；完善了非法证据排除制度，强化了证人出庭和保护制度；完善了逮捕、监视居住的条件、程序和采取强制措施后通知家属的规定；完善了辩护人在刑事诉讼中法律地位和作用的规定，扩大了法律援助的适用范围；完善了讯问犯罪嫌疑人的程序和必要的侦查措施，强化了对侦查措施的规范和监督；完善了审判程序中的重要环节；完善了暂予监外执行规定，强化了人民检察院对减刑、假释、暂予监外执行的监督。上述修改加强了刑事诉讼中的人权保障，完善了公、检、法、司之间的权力监督制约关系，提高了刑事诉讼程序的科学化程度。

《民事诉讼法》的修改完善了调解与诉讼相衔接的机制，进一步保障了

① 史立梅：《论司法改革的合法性》，《北京师范大学学报》（社会科学版）2005 年第 6 期。
② 孟建柱：《深化司法体制改革》，《人民日报》2013 年 11 月 25 日，第 6 版。

当事人的诉讼权利；完善了当事人举证制度；完善了简易程序、审判监督程序和执行程序，强化了检察机关的法律监督。修改后的《民事诉讼法》注重有效解决民事纠纷，提高诉讼效率，进一步保障当事人的诉讼权利，维护司法公正。

但是，两大诉讼法的修改基本未能触及学术界高度关注的体制性、结构性问题。修改后的《刑事诉讼法》在刑事司法职权配置方面，基本上维持了现有的刑事司法体制以及公、检、法三机关之间的权力架构，即公安机关拥有对除逮捕以外的其他强制性侦查措施的自行处分权，检察机关兼有控诉职能的行使者和法律监督者双重身份，而作为现代刑事诉讼重要特征的"司法裁判中心主义"未能在观念和制度上得到确立。这使得刑事诉讼立法未能通过司法体制改革在限制国家专门机关权力、保障公民权利方面获得长足的进步。而修改后的《民事诉讼法》未能在改革民事执行体制问题上有所建树，依旧保留了法院负责已生效的民事裁判以及刑事裁判中的财产部分的规定。

在两大诉讼法的修改中，作为中国特色存在的还有一个重要方面，那就是检察机关的法律监督职能大大加强。修改后的《刑事诉讼法》进一步明确了检察机关审查批准逮捕的程序；增加了检察机关对指定居所监视居住的决定和执行的监督、对在押人员进行羁押必要性的定期审查；规定检察机关对司法机关及其工作人员滥用对人对物的强制性措施等行为的申诉、控告，有审查核实、通知纠正权；检察机关对侦查人员的非法取证行为有调查核实、通知纠正权；检察机关对公安司法机关及其工作人员阻碍律师依法执业行为有调查核实、通知纠正权；检察机关有权对减刑、假释、暂予监外执行实行同步监督。在刑事诉讼中，一方面，检察机关承担了一些在其他国家和地区由法院承担的司法职能，如审查批准逮捕、对公安司法机关侵犯公民权利的司法救济；另一方面，检察机关可以对法院的审判活动进行监督，尤其是对于法院的生效裁判，可以提起抗诉，而法院必须对该案启动再审。与其他国家和地区的检察机关相比，中国的检察机关享有最强的司法职能，然而行使职能的方式却高度行政化。长期以来，检察机关实行的是一种"三级审批制"的办案方式，即"检察人员承办，办案部门负责人审核，检察长或者检察委员会决定"。①

修改后的《民事诉讼法》增加了检察机关法律监督的方式，在再审抗

---

① 参见《人民检察院刑事诉讼规则（试行）》第4条。

诉之外，增加了提出检察建议作为一种新的方式；扩大了监督范围，将人民法院的调解活动和民事执行活动纳入监督范围；强化了监督手段，增加规定"人民检察院因履行法律监督职责提出检察建议或者抗诉的需要，可以向当事人或者案外人调查核实有关情况"（第 211 条）。在民事诉讼中，如何处理检察监督与当事人自由处分原则、与生效民事裁判的既判力、与审判独立之间的关系，一直存在较大的理论争议。学术界对于民事诉讼检察监督制度的质疑，未能从根本上否定它，相反，在《民事诉讼法》修改中，民事诉讼检察监督制度得到很大程度的强化。

修改后的两大诉讼法均在 2013 年 1 月 1 日起施行。从某种意义上可以说，两大诉讼法的修改对于深化司法体制改革，理顺法院与检察院的关系，加强审判独立，维护法院的司法权威构成了新的制约。探讨深化司法体制改革问题，在明确改革方向的同时，需要将具体的改革举措放在现行法律的框架下予以审视，以便准确把握改革的重点与难点，明确具体的改革方案是否以及在多大程度上需要突破现行法律的限制。

二　深化司法体制改革的宏观思路

中央政法委书记孟建柱撰文指出：深化司法体制改革，必须坚持 7 个基本遵循，即坚持党的领导、坚持中国特色社会主义方向、坚持人民主体地位、坚持从中国国情出发、坚持遵循司法规律、坚持依法有序、坚持统筹协调。① 这主要从政治层面概括了深化司法体制改革的整体思路，体现了中央决策层对于深化司法体制改革的宏观思考。笔者认为，关于深化司法体制改革的宏观思路，还可以从以下两个层面予以展开。

（一）　从尊重司法规律看深化司法体制改革

司法体制改革究竟应当如何深化？对此问题的回答离不开对司法本身性质和功能的认识，只有在此基础上，才谈得上对司法规律的遵循。在一个法治社会中，司法的权威代表着法律的权威，"法律至上"在具体的司法裁判中加以体现。当公权力与公权力之间、公权力与私权利之间、私权利与私权利之间发生冲突时，将这种冲突委诸法院居中裁断，法院承担着解决纠纷、救济私权、制约公权的职责。显然，司法体制改革应当以有利于法院更好地履行司法职责为依归。据此，强化司法的本我定位、保障司法的独立性、提高司法保障人权的程度、促进司法品质的提升以及赢得民众

---

① 孟建柱：《深化司法体制改革》，《人民日报》2013 年 11 月 25 日，第 6 版。

对司法的信赖等，应当成为司法体制改革所追求的理想目标。

从世界范围内来看，在以苏联和东欧国家为代表的建立法治的国家，司法的功能因为法治作为国家基本原则的确立而重新定位，司法在国家政治力退出、社会力解放后，必须承担起维系新秩序的主要责任。在中国，以吴敬琏先生为代表的经济学家们正在呼吁"走向法治市场经济"，他们认为当前社会上存在的种种丑恶现象，从根本上说是经济改革没有完全到位、政治改革严重滞后、行政权力变本加厉地压制和干预民间正常经济活动，造成广泛寻租活动的结果。中国市场已经从人格化交换为主的"熟人市场"发展为以非人格化交换为主的"生人市场"，双边和多边声誉与惩罚机制难以发挥作用，因此需要建立一个以正式法庭为主的第三方执法体系来保证合同的实施，而从目前的情况看，司法的行政化、地方化、官僚化、政治化阻碍了司法功能的正常发挥。司法体制应当与市场机制相匹配，带有计划经济时代烙印的旧有司法体制应当予以改革。①

司法体制改革是中国政治民主化、法治化的表现之一，因此，从大的方向上来说，司法体制改革应当将构建中立、独立的法院作为主要目标，将其塑造为依"法"审判的第三者角色。只有如此，司法才能承担起对公民权利进行救济、对公共权力进行制约的功能。务实的司法体制改革应该以构建明确的司法功能为其目标，在组织上、程序上，让司法的中立、被动、事后、个案、争议等特质得到彰显，以与其他部门相区隔；建立保障法官身份、保障法官职务独立的制度，凭借裁判格式、严谨推理、程序公开等来达到"审判"的独立。

近些年来，"司法独立"似乎成了敏感词汇。在司法独立问题上，我们陷入了司法独立与司法公正的关系的纠结之中。一些人认为，因为司法不公正，所以司法独立目前尚不具备条件。但是，司法独立是法治的基石，司法不独立，法治的权威就无法树立。司法所承载的纠纷裁判功能决定了它需要以亲历性、判断性、独立性、对审性、中立性等为基本特征。司法独立是司法公正的前提条件。司法不独立，审判主体不明确，裁判的责任就难以追究，从而助长司法腐败，妨碍司法公正。如果我们能够在司法独立的问题上达成基本共识，并以此为出发点推进法官队伍的精英化，司法的信誉就能逐渐提升，民众对司法的信赖才能逐渐形成。司法独立是深化司法体制改革的瓶颈问题，也是司法体制改革的突破口。

---

①　参见吴敬琏《走向法治市场经济》，《小康》2013 年第 3 期。

司法在法治社会中功能的发挥，有赖于司法权威的建立。对于司法权威，需要从外部和内部两方面加以维护。从司法权的外部看，司法权在国家权力体系中是"最不具有危险性""最微不足道"的权力，各种权威力量都可能对司法运作构成实质影响。在这种情况下，要维护司法权威，首先需要树立法律的权威，使得"任何人和组织都不能凌驾于宪法和法律之上"，政治权力应当保持对司法的尊重，国家应当加大对司法的投入，充分保证司法的各项必要费用。党对司法工作的领导主要是路线方针的领导，政法委不应干预个案。

从司法权的内部看，司法机关应当对终审裁判予以尊重，保持终审裁判的稳定性。从中国目前司法制度的设计来看，再审制度有利于司法实现"有错必纠"，以至于错误可以一改再改，却不利于尊重终审裁判。"有错必纠"的传统观念，对司法权威具有严重影响。虽说司法错误的发生，肯定会严重危害司法权威，然而，我们在观念上应当允许一定程度的错误存在。如果所有的裁判都正确，司法才有权威，恐怕任何国家的司法都不可能有权威。当然，这绝不意味着司法可以为所欲为，也并不意味着司法的所有错误我们都应容忍，但这预示着司法权威需要刻意维护。信访是沟通民意、表达民意、听取民意的有效途径，但现实中有些信访变成救济权利、解决纠纷的途径，偏离了制度的初衷。因此，需要重新予以正确定位，减少行政对于司法的干预，改革信访考核制度，维护司法权威。法院判决执行难以及因为判决执行引发的信访问题屡见不鲜，严重影响法院的司法权威，因此，法院判决与执行有待进行外部分离。

（二）以问题为导向看深化司法体制改革

尽管进行了广泛而具有实质意义的司法改革，但中国当前的司法制度仍然存在一些根本性的问题，突出地表现在法官的非职业化、司法的行政化和司法的地方化。因此，深化司法体制改革应当以解决法官的非职业化、司法的行政化和司法的地方化为主要内容。

依法治国的指导原则和蓬勃发展的市场经济是不可分的，在市场经济下，经济行为以及国家机关作为的"可预期性"变得非常重要，它有利于降低市场的风险成本，提高经营者的积极性。如果司法人员的专业训练不够，法律的操作变成完全不可预测，司法将无法承担"依法"裁判的功能。统一司法考试在加强司法专业化方面迈出了重要一步，未来的司法改革应当朝着进一步加强司法专业化的方向努力，如建立司法职业训练制度，提高法官的专业素质。另外，司法在追求专业化的同时，也要透过适当的教育，避免专业因素加深民众对法律的排斥，要通过法庭的开放、裁判书的通俗（其中包括判决理由的阐明）与网络化等方式，减轻专业化改革可能造成的社会对司法的疏离。

司法的行政化是影响中国司法独立的体制性原因，也是制约司法体制改革的核心因素。司法的行政化体现在司法机关地位的行政化、司法机关内部人事制度的行政化、法官制度的行政化、审判业务上的行政化、审级间的行政化、司法机关职能的行政化等诸多方面。司法的行政化为行政权干涉司法权提供了可能，严重影响了法官的独立审判，严重威胁到审级监督体系，进而对司法公正造成严重影响。司法行政化问题早已受到社会各界的广泛批评，但近年来司法行政化倾向并未明显缓解，反有加重之势。这与中国的权力结构及其运行机制有关，也与司法功能设定的非司法化和资源配置的有限性以及人事管理和财政供应制度有关。司法体制改革应当将去行政化作为改革重点之一，全面实现司法行政和司法审判的分立，阻隔行政性要素进入审判。①

司法的地方化是困扰中国司法审判的另一个突出问题，它严重损害了法院作为公正执法机关的形象和声誉，严重危害到国家法制的统一和尊严。司法难以真正独立、法院受经济利益驱动、法官整体素质偏低、法制不健全以及缺乏对地方性法规、规章的合法性审查等是造成司法地方保护主义的主要原因。司法改革应当继续在遏制司法的地方化方面做出努力，通过改革现行法院管理体制，使法院在人、财、物方面摆脱地方政府的控制，在法院系统内部建立和完善跨地区、跨级别的法官交流和轮岗制度，完善现行管辖制度等措施遏制司法的地方化。

在司法体制改革中，还应当注意以下问题：认真倾听民间意见，对民间意见进行有效的整合，以弥补司法改革自上而下进行所造成的民众参与不够的缺陷；防止司法改革过程中各部门的自利化，打破部门割据、各自为政的状况；针对各地区实际情况的差异，提出不同的改革方案，避免改革中的"一刀切"。司法体制改革既要目标明确、重点突出，又要统筹兼顾、循序渐进，只有如此，才能少走弯路，推动司法体制改革走向深入。

三 深化司法体制改革的具体方案

深化司法体制改革，除了需要明确宏观思路之外，还需要拟定具体方

---

① 参见龙宗智、袁坚《深化改革背景下对司法行政化的遏制》，《法学研究》2014 年第 1 期。

案。司法体制改革由于涉及不同机关的权力重新配置和工作关系的重大调整，因此需要建立统筹协调机制，由中央决策部门出台具体的改革方案。《中共中央关于全面深化改革若干重大问题的决定》（以下简称《决定》）指出了深化司法体制改革中的若干重点问题；而中国法学界关于此问题的讨论，则希冀在中央司法改英方案的基础上，进一步加大改革的力度。这些具体的改革方案需要对照深化司法体制改革的总体目标加以审视和评估，同时也需要加以细化，使其具备可操作性。

（一）《决定》确定的改革重点

根据《决定》，深化司法体制改革，重点包括以下内容①。

1. 确保人民法院、人民检察院依法独立公正行使审判权、检察权

具体举措包括：（1）推动省以下地方法院、检察院人财物统一管理；（2）探索与行政区划适当分离的司法管辖制度。

要使法院在行使审判权时摆脱外部的干扰和控制，有必要对法院的人事编制、经费预算、基础设施的配给等给予特别保障。法院、检察院系统经费由省级财政统一拨付、将司法管辖与行政区划适当分离等改革举措，有助于解决司法的地方化问题。然而，省以下地方法院、检察院人财物统一管理，是否会加剧法院体系和检察院体系内部的行政化，值得予以观察。另外，如果建立"跨区法院"或"巡回法院"，涉及对《人民法院组织法》的修改，根据《人民法院组织法》第34条的规定，法官由同级人大及其常委会任免，任免"跨区法官"或"巡回法官"存在制度上的障碍；而通过提级管辖、集中管辖，审理行政案件或者跨地区的民商事、环境保护案件，则可能对《行政诉讼法》《民事诉讼法》所规定的管辖制度造成冲击，需要对相关法律规定进行修改。

2. 建立符合职业特点的司法人员管理制度

具体举措包括：（1）推进司法人员分类管理改革；（2）完善法官、检察官、人民警察选任招录制度；（3）完善法官、检察官任免、惩戒制度；（4）强化法官、检察官、人民警察的职业保障制度。

中国通过统一的司法考试制度提高了法官、检察官和律师的业务素质，一个法律职业共同体开始逐步形成。但是，目前在司法人员招录、遴选、培养、任用等方面，实行与普通公务员相同的模式，未能体现司法人员的

---

① 关于改革重点的归纳，见孟建柱《深化司法体制改革》，《人民日报》2013年11月25日，第6版。

职业特点，因此，司法职业化改革有待继续下去，尤其是法官的业务素质有待进一步提高。可考虑采取以下改革方案：（1）将书记员改为"书记官"，与法官纳入不同序列，进行分类、分级管理，不再将担任书记员作为培养法官的必经途径。（2）建立司法研修制度，担任法官和书记官均需通过一定时间的司法研修，学习所需要的职业技能。（3）法院院长应当从职业法官、职业检察官或律师中选拔，要求具有长时间的法律职业经历。（4）加强对法官的职业保障，如法官工资比公务员应当高1/3或1倍；法官的任期由法律明确加以规定，以确保法官的任职期间不被任意地缩短或延长；延长法官退休年龄（如法官的任职年龄不超过70岁）；等等。（5）完善司法人员纪律处分程序，对于追究法官责任的机构和程序做出明确的法律规定。（6）将法院内部从事行政管理的人员从审判人员中剥离，成立专门的法院管理机构；管理机构人员具有公务员身份，而非法官身份，保障法官队伍的纯洁性。

3. 健全司法权力运行机制

具体举措包括：（1）建立主审法官、合议庭办案责任制；（2）改革审判委员会制度；（3）明确四级法院职能定位。

建立主审法官、合议庭办案责任制，旨在让审理者裁判、由裁判者负责，体现审理与裁判的统一、权力与责任的统一，有利于推进司法独立从法院独立走向法官独立。需要注意的是，目前法院系统普遍存在案多人少问题，在法官超负荷运转的情况下，案件质量难以得到保障。要将主审法官、合议庭办案责任制落到实处，除了有审判职称的人员须全部办案之外，还需针对各地区实际情况，科学合理确定法官员额，并配套性地健全司法辅助人员分类管理制度，从根本上缓解案多人少的矛盾。

现行审判委员会制度造成审理与裁判的脱节，改革审判委员会制度应以促进审理与裁判的统一为基本方向，应当减少审判委员会讨论决定案件的数量，审判委员会的职能主要限定于研究案件的法律适用问题，应当推进院长、副院长、审判委员会委员或审判委员会直接审理重大、复杂、疑难案件。

四级法院的职能定位应当有明确的界分，"一审法院明断是非定分止争、二审法院案结事了、再审法院有错必究、最高人民法院保证法律统一正确实施"，[①] 以体现法律所规定的审级制度的基本精神。应当改变下级法

---

① 孟建柱：《深化司法体制改革》，《人民日报》2013年11月25日，第6版。

院向上级法院请示汇报或者上级法院"提前介入"等做法，确保审级独立。

4. 深化司法公开

具体包括推进审判公开、检务公开、警务公开和狱务公开。

近些年来，司法机关全面推进司法公开，扩大了公开的事项和内容，丰富了公开的形式和载体，强化了公开的效果和保障。今后的司法公开工作有待从以下几个方面加以完善：（1）强化以公开为原则、不公开为例外的理念。司法公开是中国宪法和三大诉讼法规定的基本原则，它是保护当事人和社会公众的知情权、加强对司法权力的社会监督、提升司法公信力的保障。为贯彻司法公开原则，应当保障公民旁听庭审的权利；裁判文书公开应从部分公开走向全面公开（例外情况下不公开）、从形式公开走向实质公开；推进其他司法信息公开，如司法机关的设置、职能、职责、权限与办案程序，司法机关制定的司法解释和其他规范性文件，司法机关的人事信息、诉讼费用信息及案件统计信息等。（2）正确把握司法公开的尺度。司法公开是原则，但这种公开并非没有边际，它需要权衡各种利益后由法律规制公开的范围与方式。应当严格依照法律把握司法公开的尺度；法律规定不明确或者不完善的，应当对法律进行相应的修改或者通过司法解释予以明确。（3）科学合理应对新闻媒体以及网络舆论监督。随着微博、微信等自媒体的兴起以及互联网的愈益发达，舆论对司法的监督呈日益增强之势。司法需要舆论监督，但应防止舆论监督转化成情绪化的舆论审判。在司法过程中，各种主体、各个参与者应当严格遵守法律，保持清醒的角色自律，摒弃情感冲动，避免将法律问题道德化。司法机关要科学引导舆论，提升应对舆论的能力。坚守司法工作底线，合理利用舆论的积极作用，同时防止舆论影响司法审判的独立性与公正性。

5. 改革人民陪审员制度，健全人民监督员制度

人民陪审员制度和人民监督员制度是公民参与和监督司法的重要方式。2004 年，全国人大常委会颁布了《关于完善人民陪审员制度的决定》，拓宽了人民陪审员的选任来源，加强了对人民陪审员的培训，各地法院还规范了人民陪审员参与审理案件的方式和流程，陪审案件数量呈逐年上升的趋势。但陪审制度流于形式的问题依然不同程度存在，需要进一步完善制度设计。要扩大人民陪审员的数量和来源，完善人民陪审员的参审机制，加强人民陪审员的经费保障，以切实发挥人民陪审员制度的作用。

最高人民检察院于 2003 年启动了人民监督员制度试点工作；2010 年 10 月，该制度在全国检察机关全面推行。人民监督员制度的创建旨在解决

"谁来监督监督者"的问题。目前人民监督员主要对检察机关在办理职务犯罪案件过程中出现的应当立案而不立案、不应当立案而立案、拟撤销案件、拟不起诉等情形进行监督与评议，人民监督员的作用体现得还不够充分。要推进人民监督员制度规范化，通过立法对人民监督员的产生、监督范围、监督程序、监督效力等做出明确规定。

6. 严格规范减刑、假释和保外就医程序

减刑、假释和保外就医是刑罚变更执行的重要制度，这些制度对于激励罪犯改造、促进罪犯回归社会，具有重要意义。但是，这些制度的存在，造成法院判定的刑罚与罪犯实际服刑时间之间的巨大差距，不仅有损刑罚的可信度，还易导致滥用自由裁量权。对于减刑、假释和保外就医程序，《刑法》《刑事诉讼法》仅做了原则性规定。为了防止减刑、假释和保外就医方面的司法腐败，提升司法公信力，需要对刑罚变更执行实行更加有力的司法控制，加强法院审查的实质性，完善减刑、假释和保外就医案件的审理程序，解决刑罚执行机关权力过大、法院沦为橡皮图章的问题；此外，还需健全对假释、暂予监外执行的管理和监督制度，防止漏管、脱管和重新犯罪，提高教育矫治效果。

（二）其他的改革举措

1. 完善废除劳教后的法律制度

2013 年 12 月 28 日，第十二届全国人大常委会第六次会议正式通过了《关于废止有关劳动教养法律规定的决定》。废止劳动教养制度后，需要对相关法律、法规、司法解释、规章和规范性文件依照法定程序进行清理；还需要做好劳动教养管理机关人民警察的职能转变和劳动教养场所的合理利用等工作。废止劳动教养制度之后，过去由劳动教养制度所处置的对象（包括 12 类违法人员）可通过刑事处罚、治安处罚等替代性措施分流处理。原有的劳动教养对象中有一部分属于特殊主体，包括吸毒成瘾者和卖淫嫖娼者。废止劳动教养制度之后，对于此类特殊主体，可分别适用强制隔离戒毒和收容教育。我国还存在着对违法犯罪的未成年人的收容教养制度。这些与劳动教养相类似的制度也有待加以改革。在废除劳教制度之后，为了加强对公民人身自由权的保护，过去由公安机关处理的一些案件将逐渐转由法院进行处理，这无疑会大大加重法院的负担。转处的这部分案件可称为治安案件，在性质和特点上与一般的刑事案件有别，因此需要增设专门的治安法庭，采用相对快速、简易的方式加以处理，以提高司法效率。对于强制隔离戒毒，可以考虑将公安机关管理的戒毒所统一划归司法行政

机关管理，以形成公安机关禁毒、司法行政机关戒毒的格局。

2. 涉法涉诉信访工作改革

信访制度是一种具有中国特色的政治参与形式和权利救济方式，国务院颁布的《信访条例》对这一制度做了规定。由于我国目前司法权威性和公信力不足，导致涉法涉诉类信访量多面广，"信访不信法"现象突出，我国的司法制度陷入了两难境地。实践中信访渠道确实解决了许多司法难以解决的实际问题，减轻了司法机关的压力，但是，信访渠道越有作为、越高效，法律就会越衰退，程序规则就会越受损害，司法权威也就越弱化，继而引发更大规模的信访，同时法院终将成为没有公信力和终局权威的裁判机构。为了维护司法权威，应当将可诉涉诉的信访事项纳入司法轨道处理。信访机构应当通过法治化的预设程序，将可诉、涉诉、诉讼终结的信访案件，引导至正常的审判程序或审判监督程序之中处理，以避免信访制度冲击司法制度。① 中共中央办公厅、国务院办公厅于 2014 年 3 月印发了《关于依法处理涉法涉诉信访问题的意见》。该意见的总体思路是：改变经常性集中交办、过分依靠行政推动、通过信访启动法律程序的工作方式，把解决涉法涉诉信访问题纳入法治轨道，由政法机关依法按程序处理，依法纠正执法差错，依法保障合法权益，依法维护公正结论，保护合法信访、制止违法闹访。努力实现案结事了、息诉息访，实现维护人民群众合法权益与维护司法权威的统一。该意见正式确立了诉访分离的原则。

3. 司法权力运行机制改革

关于司法权力运行机制改革，除了《决定》中所列举的改革措施外，学术界还提出了以下改革建议。

第一，关于执政党与司法的关系。正确处理党的领导与司法机关独立行使职权之间的关系，是中国司法体制改革中的关键性问题。党对司法工作的领导主要表现为政策、方针和组织上的领导，党的组织和领导干部应当尊重和支持司法机关依法独立行使职权；在刑事司法中，应当遵循公、检、法三机关分工负责、互相配合、互相制约的原则。党的组织和领导干部不宜具体参与办案，在极其例外的情况下，即便有必要协调案件，也不能协调对于案件事实和证据的评判。目前，还需要妥善处理纪委与司法机关之间的关系。反腐工作由党委领导、纪委协调，但司法机关与纪委之间不是领导与被领导的关系，而是协调与配合的关系；纪委办案，也应当严

---

① 参见刘炳君《涉法涉诉信访工作的法治化研究》，《法学论坛》2011 年第 1 期。

格遵守法律的正当程序。根据《刑事诉讼法》的有关规定，行政机关在行政执法和查办案件过程中收集的物证、书证、视听资料、电子数据等证据材料，在刑事诉讼中可以作为证据使用。这里的行政机关应当包括监察机关，而监察机关与纪委往往合署办公。依此规定，纪委在办案过程中收集的实物证据可以移送检察机关，但纪委所收集的言词证据，不得在刑事诉讼中加以使用。

学术界对于政法委的职能存在一些争议。政法委在保障党的路线、方针、政策在政法工作中得到正确实施、对政法工作做出全局性部署、指导政法工作和政法队伍建设以及协调社会治安综合治理等方面发挥着举足轻重的作用。政法委对于政法工作的领导，关键是要善于运用法治方式和法治思维进行领导，像过去那种协调个案的做法应当尽量减少。一些学者建议，省以下政法委不宜协调个案；应当明确政法委协调个案的具体范围，如仅限于大案、要案等个别案件；不能协调对案件事实和证据的评判；应当建立案件协调责任制；等等。①

第二，看守所的归属问题。2012 年的《刑事诉讼法》修改，在法条中除了"公安机关""侦查机关"等称谓之外，还出现了"看守所"的专门用语，可以解读为"看守所"成为刑事诉讼中独立的诉讼主体，承担独立的诉讼职能，不再为"公安机关""侦查机关"所包含，从而为看守所管理体制改革扫清了障碍。一些学者建议将看守所从公安机关剥离出来，归属于司法行政机关领导，这有助于加强公、检、法、司之间的权力制约，遏制刑讯逼供、超期羁押等违法现象发生。

第三，法院的判决执行权改革。根据《民事诉讼法》、《行政诉讼法》和《刑事诉讼法》的规定，发生法律效力的民事、行政判决、裁定，以及刑事判决、裁定中的财产部分，还有死刑立即执行的判决，均由人民法院负责执行。让人民法院负责执行，是因为将执行权视为审判权的一部分或者审判权的延伸。但是，执行权本质上属于行政权，且执行工作难度大、任务重，法院从事执行工作，易与当事人发生直接冲突，有损法院权威，因此，可以考虑将法院的判决与执行予以分离。

总体而言，深化司法体制改革应当以法院的改革为重点，以提高司法公信力为核心，防止其沦为公、检、法、司新一轮的权力博弈；而法院的改革应当以提高判决书和庭审质量为轴心，因为司法公信力主要体现于一

———

① 参见陈光中、龙宗智《关于深化司法改革若干问题的思考》，《中国法学》2013 年第 4 期。

纸判决书，而高质量的判决书以高质量的庭审为前提。深化司法体制改革的目的在于建立保障司法职能得以有效、充分发挥的机制，以最终实现建立公正高效权威的中国特色社会主义司法制度的改革目标。

Macro-Thinking and Concrete Plan of Deepening the Judicial Reform in China

Xiong Qiuhong[*]

【Abstract】 The judicial reform in China has undergone a process of progressive development. The deepening of the reform means that the reform is about to enter into "deep water"—namely the focus of the reform will be on systems that are incompatible with the independent, lawful and fair performance of functions by judicial organs. In the process of deepening the judicial reform, it is necessary to take a dialectic approach to the relationship between following the rules of judicial activities and adhering to the principle of carry out the reform in an orderly way and in accordance with law and strike a balance between timely revision of laws and maintaining the stability of law. From the perspective of respecting the rules of judicial activities, the objectives of deepening the judicial reform should be to safeguard the independence of administration of justice, to raise the level of judicial protection of human rights, and to improve the quality of and promote the public trust in administration of justice; from the perspective of adhering to problem-oriented approach, the deepening of the judicial reform should be focused on solving such problems as the non-professionalism of judges and the administrativization and provincialization of administration of justice. The plan for the new round of judicial reform adopted by the central government contains the following key reforms: improving the judicial administration system, establishing a judicial personnel management system suited to the professional characteristics of judicial personnel, improving the mechanism for the exercise of judicial power, increasing

* Professor, Institute of Law, Chinese Academy of Social Sciences.

judicial transparency, reforming the people's assessor system and the people's supervisor system, strictly regulating the procedures of commutation of sentence, release on parole, and medical parole, and reforming the mechanism for dealing with complaints by letters and visits that involve laws and lawsuits. The concrete plans for these key reforms still need to be made. In order to broaden the vision of the research on deepening the judicial reform, the following issues need to be brought into the ambit of discussion: the reform of the reeducation-through-labor system and similar systems, the mechanism for the handling of corruption cases, the functions of political and legal affairs commissions, the affiliation of detention houses, and reform of the system of judgment enforcement power.

【Keywords】 Deepening the Judicial Reform; Macro-thinking; Concrete Plan

保安处分与中国行政拘禁制度的改革[*]

刘仁文[**]

【摘要】 废止劳动教养制度是中国法治的重大进步，但是应当看到，我国现行行政法律体系中还有一些"类劳教"措施，如针对卖淫嫖娼者的收容教育、针对未达到刑事责任年龄者的收容教养、强制戒毒等。这些行政拘禁制度的改革方向应为经过司法裁决的保安处分。

【关键词】 保安处分　行政拘禁　司法裁决

2013 年 11 月 12 日，中共十八届三中全会通过的《中共中央关于全面深化改革若干重大问题的决定》提出，废止劳动教养制度，完善对违法犯罪行为的惩治和矫正法律，健全社区矫正制度。2013 年 12 月 28 日，全国人大常委会通过《关于废止有关劳动教养法律规定的决定》，正式废止劳动教养制度。根据该决定，在劳动教养制度废止前，依法做出的劳动教养决定有效；劳动教养制度废止后，对正在被依法执行劳动教养的人员，解除劳动教养，剩余期限不再执行。至此，诞生于 20 世纪 50 年代的劳动教养制度正式成为历史。

在劳动教养制度改革方案的讨论中，曾有不少人建议将劳动教养制度改革为保安处分。现在，虽然劳动教养制度被废止，但大家都认为，需要完善相关法律制度。例如，有学者就建议，可考虑在《社区矫正法》中规定"行为监督"这类保安处分措施，对那些屡教不改的轻微违法犯罪人员，附加由法院判处一定期间的"行为监督"，以便在社区中对其行为习惯和心

---

[*] 本文为笔者承担的北京市法学会 2013 年度重点课题"后劳教时代的保安处分构建"的研究成果。

[**] 刘仁文，中国社会科学院法学研究所研究员。

理进行矫正和治疗。① 另外，这次废止的仅是"小劳教"，学界还有所谓的
"大劳教"，即收容教育、收容教养、强制戒毒等，这些现行行政法律体系
中的"类劳教"措施，"已成为约束公权力之路上无法绕开的绊脚石"。②

本文要解决的问题是：保安处分到底是一种什么样的制度，它在当今世界
各国和地区是如何规定的，对我国后劳教时代的相关制度改革有何借鉴意义。

一　保安处分制度的缘起与演变

现代国家的刑法一般都实行刑罚和保安处分的二元制。所谓保安处分，
是指国家为了保卫社会的安全，对于具有特殊人身危险性的人，以矫治、
感化、医疗、禁戒等手段，替代或补充刑罚适用的各种保安措施的总称。

现代意义上的保安处分理论发端于18世纪末德国刑法学者克莱因，③
他在《保安处分的理论》一文中将刑罚与保安处分做了区分，认为刑罚是
基于对行为和行为人的否定评价而在判决中根据刑罚的种类和幅度来确定
的，而保安处分则是基于行为人的犯罪危险性来确定的。根据克莱因的观
点，二者的执行顺序应当是先执行刑罚，在刑罚执行完毕后，紧接着将仍
然需要矫正或者使之不能犯的行为人收容于矫正机构或保安监禁机构。

克莱因的理论提出之时，正值欧洲冲破封建罪刑擅断、野蛮司法之黑
暗，迎来近代刑法文明之光的刑事古典学派占据主流阵地。在当时崇尚自
由、建立以罪刑法定主义为基础的法治文化的历史背景下，罪刑法定主义
的代表们取得了论战的胜利。

但到19世纪末，在刑事实证学派的推动下，保安处分思想得以广泛传播
并不同程度地被刑事立法所吸收，如累犯从重处罚制度，缓刑、假释制度等，
都是在考虑行为人的人身危险性的基础上而建立的。尤其值得一提的是，1893
年德国刑法学家施托斯（又译斯托斯）受托起草的《瑞士联邦刑法草案》
（即施托斯草案），首创将保安处分与刑罚统一于一部刑法典的立法例。该草
案在承认和遵守罪刑法定原则和责任主义原则的基础上，综合报应刑思想和

---

① 参见熊秋红《完善废除劳教后的法律制度》，《中国社会科学报》2014年3月5日。

② 参见张舟逸《"类劳教"待改革》，《财经》2013年第27期。

③ 封建社会及其以前的刑罚，由于以死刑、身体刑和驱逐出境（发配）为中心，加上刑法中
并没有严格确立责任主义原则、罪刑擅断现象普遍等原因，建立有别于刑罚体系的保安处
分体系缺乏必要。尽管如此，古代法律文献中还是有一些可以被视为"保安处分"内容的
规定，如中世纪的戈斯拉尔法对丧失理智的犯罪人予以保护性监禁的规定。参见徐久生
《保安处分新论》，中国方正出版社，2006，第25页。

目的刑思想，在规定传统刑罚之外，对某些犯罪规定了矫正、监护、隔离等措施作为补充，如对累犯的保护管束、酗酒者治疗所、善行保证等。

在施托斯草案的影响下，欧洲、美洲、亚洲等许多国家的刑法改革都开始重视保安处分，例如，英国于 1907 年制定了《保护观察法》和《少年法》，1908 年制定了《犯罪预防法》，1913 年制定了《精神病法》，这些法律都包含了保安处分的内容。①

保安处分思想曾经一度有取代刑罚的势头，突出例子是 1921 年菲利起草的《意大利刑法草案》（即菲利草案），该草案试图否定刑罚的传统概念，将刑罚与保安处分融为一体，构成新型的、社会性的"制裁体系"，这就是刑罚与保安处分的一元论立法模式。菲利草案虽然最终仍然被二元论立法模式所取代，但正如有学者所观察指出的：保安处分发展至今，各国立法多是二元之中有统一，统一之中有二致，"强调刑罚和保安处分两者的互补性"。② 也就是说，今天虽然大多数国家采行刑罚与保安处分的"二元制"，但这种二元不是截然分开的，而是彼此融合的。

在保安处分的发展历史上，有过很不光彩的一页，那就是纳粹德国时期保安处分曾被希特勒恶意利用。纳粹法西斯在德国执政后，以"强化民族精神"和"保卫国家利益"为幌子，肆意扩大保安处分的适用范围，放宽保安处分的适用条件，如 1933 年纳粹德国通过的"关于危险的惯犯"和"关于保安矫正处分"两项法令，就是这方面的代表。这种保安处分的特点是，一切以所谓的国家、社会利益为中心，将保卫社会安全作为适用保安处分的根本目的，以消极镇压为主要手段，而对被处保安处分者的教育、改善则是附属于保安目的的次要内容。③ 这一惨痛教训告诉人们，如果保安

---

① 英美法系国家虽然在形式上不像大陆法系国家那样在刑法典中确立刑罚与保安处分的二元制（或称双轨制），而往往把有关保安处分的内容单独立法，但从其实质来看，仍然可以说是刑罚与保安处分的二元制。

② 参见屈学武《一体两支柱的中国刑事法体系构想》，载陈泽宪主编《犯罪定义与刑事法治》，中国社会科学出版社，2008，第 6 页。

③ 对被处保安处分者的教育、改善则应当是保安处分与防卫社会相并列的一个主要目的。美国学者曾指出：如果一个人犯重罪的可能性为 80%，没有一项法律会允许对其定罪判刑；但另一方面，如果精神病医生证明一个人有精神病且有 80% 实施危险行为的可能性，那么这个人可以被收容（但事实上，现今绝大多数国家仍然实行对精神病人收容要建立在他已经实行了危险行为的基础上——笔者注）。对这种不同对待方法的一种解释是：对患有精神病的人采取医院治疗的方法可能对他自身有益，对他的自由限制也不因此而像监禁一个"无辜的"人一样"不公平"。参见《哈佛法律评论》编辑部《精神病人的民事收容：理论与程序》，朱江译，载刘仁文等编译《哈佛法律评论·刑法学精粹》，法律出版社，2005，第 306 页。

处分没有处分法定主义等作为制度屏障，将成为对人权侵夺的一个极好借口。

由于保安处分在历史上留下过不好的名声，所以我们过去一直对保安处分颇有微词。但应当指出的是，世界上任何一个国家都会面临精神病人危害社会、未达到刑事责任年龄的人危害社会、吸毒成瘾者危害社会、某些有特殊人身危险性的人需要加以特殊防范等问题。因此，"二战"后各国从防止保安处分被滥用以及保障人权出发，在法治原则和矫正主义的基础上，对保安处分制度进行了完善，如加强对人身危险性的测量标准和技术的研究和开发，对剥夺自由的保安处分从程序和评估上进行严格限制，把剥夺自由的保安处分从消极的隔离执行方式改为对被处保安处分者进行矫治、教育的积极执行方式，从而更好地实现防卫社会和保障人权的平衡。也正因此，保安处分制度获得了更大的发展，不仅遍及传统欧陆国家以及欧陆国家以外的大陆法系国家和地区，而且英美法系国家也广泛采纳（如美国，虽然不用保安处分这个名字，但它对精神病人和毒品滥用者的"民事拘禁"措施，以及在少年司法制度中对未达到刑事责任年龄者的拘禁教育措施等，其实都与保安处分同质），甚至连苏联、东欧等社会主义国家也在各自的刑法典中纷纷对此加以全面承认。保安处分制度在全世界已经发展成为与传统刑罚制度并驾齐驱、互相支持甚至互相融合的一种制度，这是公认的事实。正如李斯特所指出："在现代刑事政策研究方面的一个重大成果，是最终达成了这样一个共识：在与犯罪作斗争中，刑罚既非唯一的，也非最安全的措施。对刑罚的效能必须批判地进行评估。出于这一原因，除刑罚制度外，还需要建立一套保安处分制度。"① 尤其需要引起我们重视的是，近年来保安处分制度还有进一步扩大的趋势，如美国的"三振出局法"，规定对第三次严重暴力犯罪者得判处不得假释的终身监禁；法国在2008年颁布的《保安拘留和保安监控法》中，特别规定了严厉的保安拘留和保安监控措施，这两类保安措施可以在刑罚执行完毕之后使用，表明其刑事政策更加偏向安全价值。

二　保安处分与刑罚的关系

从现今绝大多数国家和地区的规定来看，刑罚和保安处分的共同点是：行为人都实施了危害社会的行为；都要实行法定主义；都要经过法院的司

① 参见李斯特《德国刑法教科书》，徐久生译，法律出版社，2000，第20页。

法裁决；都要符合比例性原则。如《德国刑法典》规定："如判处矫正及保安处分与行为人的行为的严重性、将要实施的行为以及由行为人所引起的危险程度不相适应，不得科处。"

刑罚和保安处分的不同点在于：刑罚主要立足于对已然犯罪的惩罚，保安处分主要立足于对未然犯罪的预防；刑罚主要针对行为的社会危害性，保安处分主要针对行为人的人身危险性；刑罚的适用对象是达到刑事责任年龄的人和有刑事责任能力的正常人，保安处分的适用对象则既包括那些没有达到刑事责任年龄、不具有刑事责任能力但实施了与犯罪同样严重的危害社会的行为，并且通过他们的行为显示他们对社会还会继续有危险的人，如精神病人等，也包括那些虽然达到刑事责任年龄、具有刑事责任能力但需要对其人格或身体进行矫正、改善和治疗的"病人"，如屡教不改者、吸毒成瘾者等；刑罚是定期的，刑期一到就得释放，保安处分则带有一定的不定期性（但这种不定期要以定期进行人身危险性评估为条件，也就是说，被处保安处分的人有权利定期接受对其人身危险性的评估）。

在具体立法模式上，有的国家和地区是在刑法典中分别规定"刑罚"和"保安处分"，如德国；也有的是在刑法典之外单独规定保安处分，如韩国。在单独规定保安处分的国家和地区中，有的是统一制定一部《保安处分法》，也有的是针对不同的保安处分对象分别制定法律。另外，除了这种把刑罚与保安处分截然分开的制度设计外，还有越来越多的国家和地区把刑罚和保安处分糅合在一起来使用，如挪威枪击案凶手布雷维克被法院判处 21 年监禁，但法院又同时决定，罪犯在刑满后，如果依然被认定对社会构成威胁的话，可被继续收押。这前面的 21 年可以说是对他罪行的定期刑罚，后面可以说是一种不定期的保安处分；如果对社会没有威胁，则 21 年刑期服满就可出狱；如果对社会有威胁，则要继续收押，直到这种威胁消除才可以被放出来。

三　保安处分的具体种类

正如各个国家或地区的刑罚种类不完全相同，保安处分在各个国家或地区的法律制度中也不完全一致。这里，以德国、意大利、西班牙和中国台湾地区为例，介绍一下保安处分的种类。

（一）德国

《德国刑法典》在"行为的法律后果"一章中，除"刑罚"之外，还规定了"矫正与保安处分"。具体而言，有 6 种矫正与保安处分措施：

（1）收容于精神病院；（2）收容于戒除瘾癖的机构；（3）行为监督；（4）保安监禁；（5）吊销驾驶证；（6）职业禁止。其中，关于"收容于精神病院"，法律是这样规定的：实施违法行为时处于无责任能力或限制责任能力状态的，法院在对行为人及其行为进行综合评价后，如认为该人还可能实施违法行为因而对公众具有危险性，可命令将其收容于精神病院。关于"收容于戒除瘾癖的机构"，法律的规定是：如果某人有过量服用含酒精饮料或其他麻醉剂的瘾癖，且因其在昏醉中实施的或归因于瘾癖的违法行为而被判处有罪，或仅仅因为他被证实无责任能力或未被排除无责任能力而未被判处有罪，那么，如果仍然存在由于其瘾癖而实施严重违法犯罪的危险，法院可命令将其收容于戒除瘾癖的机构。关于"行为监督"的规定是：因实施了法律特别规定应予以行为监督的犯罪行为而被判处 6 个月以上有期自由刑的，如果行为人仍存在继续犯罪危险，法院除判处刑罚外还可命令在其释放后对其予以行为监督，未经行为监督机构许可，不得擅自离开住所或居所或某一特定区域。行为监督的期间不得低于 2 年高于 5 年。法院可缩短最高期限。关于保安监禁，是指在特定条件下对具有特殊危险性的犯罪行为人适用的保安监禁措施，主要适用于有严重人身危险性的累犯和惯犯。保安监督是最严厉的一种保安处分措施，具有刑事政策上的最后一个紧急措施的特点，因此实践中对其适用格外慎重，全德国每年被科处保安监禁的人也就 40－50 人（对这些人要经过专门的专家小组鉴定，并由专家小组在法庭上说服法官确信对这些人有必要科处保安监禁）。保安监禁首次科处期限为 10 年（每 2 年审查一次来确定是否有必要继续监禁），若因犯罪再次被科处保安监禁，则可无期限地监禁（当然还是要定期审查，以便决定可否宣告处分终结）。由于保安监禁理论上存在无期限监禁的可能，且执行中无法将这种监禁与刑罚中的监禁区分开来（本来保安处分带有对被处保安处分者矫正治疗的意思），因此受到欧洲人权法院的批评。在这种情况下，德国联邦宪法法院于 2010 年做出判决，要求立法机关必须在 2013 年 5 月 31 日前找到该条的替代措施，否则就是违宪。至于吊销驾驶证和职业禁止，有点类似资格刑，由法官根据具体案情判处。此外，德国的《少年法院法》还对违法少年规定有"教育处分"等带有保安处分性质的措施。

（二）意大利

《意大利刑法典》也分别规定了"刑罚"和"保安处分"。根据《意大利刑法典》的规定，适用保安处分这样一种特殊的预防性措施必须同时具备以下两项条件：一是客观条件，一般要实施了被法律规定为犯罪的行为，但"刑事法律确定在哪些情况下可以因不被法律规定为犯罪的行为而对具有社会危险性的人适用保安处分",后者的适用受到严格控制,法律对哪些情况下可以适用做了严格限定。二是主观条件,即行为人具有社会危险性。关于如何判断行为人是否有社会危险性,《意大利刑法典》规定了具体的推定方法和严格的程序。

适用保安处分的期限是不确定的,刑法典为每项保安处分只规定一个"最短持续期",在这个最短持续期结束之前,法官一般不得裁定撤销该处分。最短持续期结束之后,法官对被处以保安处分的人进行考查,如果已不具有危险性,即告解除;如果仍有危险性,法官则为下一个考查确定一个新的期限,原处分继续适用。

意大利刑法上的保安处分分为两大类:人身保安处分和财产保安处分。其中人身保安处分又分为监禁性保安处分和非监禁性保安处分。

监禁性保安处分有:(1)送往农垦区或劳动场。它一般适用于重罪的惯犯、职业犯或倾向犯,最短持续期为1年,但对于惯犯为2年,职业犯为3年,倾向犯为4年。(2)收容于医疗看守所。它一般适用于因精神病、酒精或麻醉品慢性中毒而被减轻处罚的犯罪人,最短持续期一般不低于6个月。(3)收容于司法精神病院。它一般适用于因精神病、酒精或麻醉品慢性中毒、又聋又哑而被免除处罚的人,最短持续期一般不低于2年。(4)收容于司法教养院。它一般适用于未成年人,最短持续期不低于1年。

非监禁性保安处分有:(1)监视自由。对于被监视自由的人不实行关押,由法官根据具体案情对他提出必须遵守的规定以防止其重新犯罪,最短持续期不低于1年。(2)禁止在一个或数个市镇或者一省或数省逗留。一般适用于犯有国事罪、危害公共秩序罪、出于政治动机或者利用特定地区的特定社会条件犯罪的人,最短持续期不低于1年。(3)禁止去酒店和出售含酒精饮料的公共店铺。一般适用于惯常性醉酒的犯罪人,最短持续期不低于1年。(4)驱逐出境。一般适用于被判处10年以上有期徒刑的外国人。

财产性保安处分有:(1)善行保证金。它要求被处以该处分的人将一笔20万里拉以上、400万里拉以下的款额存入罚款收款处,或者以抵押财产或连带担保的方式代替上述保证金。其持续期不得低于1年,也不得超过5年。如果在此期间,被处以该处分的人没有犯罪,法院发还保证金,撤销抵押或连带担保;如果情况相反,保证金、抵押物或担保的金额被充作罚款。如果被处以善行保证金的人交不出上述款项或者提供不出保证,法官就用监视自由取而代之。（2）没收，即没收犯罪所得和获利，并且可以没收其制造、使用、运送、持有或转让构成犯罪的任何物品。

（三）西班牙

《西班牙刑法典》也在"刑罚"之后，专门规定了"保安处分"。该法典第95条规定了适用保安处分的条件：一是行为已经构成犯罪；二是法官根据恰当的信息，认为行为人还会重新犯罪。

根据《西班牙刑法典》的规定，保安处分包括剥夺自由的措施和非剥夺自由的措施两类。

剥夺自由的措施有：

（1）拘留于精神矫正中心，因精神异常而免除刑事责任时，如确有必要，可将行为人拘留于与其异常状态相结合的或者能改变其精神状态的医疗中心或精神矫正中心。拘留的期间不得超过假设的未被免除刑事责任而应当判处的刑罚的期限，法院在判决时应确定该期限的上限。（2）拘留于习惯矫正中心。因吸食毒品、扰乱精神物质或者能产生类似效力的物质正处于其药性发作期间、阻碍当事人理解其行为的违法性而免除刑事责任时，如确有必要，可将行为人拘留于公立的以及经授权或同意的私立习惯矫正中心。拘留的期间不得超过假设的未被免除刑事责任而应当判处的刑罚的期限，法院在判决时应确定该期限的上限。（3）拘留于特殊教育中心。自出生或者幼年起理解能力发展迟缓，而造成认知力严重低下，行为人因此被免除刑事责任时，如确有必要，可将行为人拘留于特殊教育中心。拘留的期间不得超过假设的未被免除刑事责任而应当判处的刑罚的期限，法院在判决时应确定该期限的上限。

《西班牙刑法典》还规定：因前述三种原因不能完全免除刑事责任时，除相关刑罚外，法官亦可以给予行为人保安处分，但拘留性的保安处分只适用于判处剥夺自由刑的罪犯，且期限不得超过所判刑罚的期间。对于同时适合处刑罚和保安处分的罪犯，法官处以保安处分就意味着不再处刑罚。撤销保安处分后，继续处刑罚会危及刑罚的目的，法官可以中止刑罚的执行，但时效不得超过刑罚规定的时间。

非剥夺自由的措施有：（1）在医疗中心或者社会卫生性质单位内接受治疗；（2）在某地居住；（3）禁止在指定的地点或者区域居住，并有义务申报其选择的住所及由此造成的变化；（4）禁止前往某地或者进入提供酒精类饮料的地点；（5）家庭监管，罪犯应当接受指定的家庭成员的照看和监管，该家庭成员与监察法官共同实施监管；（6）接受教育、文化、教学、职业、性教育和类似类型的培训；（7）禁止接触被害人及其家人或者由法官确定的其他人，或者禁止与这些人通信。这七项措施可以在前述剥夺自由的保安处分开始时或者实施期间内，合理地加以实施，但最高不得超过5年。此外，还有不得持有武器和不得驾驶机动车辆，这两项措施也由法官判处，最高不得超过10年。法官还可以合理地对那些滥用其从事的职业的人予以5年内不得从事某项职业的处分。如果罪犯是在西班牙非法居住的外国人，法官在征求其意见后，可以将其驱逐出境以代替对其实施的剥夺自由的保安处分。该外国人在指定时间内不得重新回到西班牙，该时间不得超过10年。

在执行保安处分期间，法院应当进行定期审查（每年至少一次），以决定是否继续、终止、替代或中止原来的保安处分：（1）当罪犯的人身危险性已经消除时，应取消保安处分；（2）罪犯发生了不利的变化，对其实行的保安处分归于无效时，可以选择更为合适的保安处分予以更换；（3）实施的保安处分已达到目的时，可以中止实施该措施。该暂停期间不得超过宣判的最长期间所剩余的时间。在该期间内，不得再次实施犯罪行为，否则中止失效。

（四）中国台湾地区

中国台湾地区现在仍然沿用1935年制定颁布的《中华民国刑法》。当时这部刑法典就规定有较为完善的保安处分制度，具体分为7种：（1）感化教育处分（"因未满14岁而不罚者，得令入感化教育所施以感化教育。因未满18岁而减轻其刑者，得于刑之执行完毕或赦免后，令入感化教育处所，施以感化教育"）。（2）监护处分（又分为两种：一是对于心神丧失的人的行为不判处刑罚，根据需要可直接处监护处分；二是对于精神耗弱或喑哑人的犯罪行为，虽然可以减轻刑罚，但在执行完刑罚或赦免后，可以强制其进入特定的处所施行监护）。（3）禁戒处分（也分两种：一是对吸毒的犯罪人，可以判令其进入特定场所施行禁戒；二是对因酗酒而犯罪的，在刑罚执行完毕或赦免以后，可以令其进入特定场所施行禁戒）。（4）强制工作处分（"有犯罪之习惯或以犯罪为常业或因游荡或懒惰成习而犯罪者，得于刑之执行完毕或赦免后，令入劳动场所，强制工作"）。（5）强制治疗处分（"明知自己有花柳病或麻风病而隐瞒、与他人进行猥亵行为或奸淫，以致传染给他人的，可以判令其进入特定处所强制治疗"）。（6）保护管束处分（包括：① 以保护管束代替其他保安处分。所有的感化教育处分、监护处分、禁戒处分、强制工作处分，都可以以保护管束取代之。但是，如果在保护管束期间不能达到预期效果，可以随时撤销保护管束，继续执行原保安处分。② 对特定人的保护管束。对受缓刑宣告者在缓刑期内和获假释者在假释中可以得付保护管束。在这两种情况中，如违反保护管束规则情节严重的，即可以撤销缓刑宣告或假释，而执行其宣告刑或继续执行其剩余刑期）。(7) 驱逐出境处分（"外国人受有期徒刑以上刑之宣告者，得于刑之执行完毕或赦免后，驱逐出境"）。

四　对中国行政拘禁制度改革的启示

行政拘禁，又称行政拘留或行政羁押，是指由国家行政机关或者法律、法规授权的组织所做出的剥夺或限制公民人身自由的行政行为，它不包括公安机关等为侦查犯罪而采取的刑事拘留与逮捕等刑事强制措施，也不包括刑罚执行机关对罪犯的关押和监管。① 在中国，行政拘禁主要涉及劳动教养、② 收容教养、③ 收容教育、④ 强制医疗、⑤ 强制戒毒、治安拘留等。⑥ 正如有的国外学者所观察指出的："中国法律制度受到最猛烈批评的一个方面就是对各种形式的行政拘留的使用，包括前联合国人权高级专员玛丽·罗

---

① 参见李洪雷《我国的行政拘禁制度与改革》，载陈斯喜主编《中国人身权的法律保护及其改革》，社会科学文献出版社，2007，第242页。

② 如前所述，该制度已于2013年底被废止。

③ 针对未达到刑事责任年龄的人。

④ 针对卖淫嫖娼的人。

⑤ 针对危害社会的精神病人，2012年修订的刑事诉讼法已将其司法化。

⑥ 实践中还存在"双规""双指"，工读学校，法制学校，强制隔离，行政管束，立即拘留和留置盘问等诸多与人身自由相关的行政行为。其中，"双规""双指"应是一个与刑事强制措施一起来讨论的程序问题。法制学校本身并无法律依据，属于实践中滋生的非法治产物。工读学校因与剥夺人身自由的处罚毕竟不一样，且以自愿为主，所以相比其他剥夺人身自由的处罚而言，还不好相提并论（但强制性的工读学校可能将来还是存在一个决定权要转移到法院的问题）。强制隔离是针对严重的传染病人或者有罹患严重传染病之虞的人员，它可以在两种意义上加以运用，一是指医疗机构做出的要求有关人员接受隔离的决定本身，二是指当相对人自己不愿履行隔离决定时，由有关部门依法采取的实力性强制执行措施。行政管束包括对醉酒者的"保护性管束"和对精神病人的"安全性管束"，虽然这两种措施本身的合法性不成问题，但目前我国对其程序、期限等都缺乏规定。立即拘留是人民警察在严重危害社会治安的突发事件的当场采取的，以控制、平息事态为目的的一种行政强制措施。由于它不是对被拘留人的最后处理，在实行立即拘留之后，对被拘留的人还必须根据具体情况做出治安拘留或刑事拘留的决定，因而就立即拘留本身而言，似乎问题不大。留置盘问是指公安机关为维护社会治安秩序，在一定时间内剥夺公民的人身自由，并对其进行盘问的一种治安行政措施。留置盘问一般不超过24小时，特殊情况下可以延至48小时，它也应当属于一个程序性问题（从法治发展的长远目标来看，所有剥夺人身自由的程序性措施也都得经法庭裁决）。此外，过去还有收容遣送，现在已经废除。

宾逊在内的许多人权学者和人权活动家都建议中国废除所有或部分行政拘留制度。"①

　　我国多数行政拘禁与剥夺人身自由的保安处分存在很大的相似之处,②它们大多符合保安处分的两个基本特征:一是为了防卫社会的安全;二是为了教育、感化、治疗、矫正和保护行为人本人(至少在理论是如此)。但是,又有不同,例如,有人以劳动教养对象的"屡教不改"为由,认为劳动教养属于保安处分,但这种观点忽视了下面的问题:如果说对于仅仅是屡次一般违法甚至是违反纪律的人就因其人身危险性而需要采取劳动教养这样的"保安处分",那么对于那些屡次犯罪从而具有特别人身危险性的人为何倒不使用这样的"保安处分"?③

　　根据笔者近年来的研究心得,对于中国的行政拘禁制度,笔者认为需要向两个方向加以改革:一是对于作为惩罚性的治安拘留和劳动教养的大部分,要把其改造成为刑法中的"轻罪",④ 通过司法裁决来实现程序正当化,与此同时,建立与轻罪制度相对应的刑事简易程序,并通过前科消灭、刑事诉讼程序的分流等制度来化解犯罪圈扩大后所带来的相关问题;二是对于强制戒毒、强制医疗、收容教养、收容教育等,要把它们改造成为刑法中的"保安处分",从而真正确立起中国刑法的"刑罚与保安处分"双轨

---

①　参见（美）兰德尔·裴文睿《中国不应废除所有行政拘留》,载王家福主编《人身权与法治》,社会科学文献出版社,2007,第201页。

②　不包括作为惩罚性的治安拘留和劳动教养的大部分,它类似一种国外的轻罪或违警罪的法律后果。劳教废止后,从长远看,治安拘留的裁决权也应当归属法院。参见刘仁文《治安拘留和劳动教养纳入刑法的思考》,《国家检察官学院学报》2010年第1期。

③　这是李洪雷博士的观点,参见李洪雷《我国的行政拘禁制度与改革》,载陈斯喜主编《中国人身权的法律保护及其改革》,社会科学文献出版社,2007,第245页。虽然刑法上有对累犯从重处理的制度,但仍然是立足惩罚来设计的,所以笔者基本是同意李洪雷博士的观点的。

④　劳动教养被废止后,过去由该制度所处置的对象将做如下4种分流处理:一是对过去就属违法劳教的行为彻底放开不管,如为维稳而针对上访户的劳教;二是针对那些"大错不犯,小错不断,气死公安,难倒法院"的人,可考虑在将来的《社区矫正法》中规定"行为监督"这类保安处分措施;三是将大部分归入治安处罚;四是少部分归入刑事处罚,这一点在2013年最高人民法院、最高人民检察院的有关司法解释中已经表现得比较明显,如《关于办理盗窃刑事案件适用法律若干问题的解释》和《关于办理敲诈勒索刑事案件适用法律若干问题的解释》、《关于办理寻衅滋事刑事案件适用法律若干问题的解释》、《关于办理抢夺刑事案件适用法律若干问题的解释》均在一定程度上降低了犯罪门槛。当然,对于这种通过司法解释而非立法的方式来降低犯罪门槛的做法,笔者持保留态度。

制。关于前者，笔者已有相关论述，① 本文重点谈谈后者。

第一，我国虽然没有明文规定保安处分制度，但由于社会存在类似的问题，因此无论从对人的保安处分还是对物的保安处分，无论是剥夺人身自由还是限制人身自由的措施，其实都是大量存在的，如针对未达到刑事责任年龄者的收容教养，针对卖淫嫖娼者的收容教育，针对吸毒成瘾者的强制戒毒，针对精神病人的强制医疗，针对卖淫嫖娼人员中性病患者的强制治疗，针对不良少年的工读学校，以及曾经存在过的劳动教养、收容遣送、留场就业，还有禁止驾驶、禁止从业和没收财物等。对照前面介绍的其他国家和地区的做法，我们发现，最大的区别就是这些措施在其他国家和地区都要经过司法程序，由法院来判处，而在我国，大多为行政措施，由公安部门等行政机关来决定。其中像收容教养、收容教育、强制戒毒等剥夺人身自由较长时间的处分，近年来随着我国法治建设的发展，遇到了越来越大的合法性危机，特别是我国已经签署并正在准备批准的《公民权利和政治权利国际公约》要求对剥夺人身自由的一切措施，都要经由一个不偏不倚的法庭或类似法庭这样的司法机构来裁决。因此，最理想的办法应是把这些行政性措施加以改造，纳入刑法，作为与刑罚相对应的保安处分来予以系统规定。事实上，2012年新修订的《刑事诉讼法》，已经把对精神病人的强制医疗的决定权由原来的公安机关转移到了人民法院，这从某种意义上也代表了剥夺人身自由的众多措施的未来发展方向。②

第二，有足够的理由来说明我们应对保安处分的系统构建高度重视。一是劳动教养被废止后，在对原来劳动教养行为和对象进行分流处理的过程中，我们必须正视那些屡教不改者，对这些人应当有相应的措施，使他们的恶习得以矫正；二是过去我们对那些有严重人身危险性的暴力犯罪者，由于适用死刑比较多，因此对他们再次危害社会的担忧就不强烈，但现在，由于国家正在顺应世界废除死刑的趋势而对我国死刑适用采取了严格控制的政策，那么对那些没有判处死刑的犯罪分子，就得在刑满释放前有一个

---

① 参见刘仁文《关于调整我国刑法结构的思考》，《法商研究》2007年第5期；刘仁文《治安拘留和劳动教养纳入刑法的思考》，《国家检察官学院学报》2010年第1期；刘仁文《刑法的结构与视野》，北京大学出版社，2010，第50页以下。

② 应当指出的是，这种"司法强制医疗模式"的改造并不彻底，其中一部分严重程度低于刑事犯罪水平，或者说低于强制医疗适用标准的案件，根据《精神卫生法》的规定，将被转为可以由公安机关强制送医，并由医疗机构单方面决定是否强制入院的"行政医学强制医疗模式"，这种双重模式并存的现状，容易产生司法程序和行政程序的选择性适用，即行政程序可能产生司法程序的"后门效应"，使强制医疗司法化的意义大打折扣。

人身危险性的评估，如果确实对社会还有现实的危险，就总得采取措施来保卫社会和公众的安全；三是 2011 年的《刑法修正案（八）》，在废除部分死刑罪名的情况下，也提高了有期徒刑的门槛，并增设了诸如限制减刑和假释、社区矫正、法官禁止令等明显带有保安处分性质的制度，说明在宽严相济的刑事政策背景下，我们一方面刑罚在朝着宽缓化方向发展，死刑从立法和司法上有效减少，另一方面，也呼唤更加严密的法网和更加安全的保卫社会的措施，两者是相辅相成的。但目前这种把保安处分内容与刑罚内容混为一体的做法，会造成三方面的消极后果：一是可能造成刑罚过剩；① 二是也可能造成刑罚不足；② 三是把保安处分对行为人的关爱变相成为刑罚的惩罚。③ 因此，最好还是把刑罚与保安处分从形式上分立，当然，具体还可以在执行顺序等环节实现二者的有机结合。

　　第三，保安处分的构建是一项宏大而复杂的工程，它的具体种类到底应当有哪些，在立法中哪些内容应当与刑罚彻底分立、哪些内容又可与刑罚保持必要的相互渗透，以及在判决和执行中如何与刑罚相协调、相配合，乃至我国保安处分的立法模式等，都需要专门研究。笔者的初步想法是：关于保安处分的具体种类，目前应将重点放在已经存在的那些行政拘禁制度上，对它们加以司法化改造，因为这些措施本来就存在，现在我们把其司法化，只会更有利于人权保障，而不用担心对人权造成威胁。至于要否增设一些新的措施，特别是像德国保安处分中的"保安监禁"那种严厉的措施，则要格外慎重，因为即使在德国这样的法治国家，它也是受到很多批评的，更何况其宪法法院已经责令立法机关要寻找其替代措施。当然，对于这种预防性羁押，也不是不可探讨，只是我们要吸取国内外的教训，即使要增加，也要从各方面严加限制，把其适用面降到最低限度，并确保各项救济措施，特别是人身危险性的测量标准和程序。对于保安处分的立法模式，最好通过修改刑法典，把各类保安处分措施归到一起，置于"保安处分"名下，与"刑罚"并列，使之成为刑法中法律后果的"车之两轮、

---

① 保安处分要定期对人身危险性进行测量和评估，一旦危险性消除，就可提前释放，但若放到刑罚里，则在限制减刑和假释的制度下，无法实现这种效果。

② 即便限制减刑和假释，刑期一到就得无条件地放出来，但保安处分则不然，如果人身危险性的鉴定通不过，就不能放出来。

③ 保安处分在执行上一定要区别于刑罚，也就是说，前者侧重对行为人的治疗、矫正，旨在关爱行为人，后者虽然也强调教育，但主要是对有刑罚感知能力的人进行惩罚。这一点很重要，前述德国宪法法院对保安监禁的判决就是一个例子。

鸟之两翼”。如果条件还不成熟，也可以先对各种保安处分措施分别规定，但前提是必须对其程序进行司法化改造，当然这里的程序可以采取有别于普通刑事案件的简易程序。

Security Measures and Reform of Administrative Detention System in China

Liu Renwen [*]

【**Abstract**】 The abolition of the reeducation-through-labor system is an important process in the development of rule of law in China. However, it should be pointed out that some administrative detention measures similar to reeducation-through-labor still remain under the current administrative law system in China, such as institutionalized education of persons engaging in prostitution and whoring, of juvenile delinquents who have not reached the age for criminal liability when committing crimes, and of persons undergoing compulsory drug rehabilitation. The direction of reform of these administrative detention measures should be security measures imposed by judicial decisions.

【**Keywords**】 Security Measures; Administrative Detention; Judicial Decision

---

[*]　Professor, Institute of Law, Chinese Academy of Social Sciences.

后 记

本书收录了中国社会科学院和芬兰科学院共同举办的第四、第五届中芬比较法国际研讨会（2012年、2013年）的优秀研究成果，也是中芬比较法合作项目出版的第三本书。该项目持续而丰硕的成果充分说明了该项目的成功实施以及中芬法学交流的广阔空间，对此我们充满信心。

本书的出版得益于中国社会科学院和芬兰科学院的大力支持，也是中国社会科学院法学所和芬兰赫尔辛基大学法学院、拉普兰大学法学院、图尔库大学法学院、芬兰中国法与中国法律文化中心（The Finnish Center of Chinese Law and Chinese Legal Culture）诸位同仁共同努力的结果。中国社会科学院及其法学所和芬兰科学院及上述三所法学院之间友好、务实、高效的合作是项目成功实施和出版物持续推出的重要基础。

在此要特别感谢本书诸位作者贡献了他们富有思想和精彩观点的论文！在论文编辑中，中国社会科学院法学所聂秀时女士做了许多组织联络工作，毕小青先生翻译了论文摘要，社会科学文献出版社编辑刘骁军女士和芮素平女士为本书的出版做了大量编辑工作，在此，对他们的努力和贡献谨致谢忱。

编　者
2014年5月

Postscript

This book is a collection of papers from the fourth and fifth Sino-Finnish seminars on comparative law, co-sponsored by Chinese Academy of Social Sciences (CASS) and Academy of Finland and held in 2012 and 2013, respectively. It is the third book published under the Sino-Finish Cooperation Project on Comparative Law. The publication of these books is a proof that the project has been implemented successfully and there is a broad space for legal exchange between China and Finland.

This book is the result of energetic support of the project by CASS and Academy of Finland and the joint efforts by CASS Law Institute, Law School of Helsinki University, Law School of Lapland University, Law School of Turku University and the Finnish Center of Chinese Law and Chinese Legal Culture. The friendly, pragmatic and efficient cooperation between Chinese and Finish partners is an important base of the successful implementation of the project and the continuous publication of the results of the projects.

Here I would like to express my deep appreciation to the authors of this book for their excellent papers, which are full of innovative ideas and wonderful views, and to the following persons for their contributions to publication of this book: Ms. Nie Xiushi at the CASS Law Institute, who had done a lot of liaison work for the project, Mr. Bi Xiaoqing at the CASS Law Institute, who has translated the abstracts of all the papers in the book, and the two editors at the Social Sciences Academic Press, Ms. Liu Xiaojun and Ms. Rui Suping, who have undertaken an arduous editing work for this book.

The editor
May 2014

图书在版编目（CIP）数据

人权保障与法治建设：中国与芬兰的比较/李林，
（芬）诺迪欧（Nuotio，K.）主编．—北京：社会
科学文献出版社，2014.6
（中国法治论坛）
ISBN 978 - 7 - 5097 - 6007 - 9

Ⅰ.①人…　Ⅱ.①李…②诺…　Ⅲ.①人权 - 法律保
护 - 对比研究 - 中国、芬兰②法治 - 对比研究 - 中国、
芬兰　Ⅳ.①D92②D953.1

中国版本图书馆 CIP 数据核字（2014）第 099252 号

·中国法治论坛·
人权保障与法治建设：中国与芬兰的比较

主　　编／李　林　基莫·诺迪欧
副 主 编／谢增毅

出 版 人／谢寿光
出 版 者／社会科学文献出版社
地　　址／北京市西城区北三环中路甲 29 号院 3 号楼华龙大厦
邮政编码／100029

责任部门／社会政法分社　（010）59367156　　责任编辑／芮素平　汪　珍
电子信箱／shekebu@ ssap. cn　　　　　　　　责任校对／王绍颖
项目统筹／刘晓军　芮素平　　　　　　　　　责任印制／岳　阳
经　　销／社会科学文献出版社市场营销中心　（010）59367081　59367089
读者服务／读者服务中心　（010）59367028

印　　装／三河市东方印刷有限公司
开　　本／787mm×1092mm　1/16　　　　印　　张／24.5
版　　次／2014 年 6 月第 1 版　　　　　　　字　　数／422 千字
印　　次／2014 年 6 月第 1 次印刷
书　　号／ISBN 978 - 7 - 5097 - 6007 - 9
定　　价／98.00 元